KOYOHARU GOTOUGE

I'm Gotouge. Volume 16 is out! The story begins moving in a big way. Thank you to everyone who encourages me. I hear from people who say they have recommended the series to acquaintances and those acquaintances got absorbed in it. That makes me happy. Like an alligator, once I bite, I never let go. It also appears some people have begun reading the manga after seeing the anime—I'm grateful for your interest as well. I'll do my best to make it even more interesting, so I hope you keep reading.

DEMON SLAYER:
KIMETSU NO YAIBA
VOLUME 16
Shonen Jump Edition

Story and Art by
KOYOHARU GOTOUGE

TRANSLATION John Werry
ENGLISH ADAPTATION Stan!
TOUCH-UP ART & LETTERING John Hunt
DESIGN Jimmy Presler
EDITOR Mike Montesa

Printed in the U.S.A

Published by VIZ Media, LLC
P.O. Box 77010
San Francisco, CA 94107

10 9 8 7 6 5 4 3 2 1
First printing, September 2020

ratings.viz.com RATED T TEEN

PARENTAL ADVISORY
DEMON SLAYER: KIMETSU NO YAIBA is rated T for Teen and recommended for ages 13 and up. This volume contains realistic and fantasy violence.

VIZ MEDIA
viz.com

SHONEN JUMP
shonenjump.com

DEMON SLAYER

KIMETSU NO YAIBA

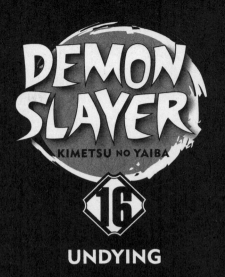

16

UNDYING

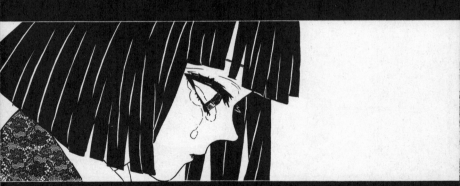

KOYOHARU
GOTOUGE

CHARACTERS

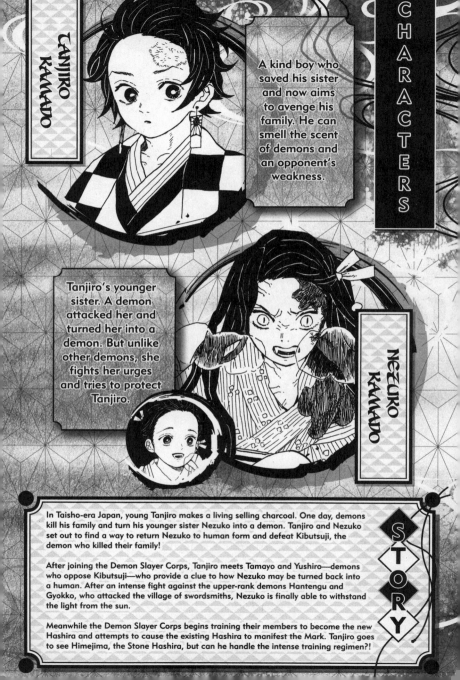

TANJIRO KAMADO

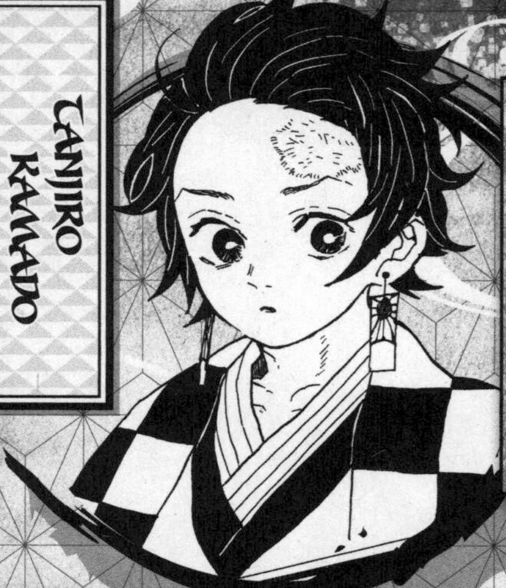

A kind boy who saved his sister and now aims to avenge his family. He can smell the scent of demons and an opponent's weakness.

NEZUKO KAMADO

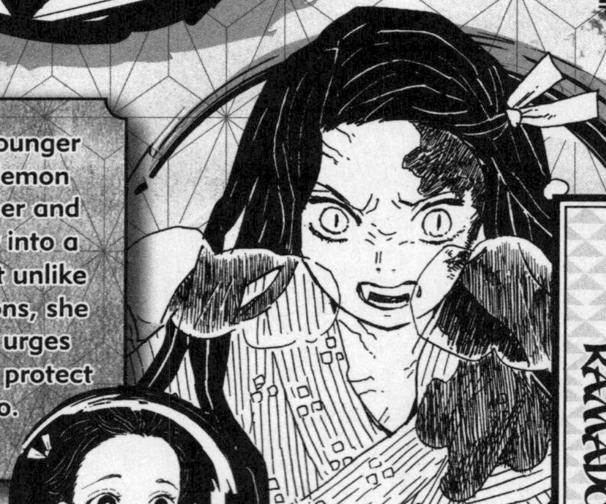

Tanjiro's younger sister. A demon attacked her and turned her into a demon. But unlike other demons, she fights her urges and tries to protect Tanjiro.

STORY

In Taisho-era Japan, young Tanjiro makes a living selling charcoal. One day, demons kill his family and turn his younger sister Nezuko into a demon. Tanjiro and Nezuko set out to find a way to return Nezuko to human form and defeat Kibutsuji, the demon who killed their family!

After joining the Demon Slayer Corps, Tanjiro meets Tamayo and Yushiro—demons who oppose Kibutsuji—who provide a clue to how Nezuko may be turned back into a human. After an intense fight against the upper-rank demons Hantengu and Gyokko, who attacked the village of swordsmiths, Nezuko is finally able to withstand the light from the sun.

Meanwhile the Demon Slayer Corps begins training their members to become the new Hashira and attempts to cause the existing Hashira to manifest the Mark. Tanjiro goes to see Himejima, the Stone Hashira, but can he handle the intense training regimen?!

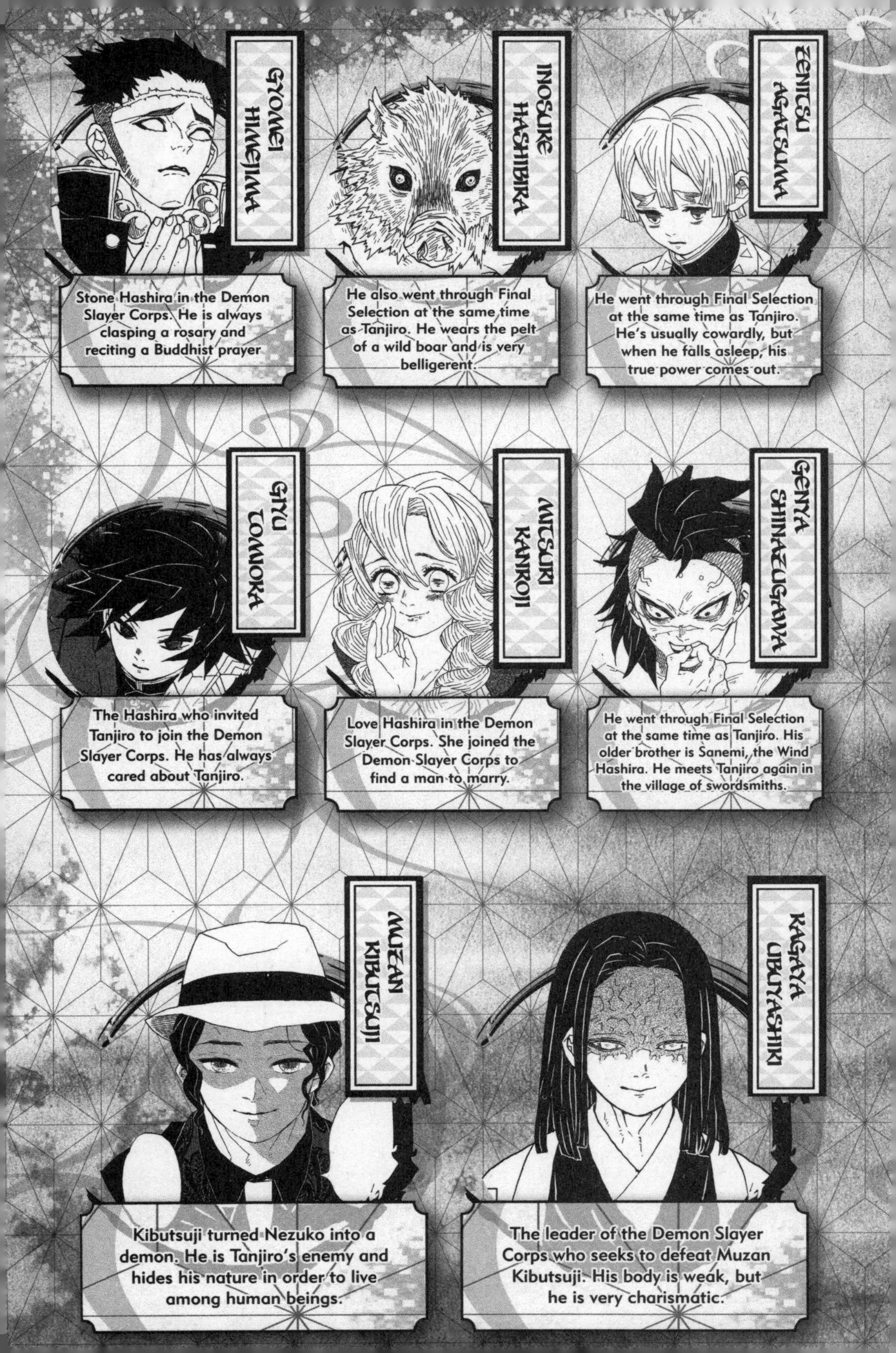

ZENITSU AGATSUMA
He went through Final Selection at the same time as Tanjiro. He's usually cowardly, but when he falls asleep, his true power comes out.
INOSUKE HASHIBIRA
He also went through Final Selection at the same time as Tanjiro. He wears the pelt of a wild boar and is very belligerent.
GYOMEI HIMEJIMA
Stone Hashira in the Demon Slayer Corps. He is always clasping a rosary and reciting a Buddhist prayer
GENYA SHINAZUGAWA
He went through Final Selection at the same time as Tanjiro. His older brother is Sanemi, the Wind Hashira. He meets Tanjiro again in the village of swordsmiths.
MITSURI KANROJI
Love Hashira in the Demon Slayer Corps. She joined the Demon Slayer Corps to find a man to marry.
GIYU TOMIOKA
The Hashira who invited Tanjiro to join the Demon Slayer Corps. He has always cared about Tanjiro.
KAGAYA UBUYASHIKI
The leader of the Demon Slayer Corps who seeks to defeat Muzan Kibutsuji. His body is weak, but he is very charismatic.
MUZAN KIBUTSUJI
Kibutsuji turned Nezuko into a demon. He is Tanjiro's enemy and hides his nature in order to live among human beings.

CONTENTS

DEMON SLAYER

KIMETSU NO YAIBA

16

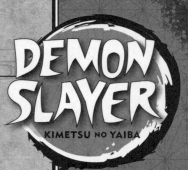

UNDYING

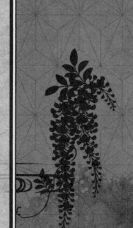

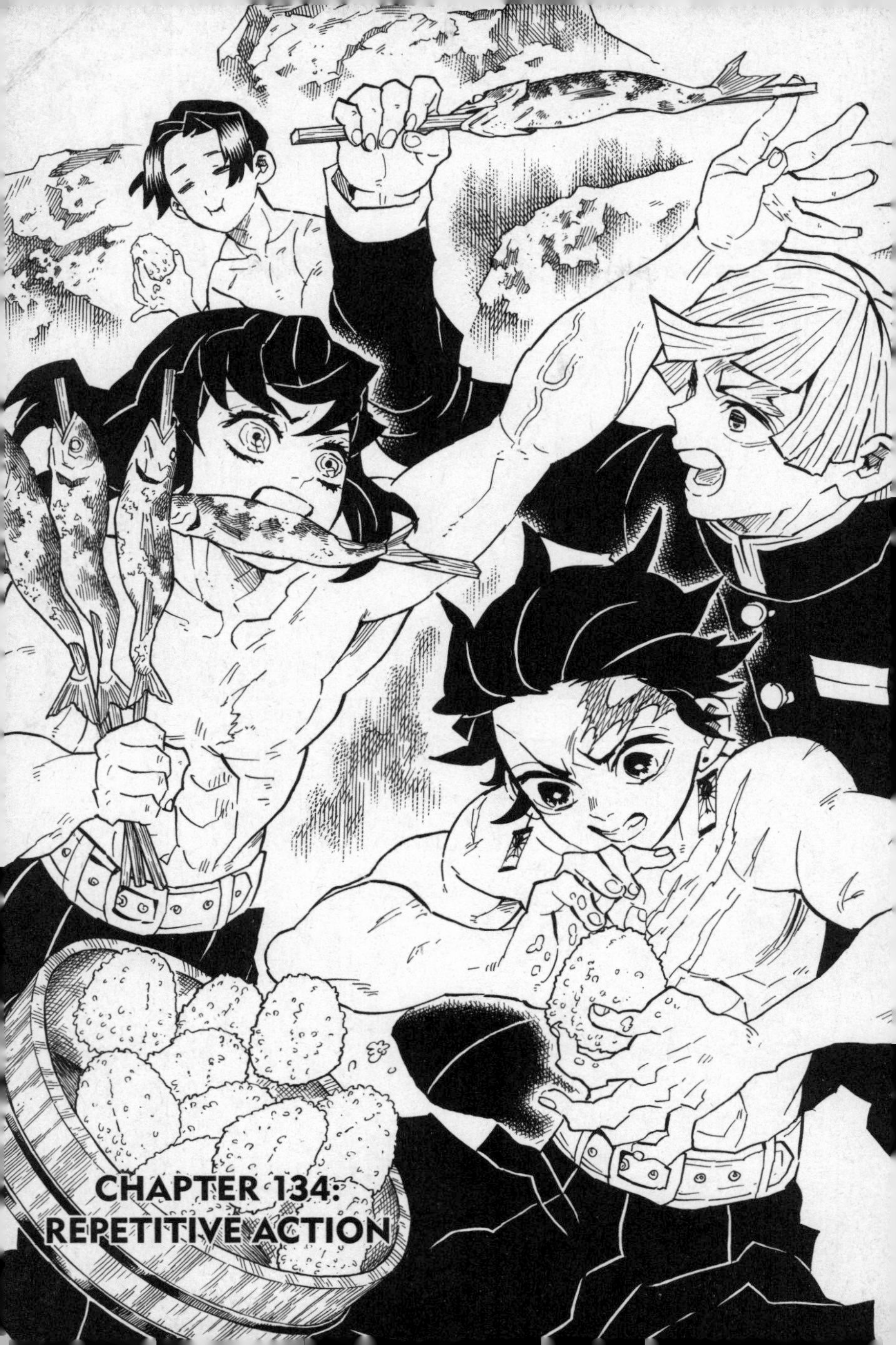
CHAPTER 134:
REPETITIVE ACTION

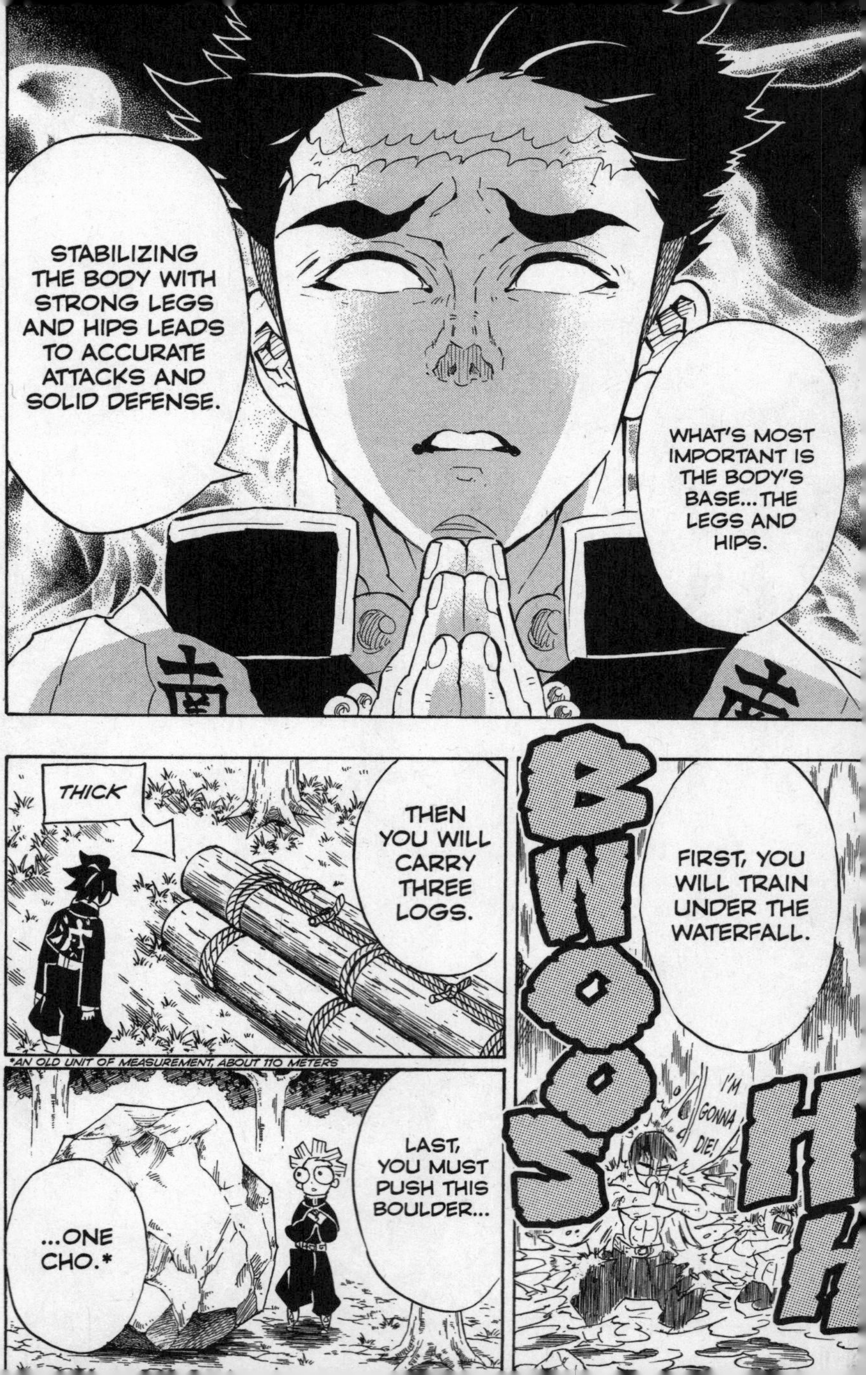
WHAT'S MOST IMPORTANT IS THE BODY'S BASE...THE LEGS AND HIPS.
STABILIZING THE BODY WITH STRONG LEGS AND HIPS LEADS TO ACCURATE ATTACKS AND SOLID DEFENSE.
FIRST, YOU WILL TRAIN UNDER THE WATERFALL.
BWOOSH
I'M GONNA DIE!
THEN YOU WILL CARRY THREE LOGS.
THICK
LAST, YOU MUST PUSH THIS BOULDER...
...ONE CHO.*

*AN OLD UNIT OF MEASUREMENT, ABOUT 110 METERS

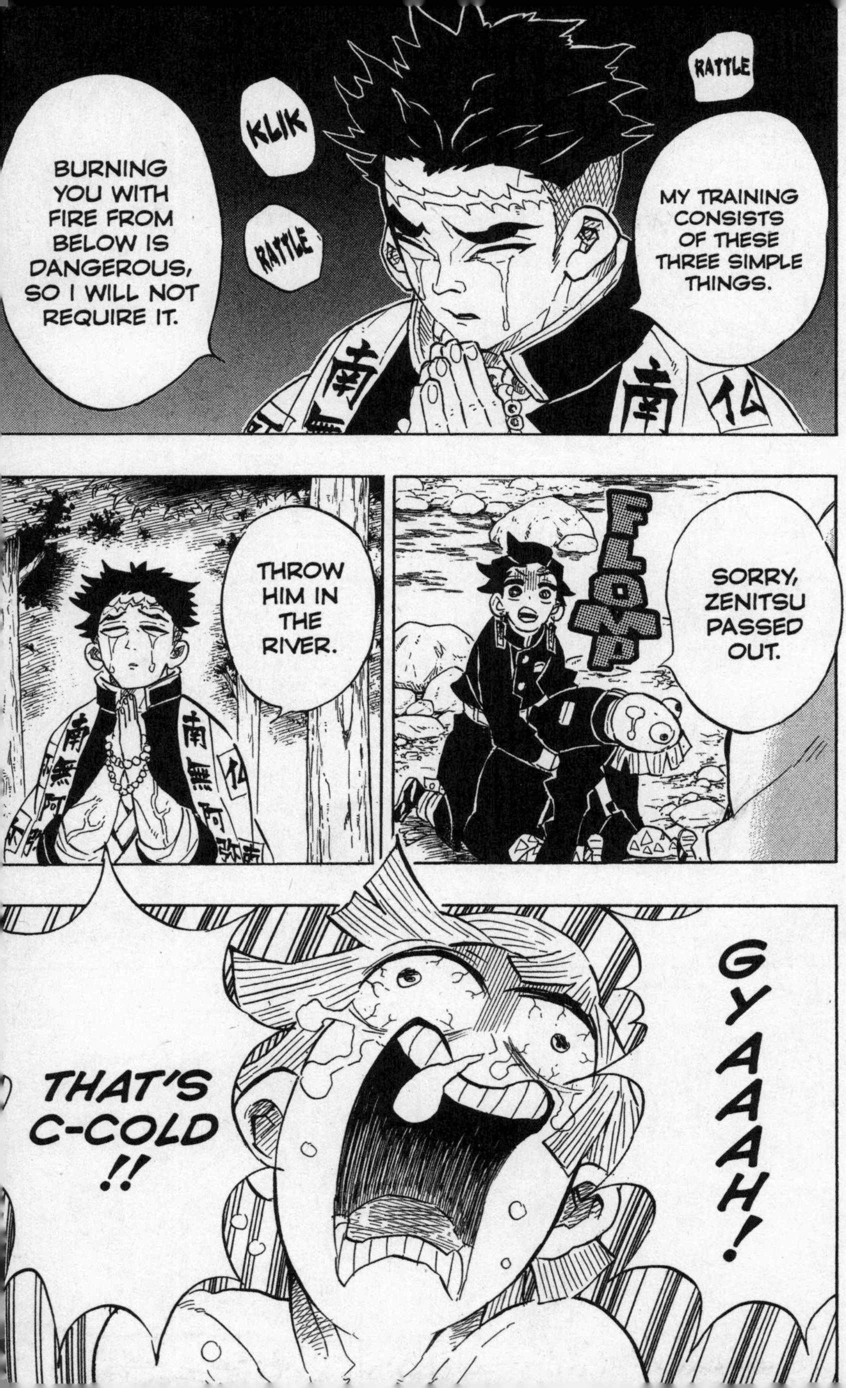
RATTLE
MY TRAINING CONSISTS OF THESE THREE SIMPLE THINGS.
KLIK
RATTLE
BURNING YOU WITH FIRE FROM BELOW IS DANGEROUS, SO I WILL NOT REQUIRE IT.
FLOMP
SORRY, ZENITSU PASSED OUT.
THROW HIM IN THE RIVER.
GYAAAH!
THAT'S C-COLD!!

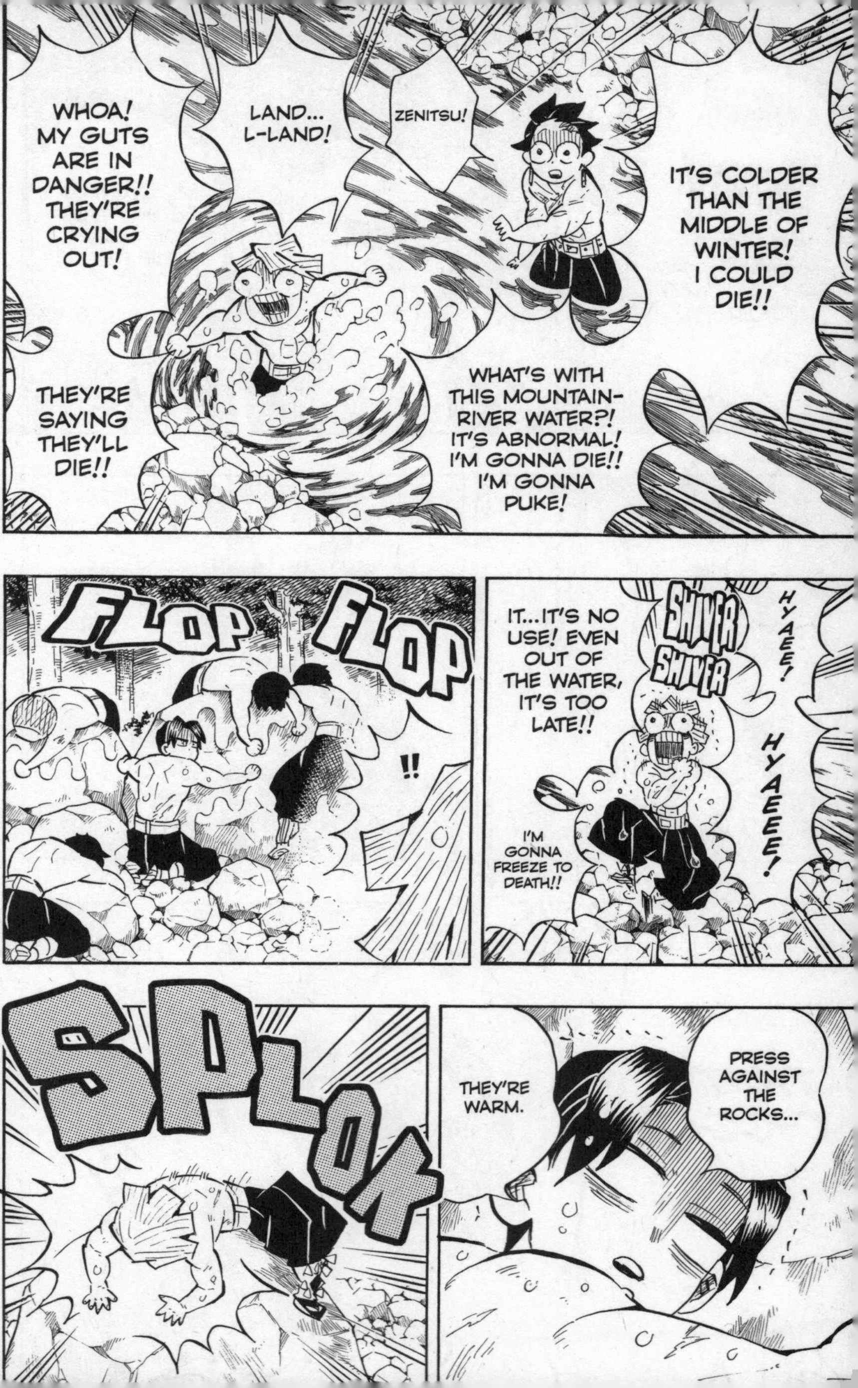
IT'S COLDER THAN THE MIDDLE OF WINTER! I COULD DIE!!
ZENITSU!
LAND... L-LAND!
WHOA! MY GUTS ARE IN DANGER!! THEY'RE CRYING OUT!
WHAT'S WITH THIS MOUNTAIN-RIVER WATER?! IT'S ABNORMAL! I'M GONNA DIE!! I'M GONNA PUKE!
THEY'RE SAYING THEY'LL DIE!!
HYAEE!
HYAEEE!
SHIVER SHIVER
IT...IT'S NO USE! EVEN OUT OF THE WATER, IT'S TOO LATE!!
I'M GONNA FREEZE TO DEATH!!
FLOP
FLOP
!!
PRESS AGAINST THE ROCKS...
THEY'RE WARM.
SPLOT

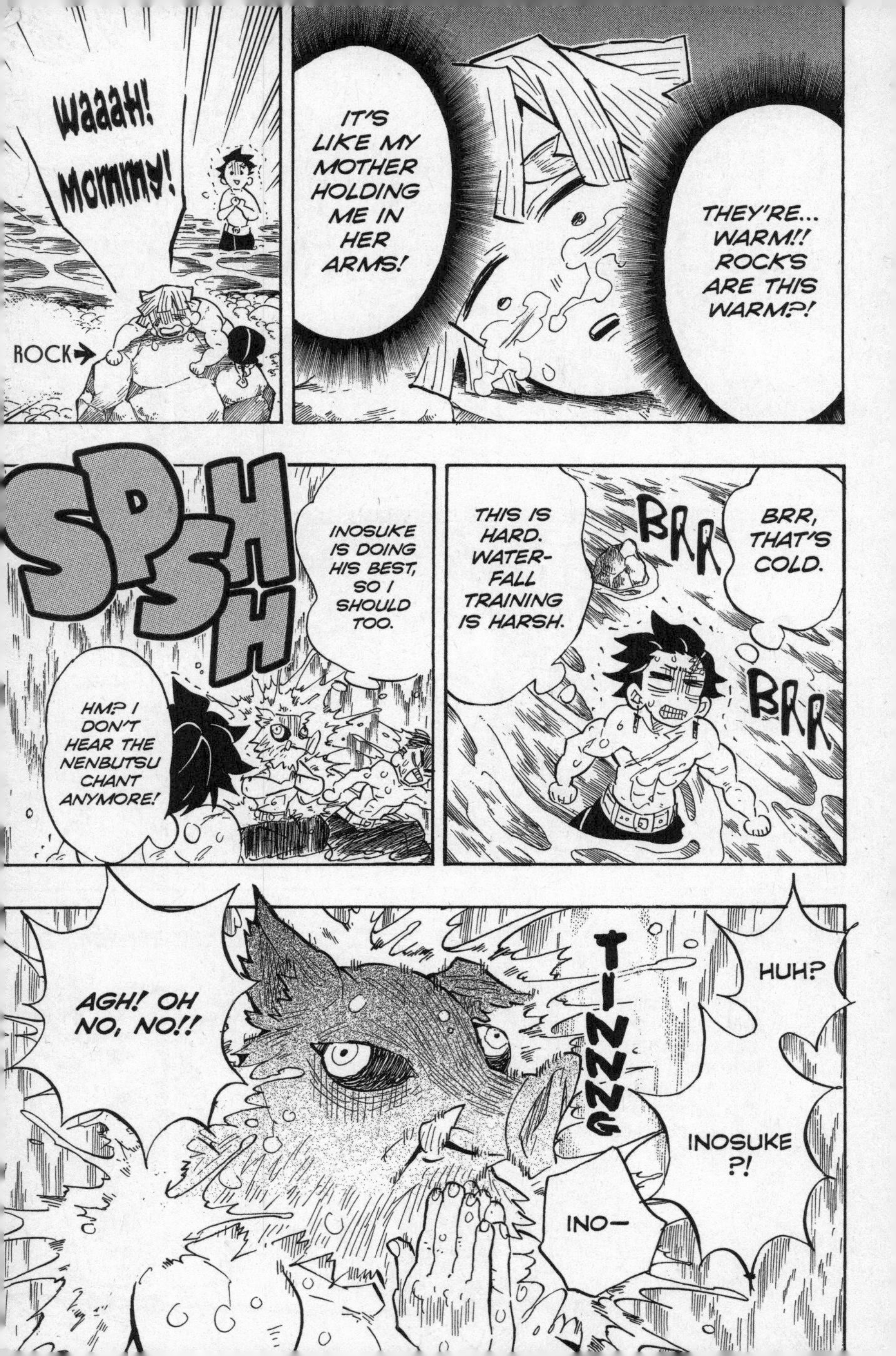
THEY'RE... WARM!! ROCKS ARE THIS WARM?!
IT'S LIKE MY MOTHER HOLDING ME IN HER ARMS!
Waaah! Mommy!
ROCK→
BRR, THAT'S COLD.
BRR
THIS IS HARD. WATER-FALL TRAINING IS HARSH.
BRR
INOSUKE IS DOING HIS BEST, SO I SHOULD TOO.
SPSHHH
HM? I DON'T HEAR THE NENBUTSU CHANT ANYMORE!
HUH?
TINNNG
INOSUKE ?!
INO—
AGH! OH NO, NO!!

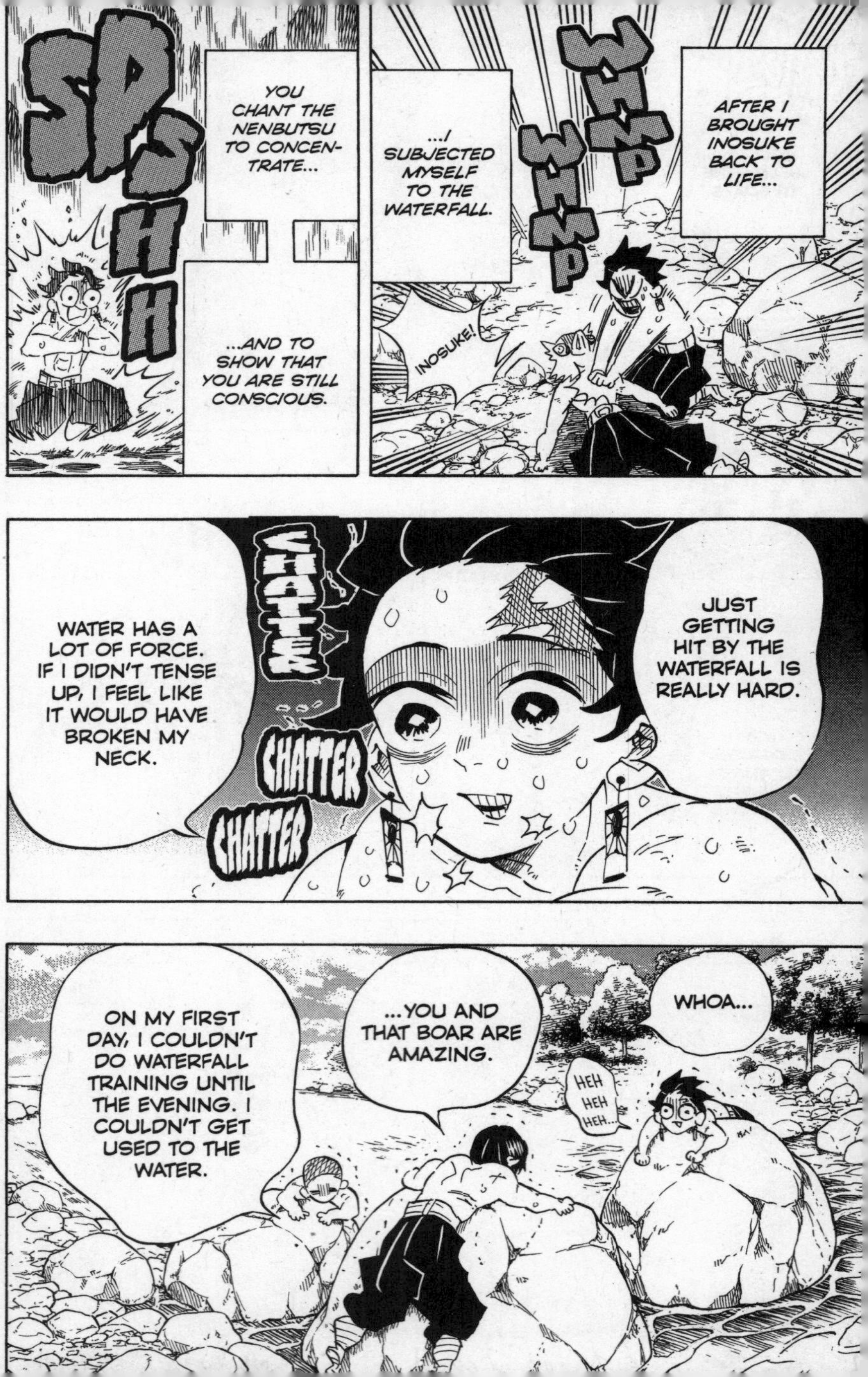

AFTER I BROUGHT INOSUKE BACK TO LIFE...
...I SUBJECTED MYSELF TO THE WATERFALL.
WHMP
WHMP
INOSUKE!
YOU CHANT THE NENBUTSU TO CONCEN-TRATE...
SPSHH
...AND TO SHOW THAT YOU ARE STILL CONSCIOUS.
JUST GETTING HIT BY THE WATERFALL IS REALLY HARD.
CHATTER
CHATTER
CHATTER
WATER HAS A LOT OF FORCE. IF I DIDN'T TENSE UP, I FEEL LIKE IT WOULD HAVE BROKEN MY NECK.
WHOA...
HEH HEH HEH...
...YOU AND THAT BOAR ARE AMAZING.
ON MY FIRST DAY, I COULDN'T DO WATERFALL TRAINING UNTIL THE EVENING. I COULDN'T GET USED TO THE WATER.

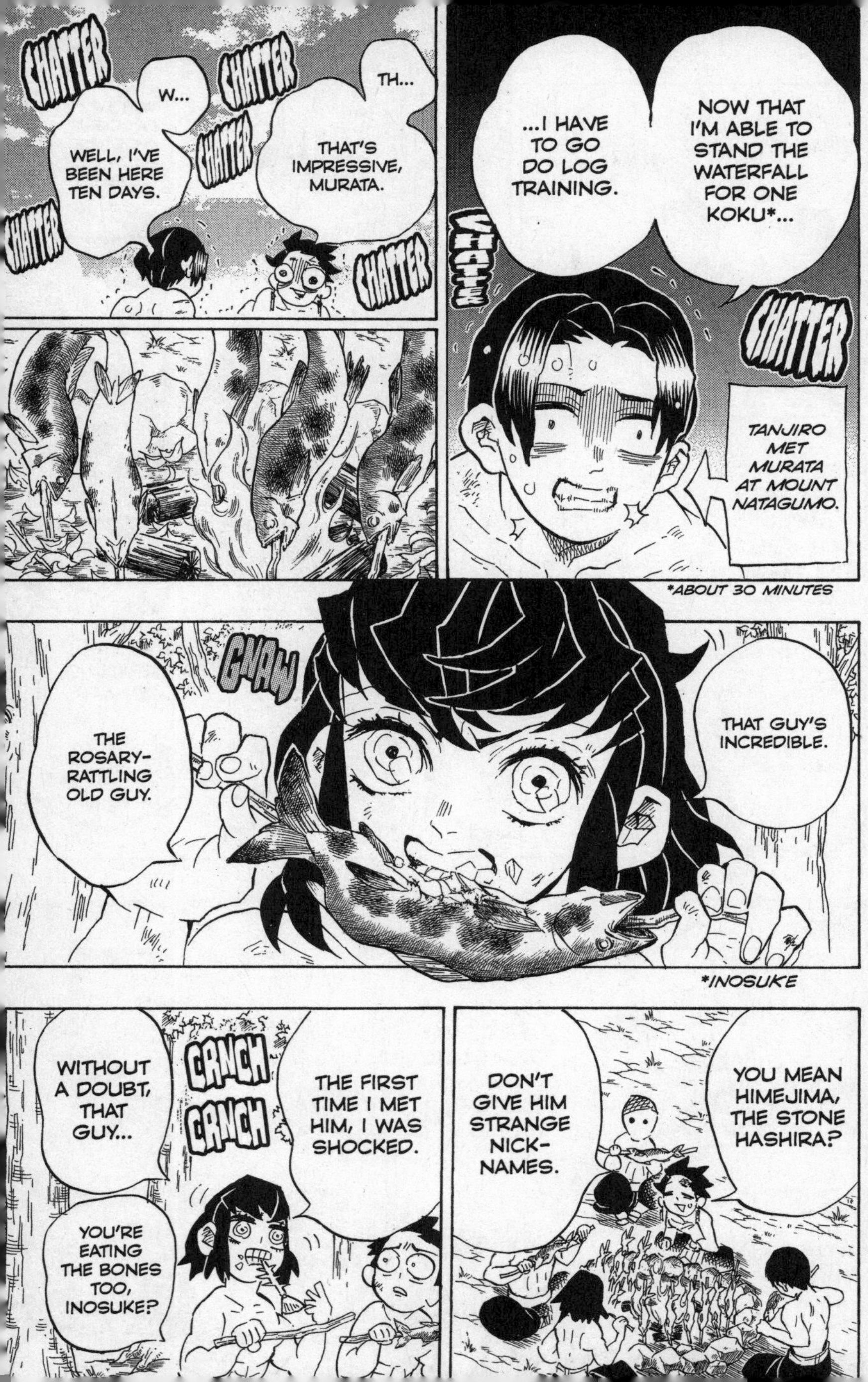
NOW THAT I'M ABLE TO STAND THE WATERFALL FOR ONE KOKU*...
...I HAVE TO GO DO LOG TRAINING.
CHATTER
TANJIRO MET MURATA AT MOUNT NATAGUMO.
CHATTER
TH...
THAT'S IMPRESSIVE, MURATA.
CHATTER
CHATTER
W...
WELL, I'VE BEEN HERE TEN DAYS.
CHATTER
CHATTER
*ABOUT 30 MINUTES
THAT GUY'S INCREDIBLE.
GNAW
THE ROSARY-RATTLING OLD GUY.
*INOSUKE
YOU MEAN HIMEJIMA, THE STONE HASHIRA?
DON'T GIVE HIM STRANGE NICK-NAMES.
THE FIRST TIME I MET HIM, I WAS SHOCKED.
CRNCH
CRNCH
WITHOUT A DOUBT, THAT GUY...
YOU'RE EATING THE BONES TOO, INOSUKE?

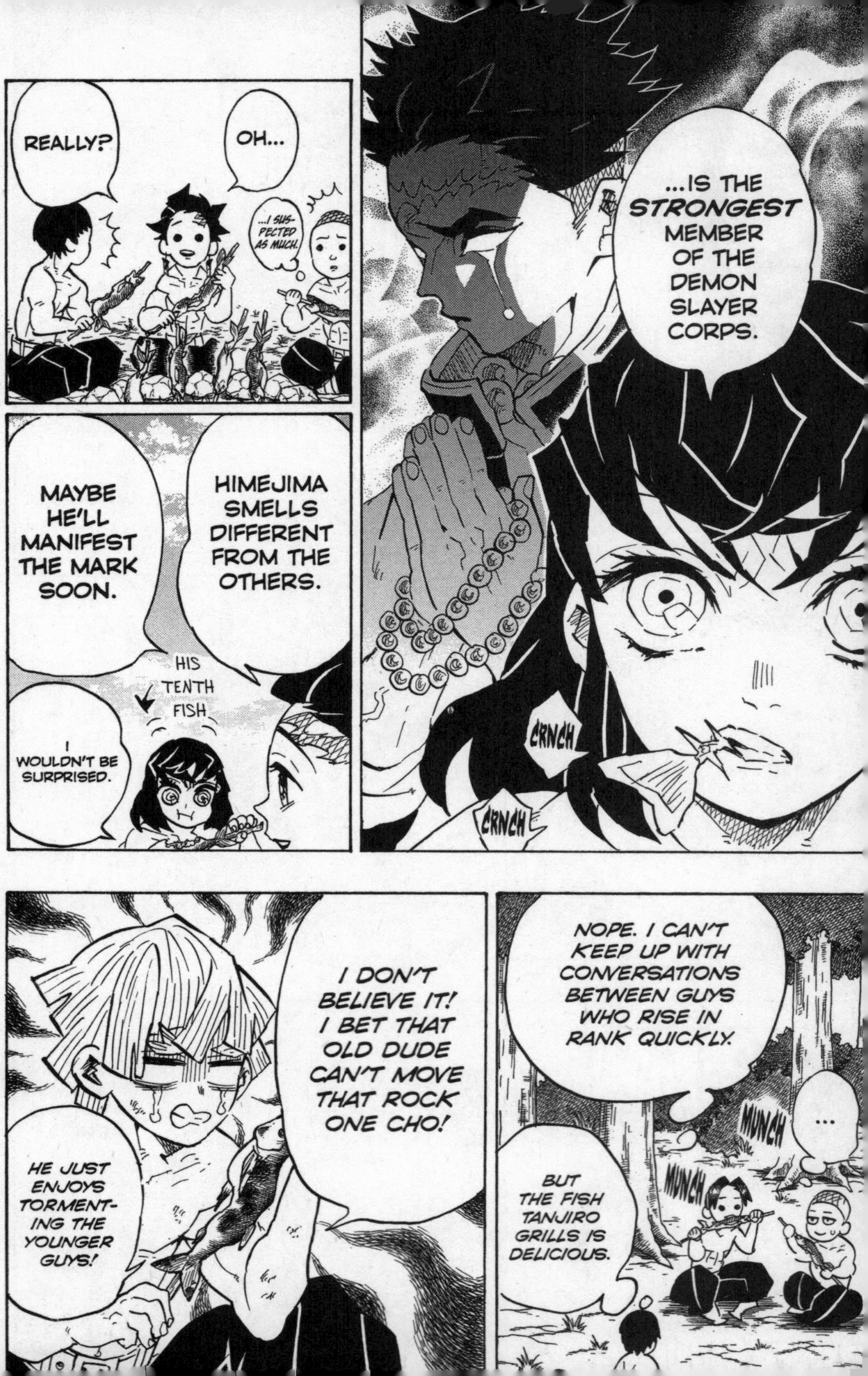
...IS THE STRONGEST MEMBER OF THE DEMON SLAYER CORPS.
CRNCH
CRNCH
OH...
REALLY?
...I SUSPECTED AS MUCH.
HIMEJIMA SMELLS DIFFERENT FROM THE OTHERS.
MAYBE HE'LL MANIFEST THE MARK SOON.
HIS TENTH FISH
I WOULDN'T BE SURPRISED.
NOPE. I CAN'T KEEP UP WITH CONVERSATIONS BETWEEN GUYS WHO RISE IN RANK QUICKLY.
...
MUNCH
MUNCH
BUT THE FISH TANJIRO GRILLS IS DELICIOUS.
I DON'T BELIEVE IT! I BET THAT OLD DUDE CAN'T MOVE THAT ROCK ONE CHO!
HE JUST ENJOYS TORMENTING THE YOUNGER GUYS!

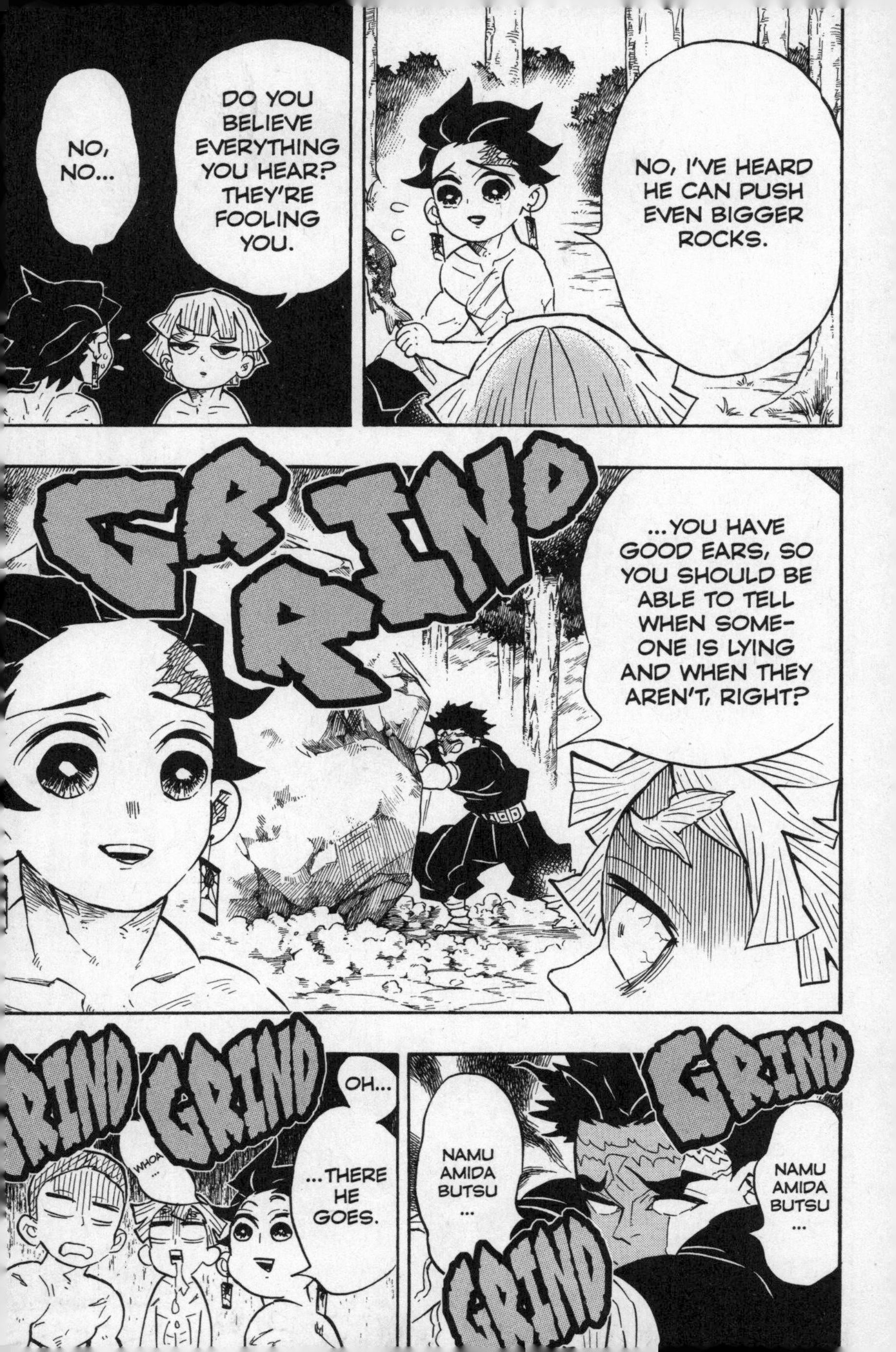
NO, I'VE HEARD HE CAN PUSH EVEN BIGGER ROCKS.
DO YOU BELIEVE EVERYTHING YOU HEAR? THEY'RE FOOLING YOU.
NO, NO...
...YOU HAVE GOOD EARS, SO YOU SHOULD BE ABLE TO TELL WHEN SOME-ONE IS LYING AND WHEN THEY AREN'T, RIGHT?
GRIND
GRIND
NAMU AMIDA BUTSU...
NAMU AMIDA BUTSU...
GRIND
OH...
...THERE HE GOES.
GRIND
WHOA...
RIND

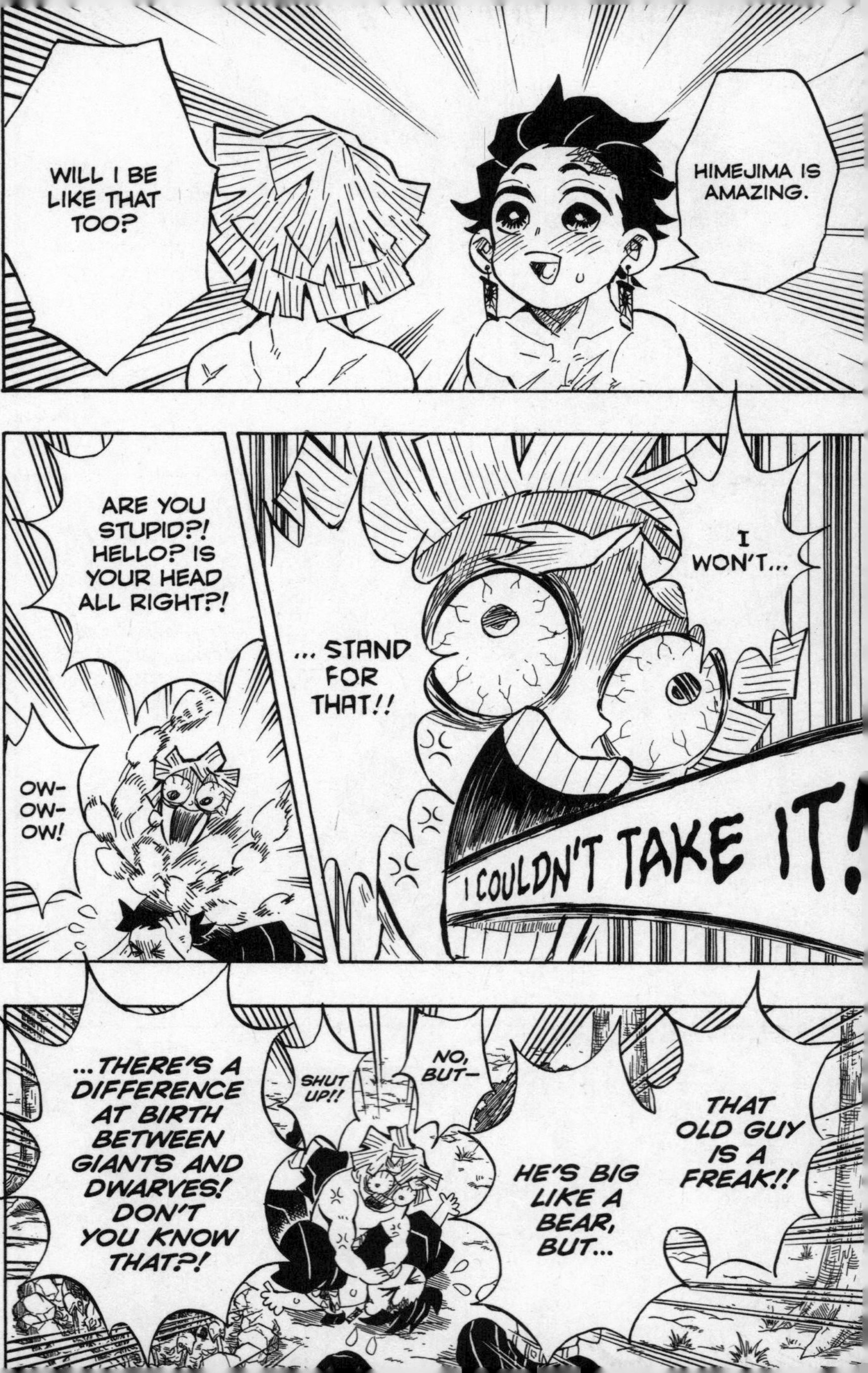

HIMEJIMA IS AMAZING.
WILL I BE LIKE THAT TOO?
I WON'T...
... STAND FOR THAT!!
I COULDN'T TAKE IT!
ARE YOU STUPID?! HELLO? IS YOUR HEAD ALL RIGHT?!
OW-OW-OW!
THAT OLD GUY IS A FREAK!!
HE'S BIG LIKE A BEAR, BUT...
NO, BUT—
SHUT UP!!
...THERE'S A DIFFERENCE AT BIRTH BETWEEN GIANTS AND DWARVES! DON'T YOU KNOW THAT?!

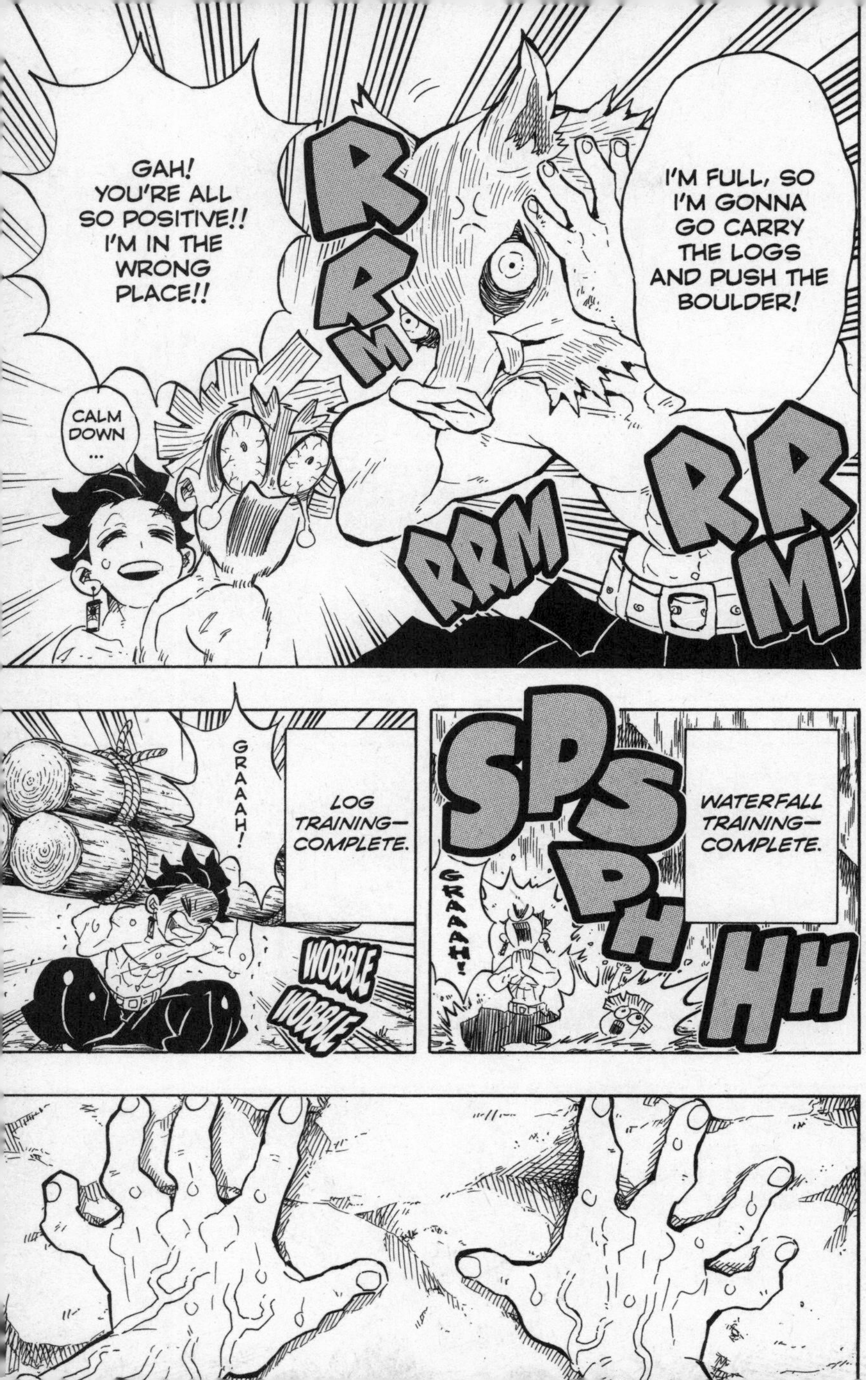
I'M FULL, SO I'M GONNA GO CARRY THE LOGS AND PUSH THE BOULDER!
RRM
GAH! YOU'RE ALL SO POSITIVE!! I'M IN THE WRONG PLACE!!
RRRM
RRM
CALM DOWN ...
WATERFALL TRAINING— COMPLETE.
SPSPHHH
GRAAAAH!
LOG TRAINING— COMPLETE.
GRAAAH!
WOBBLE WOBBLE

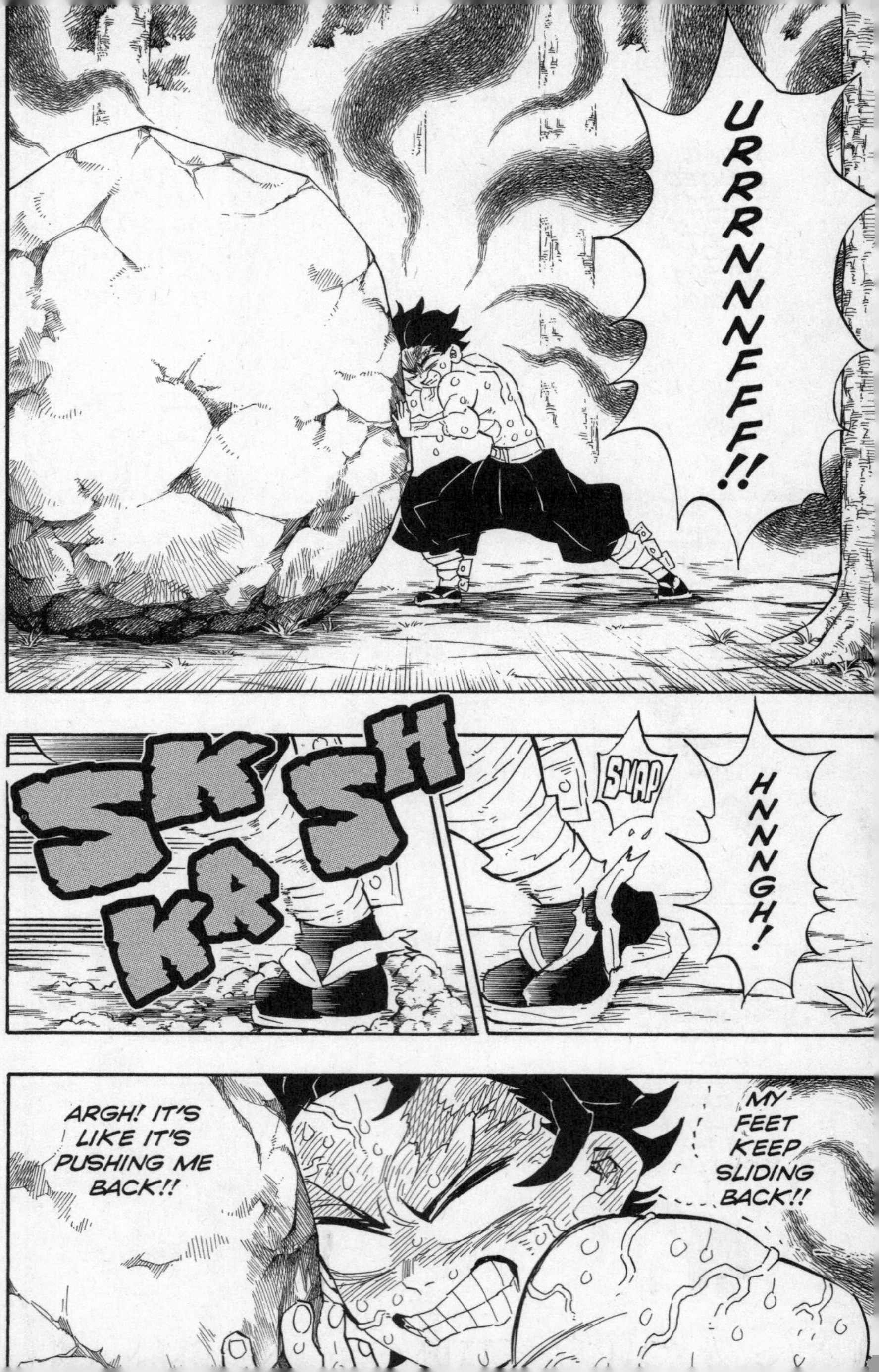
URRRNNNFFF!!
HNNNGH!
SNAP
SKKRSH
MY FEET KEEP SLIDING BACK!!
ARGH! IT'S LIKE IT'S PUSHING ME BACK!!

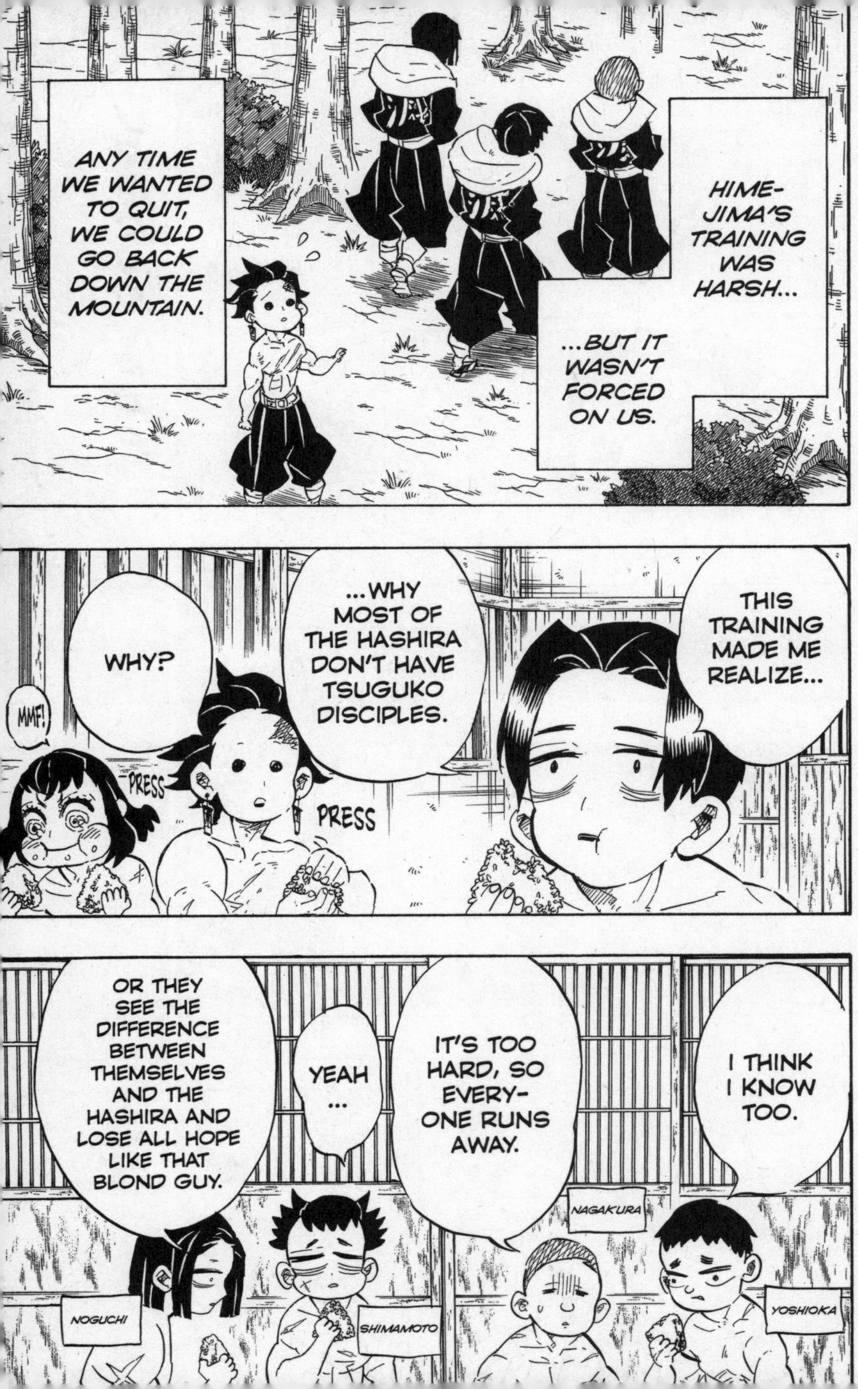
HIME-JIMA'S TRAINING WAS HARSH...
...BUT IT WASN'T FORCED ON US.
ANY TIME WE WANTED TO QUIT, WE COULD GO BACK DOWN THE MOUNTAIN.
THIS TRAINING MADE ME REALIZE...
...WHY MOST OF THE HASHIRA DON'T HAVE TSUGUKO DISCIPLES.
PRESS
PRESS
WHY?
MMF!
I THINK I KNOW TOO.
YOSHIOKA
NAGAKURA
IT'S TOO HARD, SO EVERY-ONE RUNS AWAY.
YEAH...
SHIMAMOTO
OR THEY SEE THE DIFFERENCE BETWEEN THEMSELVES AND THE HASHIRA AND LOSE ALL HOPE LIKE THAT BLOND GUY.
NOGUCHI

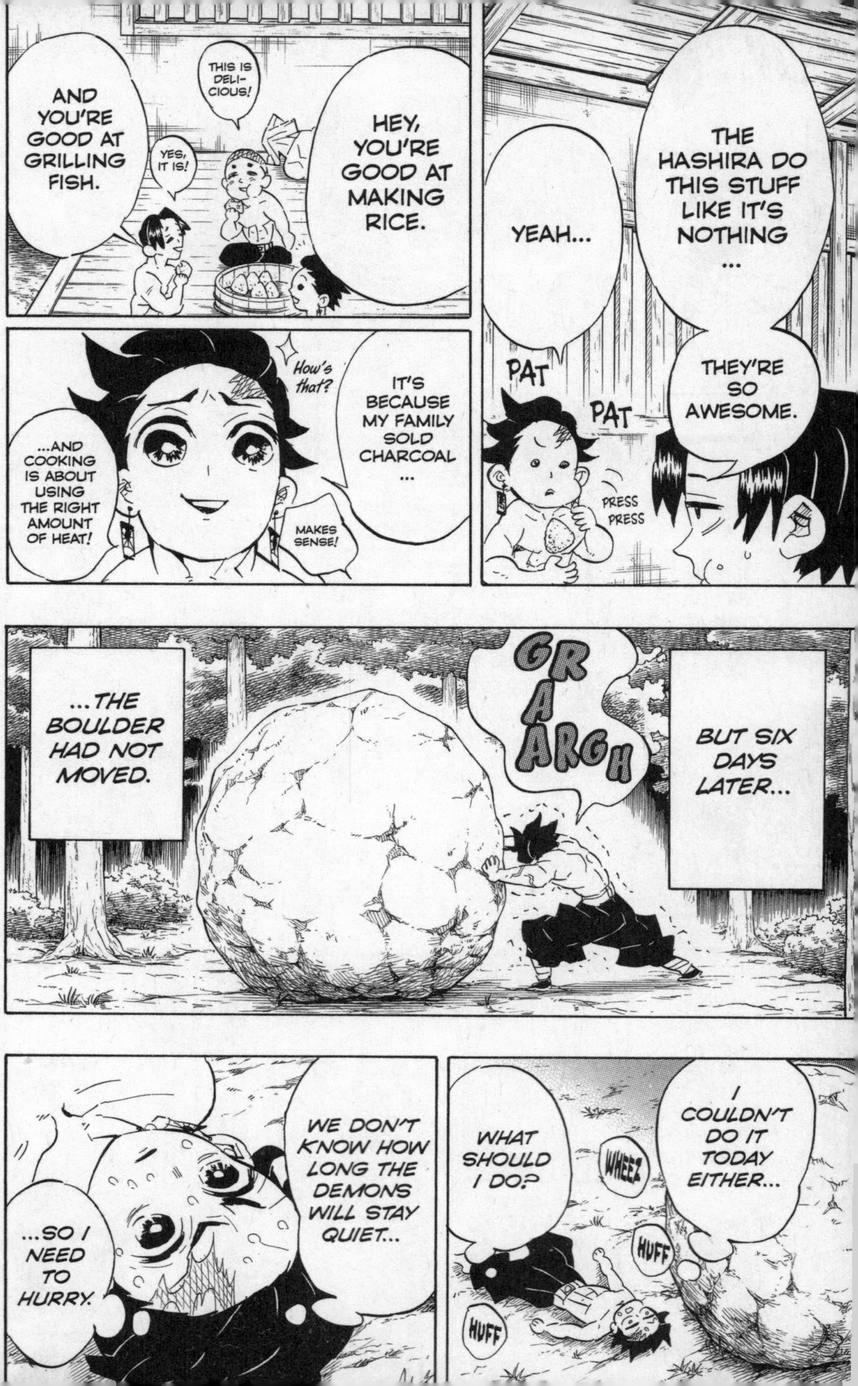
THE HASHIRA DO THIS STUFF LIKE IT'S NOTHING...
YEAH...
THEY'RE SO AWESOME.
PAT
PAT
PRESS PRESS
HEY, YOU'RE GOOD AT MAKING RICE.
THIS IS DELI-CIOUS!
YES, IT IS!
AND YOU'RE GOOD AT GRILLING FISH.
IT'S BECAUSE MY FAMILY SOLD CHARCOAL...
How's that?
MAKES SENSE!
...AND COOKING IS ABOUT USING THE RIGHT AMOUNT OF HEAT!
BUT SIX DAYS LATER...
GRAARGH
...THE BOULDER HAD NOT MOVED.
I COULDN'T DO IT TODAY EITHER...
WHAT SHOULD I DO?
WHEEZ
HUFF
HUFF
WE DON'T KNOW HOW LONG THE DEMONS WILL STAY QUIET...
...SO I NEED TO HURRY.

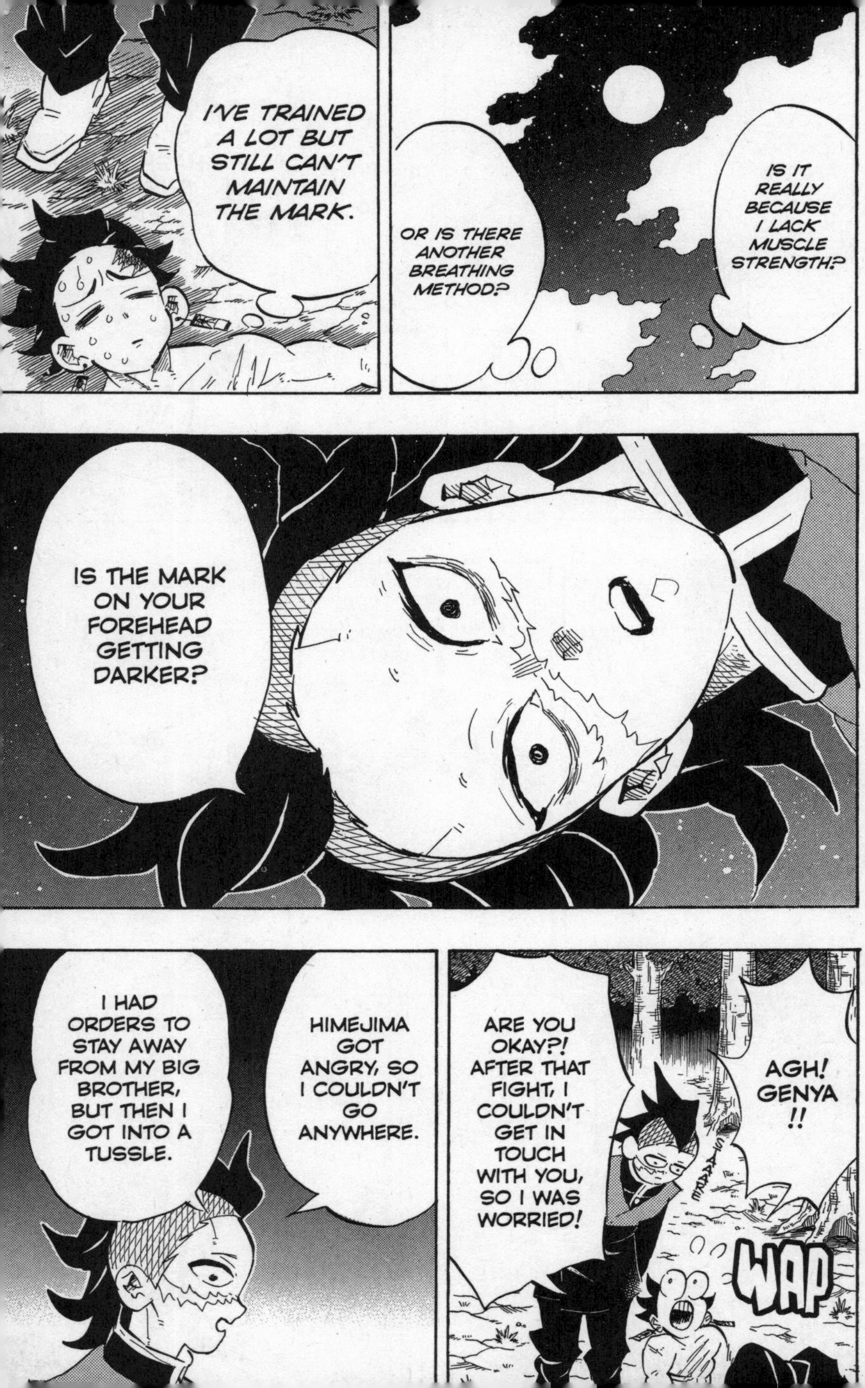
IS IT REALLY BECAUSE I LACK MUSCLE STRENGTH?
OR IS THERE ANOTHER BREATHING METHOD?
I'VE TRAINED A LOT BUT STILL CAN'T MAINTAIN THE MARK.
IS THE MARK ON YOUR FOREHEAD GETTING DARKER?
AGH! GENYA !!
WAP
ARE YOU OKAY?! AFTER THAT FIGHT, I COULDN'T GET IN TOUCH WITH YOU, SO I WAS WORRIED!
HIMEJIMA GOT ANGRY, SO I COULDN'T GO ANYWHERE.
I HAD ORDERS TO STAY AWAY FROM MY BIG BROTHER, BUT THEN I GOT INTO A TUSSLE.

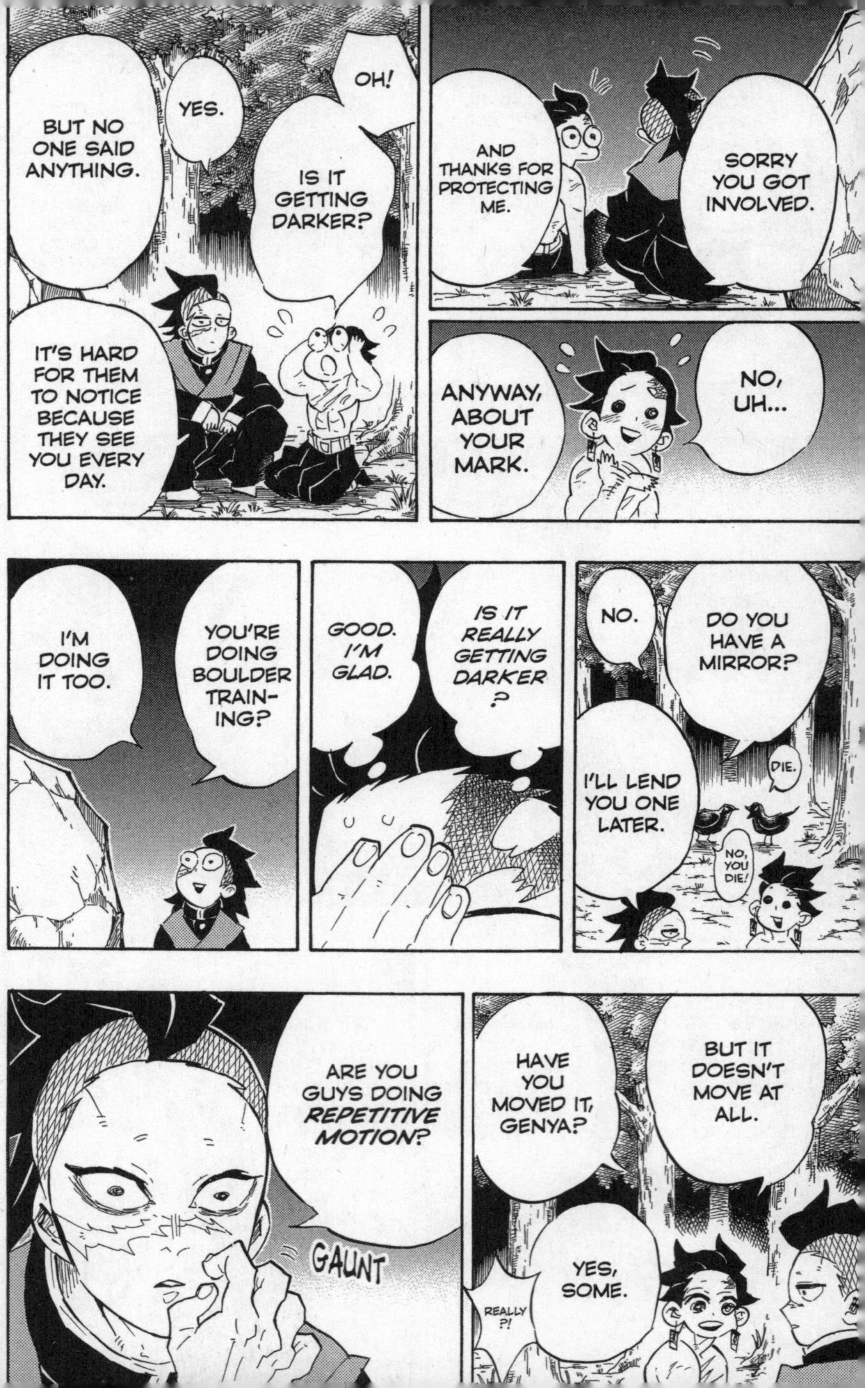
SORRY YOU GOT INVOLVED.
AND THANKS FOR PROTECTING ME.
NO, UH...
ANYWAY, ABOUT YOUR MARK.
OH!
IS IT GETTING DARKER?
YES.
BUT NO ONE SAID ANYTHING.
IT'S HARD FOR THEM TO NOTICE BECAUSE THEY SEE YOU EVERY DAY.
DO YOU HAVE A MIRROR?
NO.
I'LL LEND YOU ONE LATER.
DIE.
NO, YOU DIE!
IS IT REALLY GETTING DARKER?
GOOD. I'M GLAD.
YOU'RE DOING BOULDER TRAIN-ING?
I'M DOING IT TOO.
BUT IT DOESN'T MOVE AT ALL.
HAVE YOU MOVED IT, GENYA?
YES, SOME.
REALLY?!
ARE YOU GUYS DOING REPETITIVE MOTION?
GAUNT

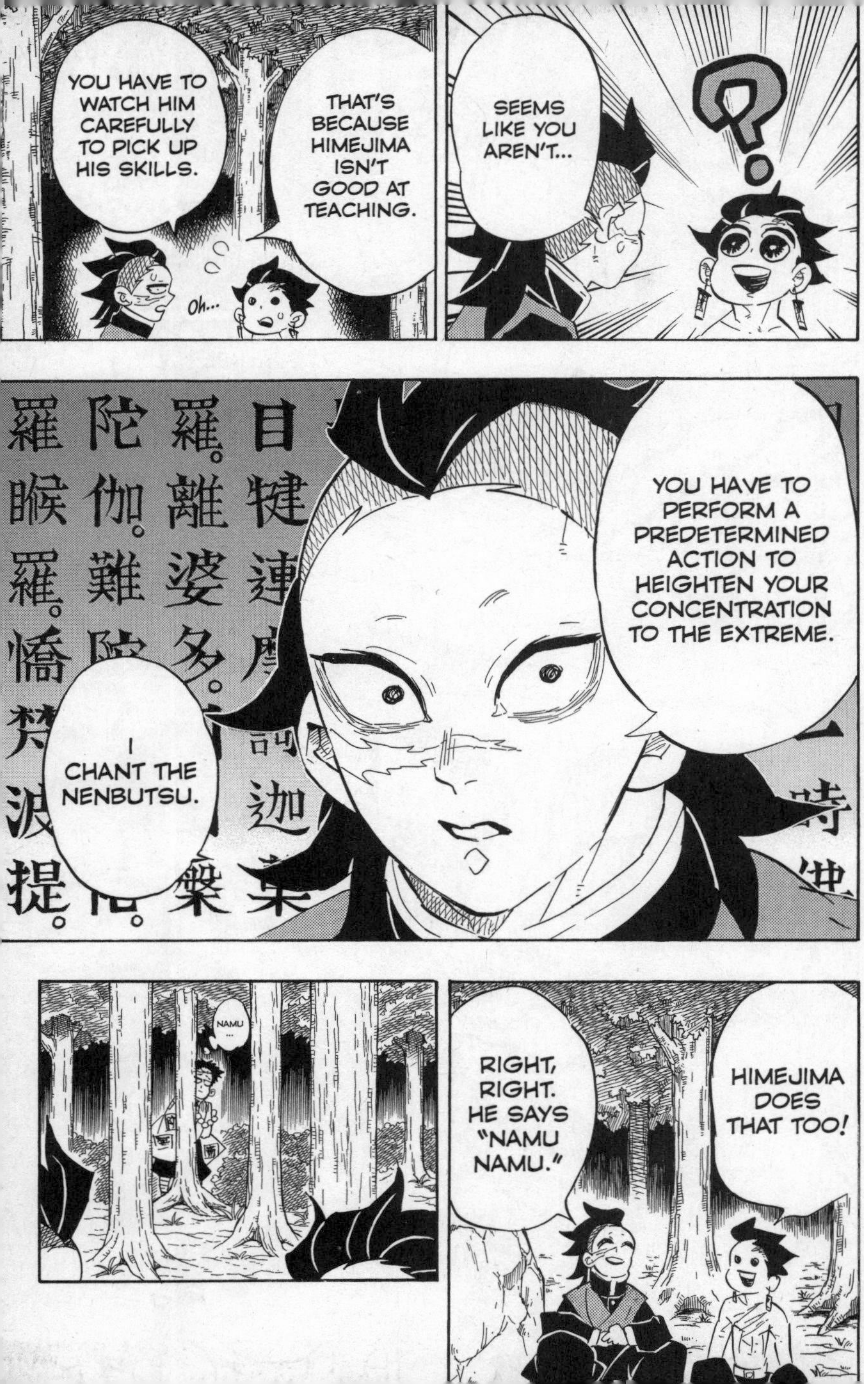
?
SEEMS LIKE YOU AREN'T...
THAT'S BECAUSE HIMEJIMA ISN'T GOOD AT TEACHING.
YOU HAVE TO WATCH HIM CAREFULLY TO PICK UP HIS SKILLS.
Oh...
YOU HAVE TO PERFORM A PREDETERMINED ACTION TO HEIGHTEN YOUR CONCENTRATION TO THE EXTREME.
I CHANT THE NENBUTSU.
HIMEJIMA DOES THAT TOO!
RIGHT, RIGHT. HE SAYS "NAMU NAMU."
NAMU ...

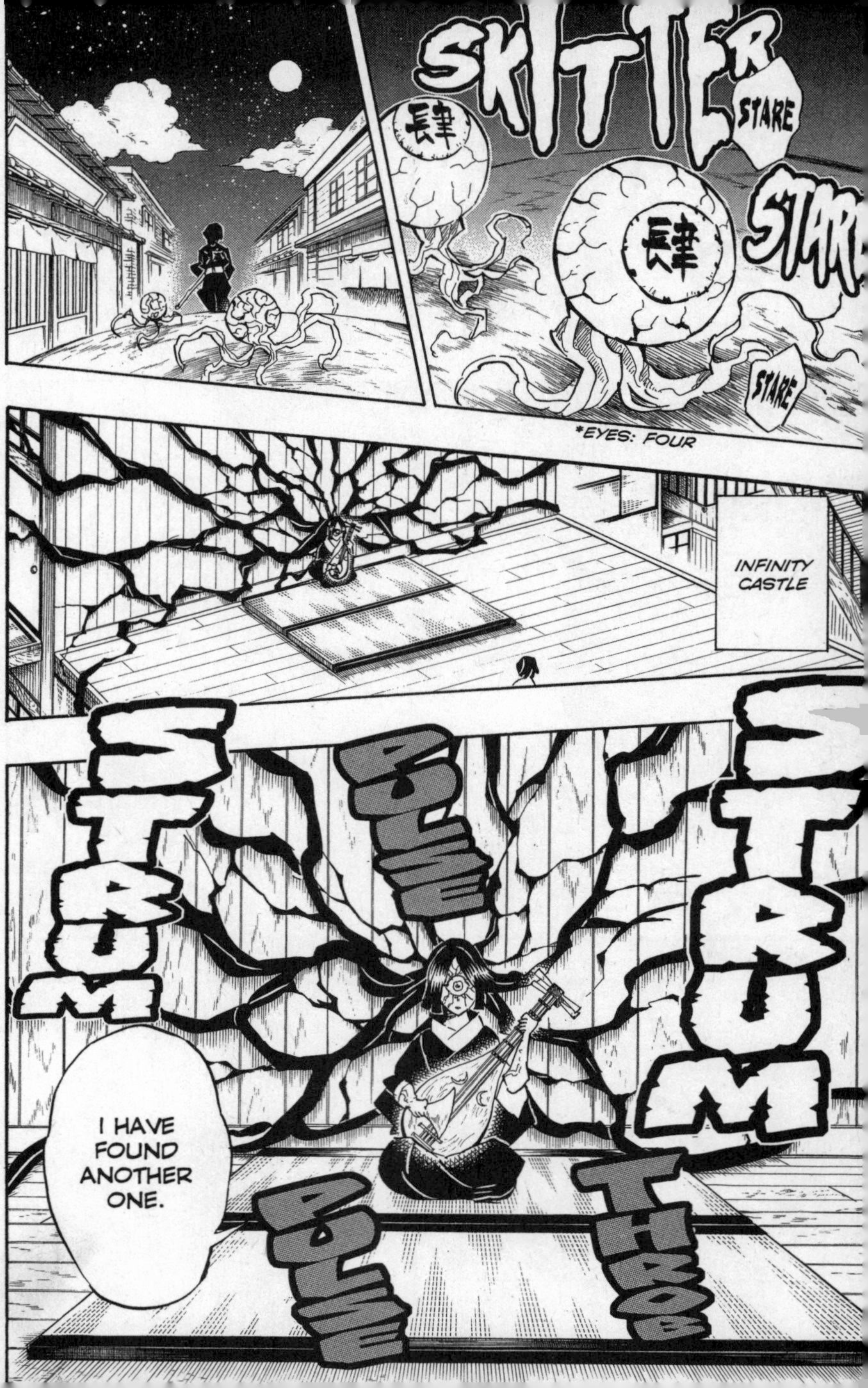
SKITTER
STARE
STARE
STARE
*EYES: FOUR
INFINITY CASTLE
STRUM
STRUM
THROB
I HAVE FOUND ANOTHER ONE.

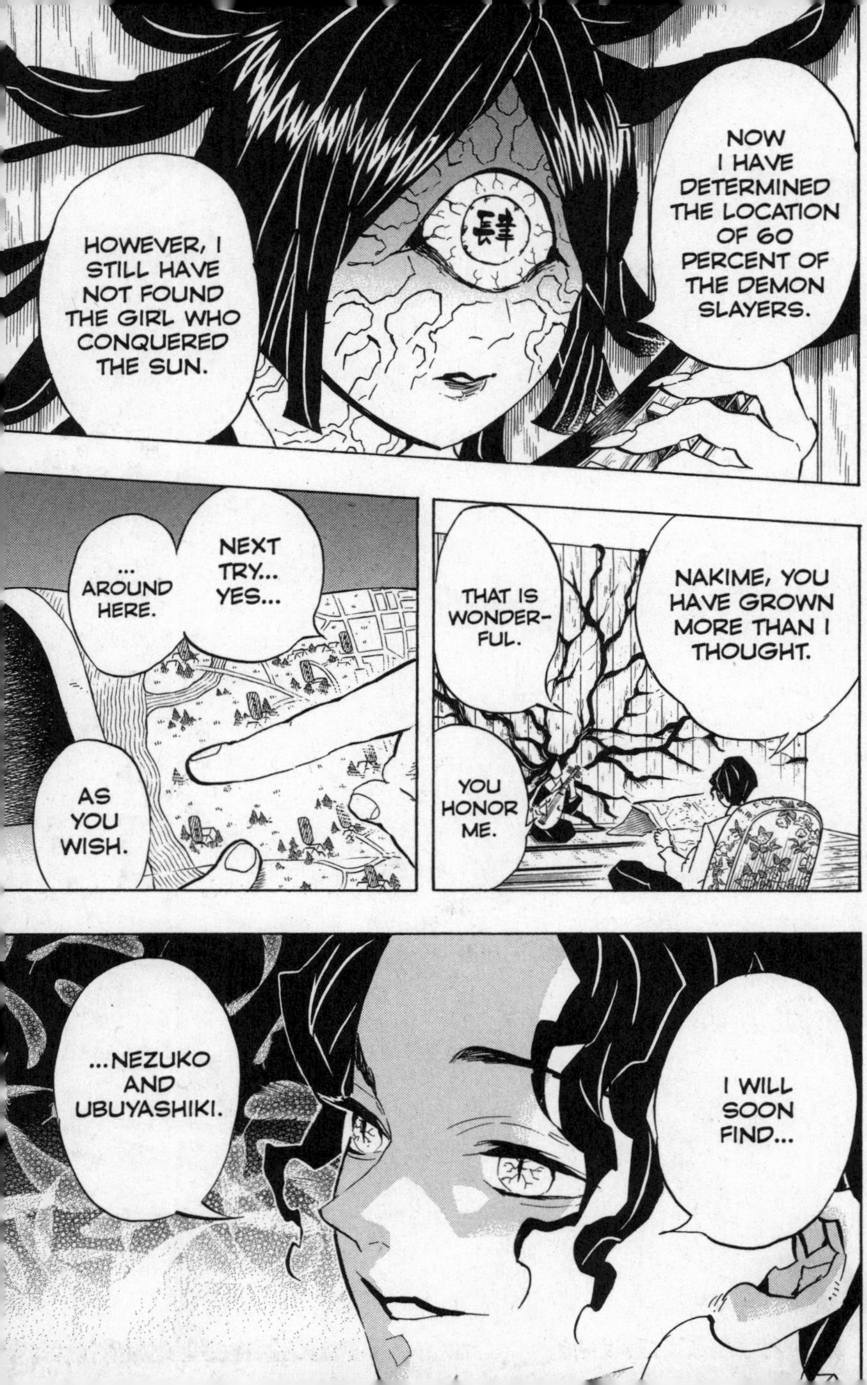
NOW I HAVE DETERMINED THE LOCATION OF 60 PERCENT OF THE DEMON SLAYERS.
肆
HOWEVER, I STILL HAVE NOT FOUND THE GIRL WHO CONQUERED THE SUN.
NAKIME, YOU HAVE GROWN MORE THAN I THOUGHT.
THAT IS WONDERFUL.
YOU HONOR ME.
NEXT TRY... YES...
...AROUND HERE.
AS YOU WISH.
I WILL SOON FIND...
...NEZUKO AND UBUYASHIKI.

During Hashira Training, Tanjiro was nicknamed "Mom."

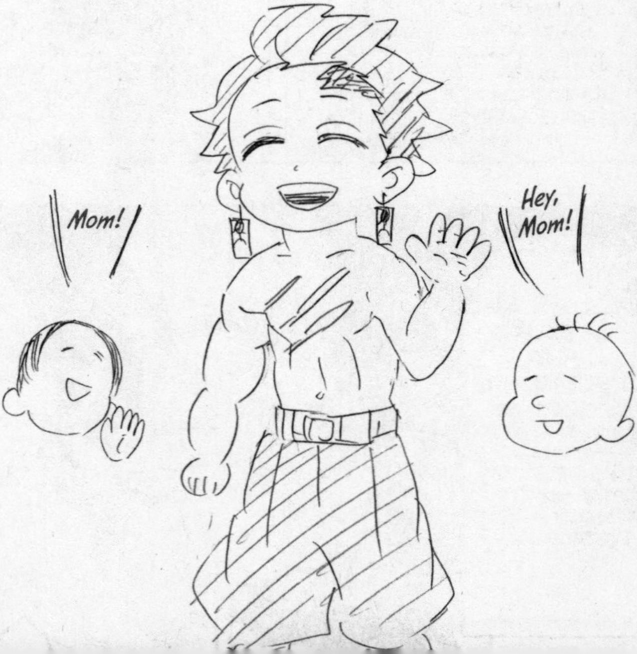
Hey, Mom!
Mom!

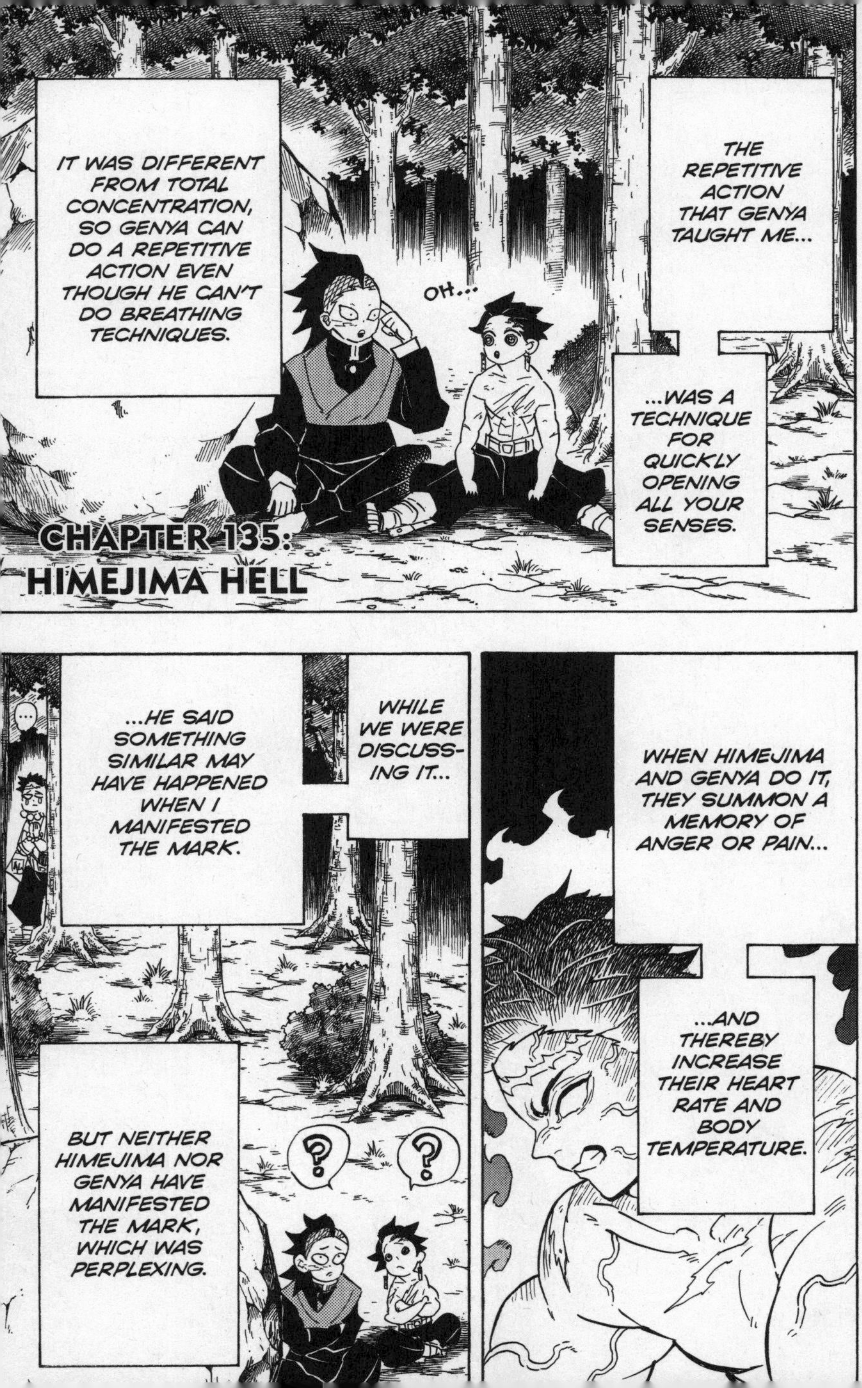
THE REPETITIVE ACTION THAT GENYA TAUGHT ME...
...WAS A TECHNIQUE FOR QUICKLY OPENING ALL YOUR SENSES.
OH...
IT WAS DIFFERENT FROM TOTAL CONCENTRATION, SO GENYA CAN DO A REPETITIVE ACTION EVEN THOUGH HE CAN'T DO BREATHING TECHNIQUES.
CHAPTER 135: HIMEJIMA HELL
WHEN HIMEJIMA AND GENYA DO IT, THEY SUMMON A MEMORY OF ANGER OR PAIN...
...AND THEREBY INCREASE THEIR HEART RATE AND BODY TEMPERATURE.
WHILE WE WERE DISCUSSING IT...
...HE SAID SOMETHING SIMILAR MAY HAVE HAPPENED WHEN I MANIFESTED THE MARK.
...
BUT NEITHER HIMEJIMA NOR GENYA HAVE MANIFESTED THE MARK, WHICH WAS PERPLEXING.
?
?

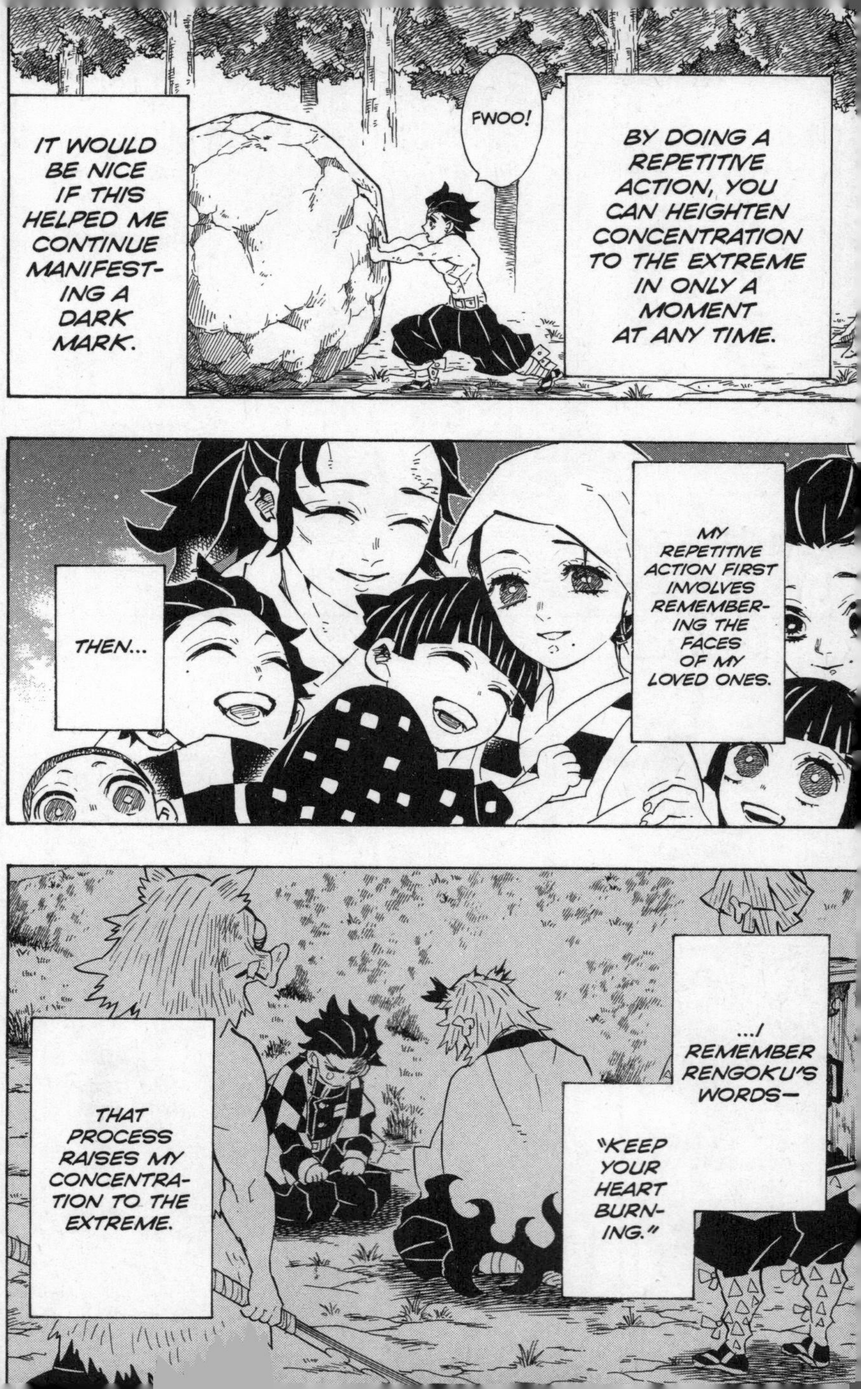
BY DOING A REPETITIVE ACTION, YOU CAN HEIGHTEN CONCENTRATION TO THE EXTREME IN ONLY A MOMENT AT ANY TIME.
FWOO!
IT WOULD BE NICE IF THIS HELPED ME CONTINUE MANIFESTING A DARK MARK.
MY REPETITIVE ACTION FIRST INVOLVES REMEMBERING THE FACES OF MY LOVED ONES.
THEN...
...I REMEMBER RENGOKU'S WORDS—
"KEEP YOUR HEART BURNING."
THAT PROCESS RAISES MY CONCENTRATION TO THE EXTREME.

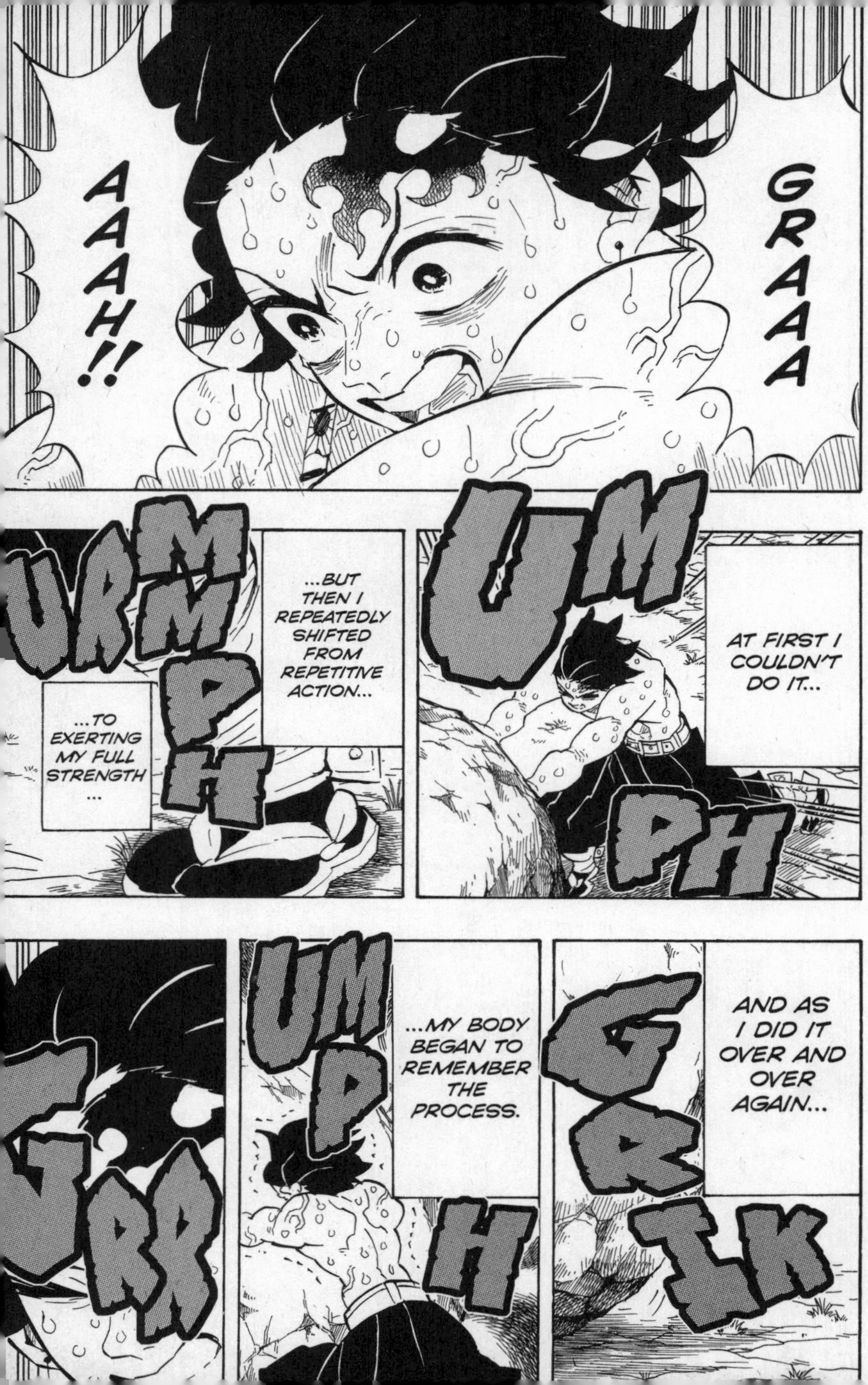
GRAAAA
AAAAH!!
AT FIRST I COULDN'T DO IT...
UMPH
...BUT THEN I REPEATEDLY SHIFTED FROM REPETITIVE ACTION...
URMMPH
...TO EXERTING MY FULL STRENGTH ...
AND AS I DID IT OVER AND OVER AGAIN...
GRILK
UMPH
...MY BODY BEGAN TO REMEMBER THE PROCESS.
URP

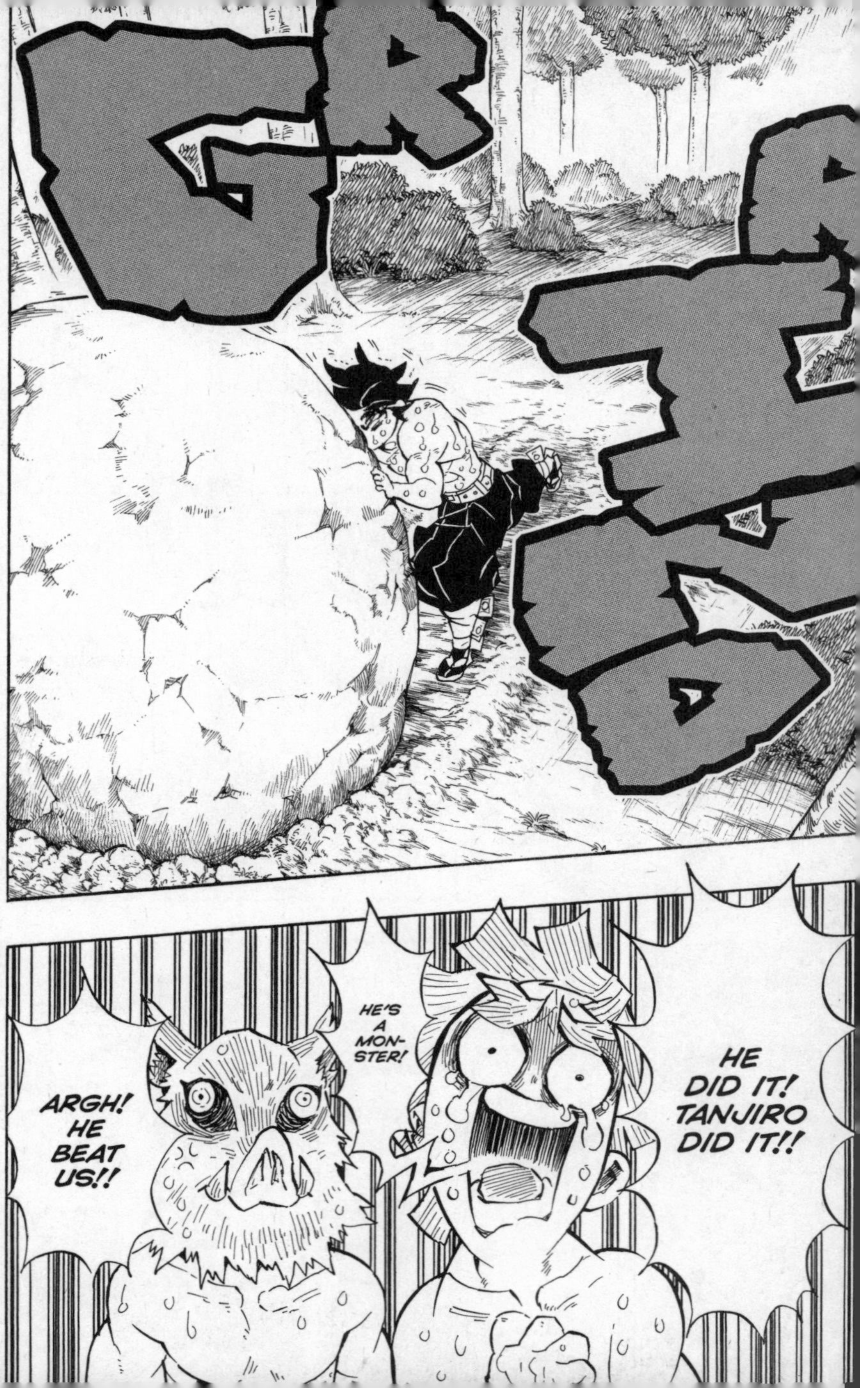
HE DID IT! TANJIRO DID IT!!
HE'S A MON-STER!
ARGH! HE BEAT US!!

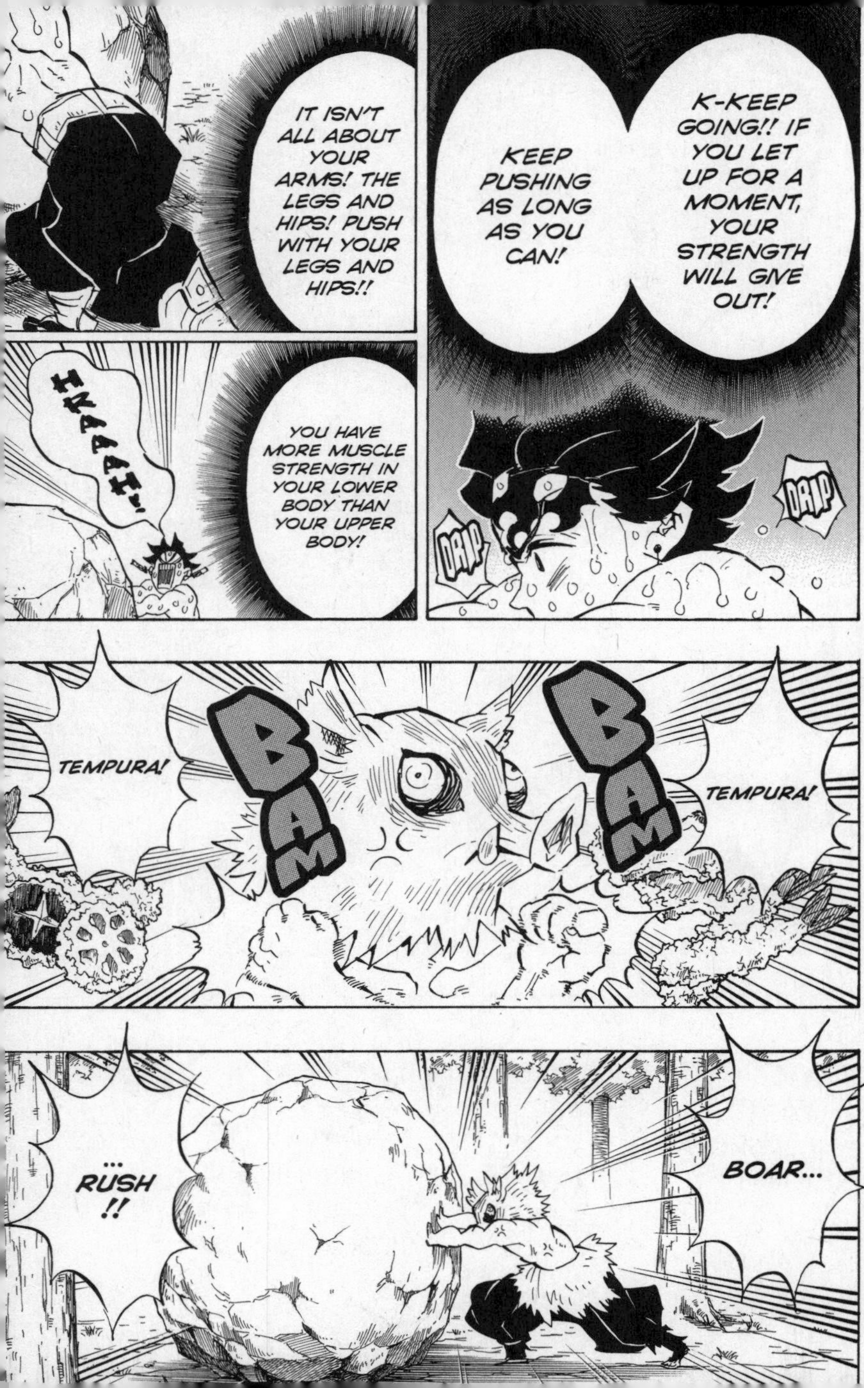

K-KEEP GOING!! IF YOU LET UP FOR A MOMENT, YOUR STRENGTH WILL GIVE OUT!
KEEP PUSHING AS LONG AS YOU CAN!
DRIP
DRIP
IT ISN'T ALL ABOUT YOUR ARMS! THE LEGS AND HIPS! PUSH WITH YOUR LEGS AND HIPS!!
YOU HAVE MORE MUSCLE STRENGTH IN YOUR LOWER BODY THAN YOUR UPPER BODY!
HRAAAH!!
TEMPURA!
BAM
BAM
TEMPURA!
BOAR...
...RUSH!!

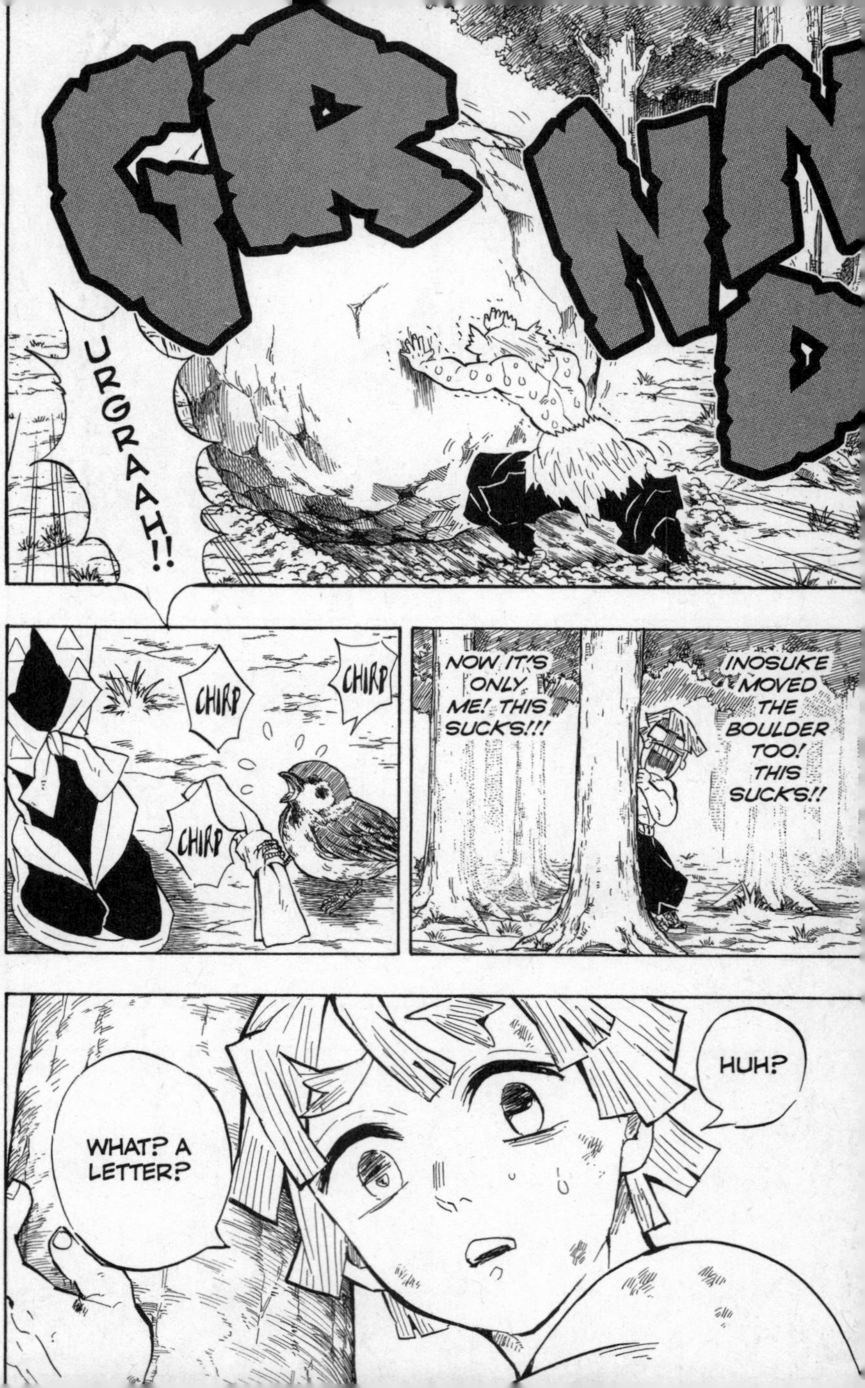
URGRAAH!!
INOSUKE MOVED THE BOULDER TOO! THIS SUCKS!!
NOW IT'S ONLY ME! THIS SUCKS!!!
CHIRP
CHIRP
CHIRP
HUH?
WHAT? A LETTER?

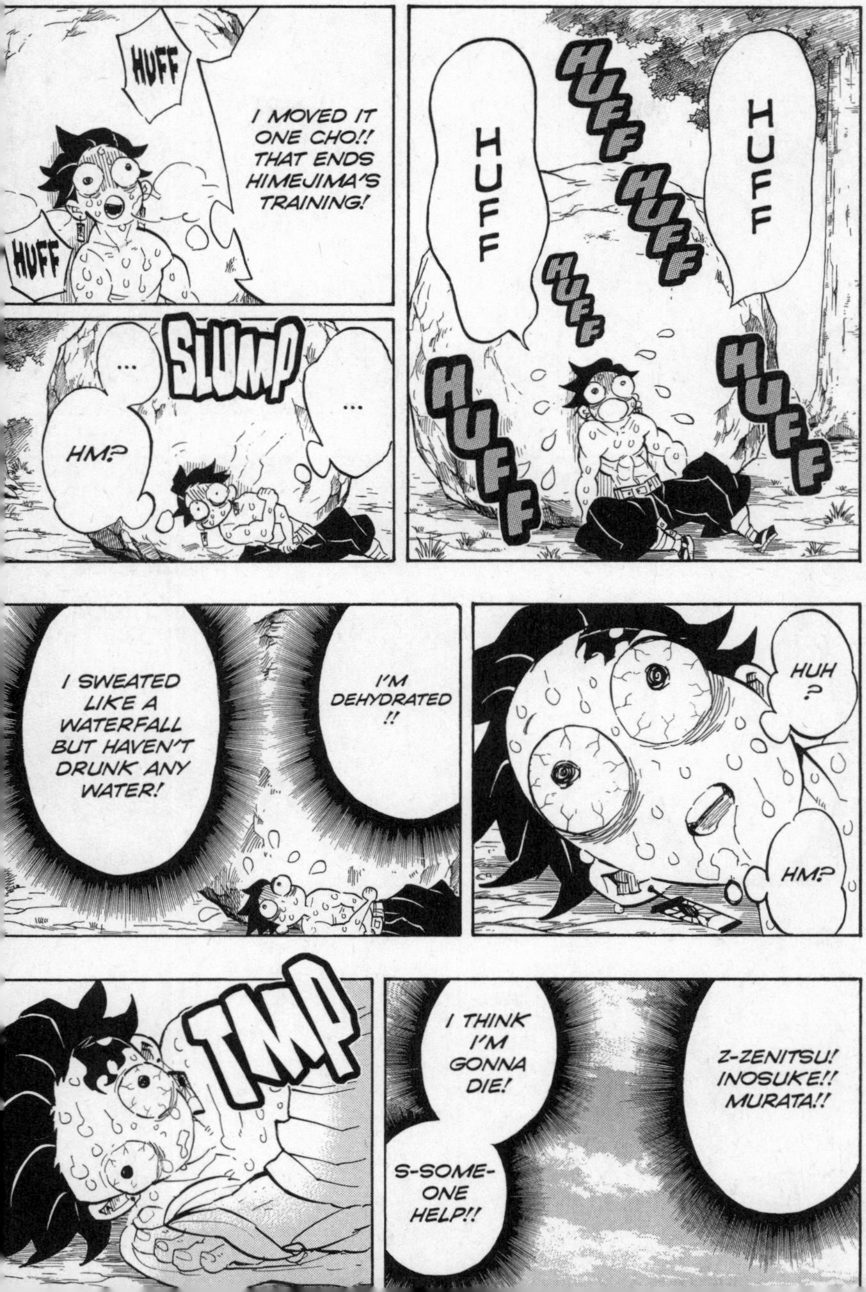
HUFF
HUFF
HUFF
HUFF
HUFF
HUFF
HUFF
HUFF
I MOVED IT ONE CHO!! THAT ENDS HIMEJIMA'S TRAINING!
HUFF
...
SLUMP
...
HM?
HUH?
HM?
I'M DEHYDRATED!!
I SWEATED LIKE A WATERFALL BUT HAVEN'T DRUNK ANY WATER!
Z-ZENITSU! INOSUKE!! MURATA!!
I THINK I'M GONNA DIE!
S-SOME-ONE HELP!!
TMP

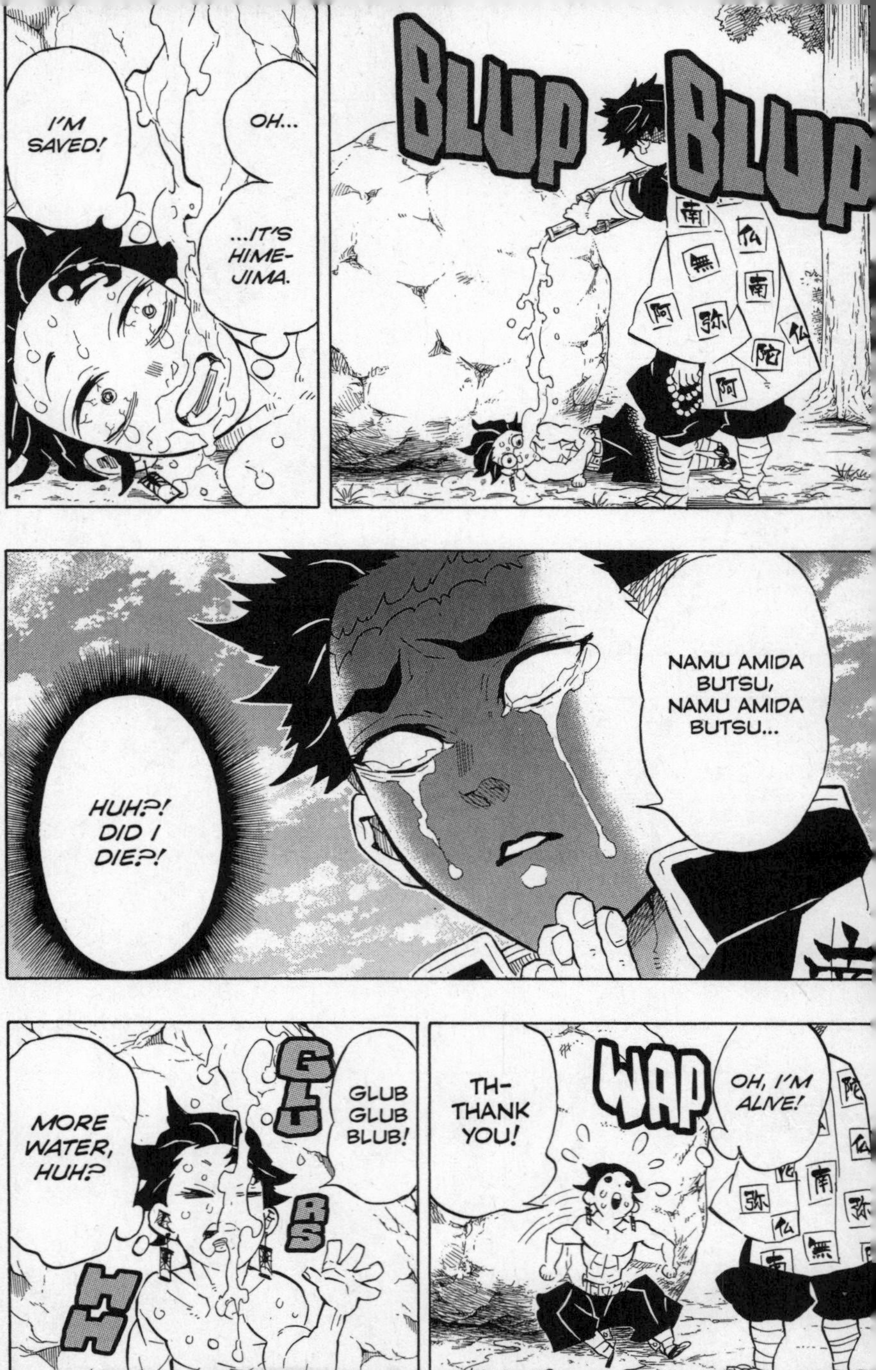
BLUP BLUP
OH...
...IT'S HIME-JIMA.
I'M SAVED!
NAMU AMIDA BUTSU, NAMU AMIDA BUTSU...
HUH?! DID I DIE?!
OH, I'M ALIVE!
WAP
TH-THANK YOU!
GLUB GLUB BLUB!
GLURS
MORE WATER, HUH?

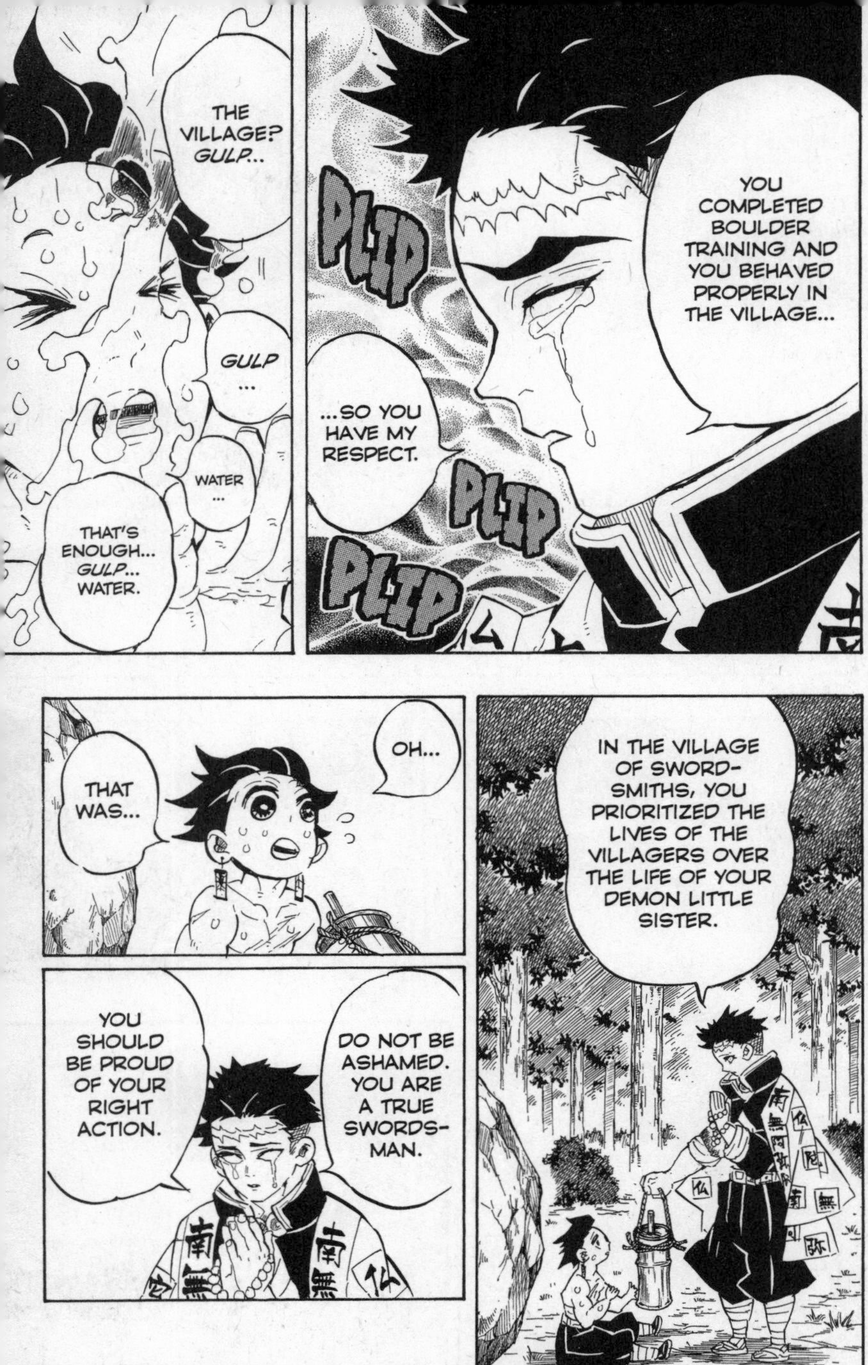
YOU COMPLETED BOULDER TRAINING AND YOU BEHAVED PROPERLY IN THE VILLAGE...
PLIP
...SO YOU HAVE MY RESPECT.
PLIP
PLIP
THE VILLAGE? GULP...
GULP...
WATER...
THAT'S ENOUGH... GULP... WATER.
IN THE VILLAGE OF SWORD-SMITHS, YOU PRIORITIZED THE LIVES OF THE VILLAGERS OVER THE LIFE OF YOUR DEMON LITTLE SISTER.
OH...
THAT WAS...
DO NOT BE ASHAMED. YOU ARE A TRUE SWORDS-MAN.
YOU SHOULD BE PROUD OF YOUR RIGHT ACTION.

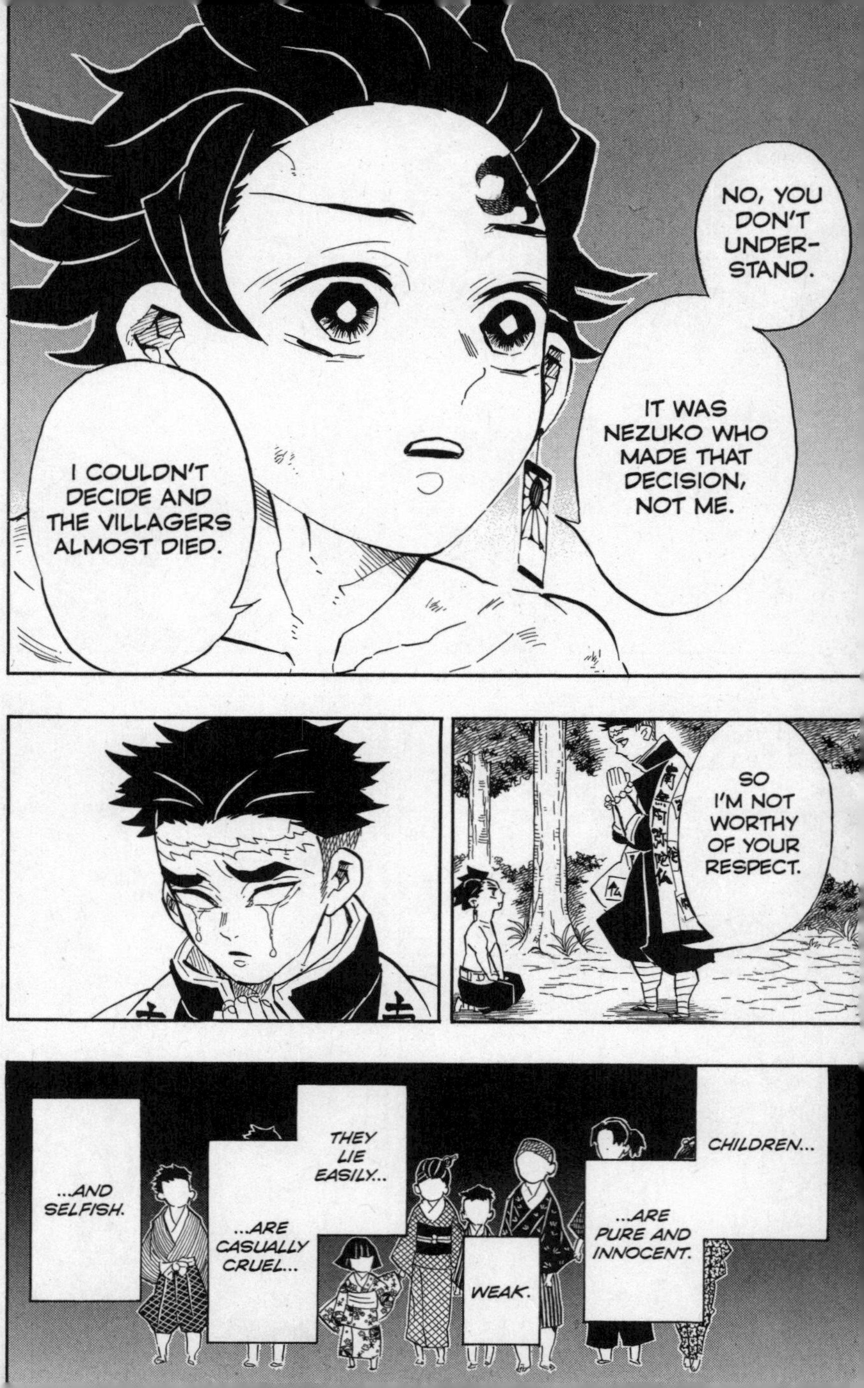
NO, YOU DON'T UNDER-STAND.
IT WAS NEZUKO WHO MADE THAT DECISION, NOT ME.
I COULDN'T DECIDE AND THE VILLAGERS ALMOST DIED.
SO I'M NOT WORTHY OF YOUR RESPECT.
CHILDREN...
...ARE PURE AND INNOCENT.
WEAK.
THEY LIE EASILY...
...ARE CASUALLY CRUEL...
...AND SELFISH.

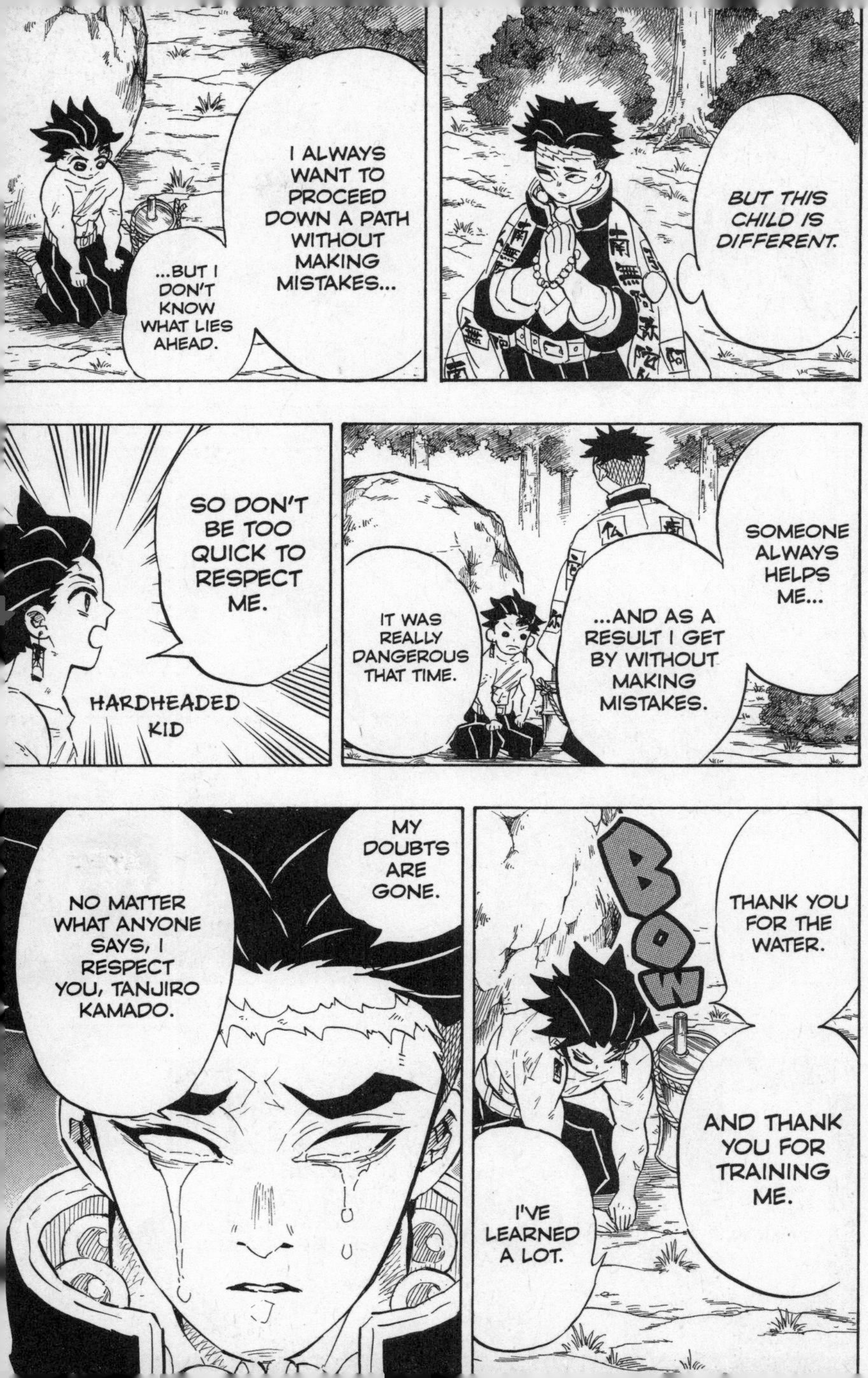
BUT THIS CHILD IS DIFFERENT.
I ALWAYS WANT TO PROCEED DOWN A PATH WITHOUT MAKING MISTAKES...
...BUT I DON'T KNOW WHAT LIES AHEAD.
SOMEONE ALWAYS HELPS ME...
...AND AS A RESULT I GET BY WITHOUT MAKING MISTAKES.
IT WAS REALLY DANGEROUS THAT TIME.
SO DON'T BE TOO QUICK TO RESPECT ME.
HARDHEADED KID
THANK YOU FOR THE WATER.
BOW
AND THANK YOU FOR TRAINING ME.
I'VE LEARNED A LOT.
MY DOUBTS ARE GONE.
NO MATTER WHAT ANYONE SAYS, I RESPECT YOU, TANJIRO KAMADO.

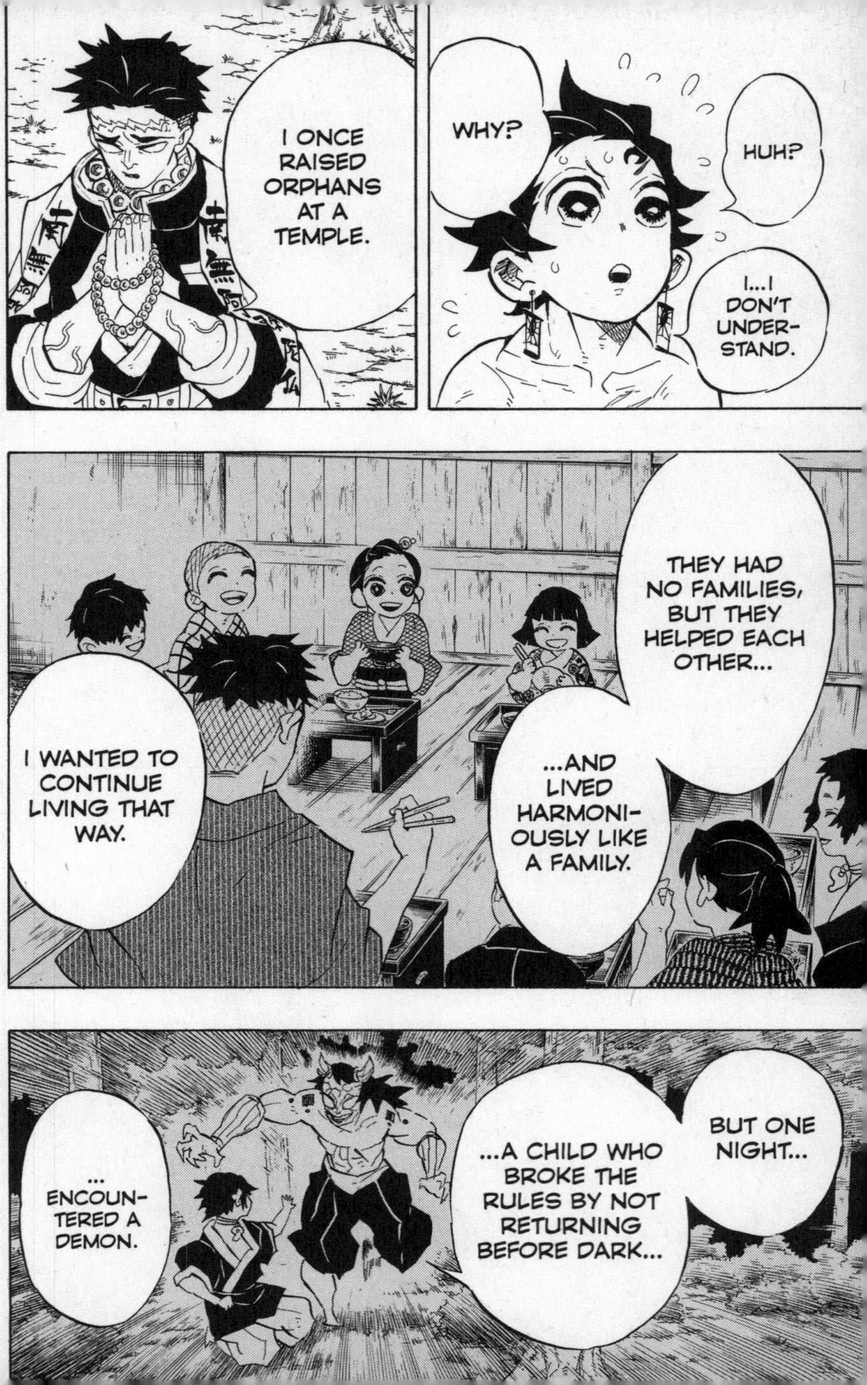
HUH?
WHY?
I...I DON'T UNDER-STAND.
I ONCE RAISED ORPHANS AT A TEMPLE.
THEY HAD NO FAMILIES, BUT THEY HELPED EACH OTHER...
...AND LIVED HARMONI-OUSLY LIKE A FAMILY.
I WANTED TO CONTINUE LIVING THAT WAY.
BUT ONE NIGHT...
...A CHILD WHO BROKE THE RULES BY NOT RETURNING BEFORE DARK...
... ENCOUN-TERED A DEMON.

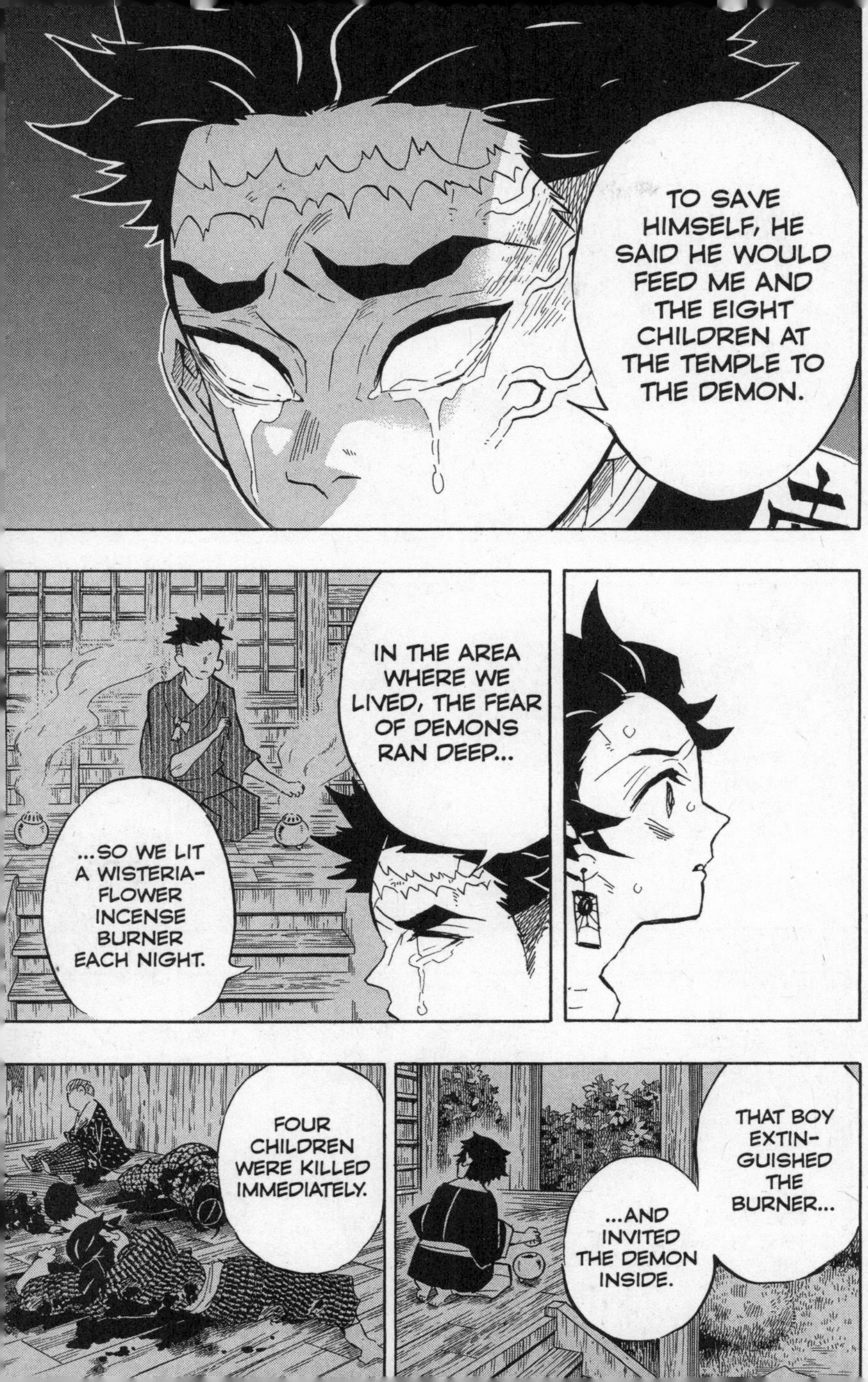
TO SAVE HIMSELF, HE SAID HE WOULD FEED ME AND THE EIGHT CHILDREN AT THE TEMPLE TO THE DEMON.
IN THE AREA WHERE WE LIVED, THE FEAR OF DEMONS RAN DEEP...
...SO WE LIT A WISTERIA-FLOWER INCENSE BURNER EACH NIGHT.
THAT BOY EXTIN-GUISHED THE BURNER...
...AND INVITED THE DEMON INSIDE.
FOUR CHILDREN WERE KILLED IMMEDIATELY.

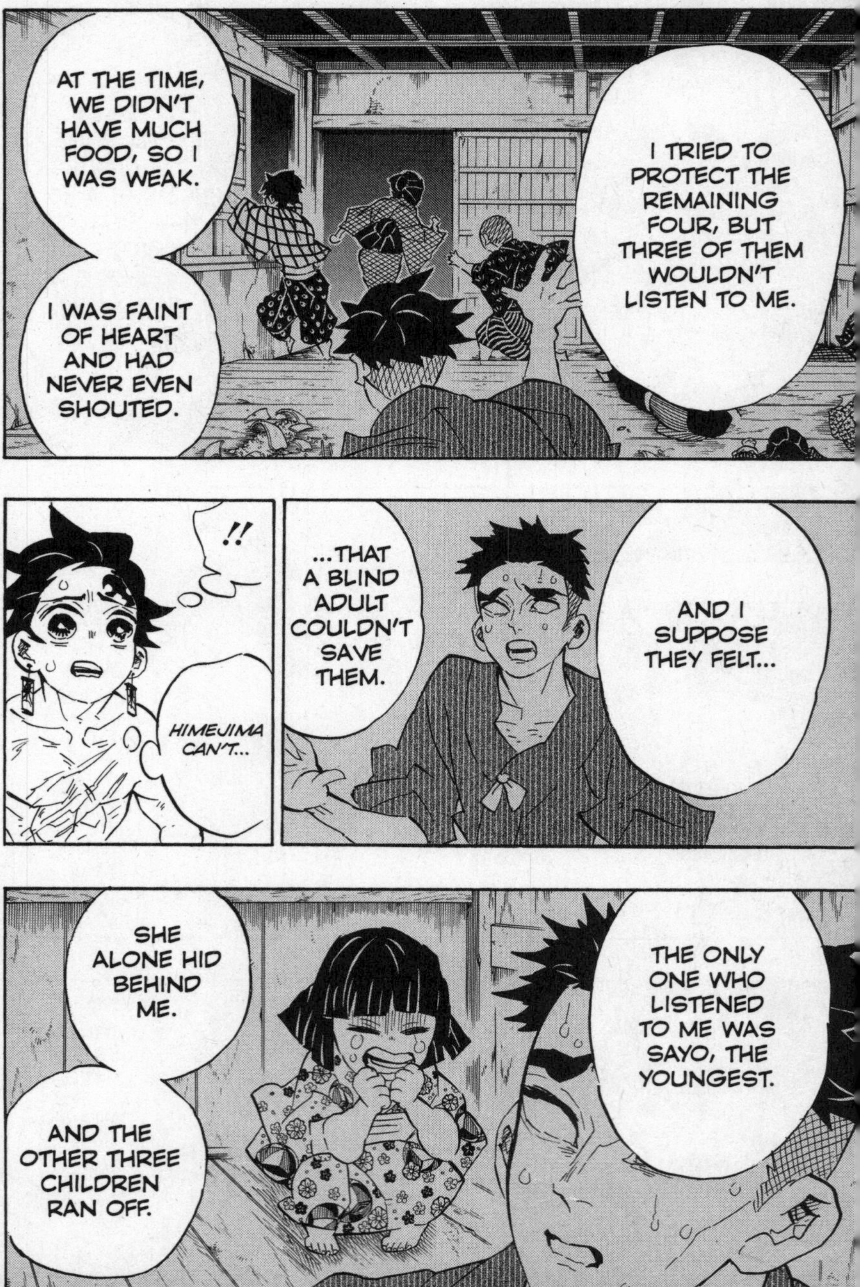
I TRIED TO PROTECT THE REMAINING FOUR, BUT THREE OF THEM WOULDN'T LISTEN TO ME.
AT THE TIME, WE DIDN'T HAVE MUCH FOOD, SO I WAS WEAK.
I WAS FAINT OF HEART AND HAD NEVER EVEN SHOUTED.
AND I SUPPOSE THEY FELT...
...THAT A BLIND ADULT COULDN'T SAVE THEM.
!!
HIMEJIMA CAN'T...
THE ONLY ONE WHO LISTENED TO ME WAS SAYO, THE YOUNGEST.
SHE ALONE HID BEHIND ME.
AND THE OTHER THREE CHILDREN RAN OFF.

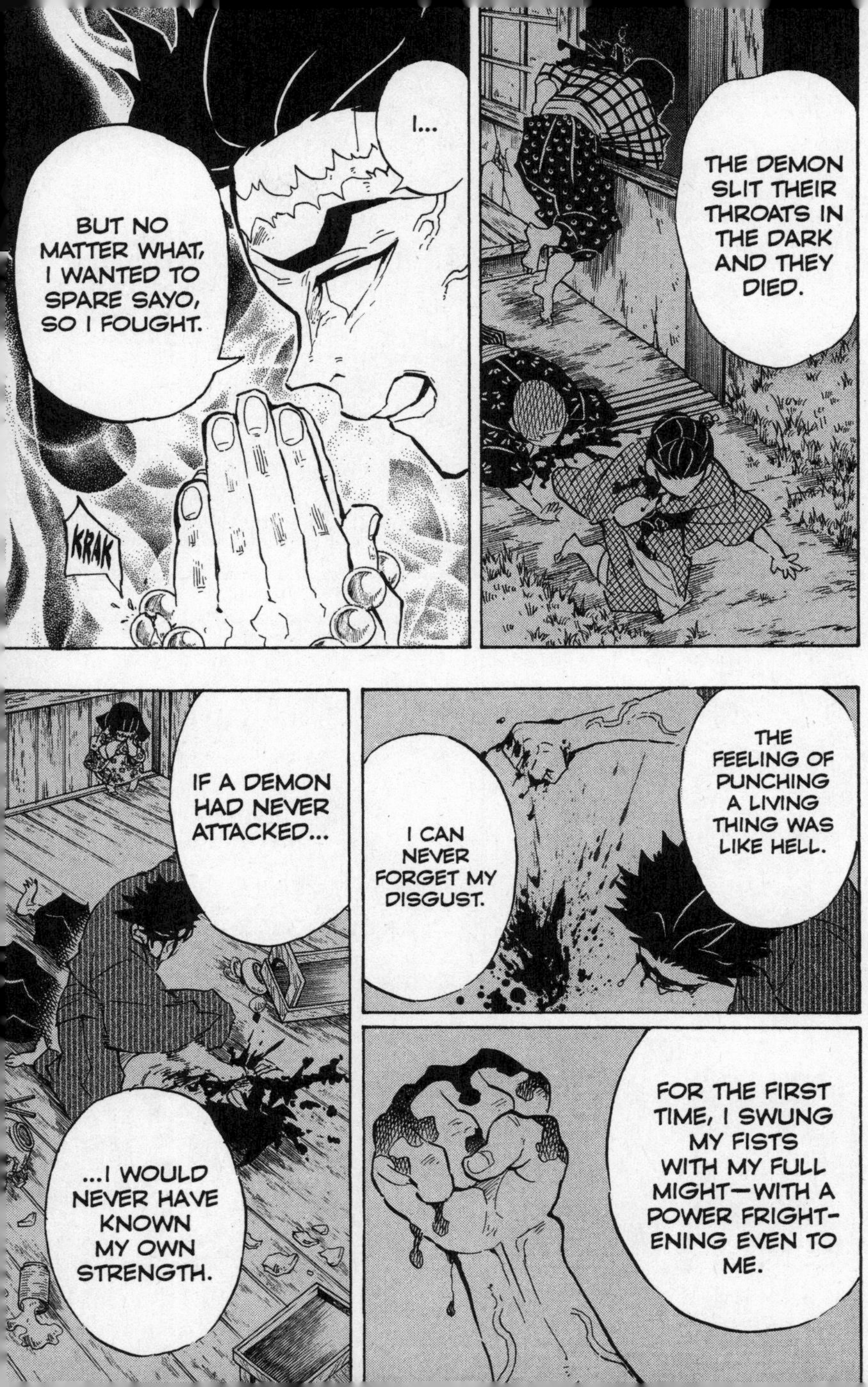
THE DEMON SLIT THEIR THROATS IN THE DARK AND THEY DIED.
I...
BUT NO MATTER WHAT, I WANTED TO SPARE SAYO, SO I FOUGHT.
KRAK
THE FEELING OF PUNCHING A LIVING THING WAS LIKE HELL.
I CAN NEVER FORGET MY DISGUST.
FOR THE FIRST TIME, I SWUNG MY FISTS WITH MY FULL MIGHT—WITH A POWER FRIGHT-ENING EVEN TO ME.
IF A DEMON HAD NEVER ATTACKED...
...I WOULD NEVER HAVE KNOWN MY OWN STRENGTH.

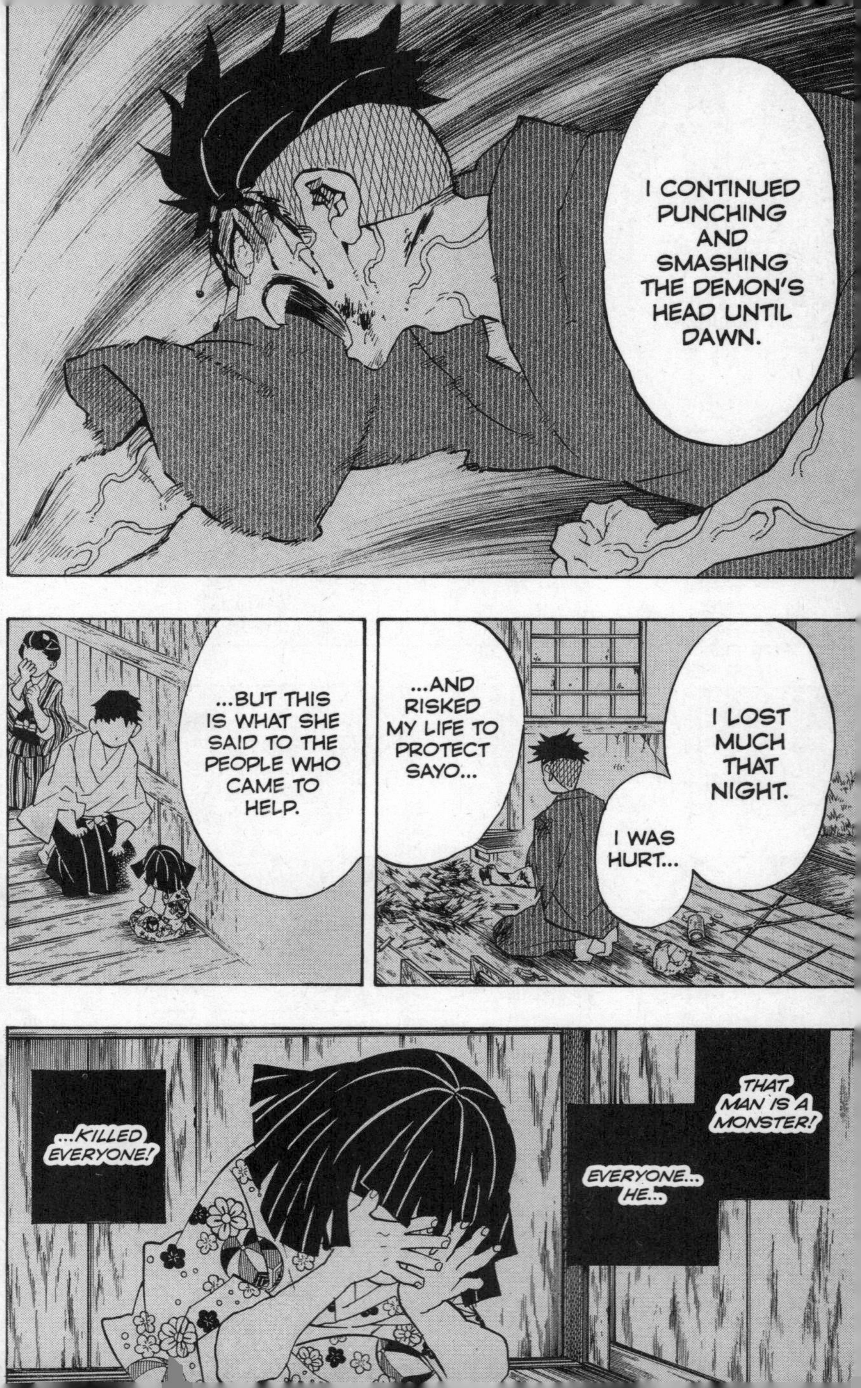
I CONTINUED PUNCHING AND SMASHING THE DEMON'S HEAD UNTIL DAWN.
I LOST MUCH THAT NIGHT.
I WAS HURT...
...AND RISKED MY LIFE TO PROTECT SAYO...
...BUT THIS IS WHAT SHE SAID TO THE PEOPLE WHO CAME TO HELP.
THAT MAN IS A MONSTER!
EVERYONE... HE...
...KILLED EVERYONE!

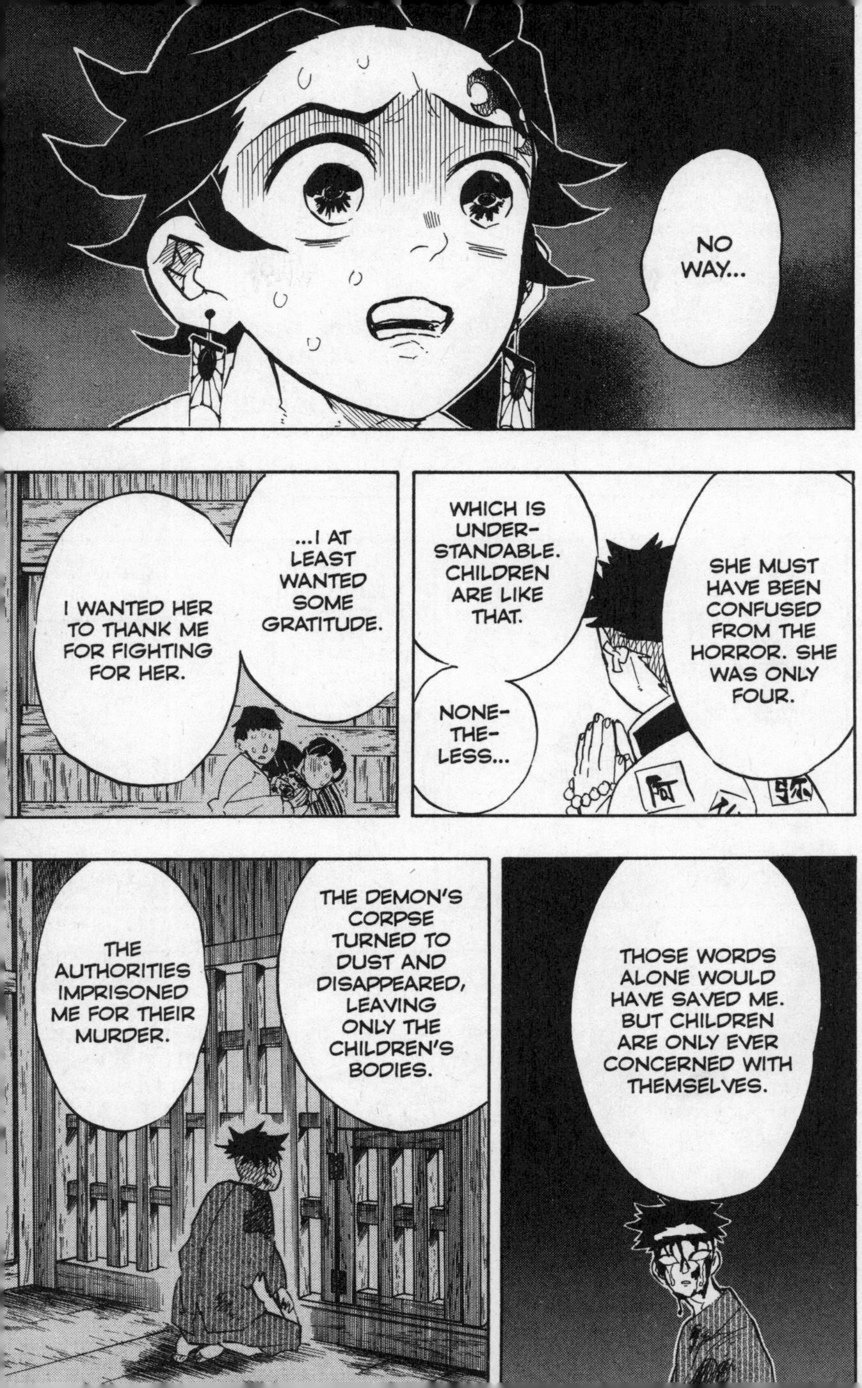
NO WAY...
SHE MUST HAVE BEEN CONFUSED FROM THE HORROR. SHE WAS ONLY FOUR.
WHICH IS UNDER-STANDABLE. CHILDREN ARE LIKE THAT.
NONE-THE-LESS...
...I AT LEAST WANTED SOME GRATITUDE.
I WANTED HER TO THANK ME FOR FIGHTING FOR HER.
THOSE WORDS ALONE WOULD HAVE SAVED ME. BUT CHILDREN ARE ONLY EVER CONCERNED WITH THEMSELVES.
THE DEMON'S CORPSE TURNED TO DUST AND DISAPPEARED, LEAVING ONLY THE CHILDREN'S BODIES.
THE AUTHORITIES IMPRISONED ME FOR THEIR MURDER.

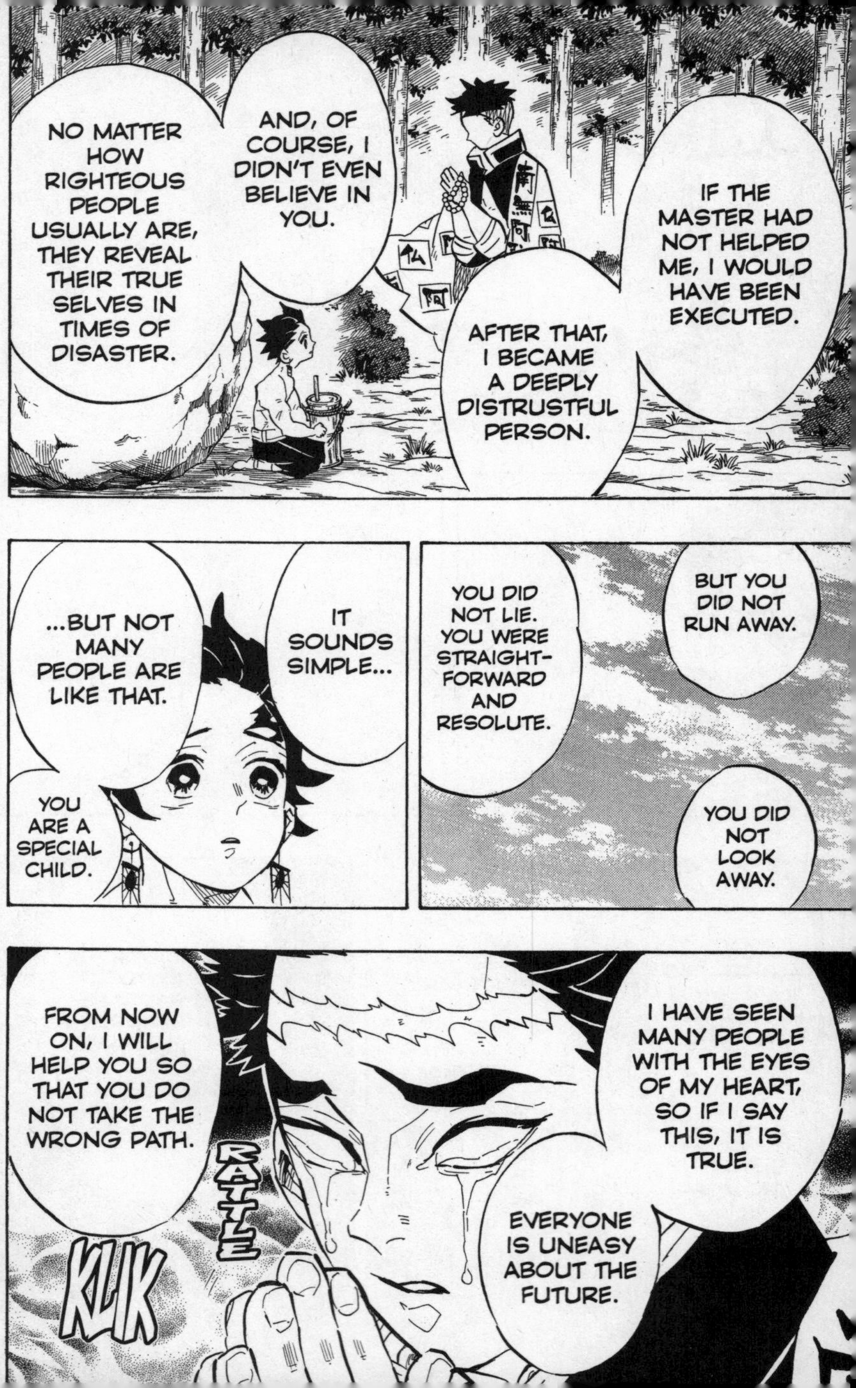
IF THE MASTER HAD NOT HELPED ME, I WOULD HAVE BEEN EXECUTED.
AFTER THAT, I BECAME A DEEPLY DISTRUSTFUL PERSON.
AND, OF COURSE, I DIDN'T EVEN BELIEVE IN YOU.
NO MATTER HOW RIGHTEOUS PEOPLE USUALLY ARE, THEY REVEAL THEIR TRUE SELVES IN TIMES OF DISASTER.
BUT YOU DID NOT RUN AWAY.
YOU DID NOT LOOK AWAY.
YOU DID NOT LIE. YOU WERE STRAIGHT-FORWARD AND RESOLUTE.
IT SOUNDS SIMPLE...
...BUT NOT MANY PEOPLE ARE LIKE THAT.
YOU ARE A SPECIAL CHILD.
I HAVE SEEN MANY PEOPLE WITH THE EYES OF MY HEART, SO IF I SAY THIS, IT IS TRUE.
EVERYONE IS UNEASY ABOUT THE FUTURE.
RATTLE
FROM NOW ON, I WILL HELP YOU SO THAT YOU DO NOT TAKE THE WRONG PATH.
KLIK

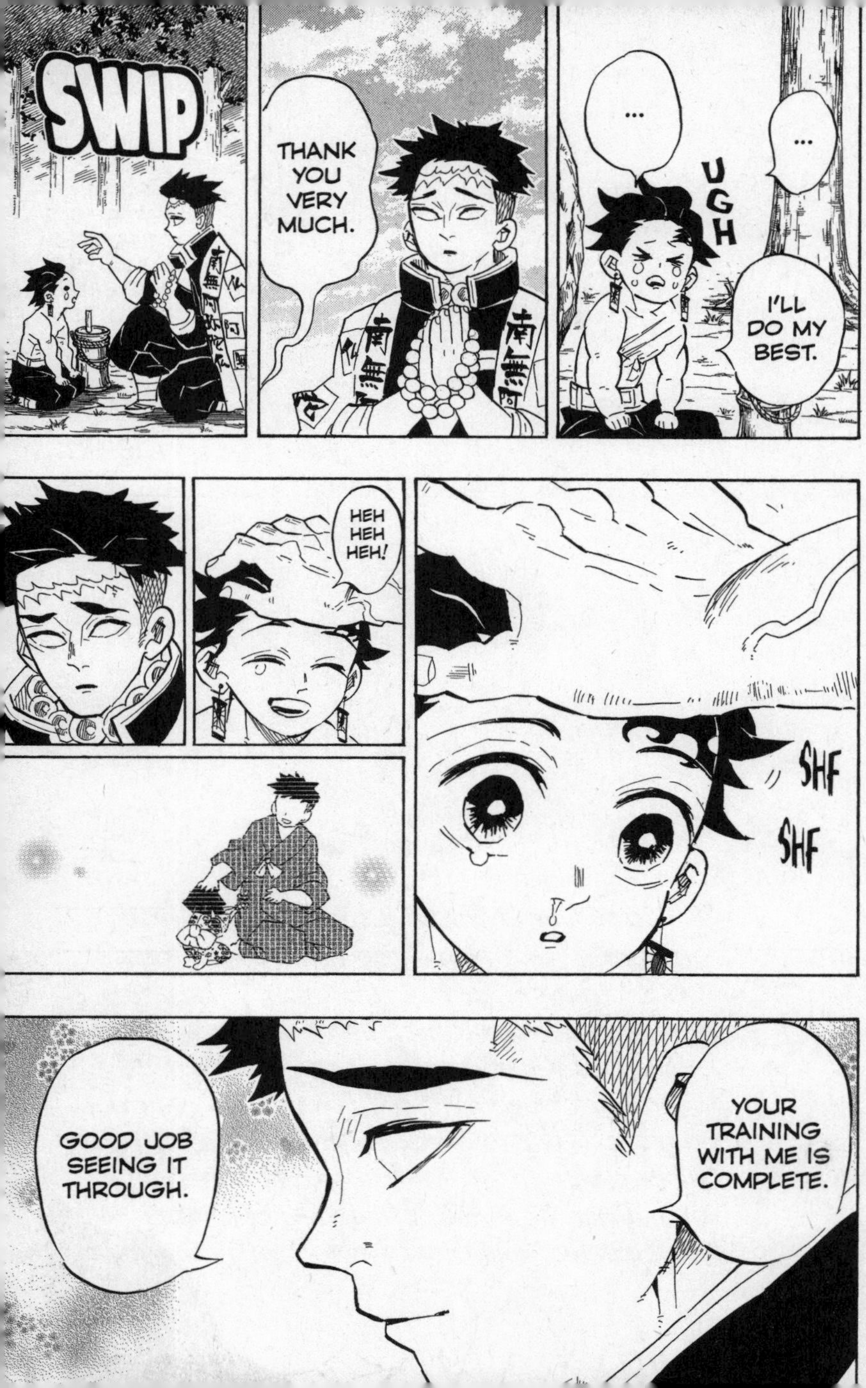
...
...
UGH
I'LL DO MY BEST.
THANK YOU VERY MUCH.
SWIP
SHF
SHF
HEH HEH HEH!
YOUR TRAINING WITH ME IS COMPLETE.
GOOD JOB SEEING IT THROUGH.

Sayo's Story

According to Sayo's account of the demon attack, "that man," was a "monster" who killed everyone, but by "that man," she meant the demon who snuck into the temple, not Himejima. However, the demon had burned up in the morning sun, and Sayo couldn't speak properly due to shock from the incident, so she couldn't dispel the suspicion that fell on Himejima. Even now, at age 14, Sayo worries about that and wishes she could apologize.

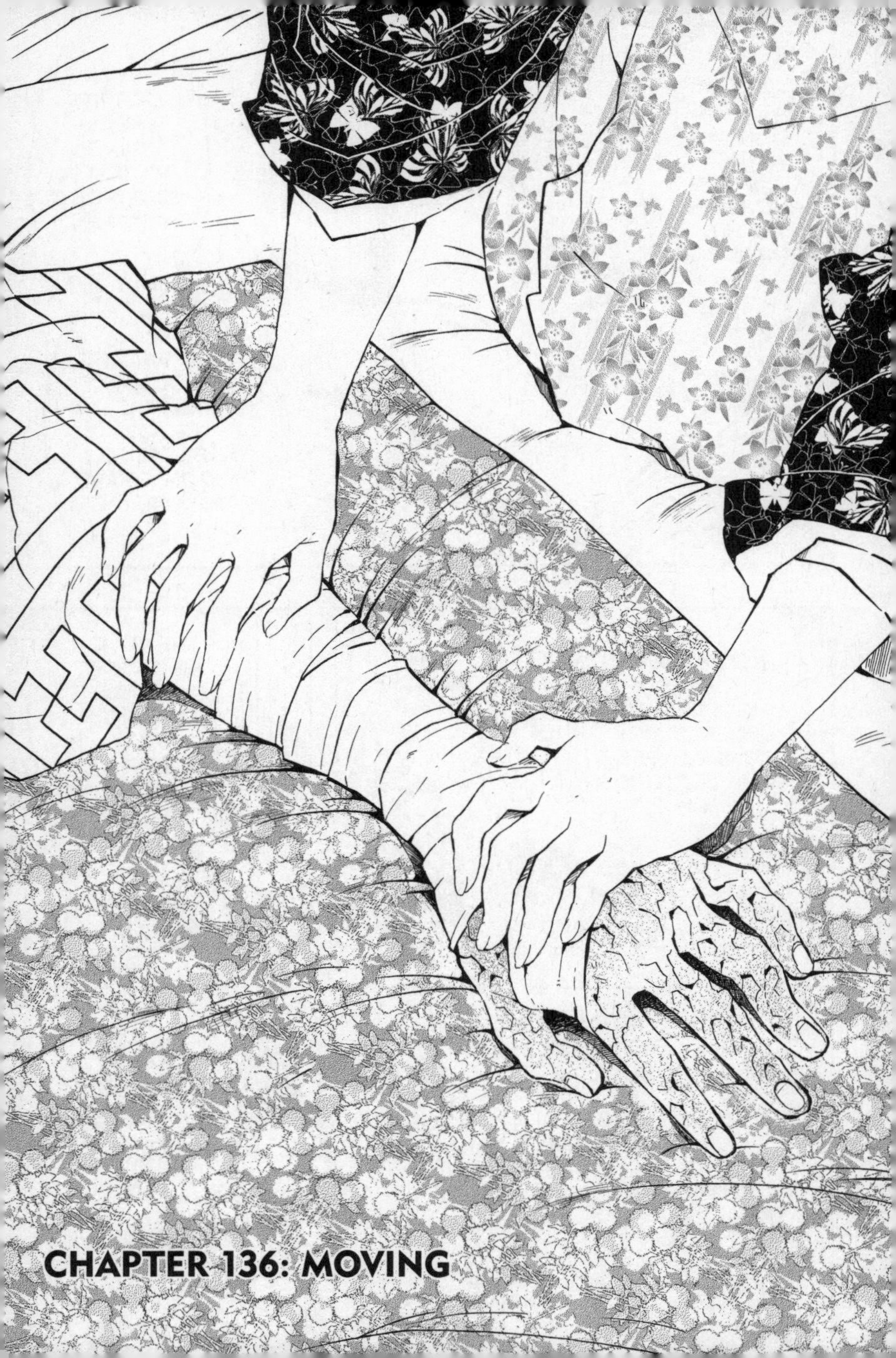

CHAPTER 136: MOVING

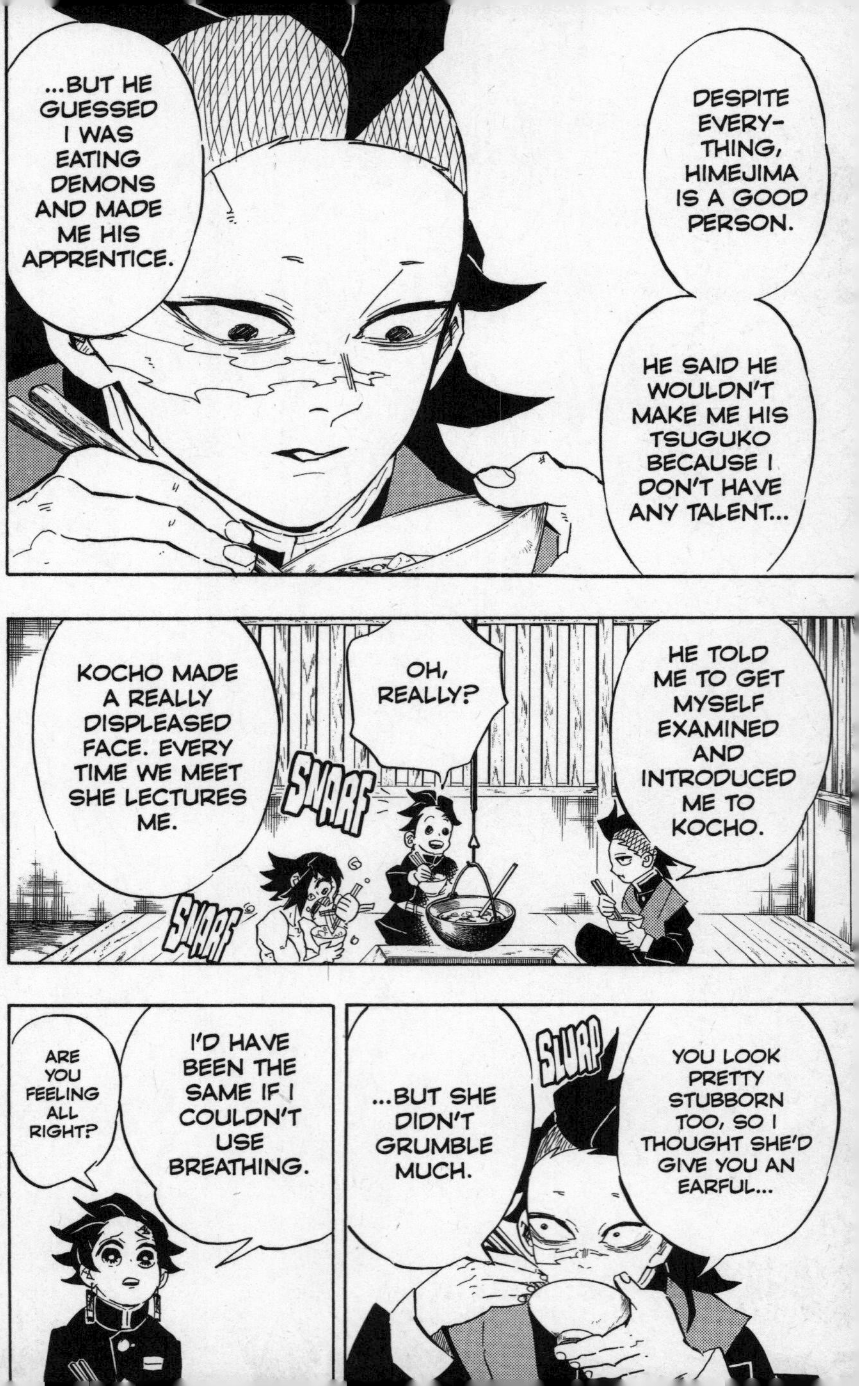
DESPITE EVERY-THING, HIMEJIMA IS A GOOD PERSON.
HE SAID HE WOULDN'T MAKE ME HIS TSUGUKO BECAUSE I DON'T HAVE ANY TALENT...
...BUT HE GUESSED I WAS EATING DEMONS AND MADE ME HIS APPRENTICE.
HE TOLD ME TO GET MYSELF EXAMINED AND INTRODUCED ME TO KOCHO.
OH, REALLY?
SNARF
SNARF
KOCHO MADE A REALLY DISPLEASED FACE. EVERY TIME WE MEET SHE LECTURES ME.
YOU LOOK PRETTY STUBBORN TOO, SO I THOUGHT SHE'D GIVE YOU AN EARFUL...
SLURP
...BUT SHE DIDN'T GRUMBLE MUCH.
I'D HAVE BEEN THE SAME IF I COULDN'T USE BREATHING.
ARE YOU FEELING ALL RIGHT?

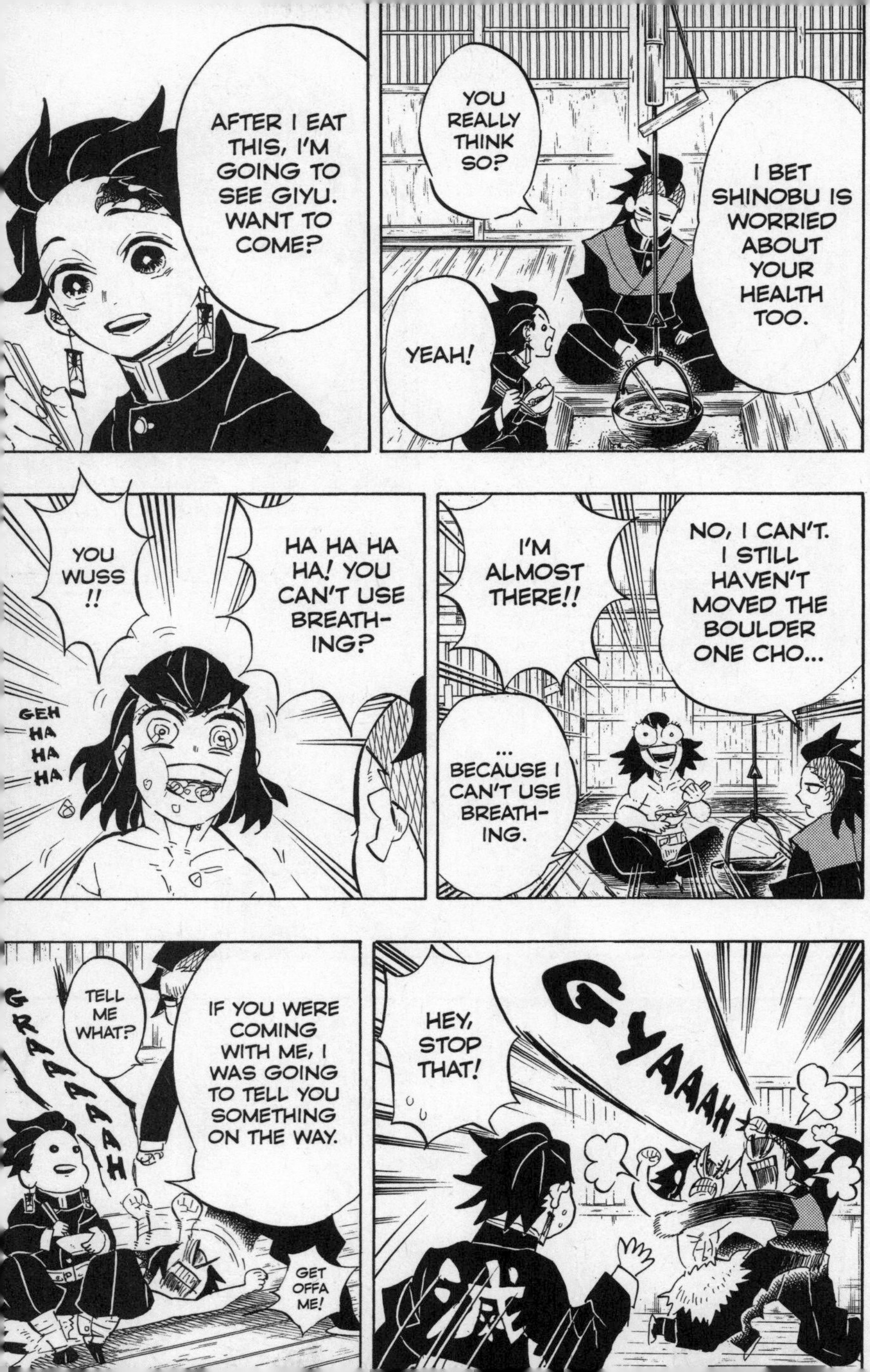
I BET SHINOBU IS WORRIED ABOUT YOUR HEALTH TOO.
YOU REALLY THINK SO?
YEAH!
AFTER I EAT THIS, I'M GOING TO SEE GIYU. WANT TO COME?
NO, I CAN'T. I STILL HAVEN'T MOVED THE BOULDER ONE CHO...
I'M ALMOST THERE!!
... BECAUSE I CAN'T USE BREATH-ING.
HA HA HA HA! YOU CAN'T USE BREATH-ING?
YOU WUSS !!
GEH HA HA HA
GYAAAAH
HEY, STOP THAT!
IF YOU WERE COMING WITH ME, I WAS GOING TO TELL YOU SOMETHING ON THE WAY.
TELL ME WHAT?
GRAAAAAAH
GET OFFA ME!

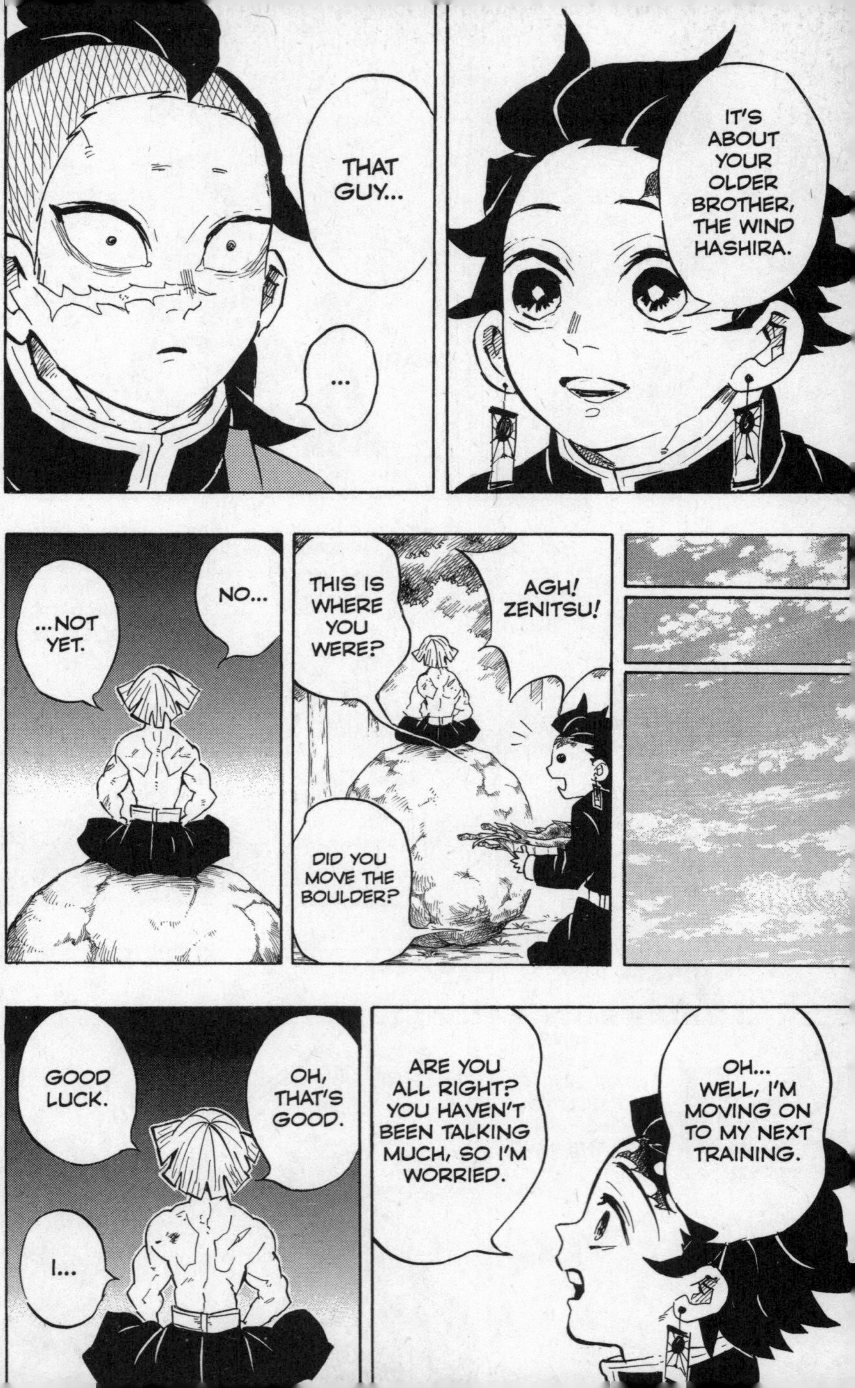
IT'S ABOUT YOUR OLDER BROTHER, THE WIND HASHIRA.
THAT GUY...
...
AGH! ZENITSU!
THIS IS WHERE YOU WERE?
DID YOU MOVE THE BOULDER?
NO...
...NOT YET.
OH... WELL, I'M MOVING ON TO MY NEXT TRAINING.
ARE YOU ALL RIGHT? YOU HAVEN'T BEEN TALKING MUCH, SO I'M WORRIED.
OH, THAT'S GOOD.
GOOD LUCK.
I...

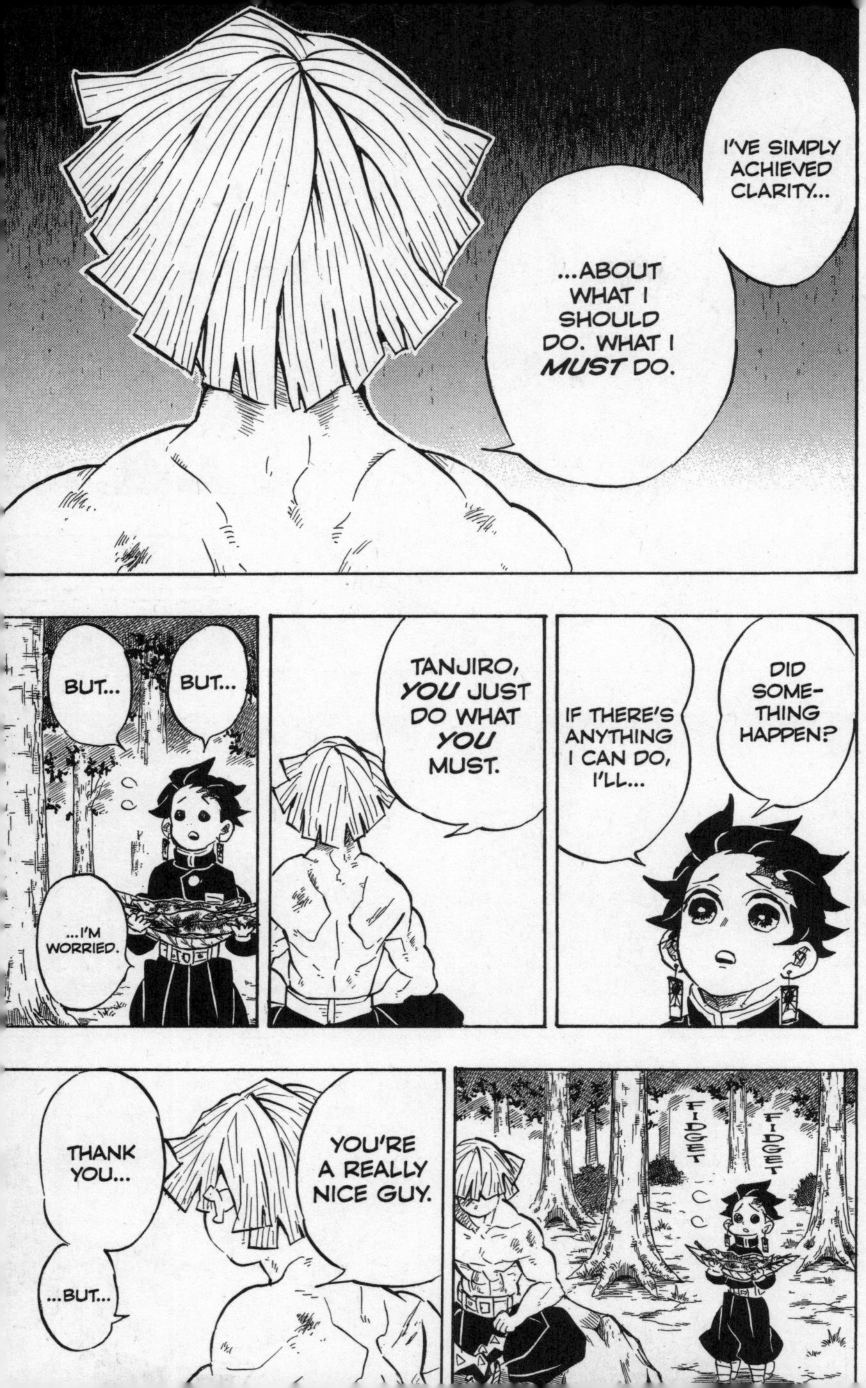
I'VE SIMPLY ACHIEVED CLARITY...
...ABOUT WHAT I SHOULD DO. WHAT I *MUST* DO.
DID SOME-THING HAPPEN?
IF THERE'S ANYTHING I CAN DO, I'LL...
TANJIRO, *YOU* JUST DO WHAT *YOU* MUST.
BUT...
BUT...
...I'M WORRIED.
FIDGET
FIDGET
YOU'RE A REALLY NICE GUY.
THANK YOU...
...BUT...

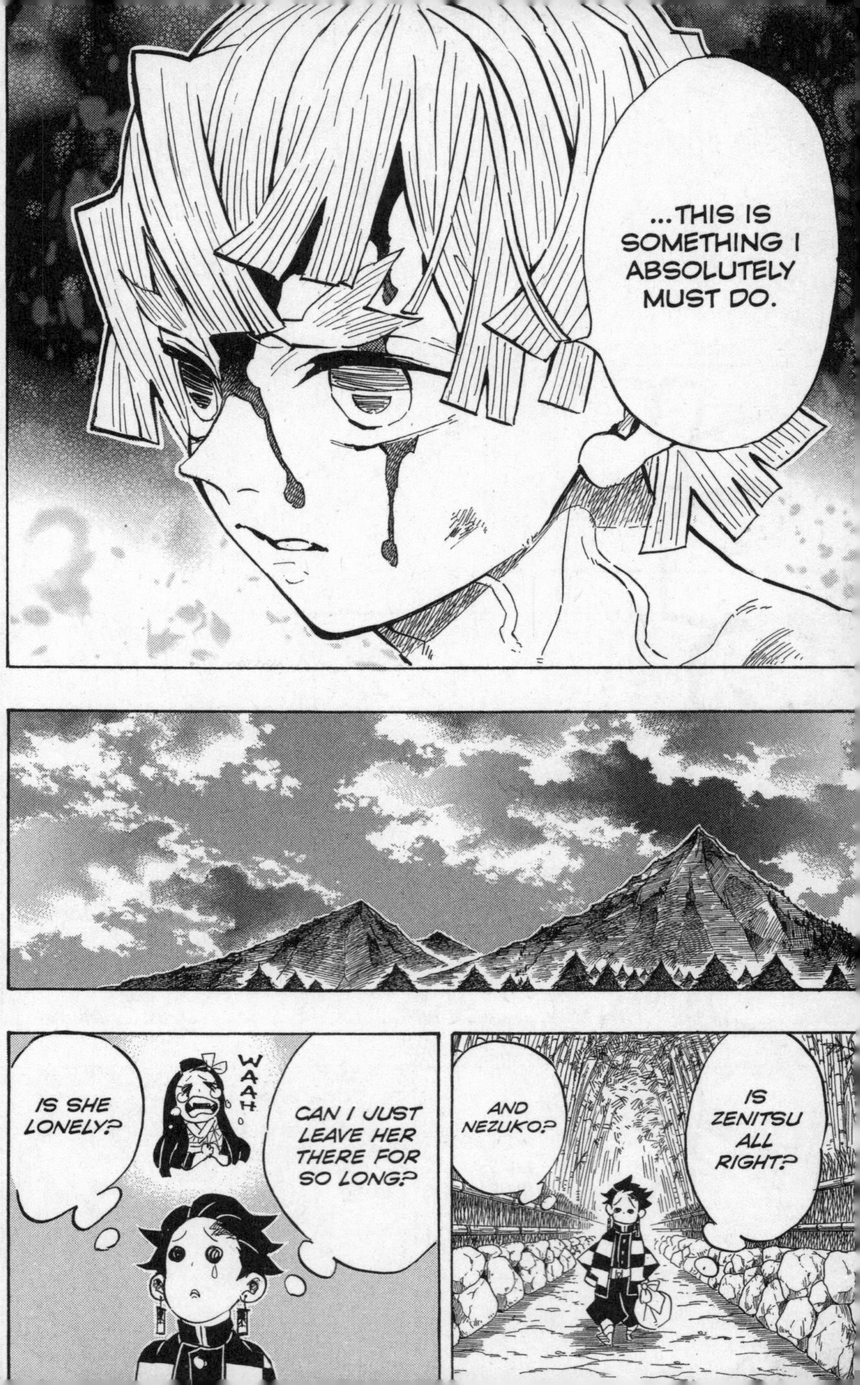
...THIS IS SOMETHING I ABSOLUTELY MUST DO.
IS ZENITSU ALL RIGHT?
AND NEZUKO?
CAN I JUST LEAVE HER THERE FOR SO LONG?
WAAH
IS SHE LONELY?

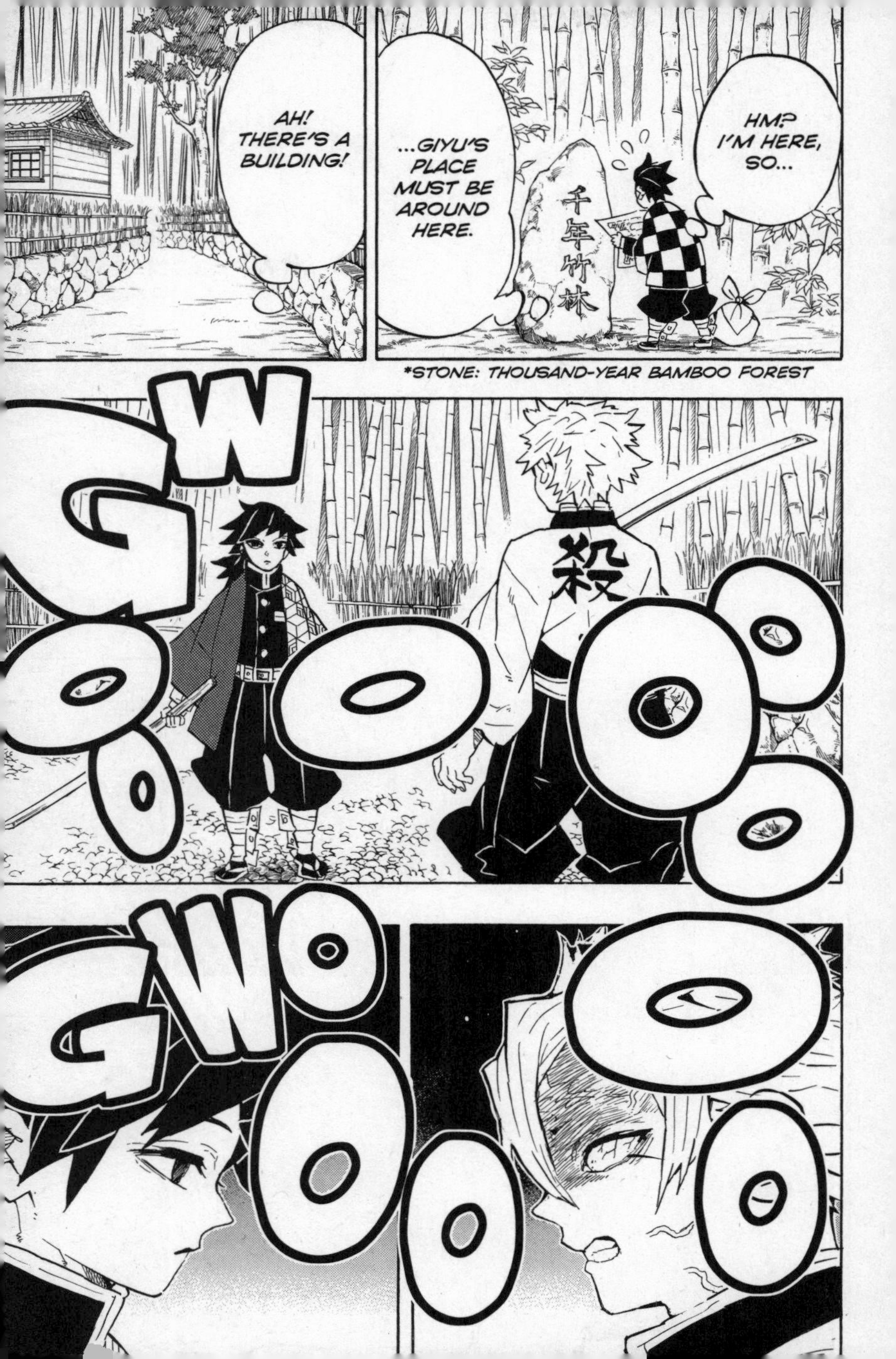
HM? I'M HERE, SO...
...GIYU'S PLACE MUST BE AROUND HERE.
AH! THERE'S A BUILDING!
千年竹林
*STONE: THOUSAND-YEAR BAMBOO FOREST
殺
GWOOOOOO
GWOOOOO

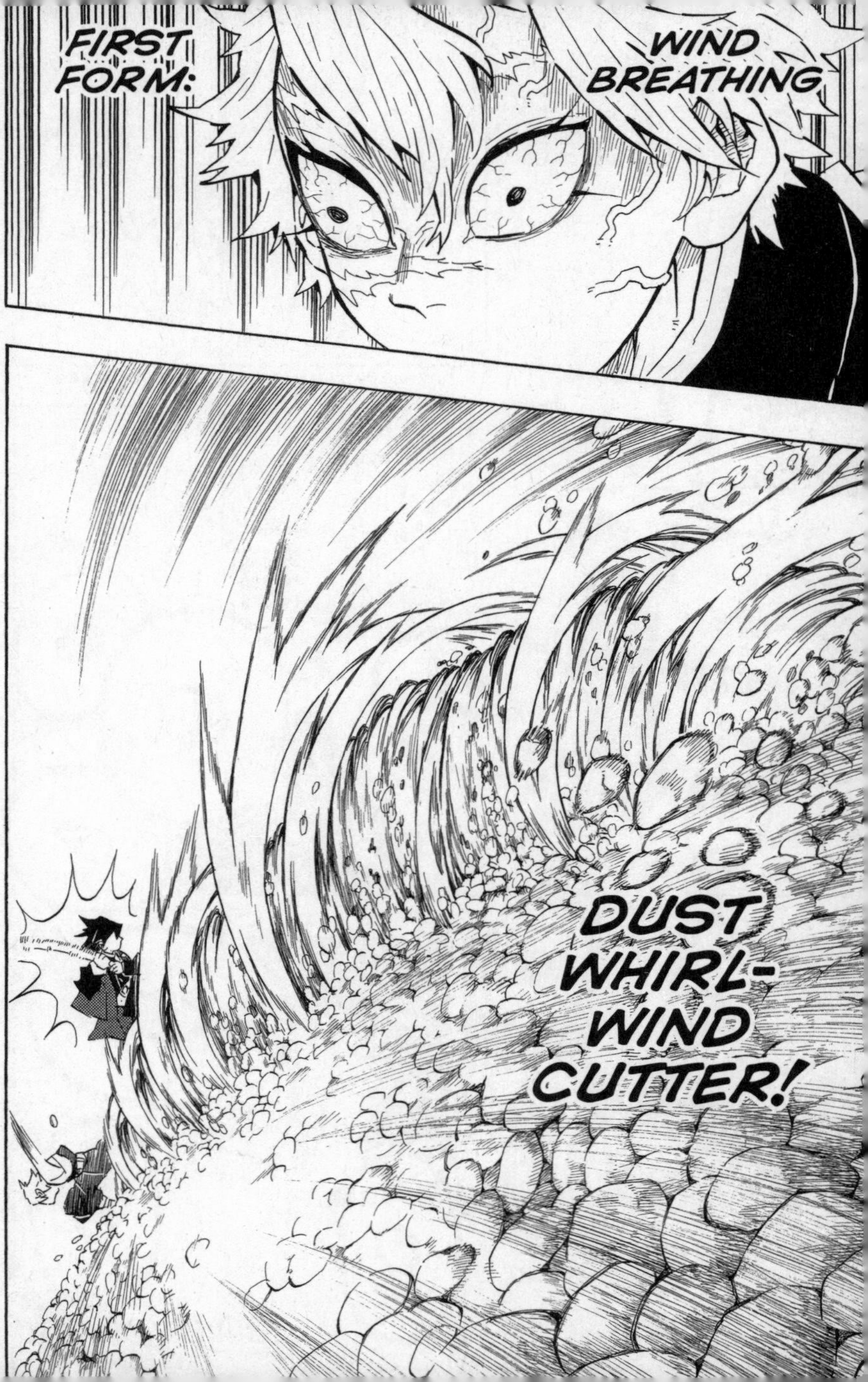
WIND BREATHING
FIRST FORM:
DUST WHIRL-WIND CUTTER!

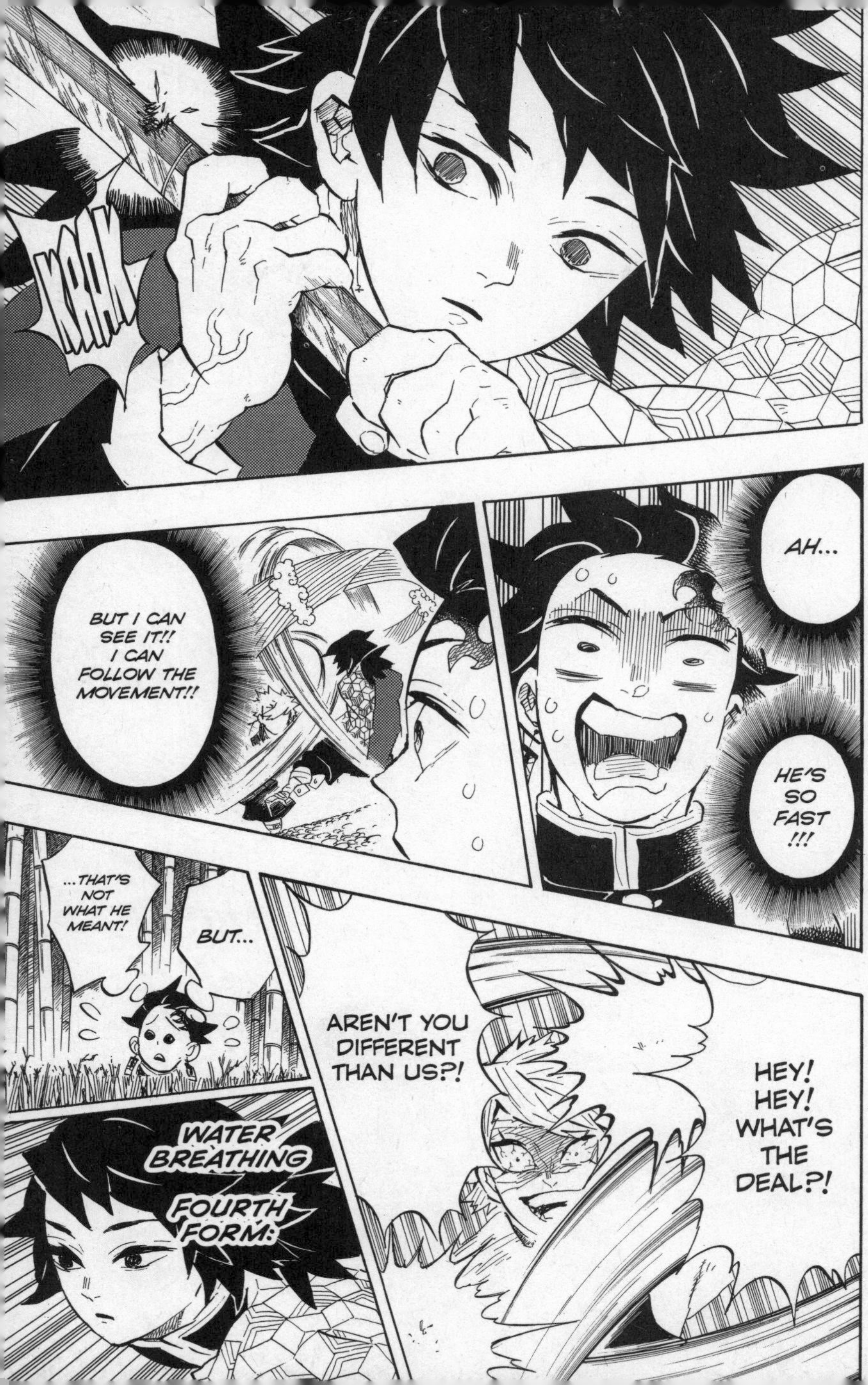
KRAK
AH...
HE'S SO FAST!!!
BUT I CAN SEE IT!! I CAN FOLLOW THE MOVEMENT!!
HEY! HEY! WHAT'S THE DEAL?!
AREN'T YOU DIFFERENT THAN US?!
BUT...
...THAT'S NOT WHAT HE MEANT!
WATER BREATHING
FOURTH FORM:

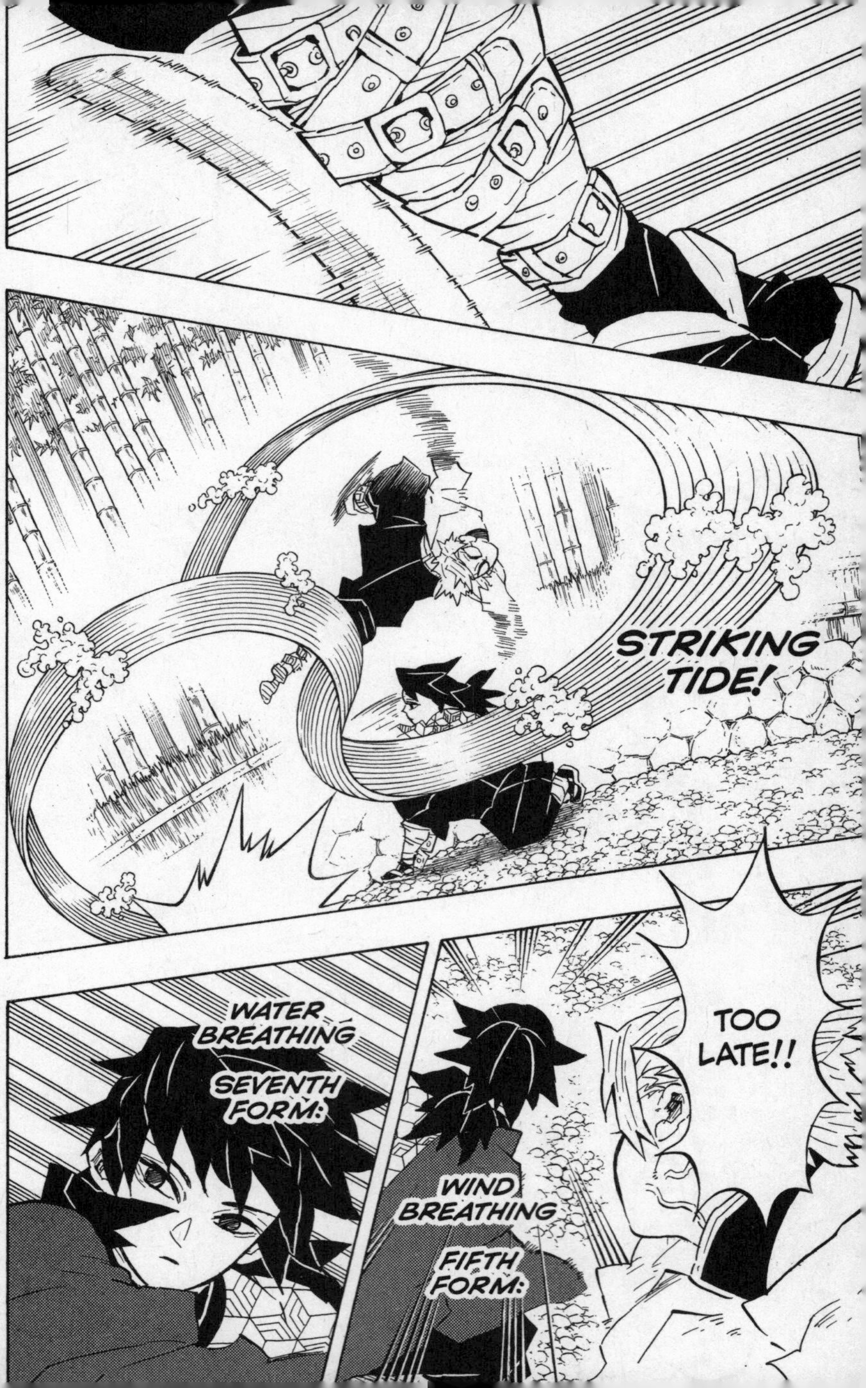
STRIKING TIDE!
TOO LATE!!
WIND BREATHING
FIFTH FORM:
WATER BREATHING
SEVENTH FORM:

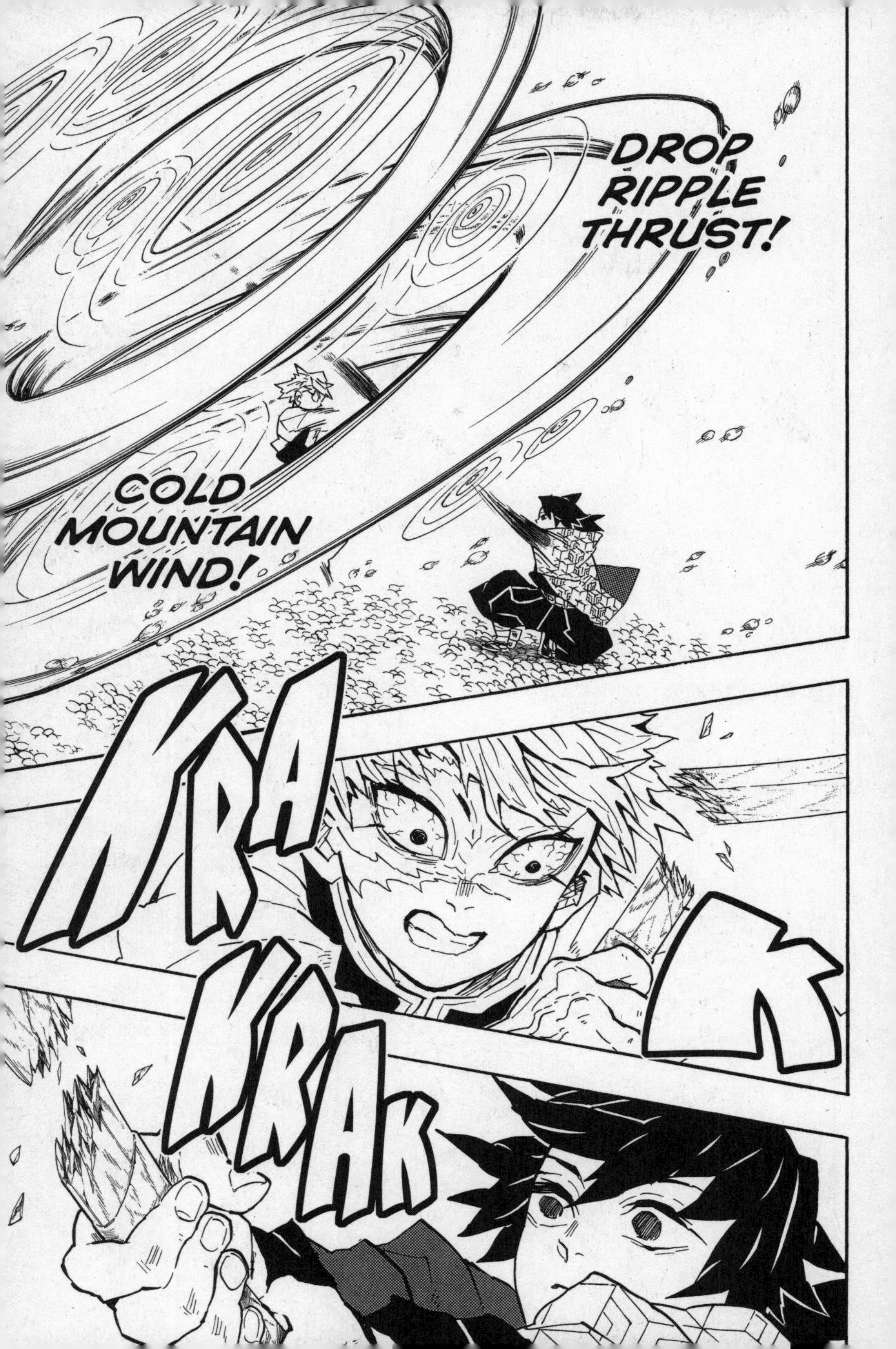
DROP RIPPLE THRUST!
COLD MOUNTAIN WIND!
KRAK
KRAK

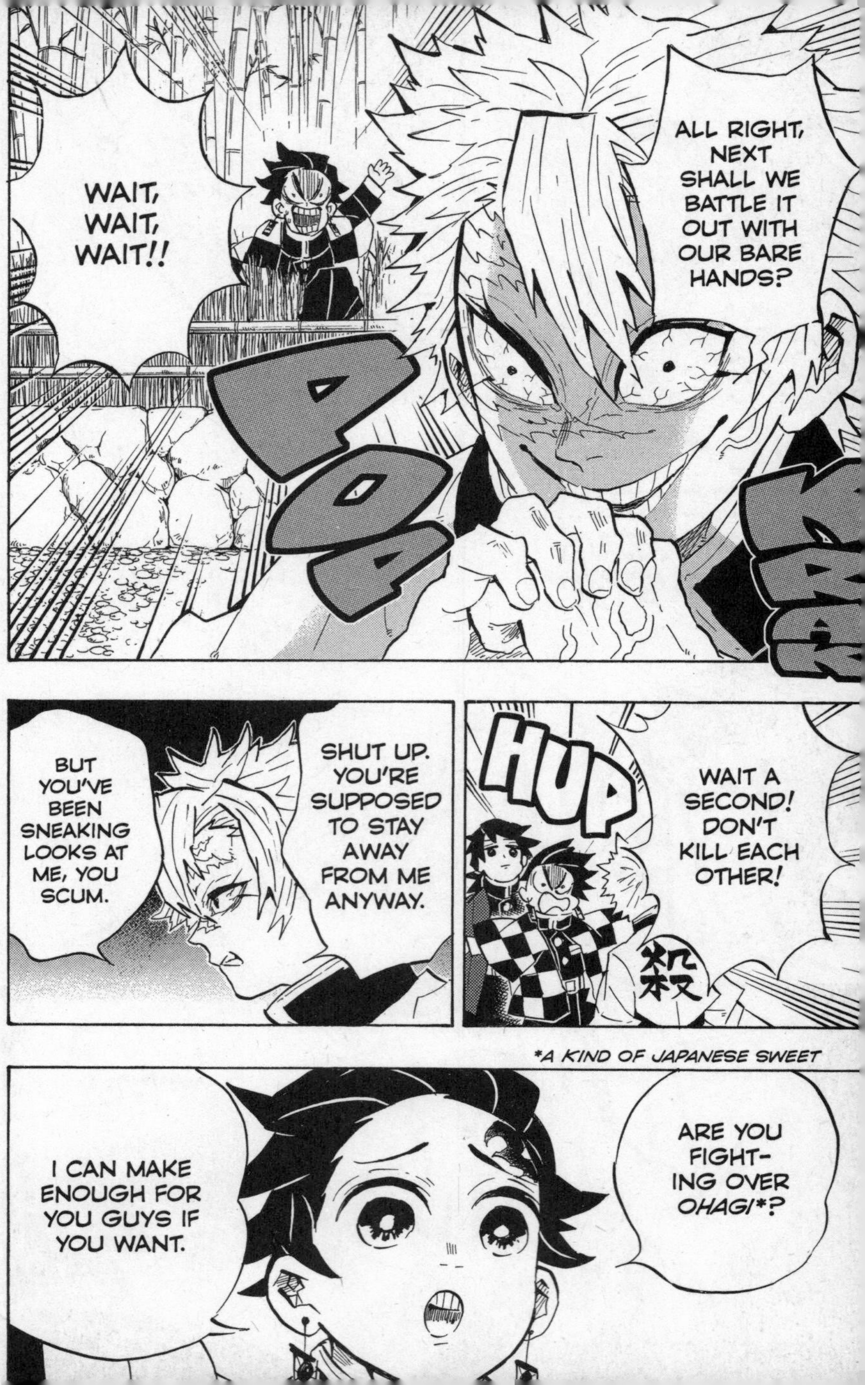
ALL RIGHT, NEXT SHALL WE BATTLE IT OUT WITH OUR BARE HANDS?
WAIT, WAIT, WAIT!!
HUP
WAIT A SECOND! DON'T KILL EACH OTHER!
殺
SHUT UP. YOU'RE SUPPOSED TO STAY AWAY FROM ME ANYWAY.
BUT YOU'VE BEEN SNEAKING LOOKS AT ME, YOU SCUM.
ARE YOU FIGHT-ING OVER *OHAGI**?
I CAN MAKE ENOUGH FOR YOU GUYS IF YOU WANT.

**A KIND OF JAPANESE SWEET*

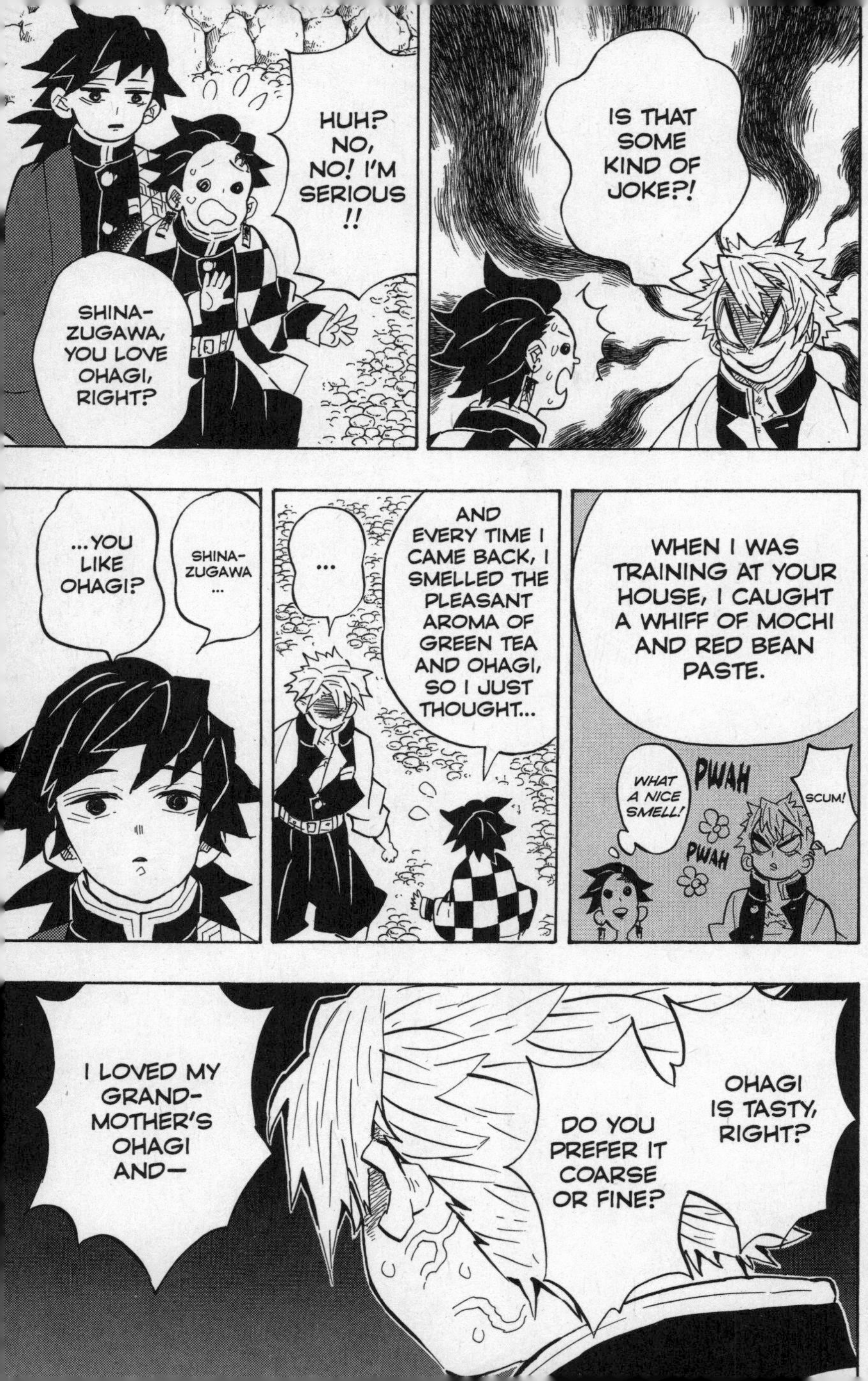
IS THAT SOME KIND OF JOKE?!
HUH? NO, NO! I'M SERIOUS!!
SHINA-ZUGAWA, YOU LOVE OHAGI, RIGHT?
WHEN I WAS TRAINING AT YOUR HOUSE, I CAUGHT A WHIFF OF MOCHI AND RED BEAN PASTE.
SCUM!
PWAH
WHAT A NICE SMELL!
PWAH
AND EVERY TIME I CAME BACK, I SMELLED THE PLEASANT AROMA OF GREEN TEA AND OHAGI, SO I JUST THOUGHT...
...
SHINA-ZUGAWA...
...YOU LIKE OHAGI?
OHAGI IS TASTY, RIGHT?
DO YOU PREFER IT COARSE OR FINE?
I LOVED MY GRAND-MOTHER'S OHAGI AND—

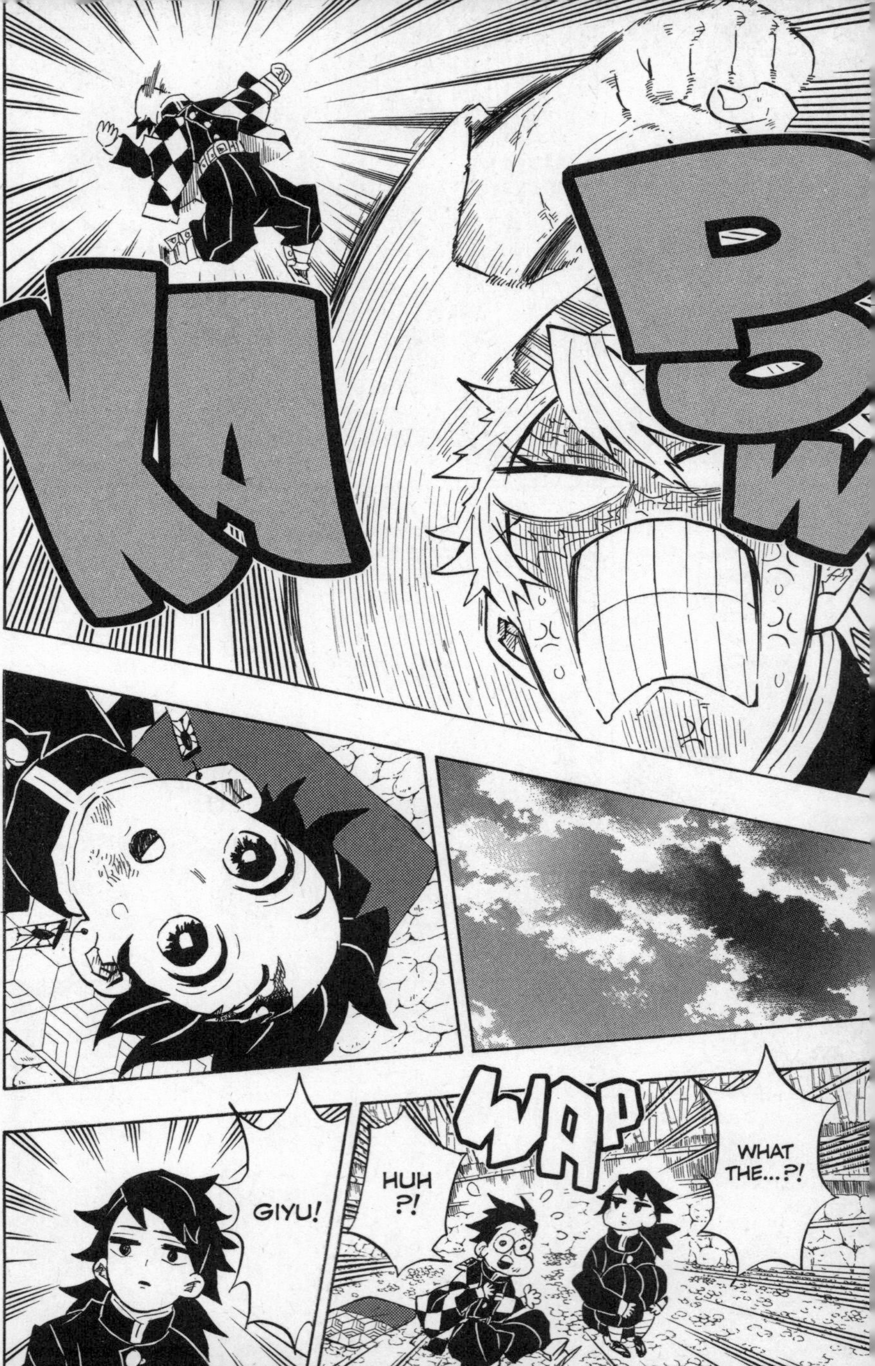
KAPOW
WHAT THE...?!
WAP
HUH ?!
GIYU!

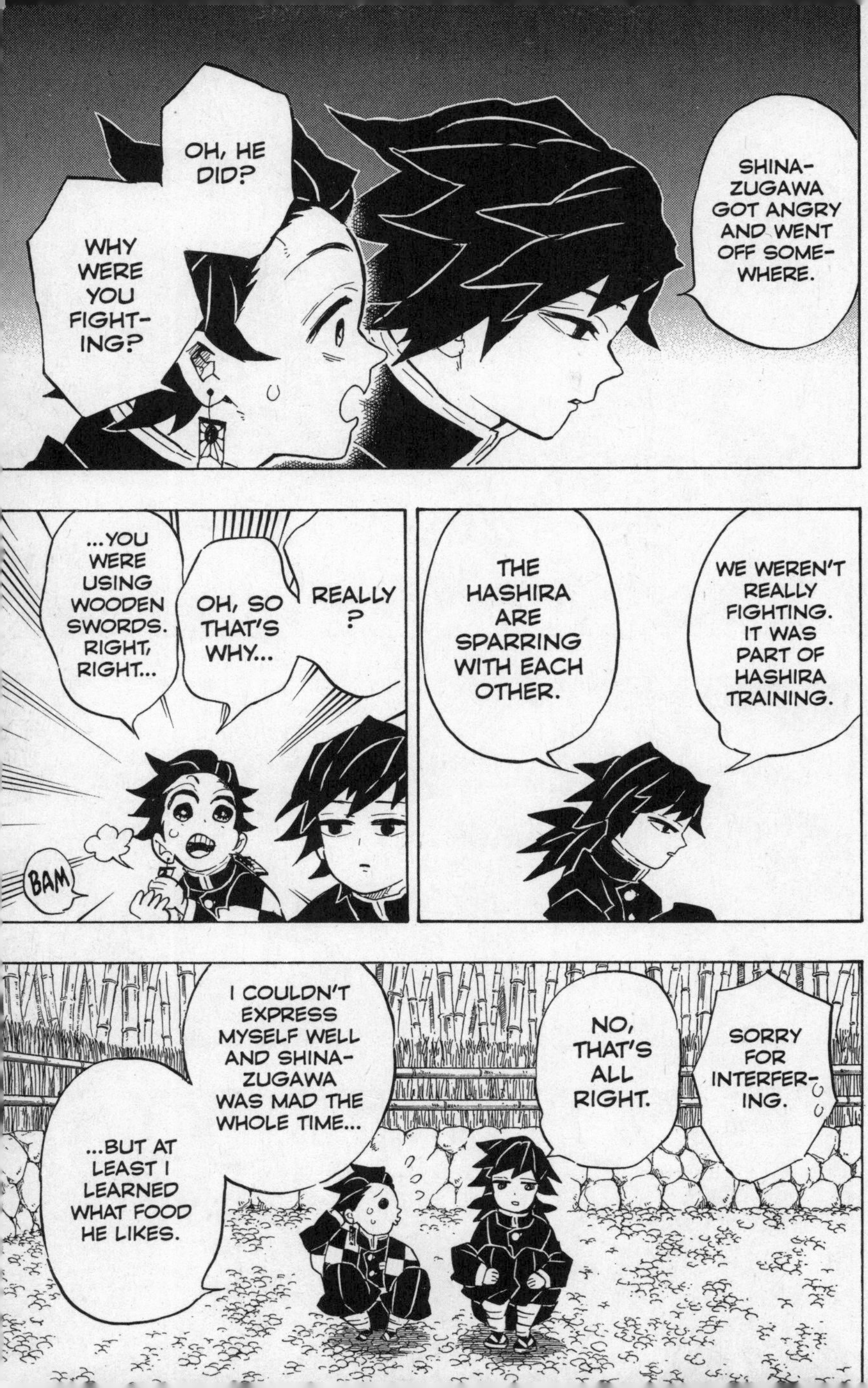
SHINAZUGAWA GOT ANGRY AND WENT OFF SOMEWHERE.
OH, HE DID?
WHY WERE YOU FIGHTING?
WE WEREN'T REALLY FIGHTING. IT WAS PART OF HASHIRA TRAINING.
THE HASHIRA ARE SPARRING WITH EACH OTHER.
REALLY ?
OH, SO THAT'S WHY...
...YOU WERE USING WOODEN SWORDS. RIGHT, RIGHT...
BAM
SORRY FOR INTERFERING.
NO, THAT'S ALL RIGHT.
I COULDN'T EXPRESS MYSELF WELL AND SHINAZUGAWA WAS MAD THE WHOLE TIME...
...BUT AT LEAST I LEARNED WHAT FOOD HE LIKES.

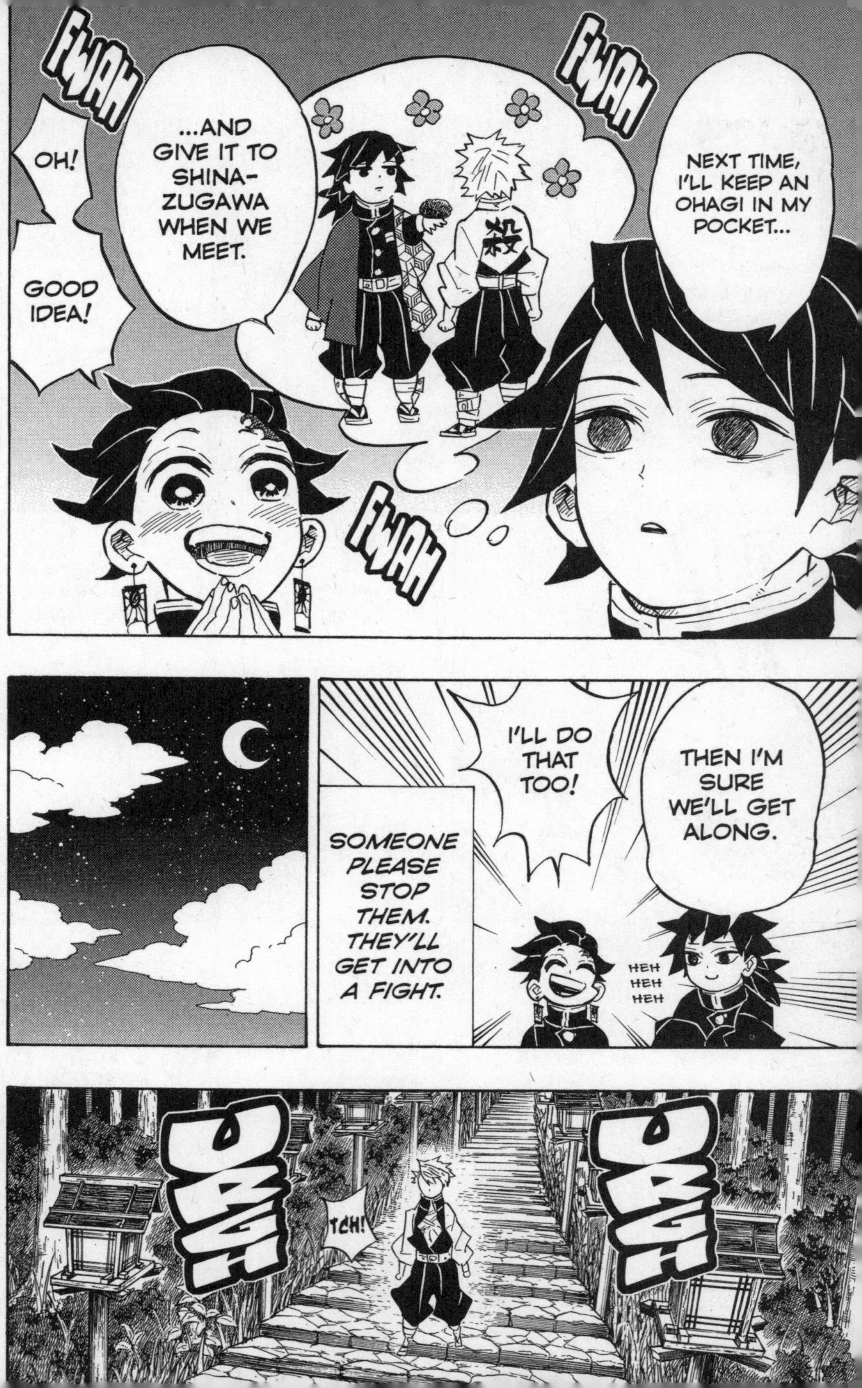
FWAH
NEXT TIME, I'LL KEEP AN OHAGI IN MY POCKET...
FWAH
...AND GIVE IT TO SHINA-ZUGAWA WHEN WE MEET.
FWAH
FWAH
OH!
GOOD IDEA!
THEN I'M SURE WE'LL GET ALONG.
I'LL DO THAT TOO!
HEH HEH HEH
SOMEONE PLEASE STOP THEM. THEY'LL GET INTO A FIGHT.
TCH!

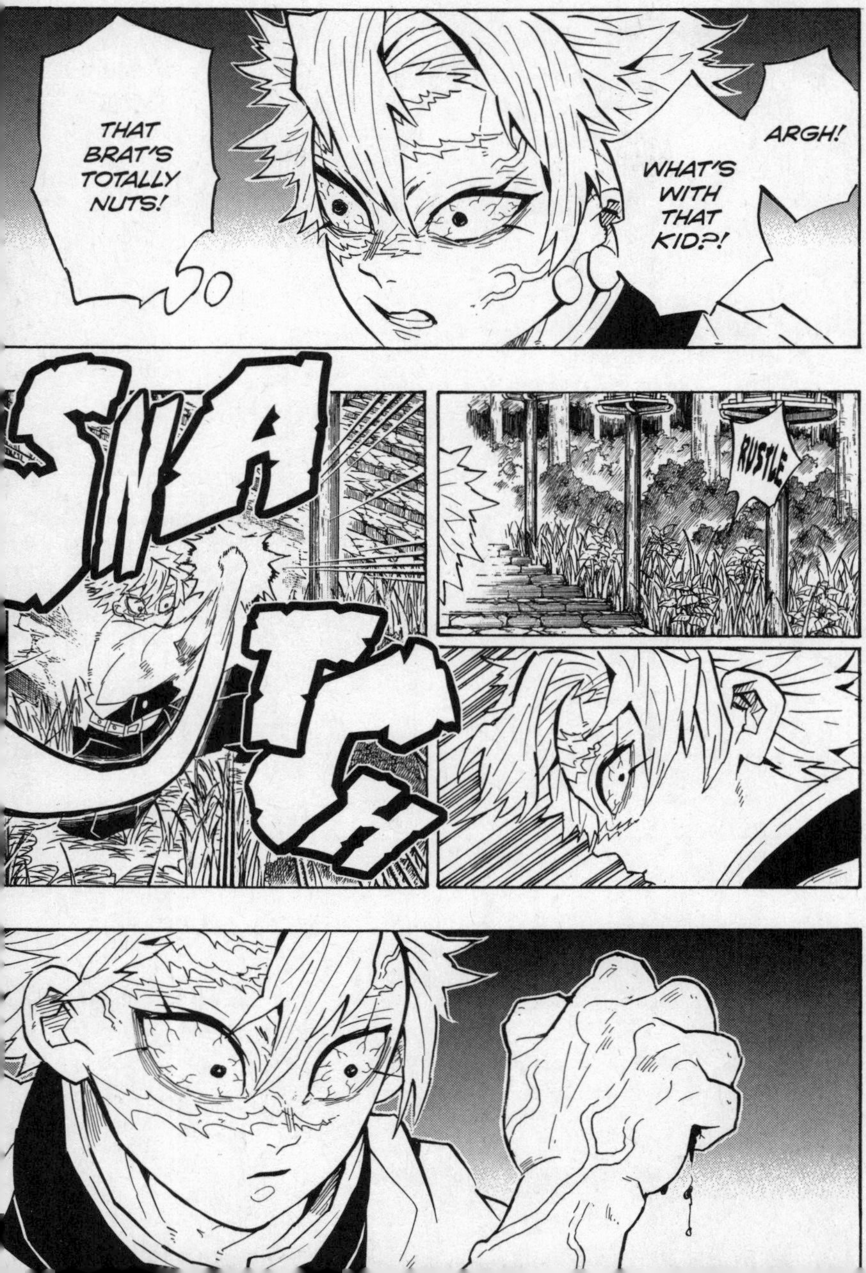
ARGH!
WHAT'S WITH THAT KID?!
THAT BRAT'S TOTALLY NUTS!
RUSTLE

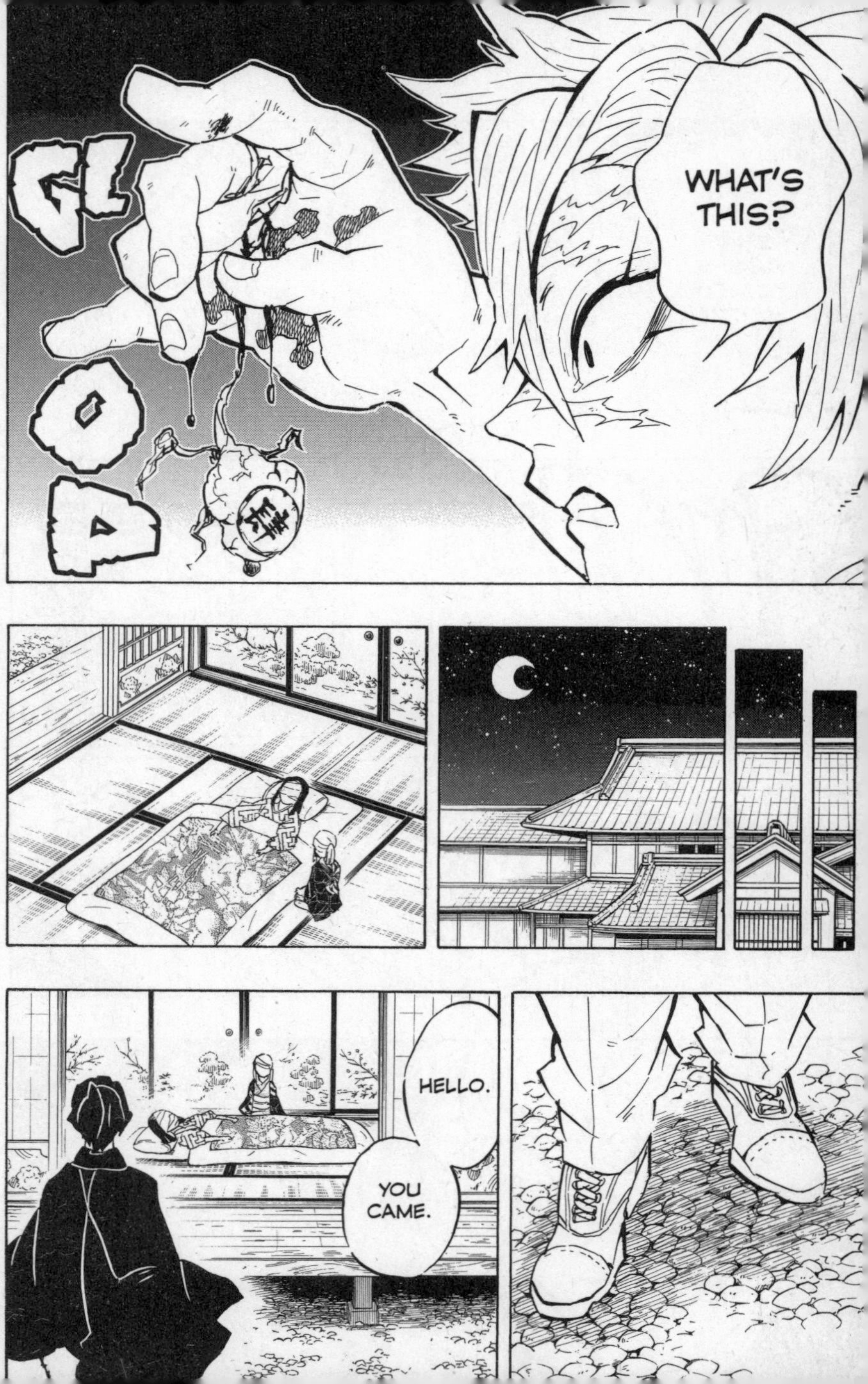
WHAT'S THIS?
GLOP
HELLO.
YOU CAME.

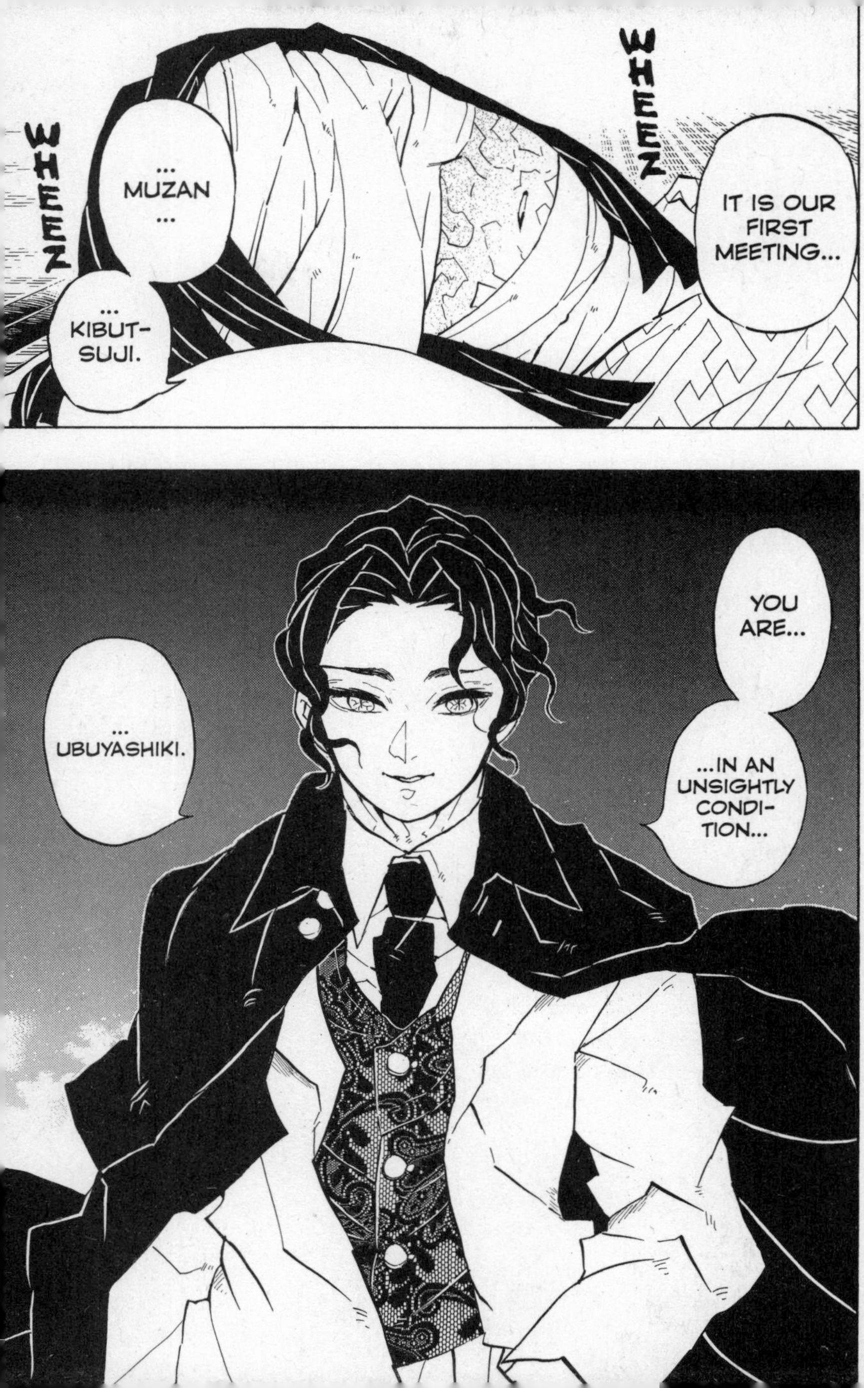
WHEEZ
IT IS OUR FIRST MEETING...
WHEEZ
... MUZAN ...
... KIBUTSUJI.
YOU ARE...
...IN AN UNSIGHTLY CONDITION...
... UBUYASHIKI.

Amane Ubuyashiki (27 yrs.).
She was 17 when she married
a 13-year-old Kagaya. Kagaya
said that if she didn't want to
marry him, he himself would
refuse. This statement, which
showed consideration for
her circumstances, was what
made her decide to marry him.

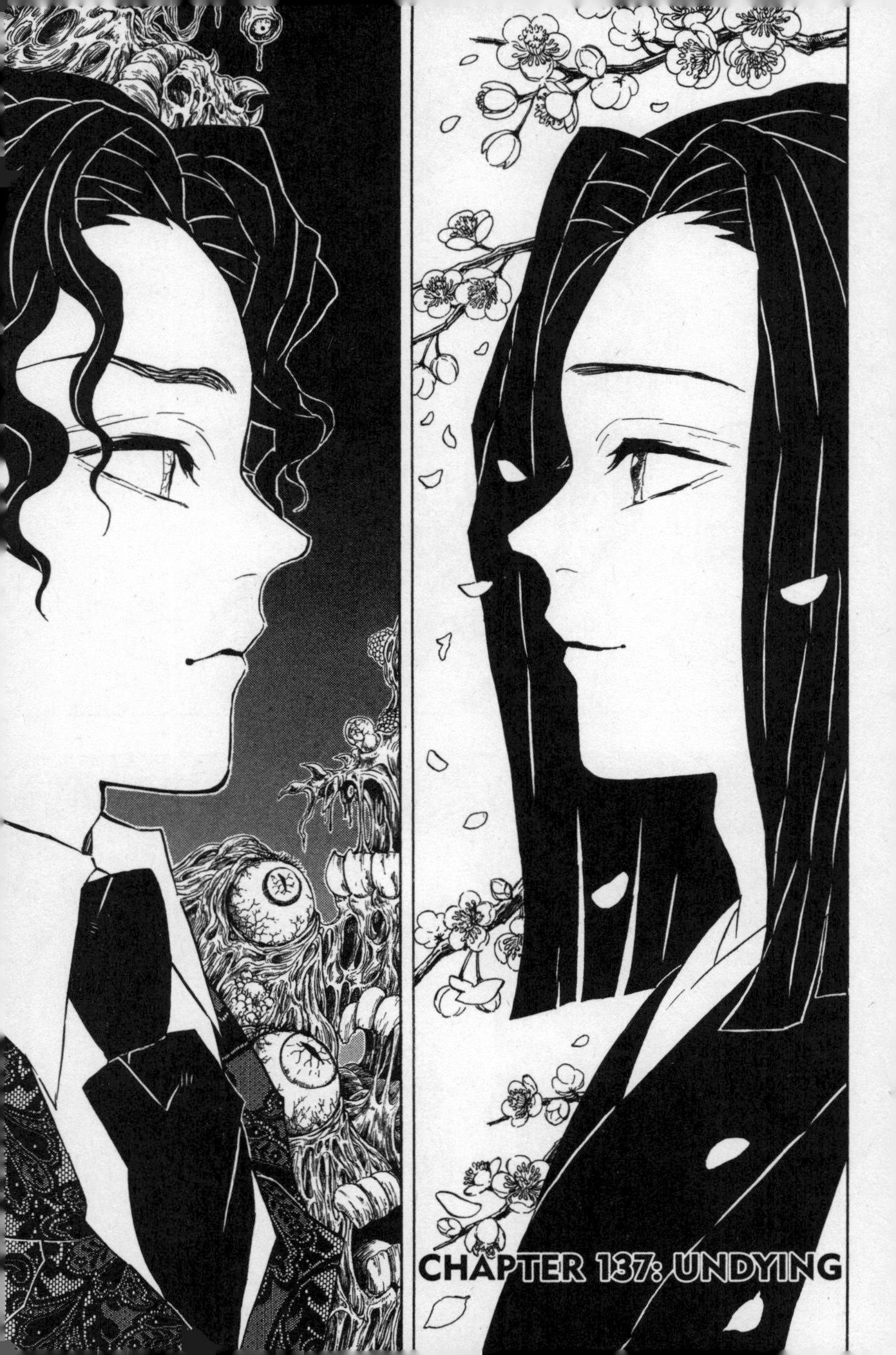
CHAPTER 137: UNDYING

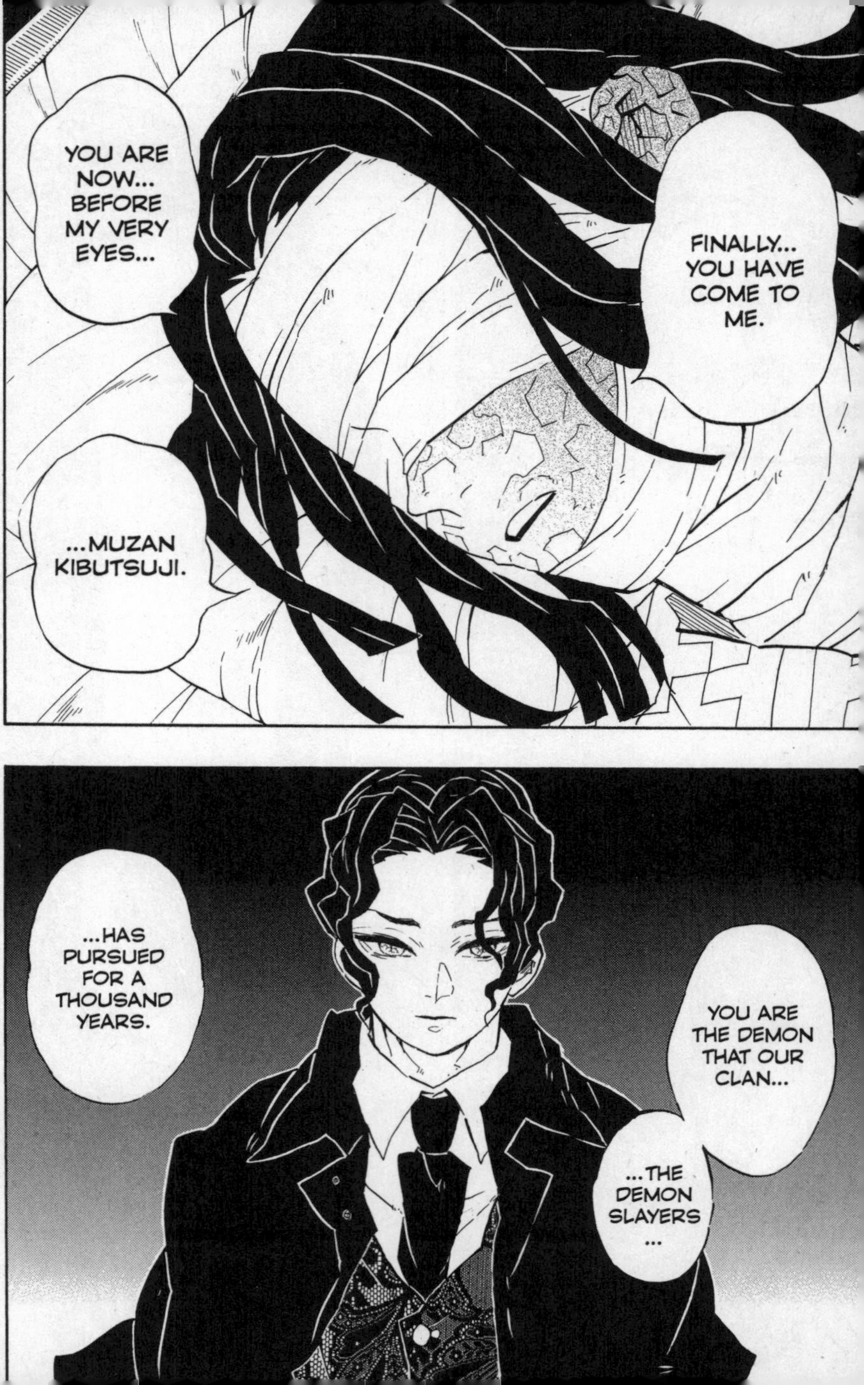
FINALLY... YOU HAVE COME TO ME.
YOU ARE NOW... BEFORE MY VERY EYES...
...MUZAN KIBUTSUJI.
YOU ARE THE DEMON THAT OUR CLAN...
...THE DEMON SLAYERS ...
...HAS PURSUED FOR A THOUSAND YEARS.

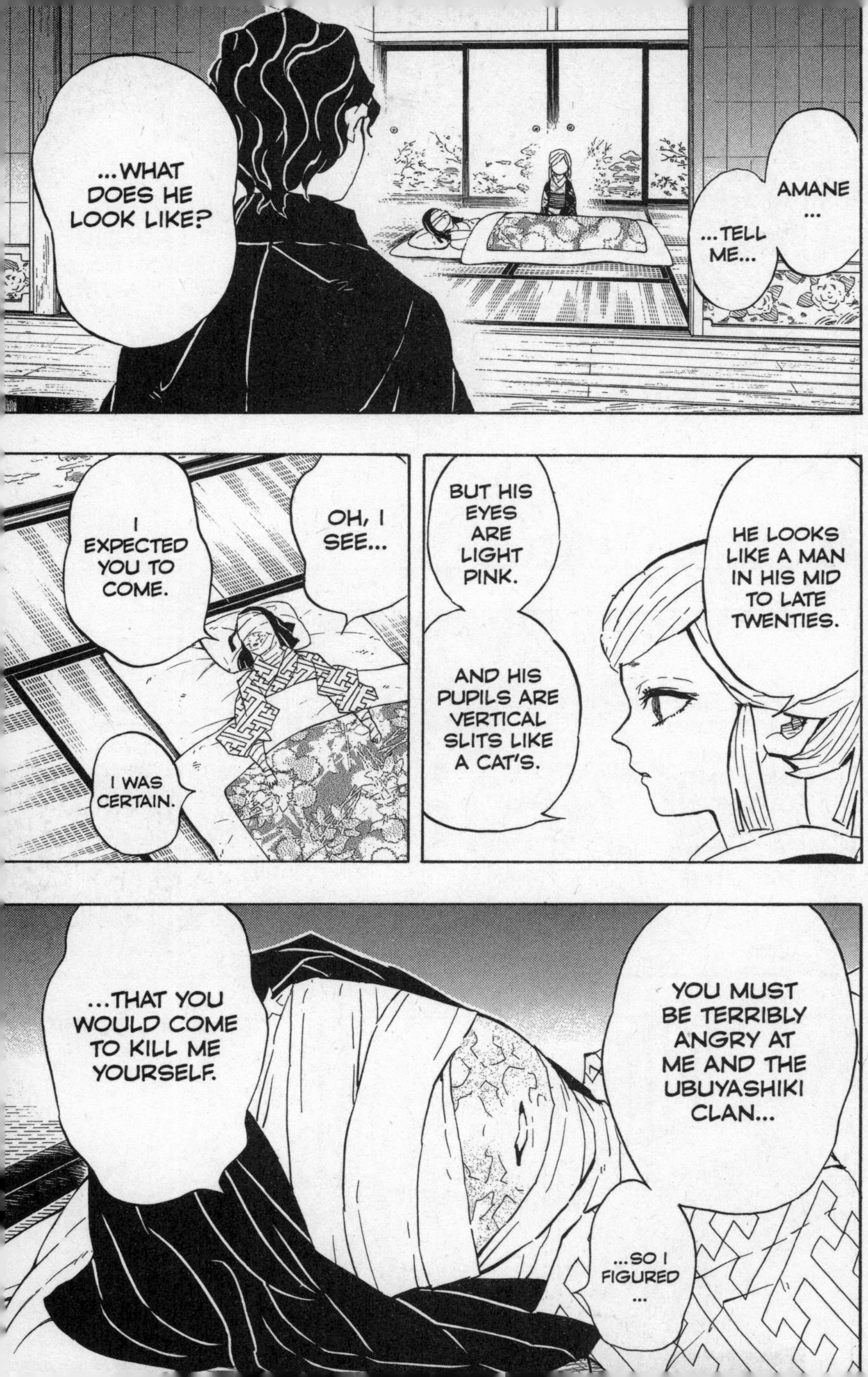
AMANE ...
...TELL ME...
...WHAT DOES HE LOOK LIKE?
HE LOOKS LIKE A MAN IN HIS MID TO LATE TWENTIES.
BUT HIS EYES ARE LIGHT PINK.
AND HIS PUPILS ARE VERTICAL SLITS LIKE A CAT'S.
OH, I SEE...
I EXPECTED YOU TO COME.
I WAS CERTAIN.
YOU MUST BE TERRIBLY ANGRY AT ME AND THE UBUYASHIKI CLAN...
...SO I FIGURED ...
...THAT YOU WOULD COME TO KILL ME YOURSELF.

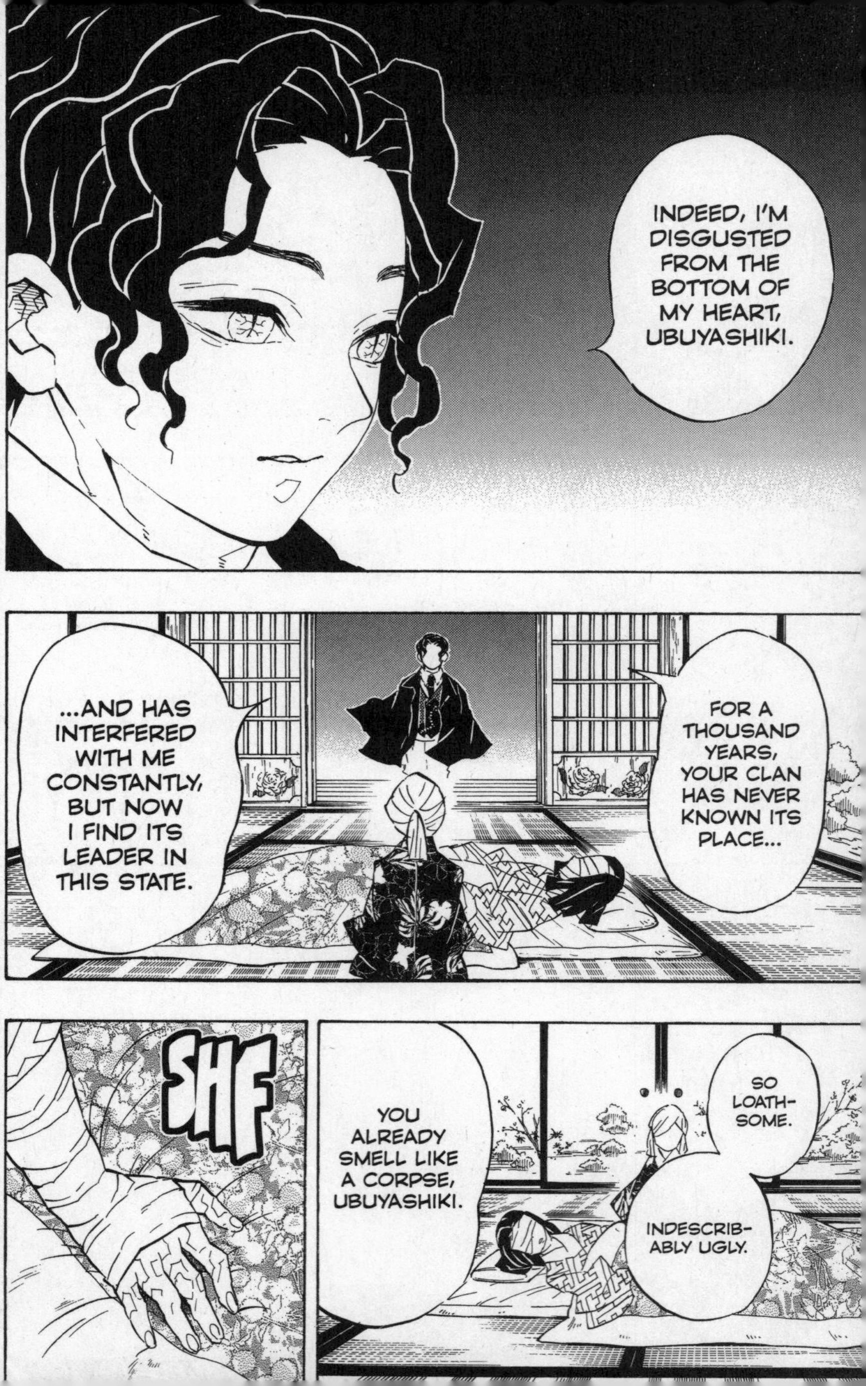
INDEED, I'M DISGUSTED FROM THE BOTTOM OF MY HEART, UBUYASHIKI.
FOR A THOUSAND YEARS, YOUR CLAN HAS NEVER KNOWN ITS PLACE...
...AND HAS INTERFERED WITH ME CONSTANTLY, BUT NOW I FIND ITS LEADER IN THIS STATE.
SO LOATHSOME.
INDESCRIBABLY UGLY.
YOU ALREADY SMELL LIKE A CORPSE, UBUYASHIKI.
SHF

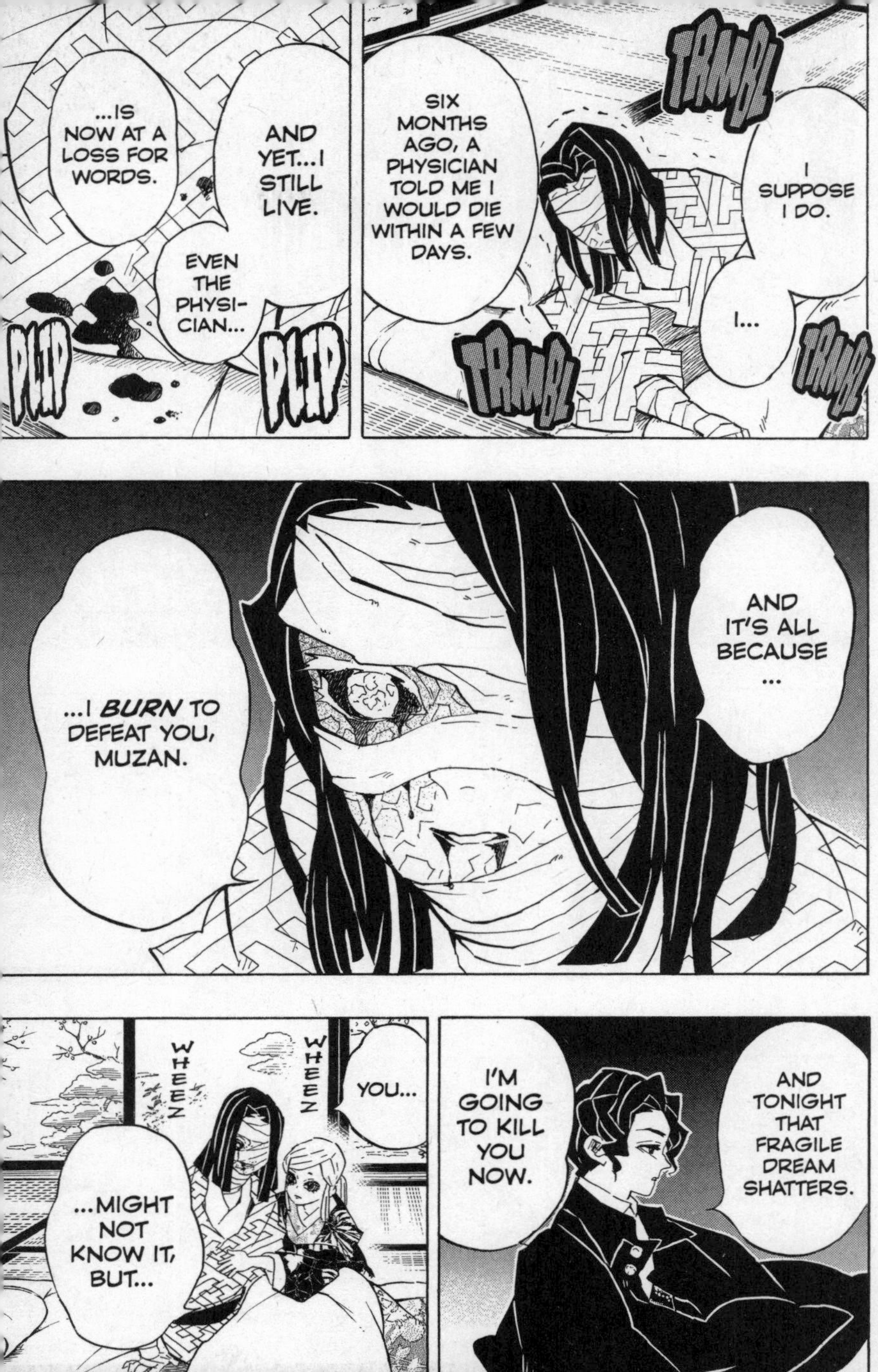
TRMBL
I SUPPOSE I DO.
I...
TRMBL
TRMBL
SIX MONTHS AGO, A PHYSICIAN TOLD ME I WOULD DIE WITHIN A FEW DAYS.
AND YET...I STILL LIVE.
EVEN THE PHYSICIAN...
...IS NOW AT A LOSS FOR WORDS.
PLIP
PLIP
AND IT'S ALL BECAUSE ...
...I BURN TO DEFEAT YOU, MUZAN.
AND TONIGHT THAT FRAGILE DREAM SHATTERS.
I'M GOING TO KILL YOU NOW.
WHEEZ
YOU...
WHEEZ
...MIGHT NOT KNOW IT, BUT...

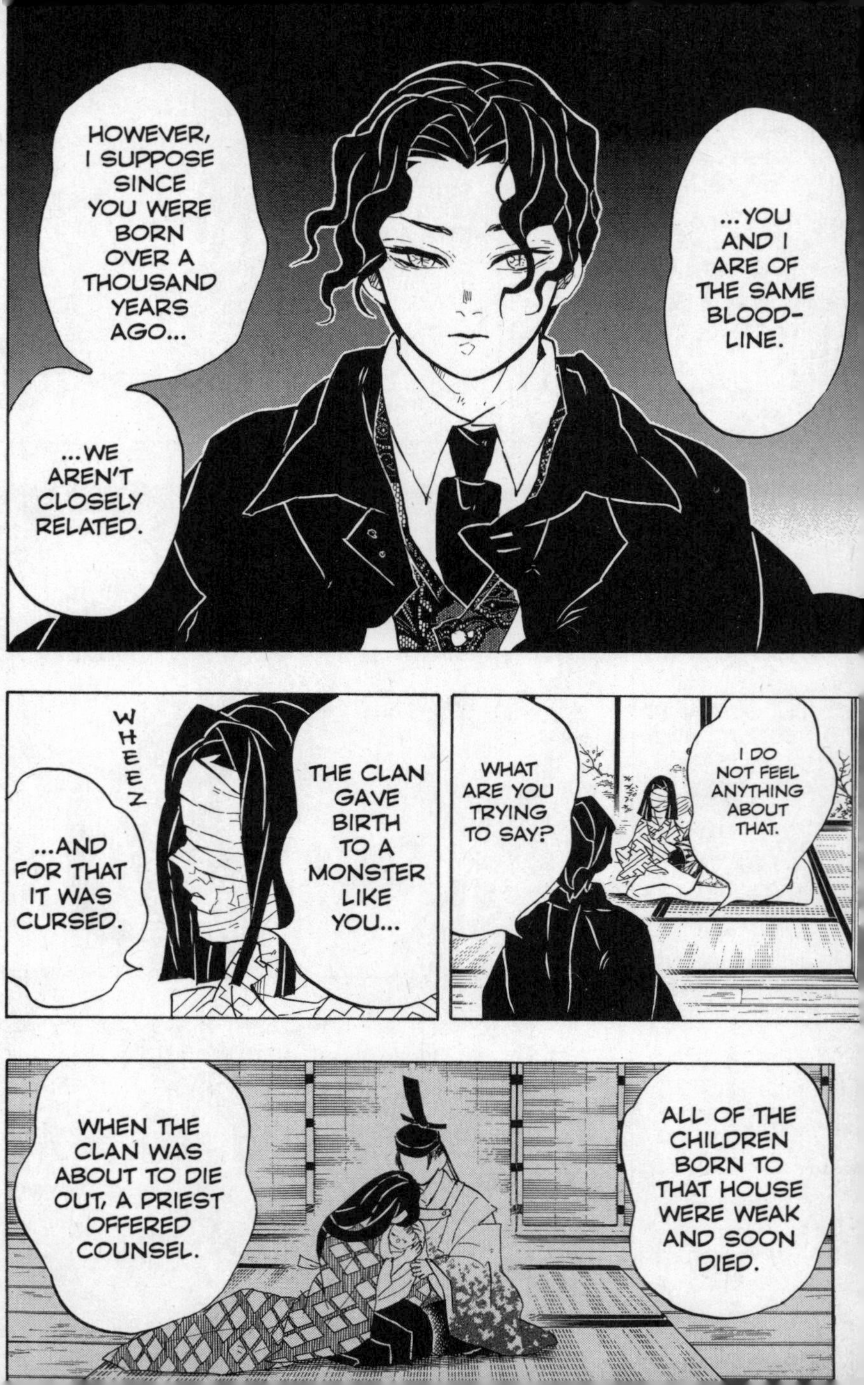
...YOU AND I ARE OF THE SAME BLOOD-LINE.
HOWEVER, I SUPPOSE SINCE YOU WERE BORN OVER A THOUSAND YEARS AGO...
...WE AREN'T CLOSELY RELATED.
I DO NOT FEEL ANYTHING ABOUT THAT.
WHAT ARE YOU TRYING TO SAY?
THE CLAN GAVE BIRTH TO A MONSTER LIKE YOU...
WHEEZ
...AND FOR THAT IT WAS CURSED.
ALL OF THE CHILDREN BORN TO THAT HOUSE WERE WEAK AND SOON DIED.
WHEN THE CLAN WAS ABOUT TO DIE OUT, A PRIEST OFFERED COUNSEL.

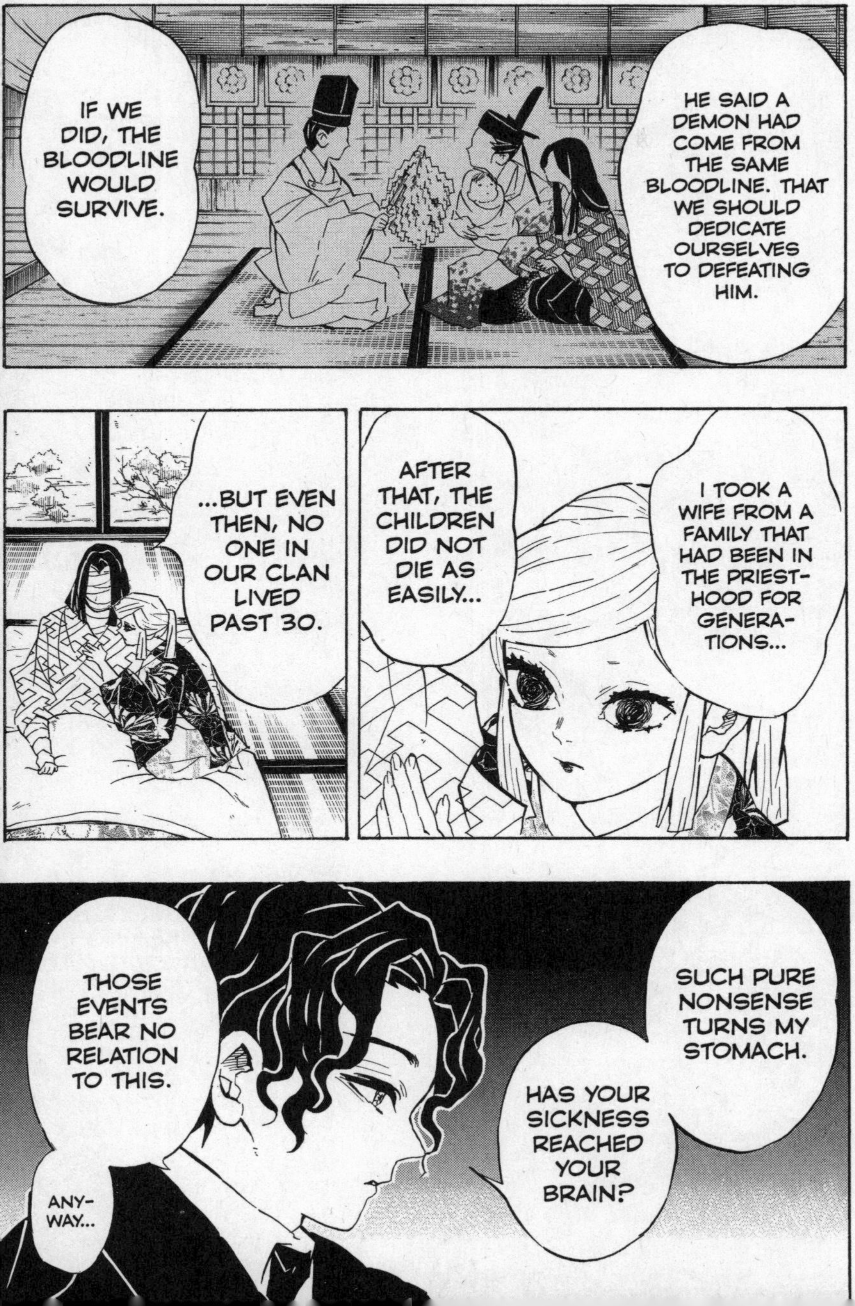
HE SAID A DEMON HAD COME FROM THE SAME BLOODLINE. THAT WE SHOULD DEDICATE OURSELVES TO DEFEATING HIM.
IF WE DID, THE BLOODLINE WOULD SURVIVE.
I TOOK A WIFE FROM A FAMILY THAT HAD BEEN IN THE PRIEST-HOOD FOR GENERA-TIONS...
AFTER THAT, THE CHILDREN DID NOT DIE AS EASILY...
...BUT EVEN THEN, NO ONE IN OUR CLAN LIVED PAST 30.
SUCH PURE NONSENSE TURNS MY STOMACH.
HAS YOUR SICKNESS REACHED YOUR BRAIN?
THOSE EVENTS BEAR NO RELATION TO THIS.
ANY-WAY...

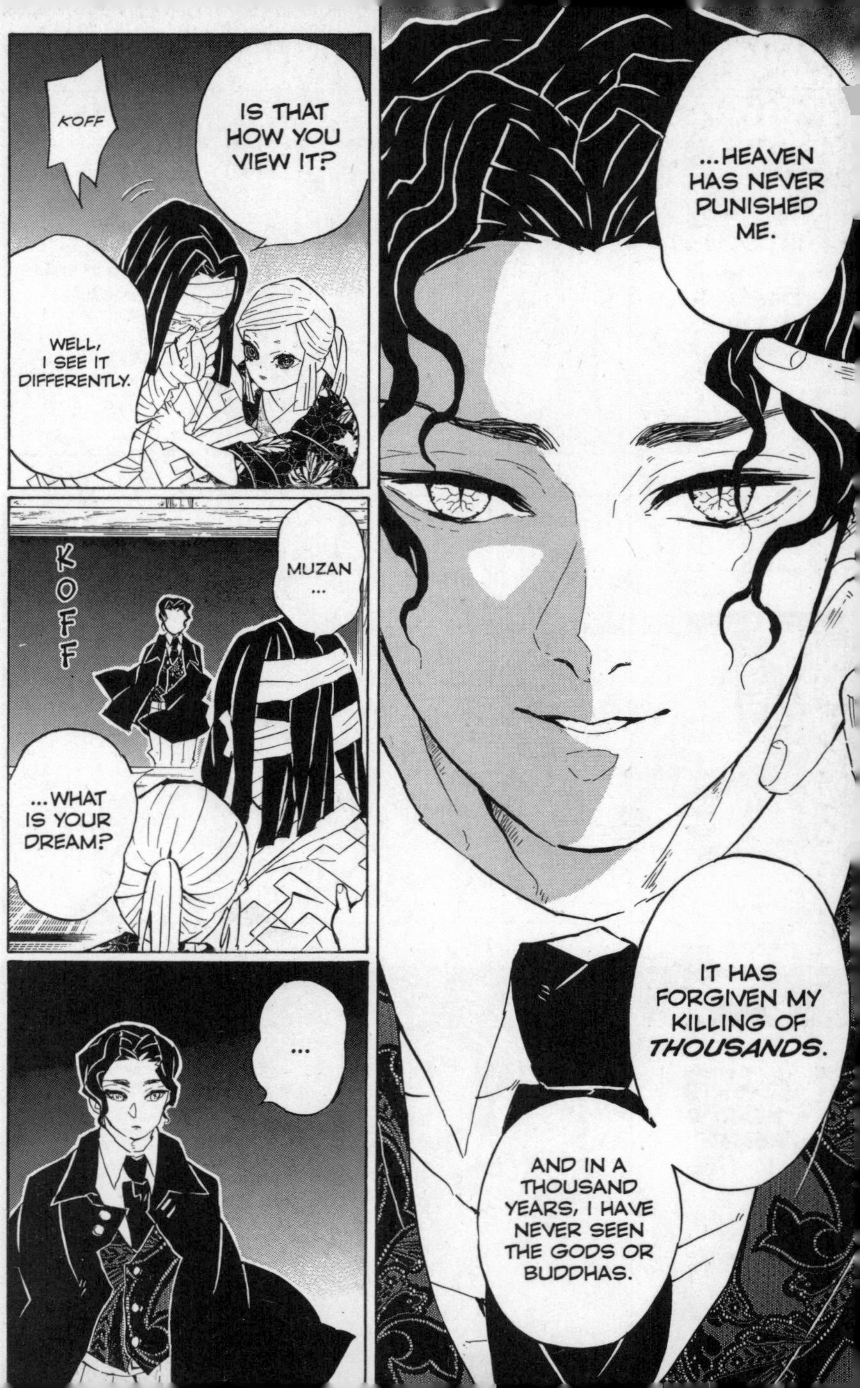
...HEAVEN HAS NEVER PUNISHED ME.
IT HAS FORGIVEN MY KILLING OF *THOUSANDS*.
AND IN A THOUSAND YEARS, I HAVE NEVER SEEN THE GODS OR BUDDHAS.
IS THAT HOW YOU VIEW IT?
KOFF
WELL, I SEE IT DIFFERENTLY.
MUZAN...
KOFF
...WHAT IS YOUR DREAM?
...

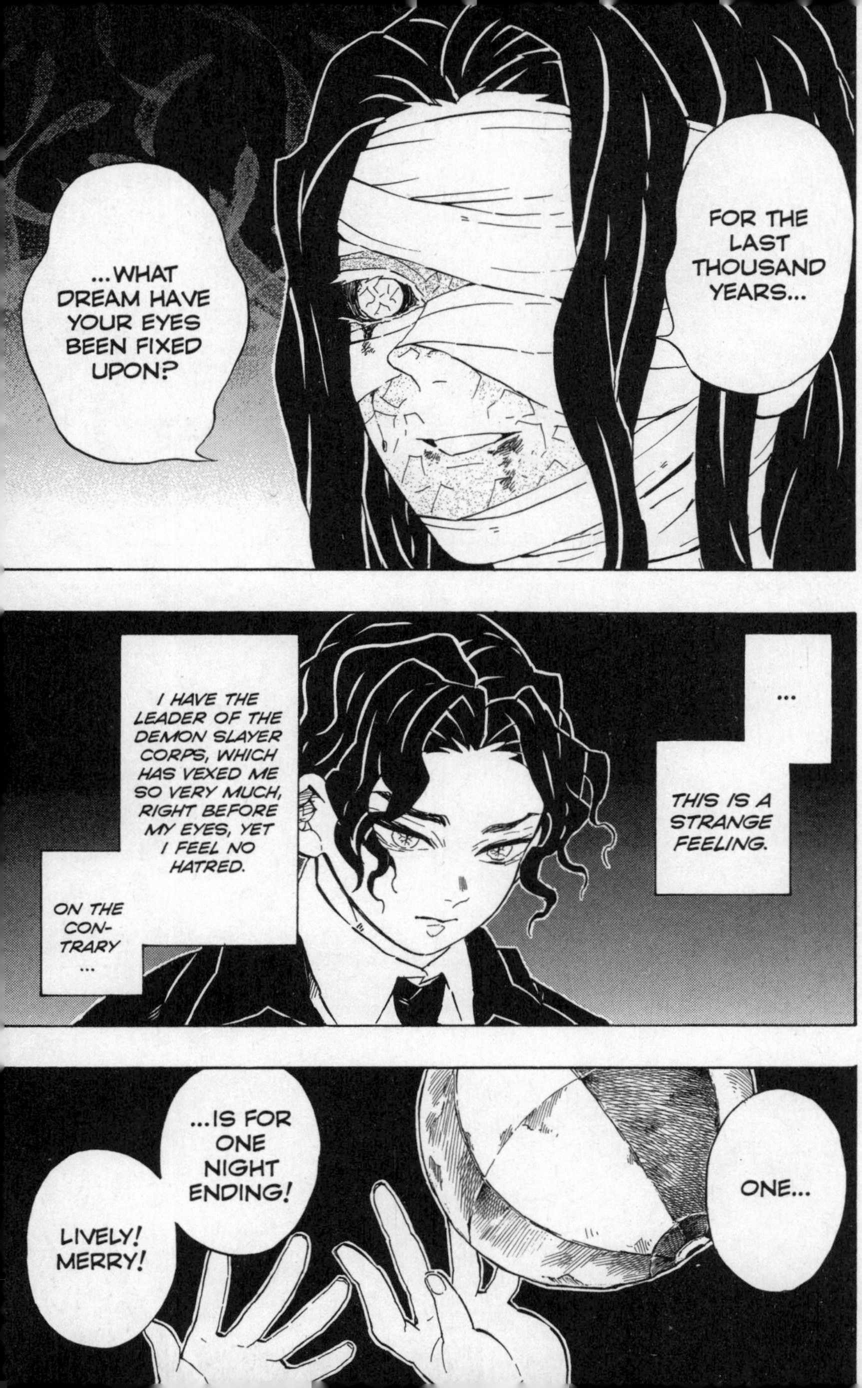
FOR THE LAST THOUSAND YEARS...
...WHAT DREAM HAVE YOUR EYES BEEN FIXED UPON?
...
THIS IS A STRANGE FEELING.
I HAVE THE LEADER OF THE DEMON SLAYER CORPS, WHICH HAS VEXED ME SO VERY MUCH, RIGHT BEFORE MY EYES, YET I FEEL NO HATRED.
ON THE CON-TRARY...
ONE...
...IS FOR ONE NIGHT ENDING!
LIVELY! MERRY!

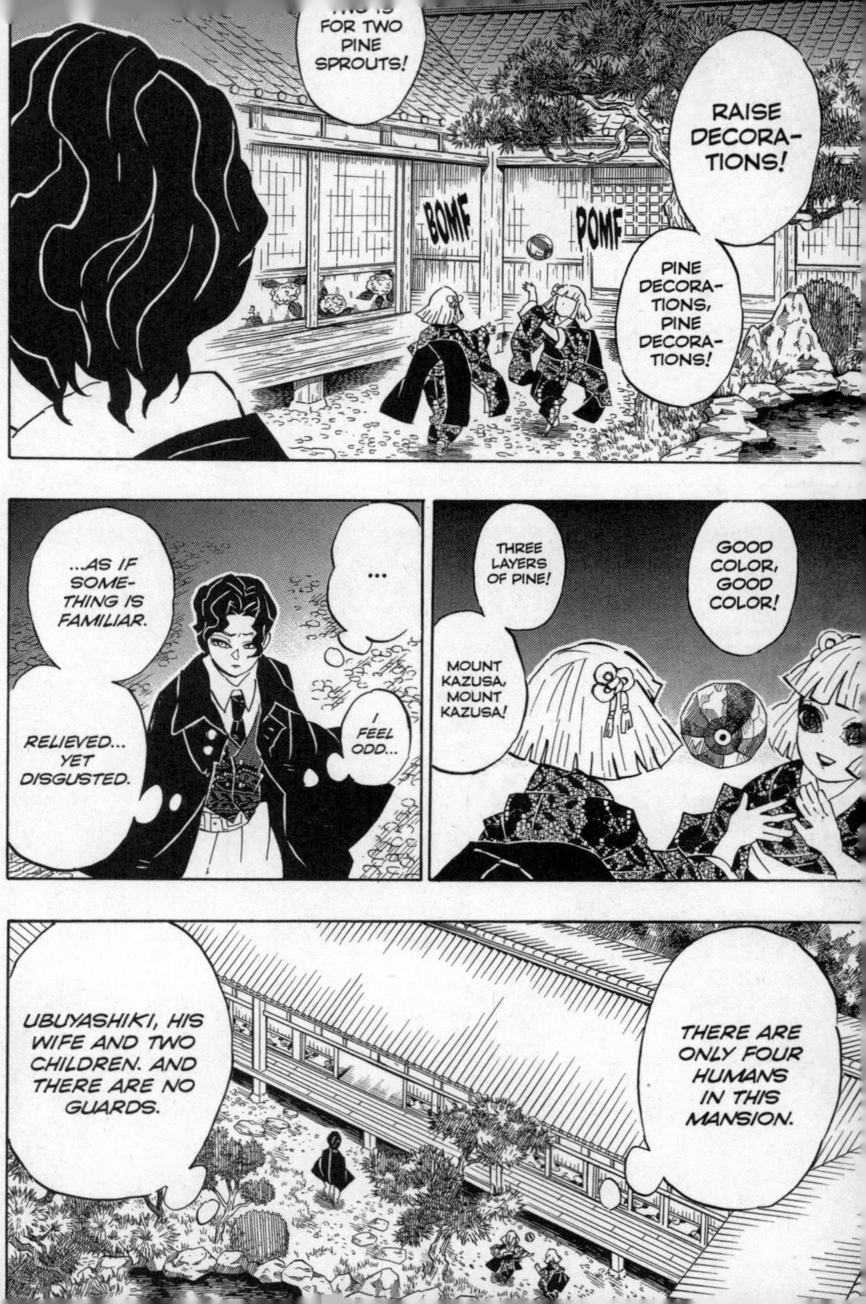
RAISE DECORATIONS!
PINE DECORATIONS, PINE DECORATIONS!
FOR TWO PINE SPROUTS!
POMF
BOMF
GOOD COLOR, GOOD COLOR!
THREE LAYERS OF PINE!
MOUNT KAZUSA, MOUNT KAZUSA!
...
I FEEL ODD...
...AS IF SOMETHING IS FAMILIAR.
RELIEVED... YET DISGUSTED.
THERE ARE ONLY FOUR HUMANS IN THIS MANSION.
UBUYASHIKI, HIS WIFE AND TWO CHILDREN. AND THERE ARE NO GUARDS.

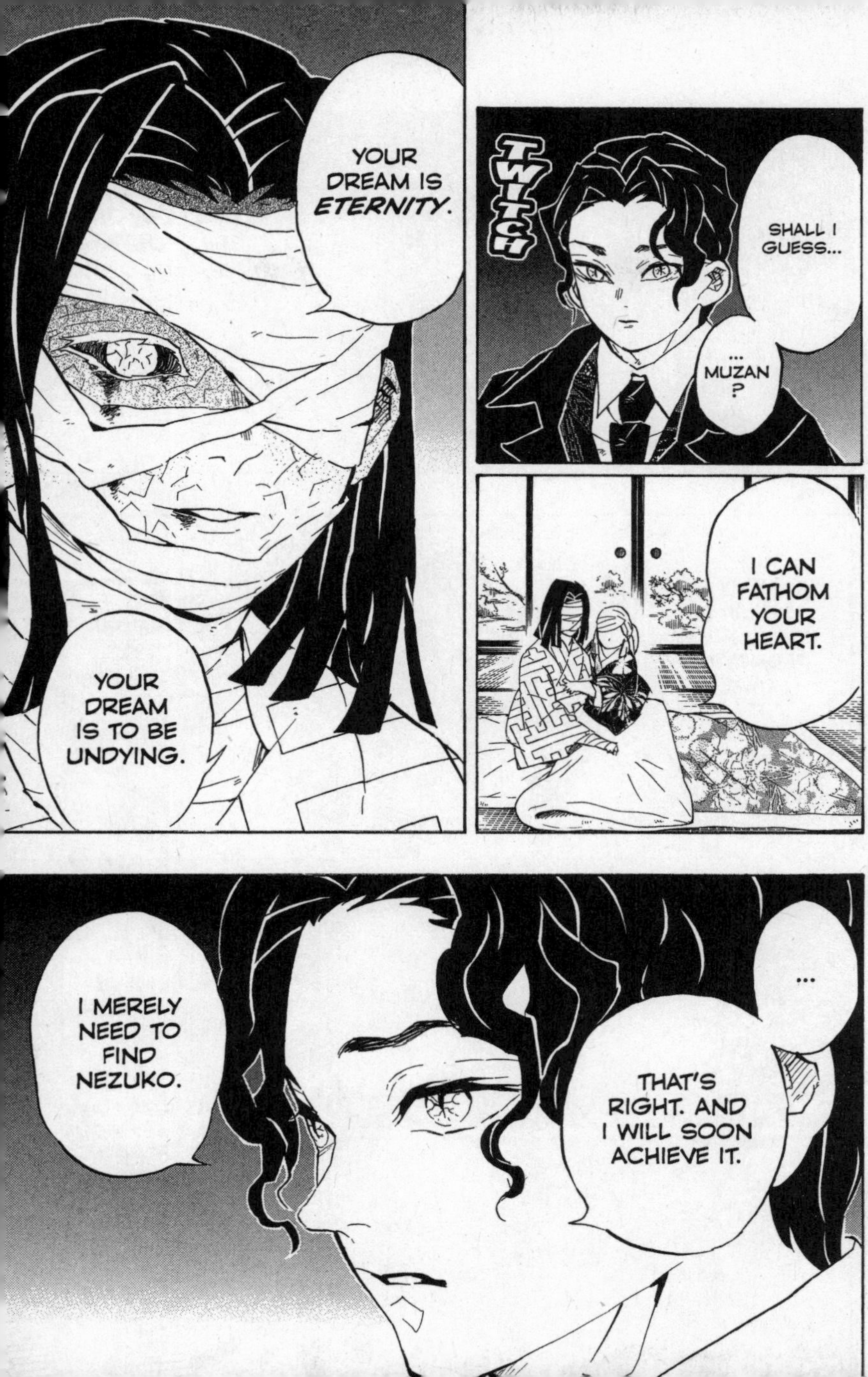
SHALL I GUESS...
... MUZAN?
TWITCH
I CAN FATHOM YOUR HEART.
YOUR DREAM IS *ETERNITY*.
YOUR DREAM IS TO BE UNDYING.
...
THAT'S RIGHT. AND I WILL SOON ACHIEVE IT.
I MERELY NEED TO FIND NEZUKO.

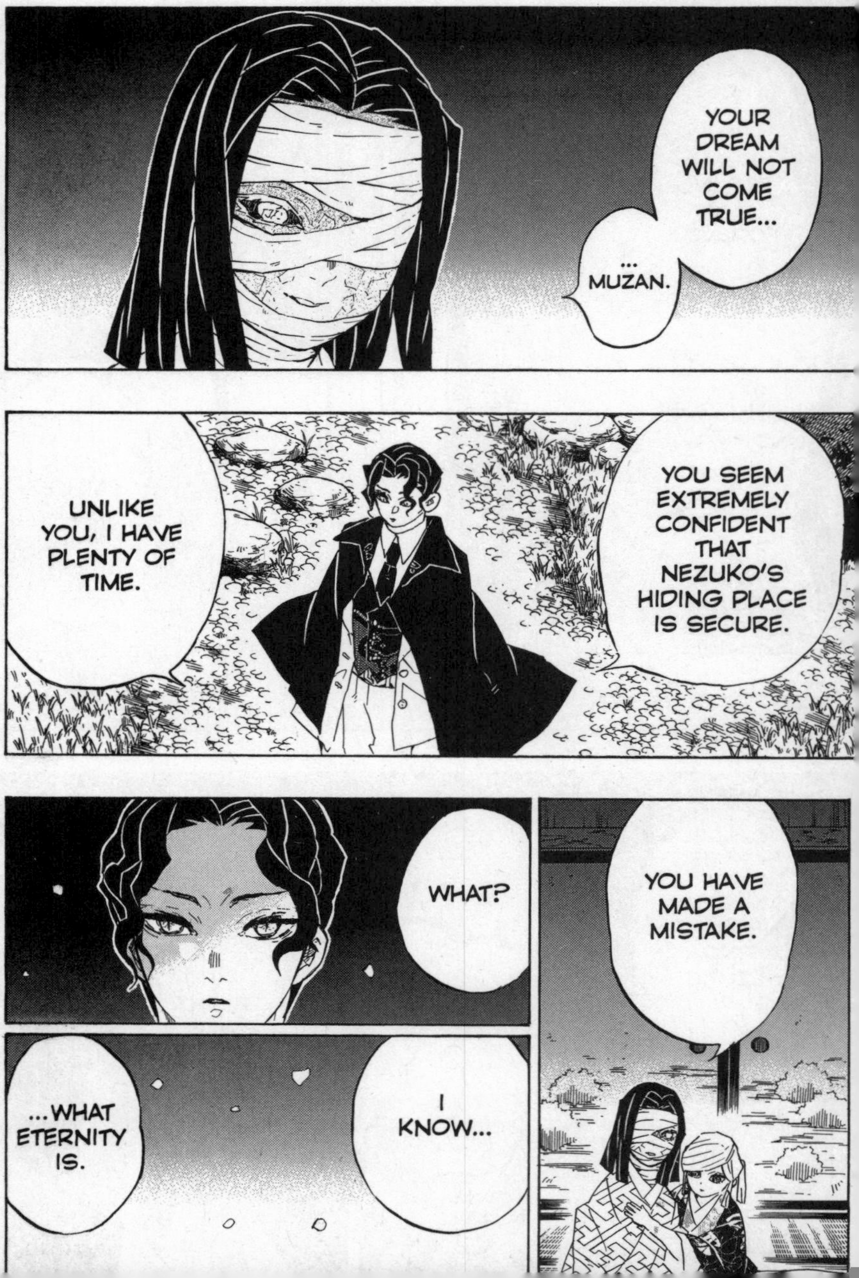
YOUR DREAM WILL NOT COME TRUE...
... MUZAN.
YOU SEEM EXTREMELY CONFIDENT THAT NEZUKO'S HIDING PLACE IS SECURE.
UNLIKE YOU, I HAVE PLENTY OF TIME.
YOU HAVE MADE A MISTAKE.
WHAT?
I KNOW...
...WHAT ETERNITY IS.

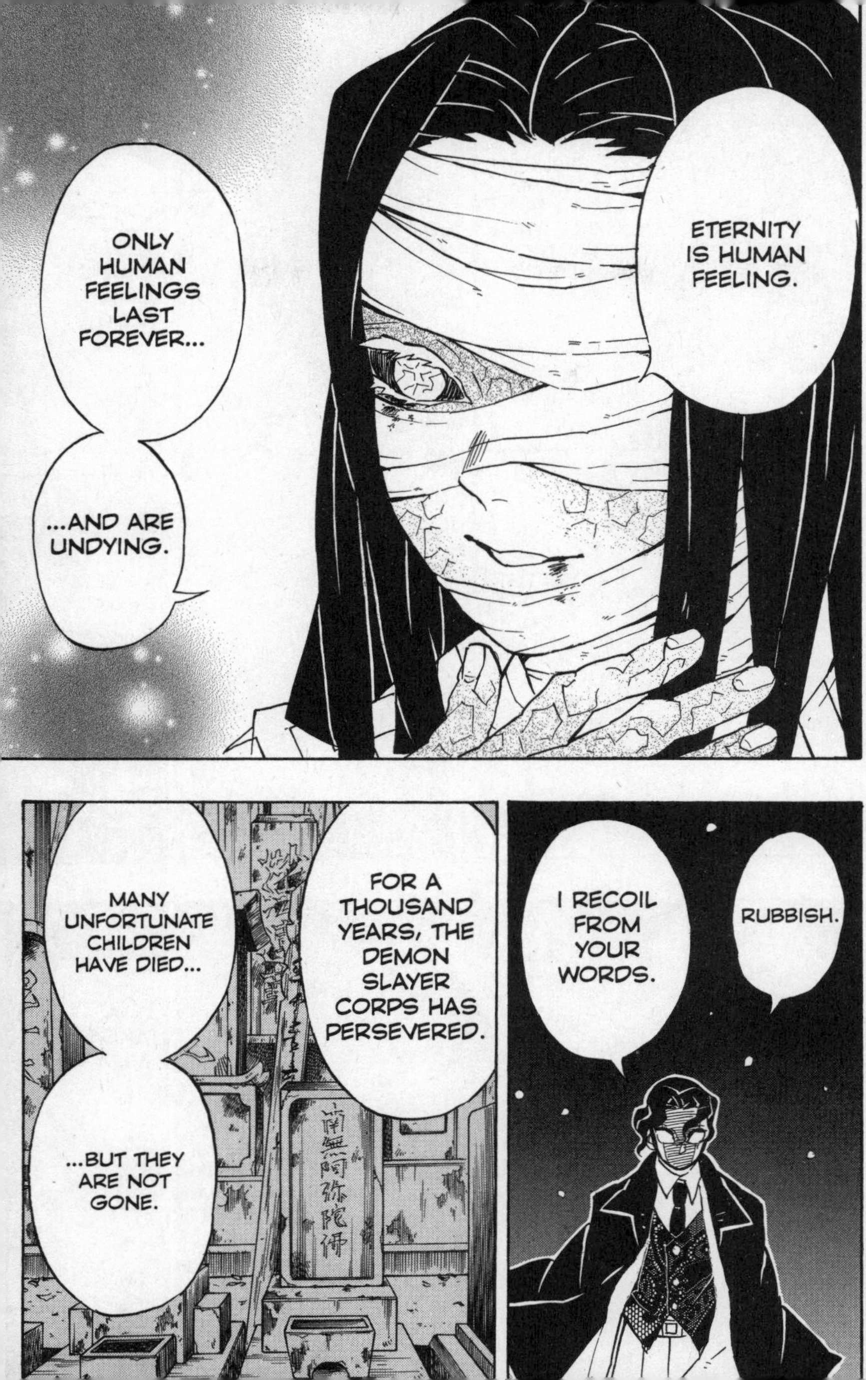
ETERNITY IS HUMAN FEELING.
ONLY HUMAN FEELINGS LAST FOREVER...
...AND ARE UNDYING.
RUBBISH.
I RECOIL FROM YOUR WORDS.
FOR A THOUSAND YEARS, THE DEMON SLAYER CORPS HAS PERSEVERED.
MANY UNFORTUNATE CHILDREN HAVE DIED...
...BUT THEY ARE NOT GONE.
南無阿弥陀佛

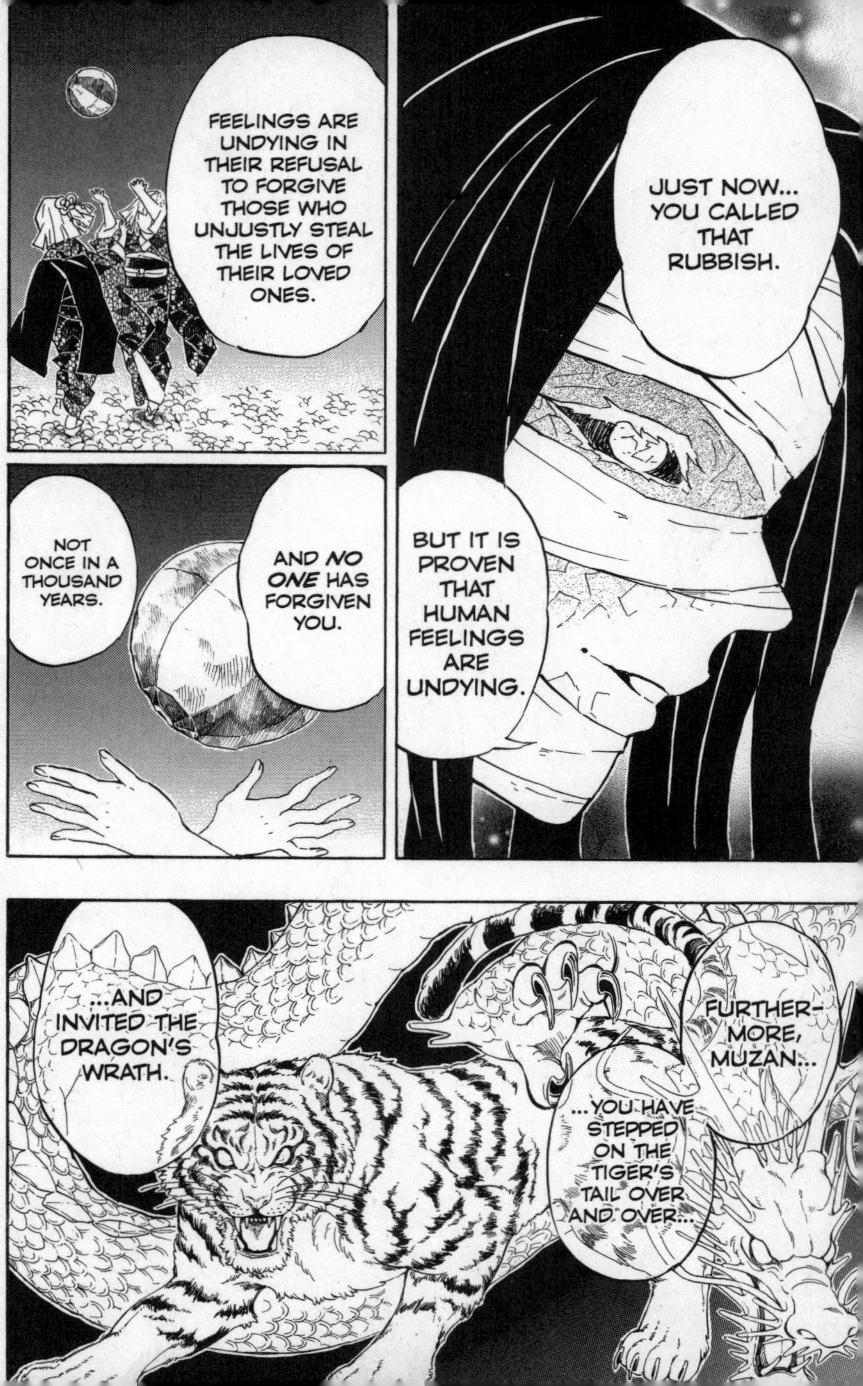
JUST NOW... YOU CALLED THAT RUBBISH.
BUT IT IS PROVEN THAT HUMAN FEELINGS ARE UNDYING.
FEELINGS ARE UNDYING IN THEIR REFUSAL TO FORGIVE THOSE WHO UNJUSTLY STEAL THE LIVES OF THEIR LOVED ONES.
AND *NO ONE* HAS FORGIVEN YOU.
NOT ONCE IN A THOUSAND YEARS.
FURTHERMORE, MUZAN...
...YOU HAVE STEPPED ON THE TIGER'S TAIL OVER AND OVER...
...AND INVITED THE DRAGON'S WRATH.

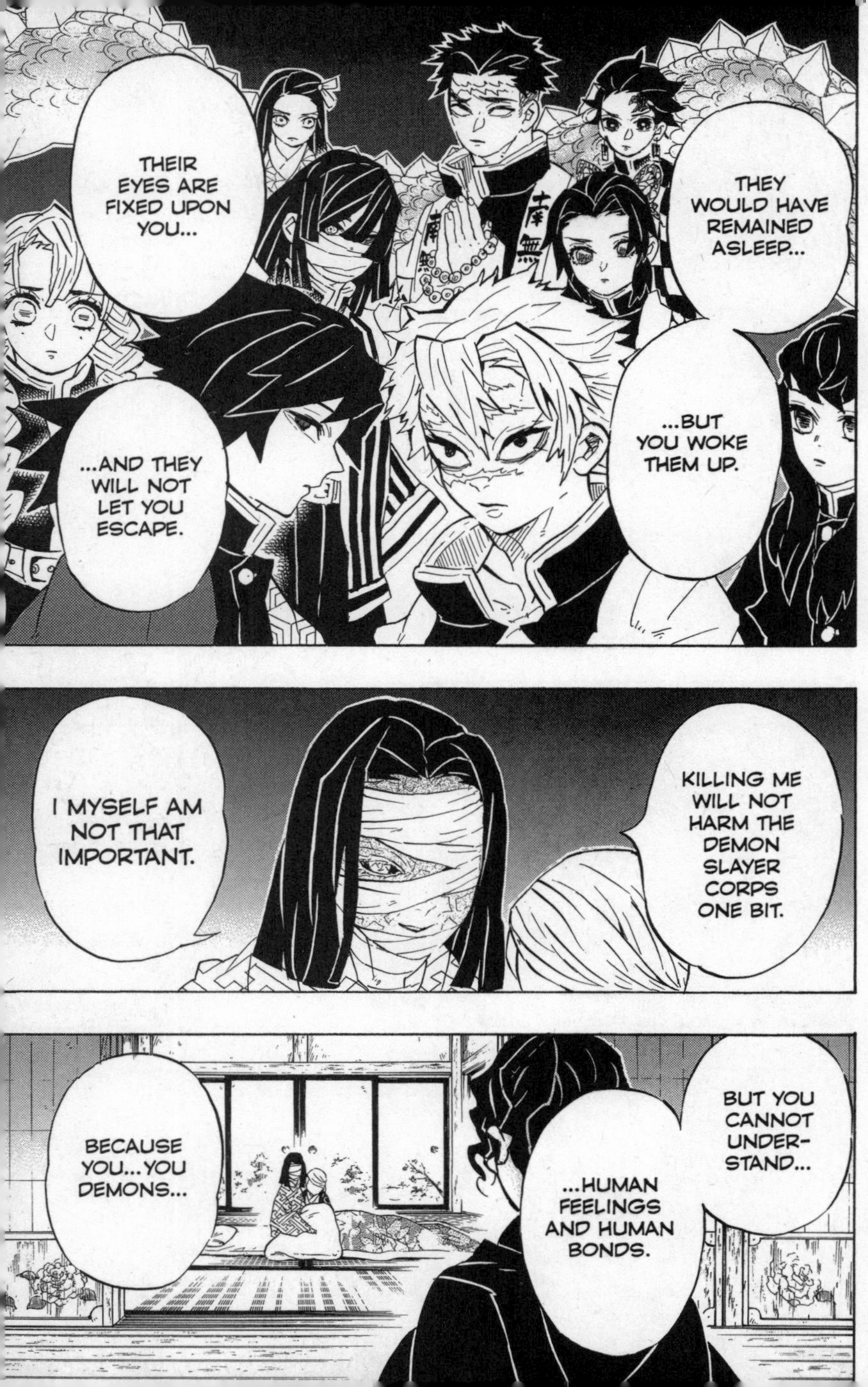
THEY WOULD HAVE REMAINED ASLEEP...
...BUT YOU WOKE THEM UP.
THEIR EYES ARE FIXED UPON YOU...
...AND THEY WILL NOT LET YOU ESCAPE.
KILLING ME WILL NOT HARM THE DEMON SLAYER CORPS ONE BIT.
I MYSELF AM NOT THAT IMPORTANT.
BUT YOU CANNOT UNDER-STAND...
...HUMAN FEELINGS AND HUMAN BONDS.
BECAUSE YOU...YOU DEMONS...

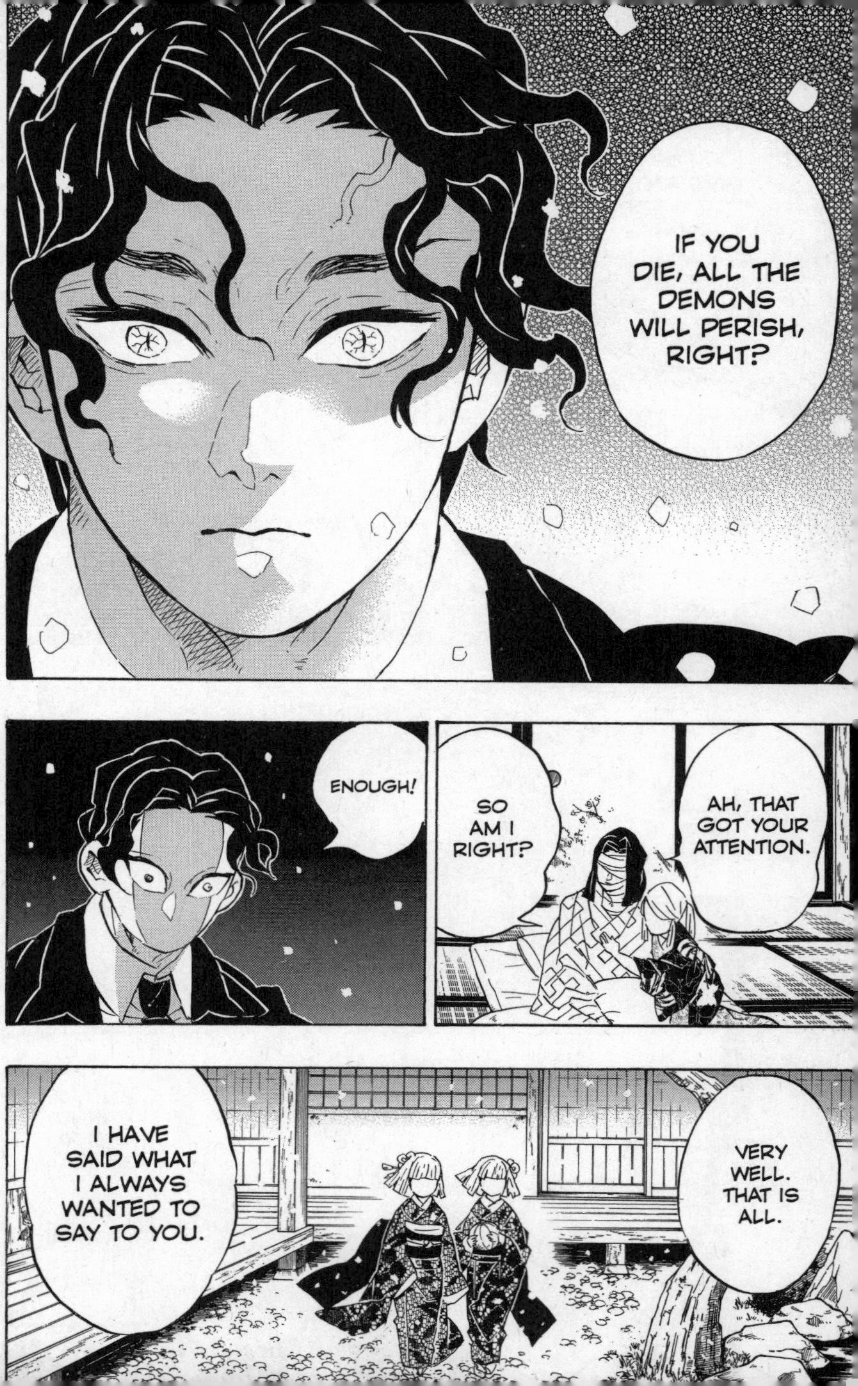
IF YOU DIE, ALL THE DEMONS WILL PERISH, RIGHT?
AH, THAT GOT YOUR ATTENTION.
SO AM I RIGHT?
ENOUGH!
VERY WELL. THAT IS ALL.
I HAVE SAID WHAT I ALWAYS WANTED TO SAY TO YOU.

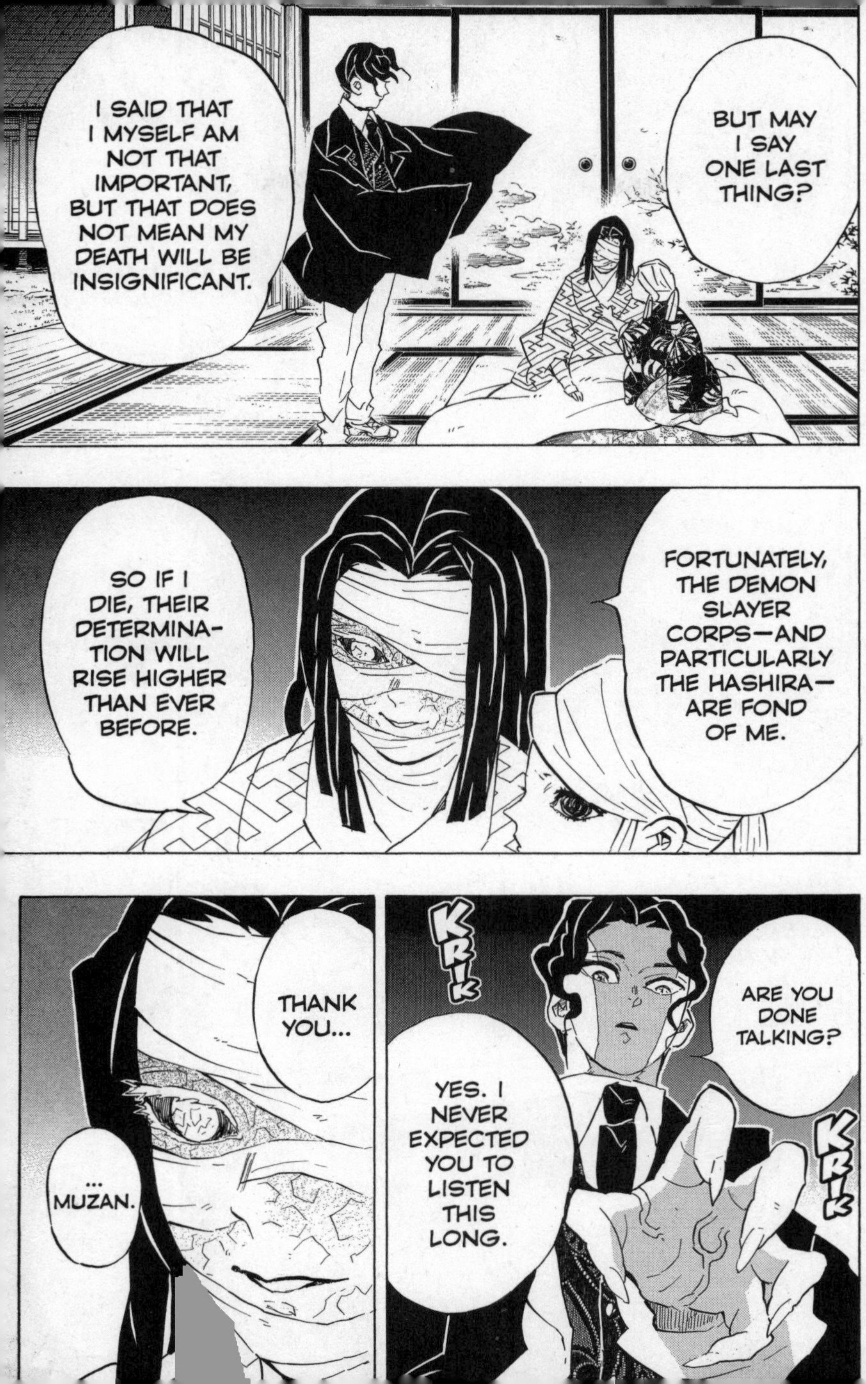
BUT MAY I SAY ONE LAST THING?
I SAID THAT I MYSELF AM NOT THAT IMPORTANT, BUT THAT DOES NOT MEAN MY DEATH WILL BE INSIGNIFICANT.
FORTUNATELY, THE DEMON SLAYER CORPS—AND PARTICULARLY THE HASHIRA—ARE FOND OF ME.
SO IF I DIE, THEIR DETERMINATION WILL RISE HIGHER THAN EVER BEFORE.
KRIK
ARE YOU DONE TALKING?
YES. I NEVER EXPECTED YOU TO LISTEN THIS LONG.
KRIK
THANK YOU...
...MUZAN.

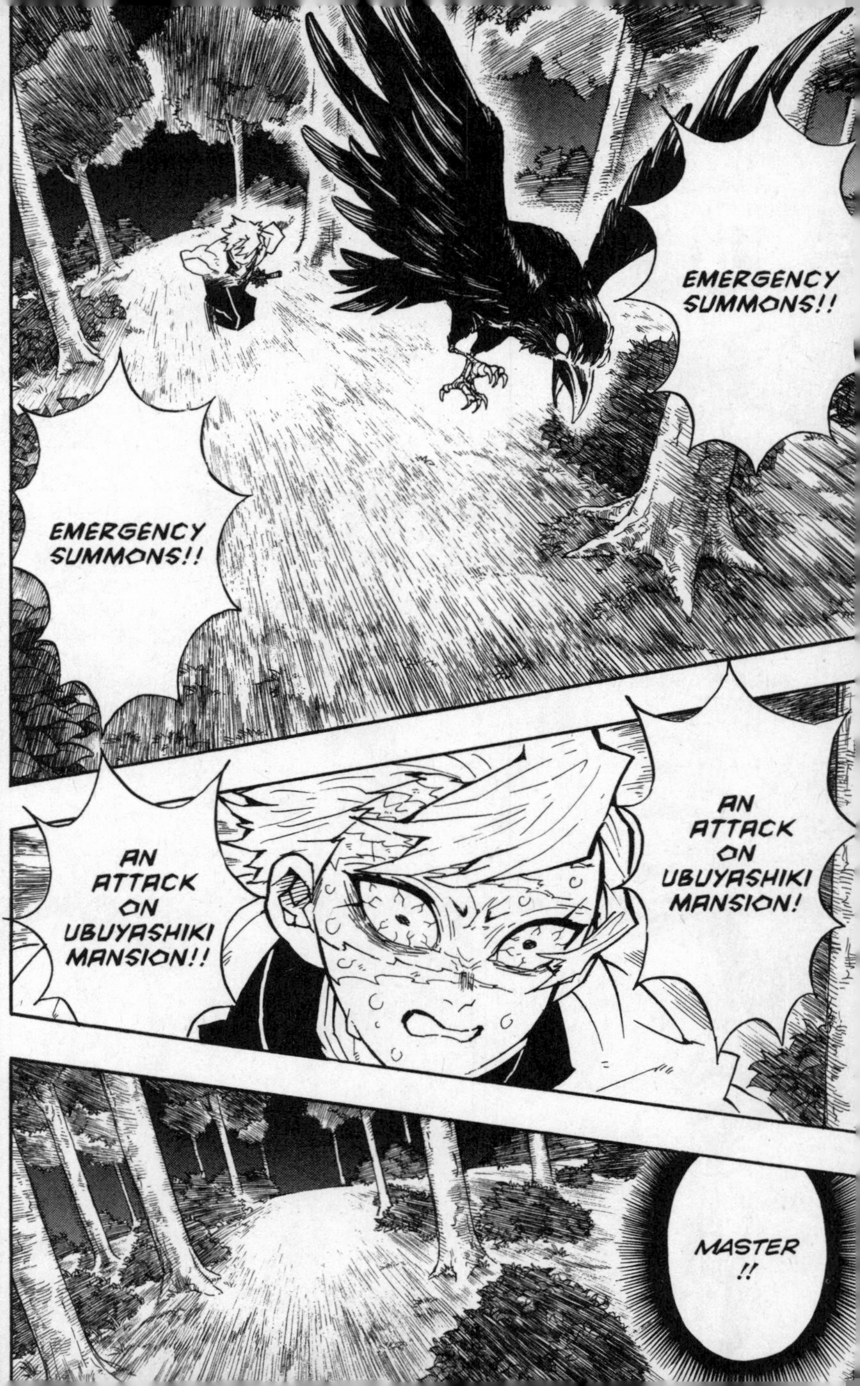
EMERGENCY SUMMONS!!
EMERGENCY SUMMONS!!
AN ATTACK ON UBUYASHIKI MANSION!
AN ATTACK ON UBUYASHIKI MANSION!!
MASTER !!

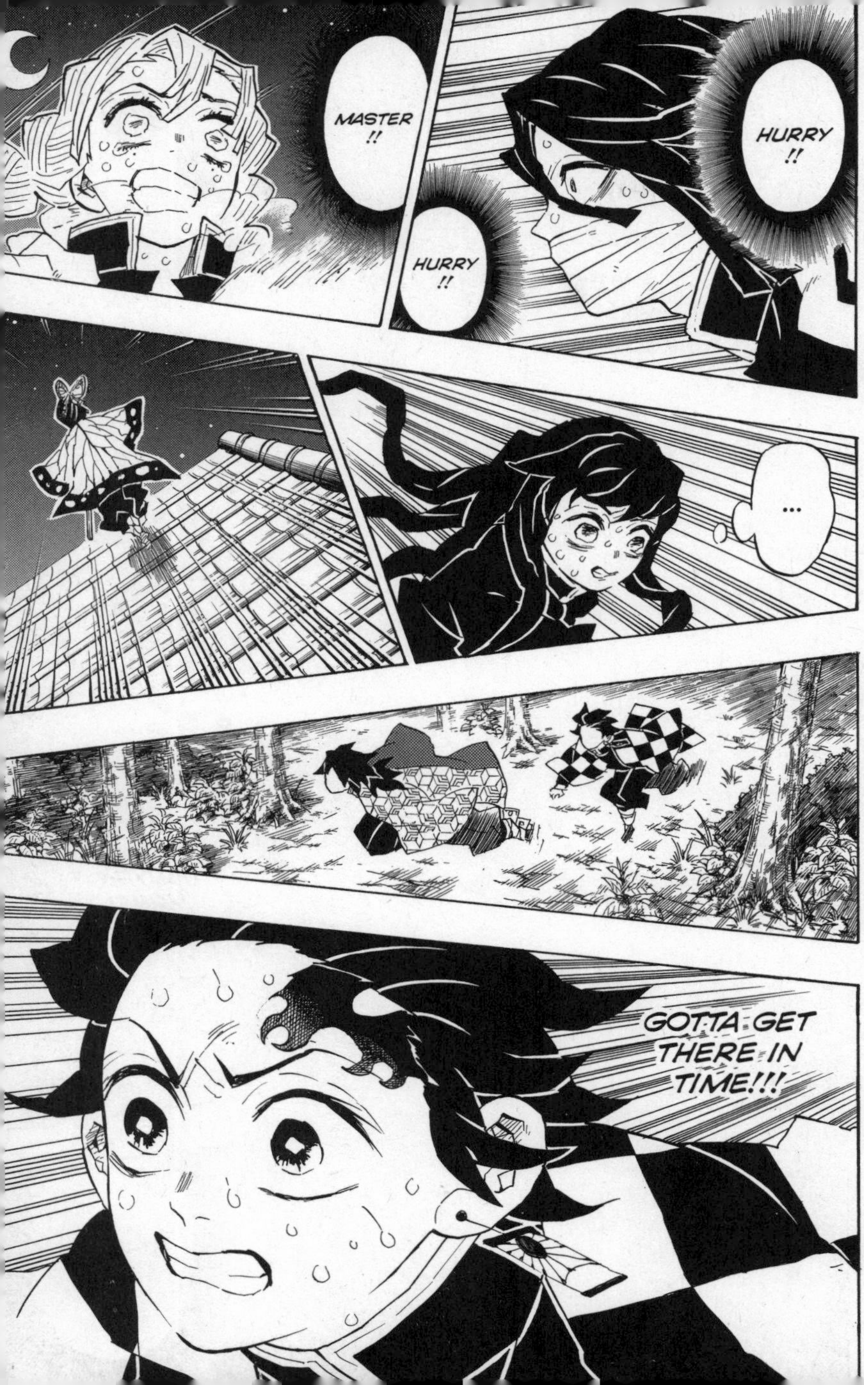
HURRY !!
HURRY !!
MASTER !!
...
GOTTA GET THERE IN TIME!!!

A scrapped illustration for a front page. Muzan and Kagaya's faces resemble each other as if they are twins.

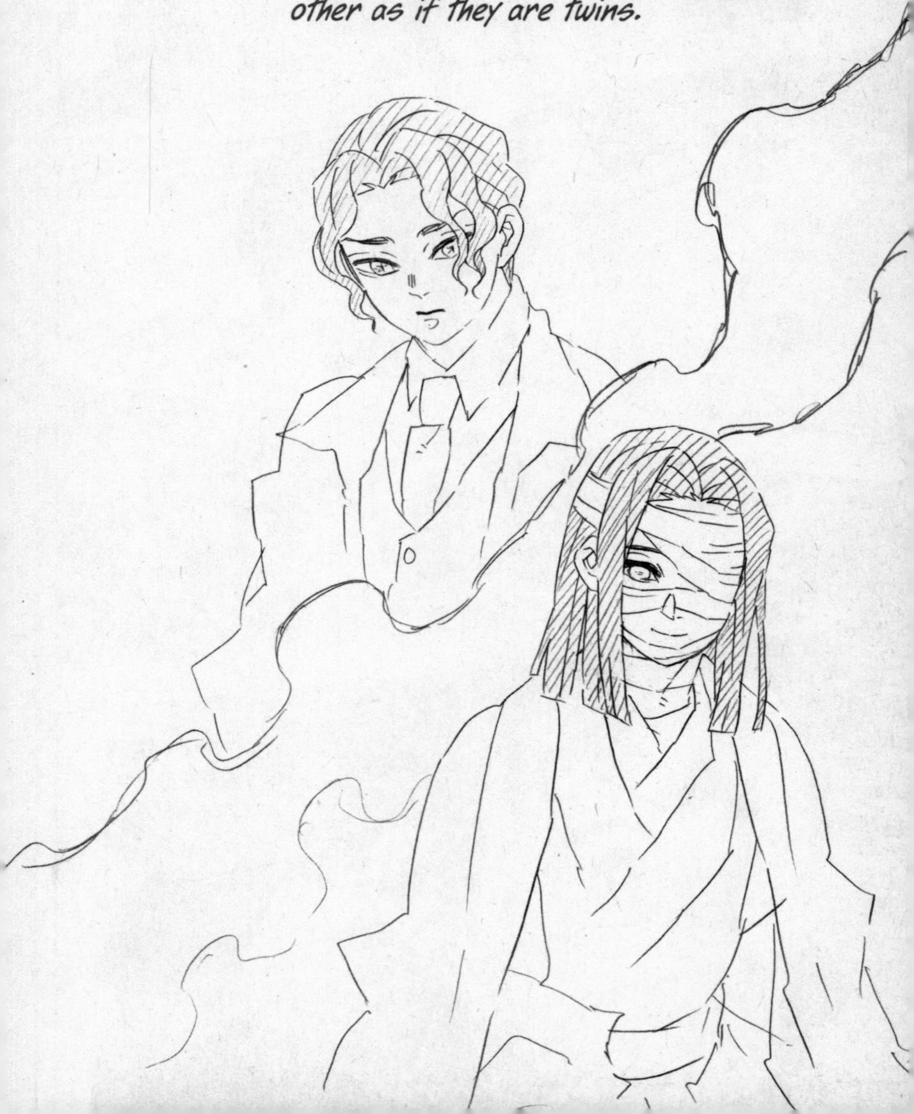

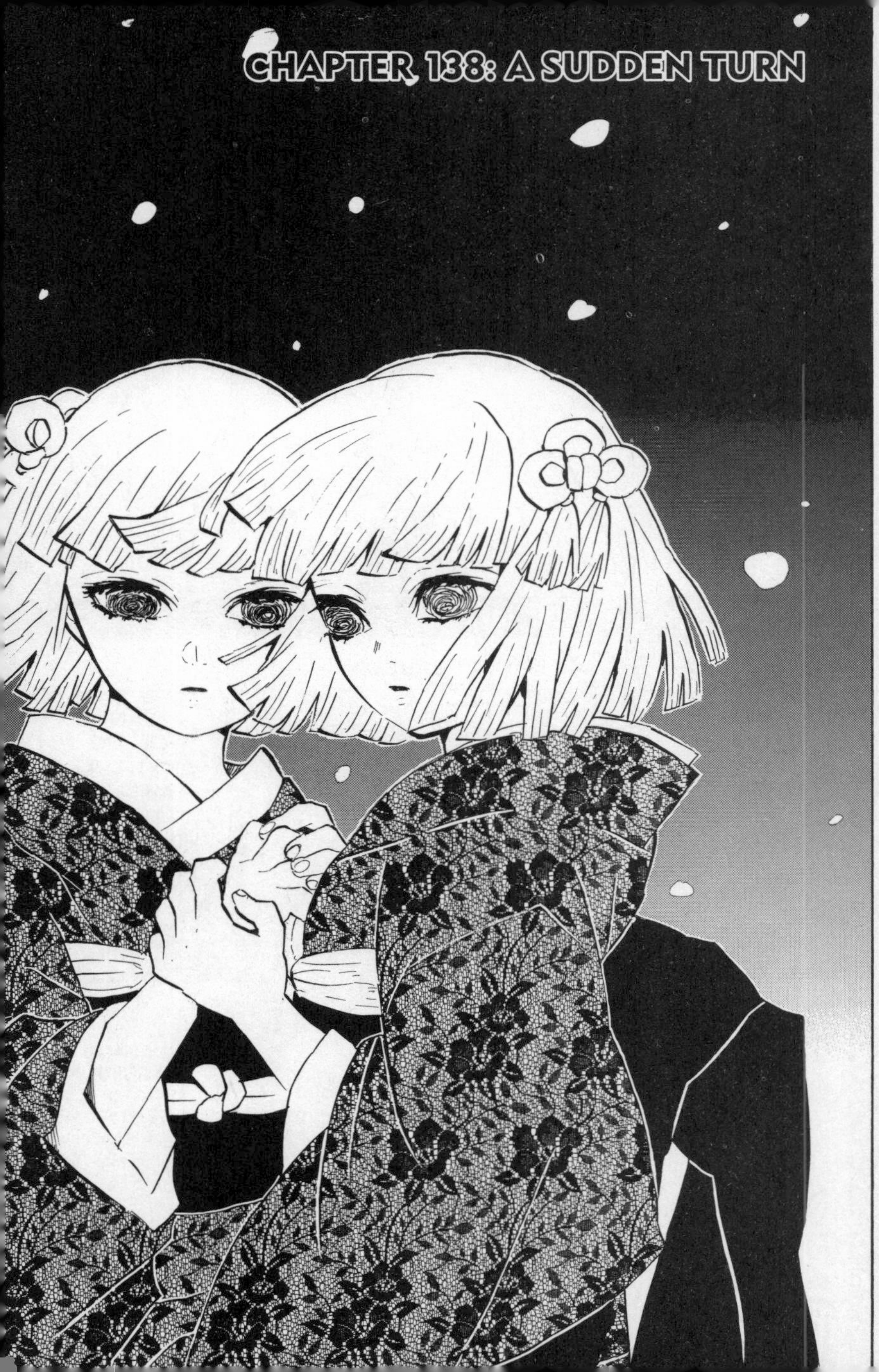
CHAPTER 138: A SUDDEN TURN

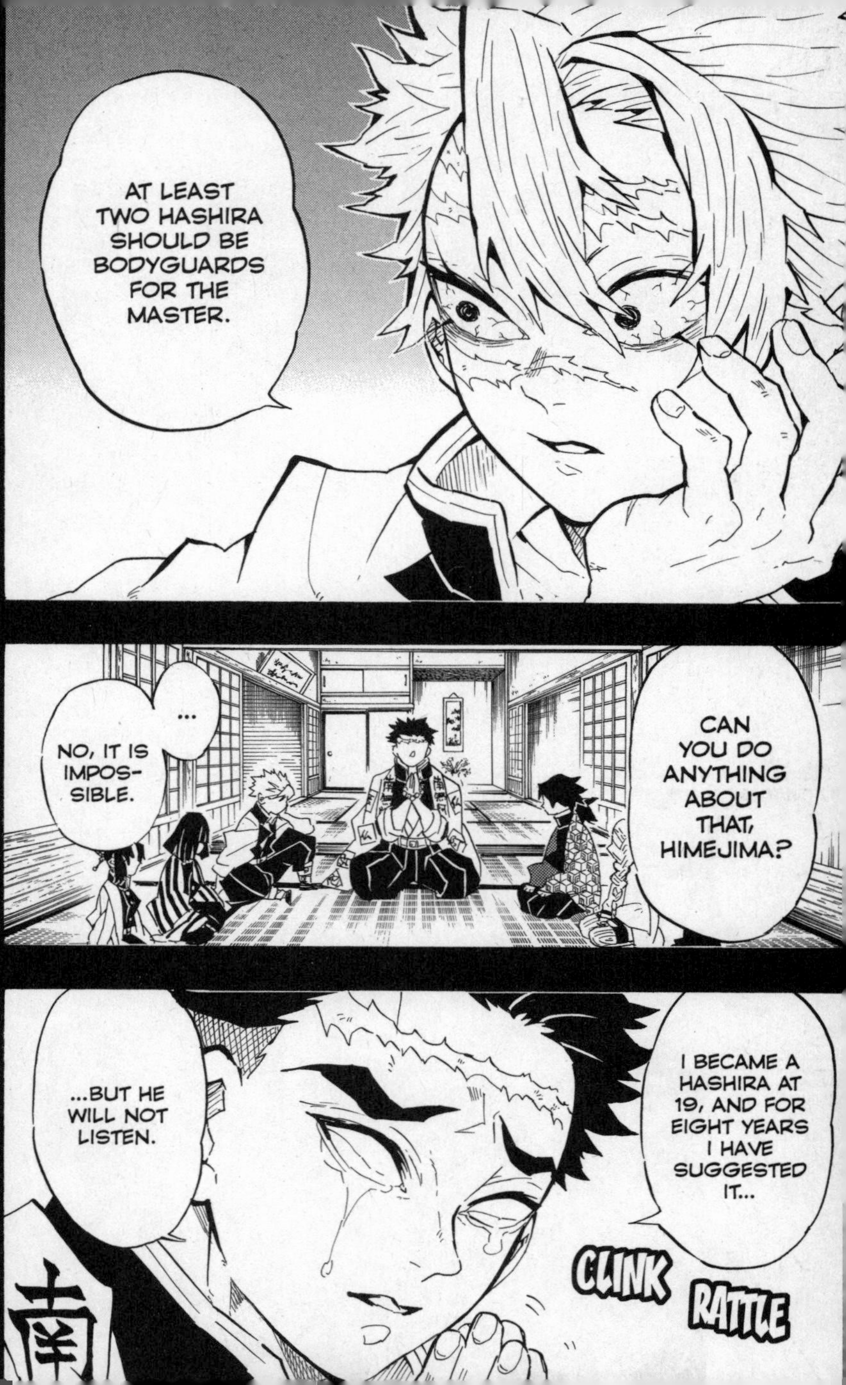
AT LEAST TWO HASHIRA SHOULD BE BODYGUARDS FOR THE MASTER.
CAN YOU DO ANYTHING ABOUT THAT, HIMEJIMA?
...
NO, IT IS IMPOSSIBLE.
I BECAME A HASHIRA AT 19, AND FOR EIGHT YEARS I HAVE SUGGESTED IT...
...BUT HE WILL NOT LISTEN.
CLINK
RATTLE

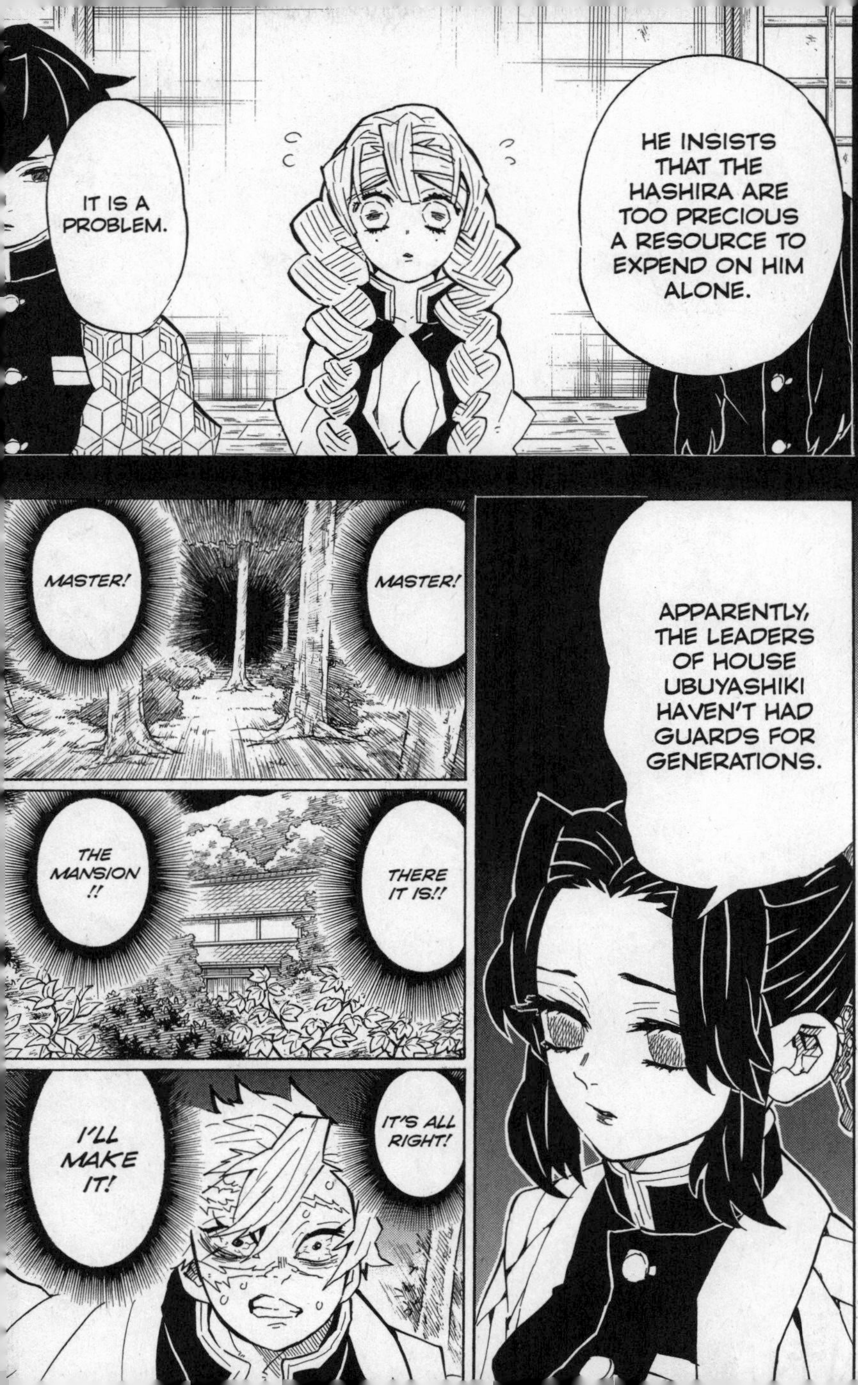
HE INSISTS THAT THE HASHIRA ARE TOO PRECIOUS A RESOURCE TO EXPEND ON HIM ALONE.
IT IS A PROBLEM.
APPARENTLY, THE LEADERS OF HOUSE UBUYASHIKI HAVEN'T HAD GUARDS FOR GENERATIONS.
MASTER!
MASTER!
THERE IT IS!!
THE MANSION!!
IT'S ALL RIGHT!
I'LL MAKE IT!

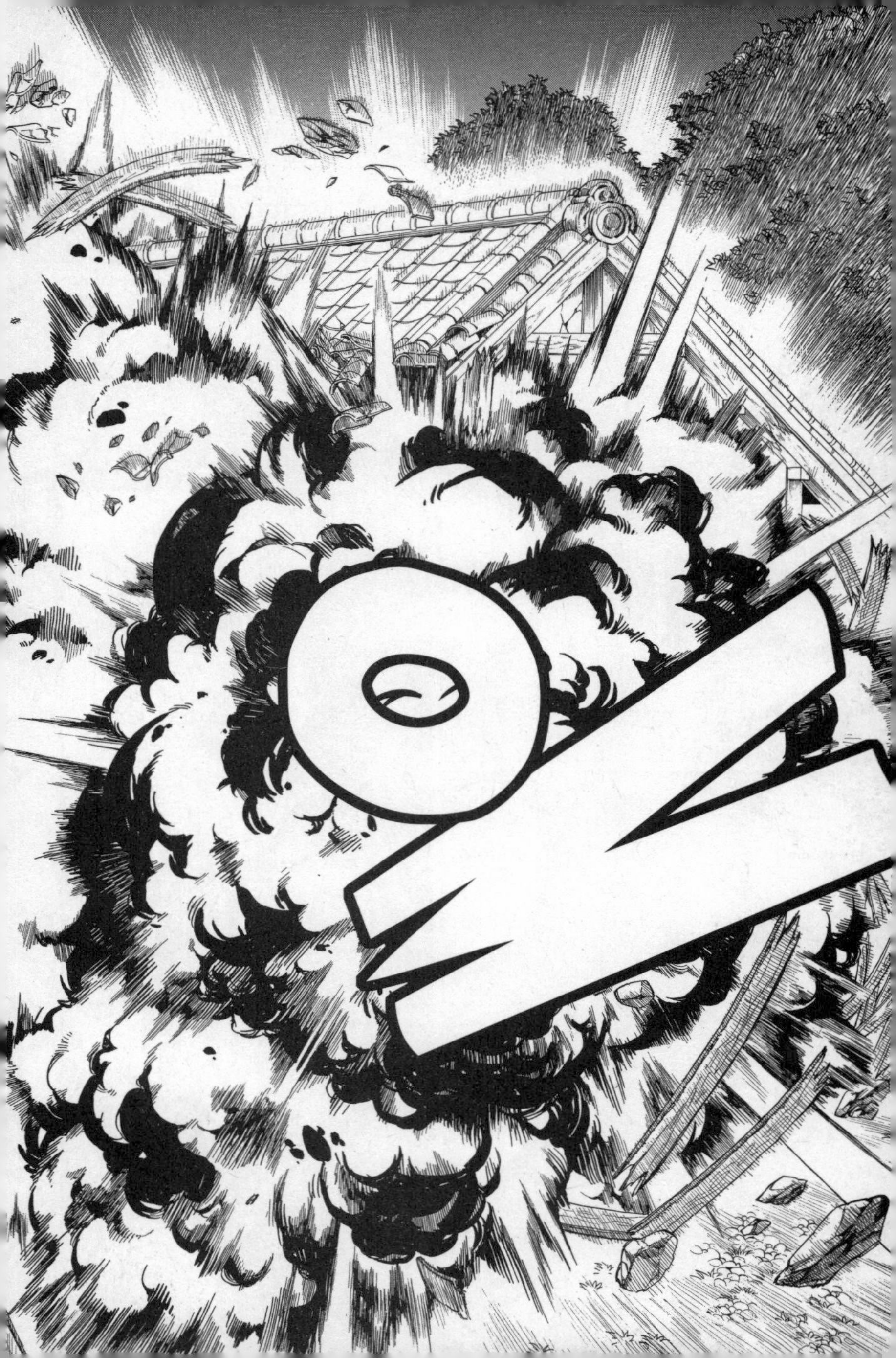

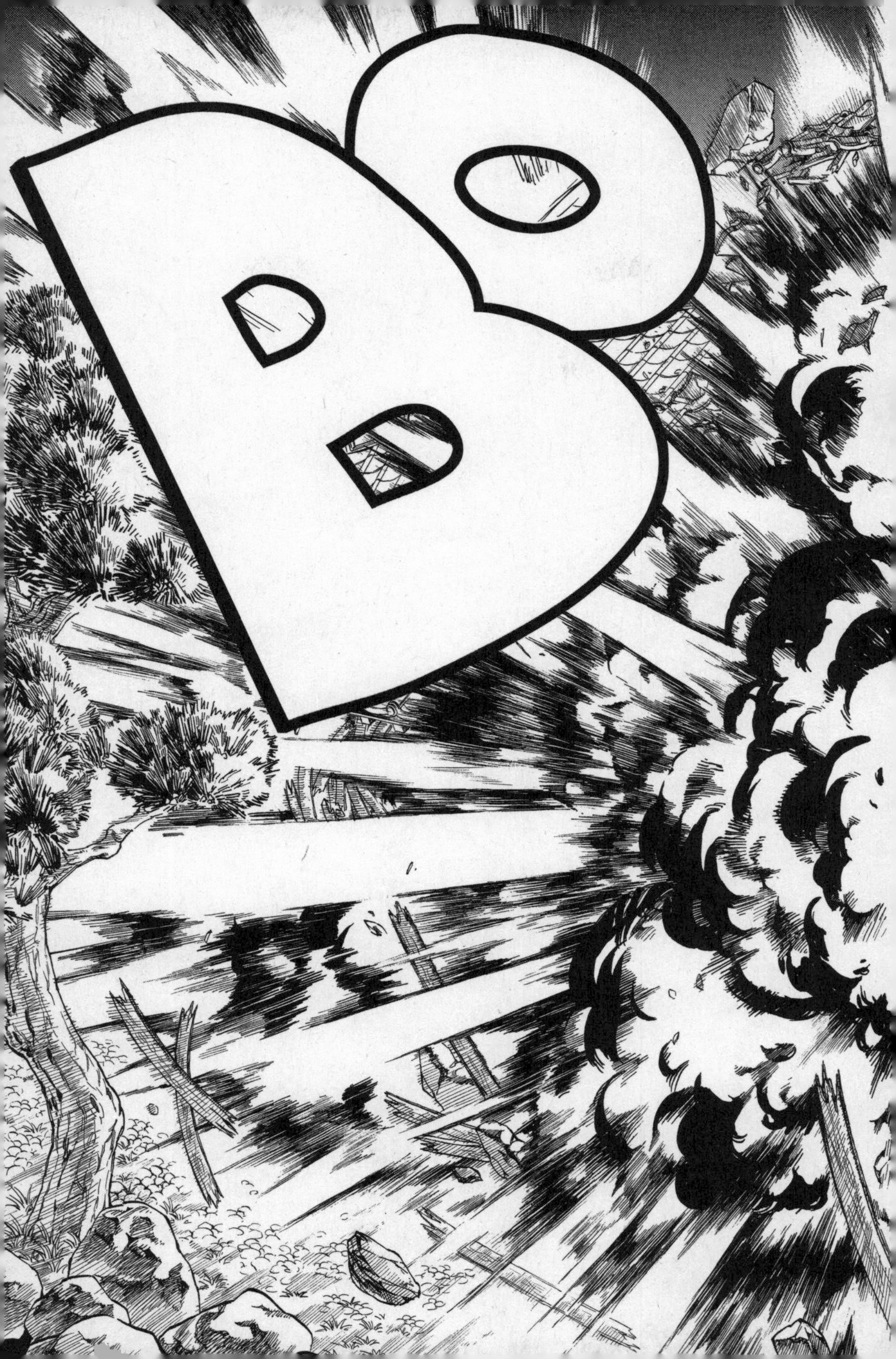
BB

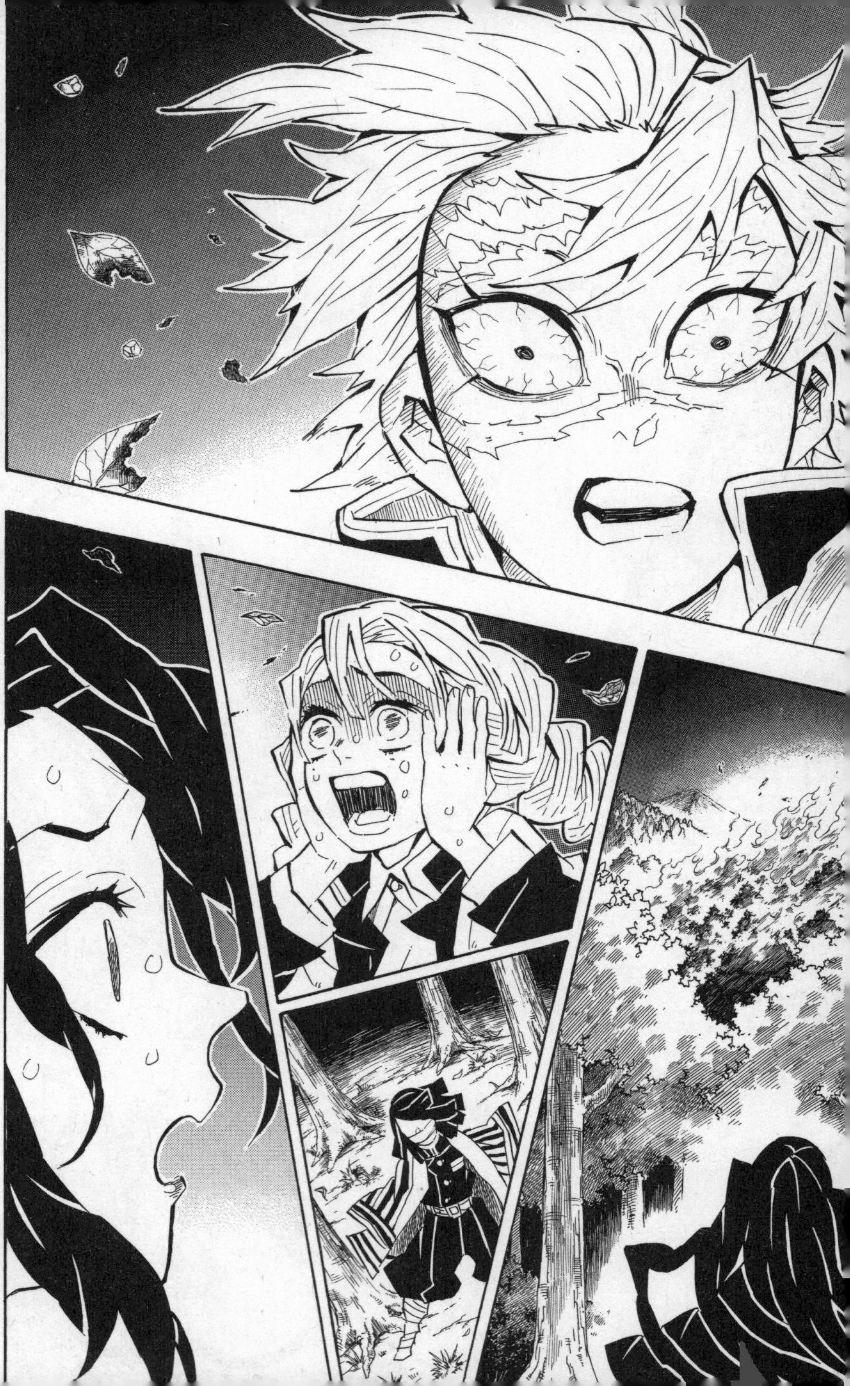

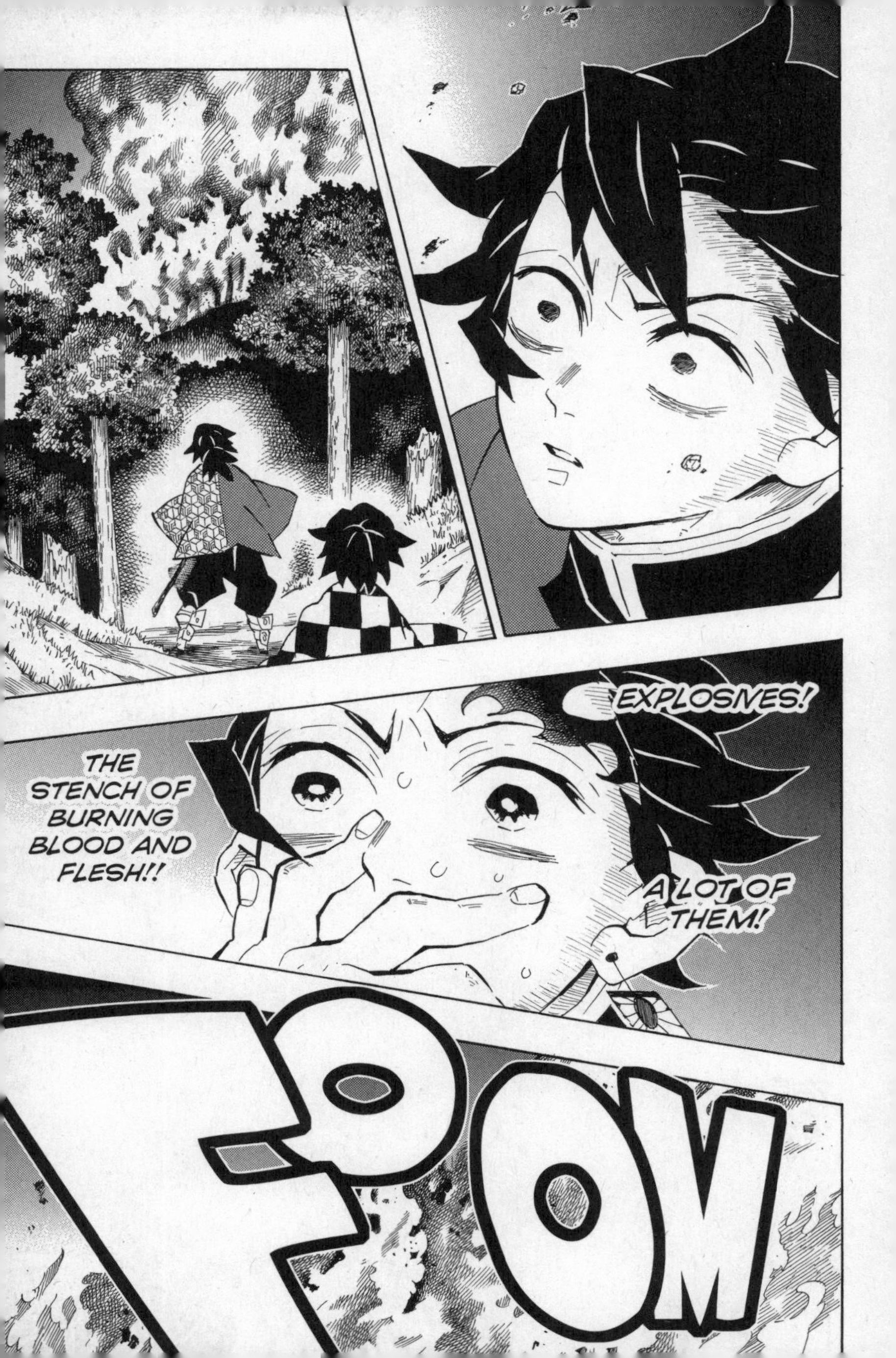
EXPLOSIVES!
A LOT OF THEM!
THE STENCH OF BURNING BLOOD AND FLESH!!

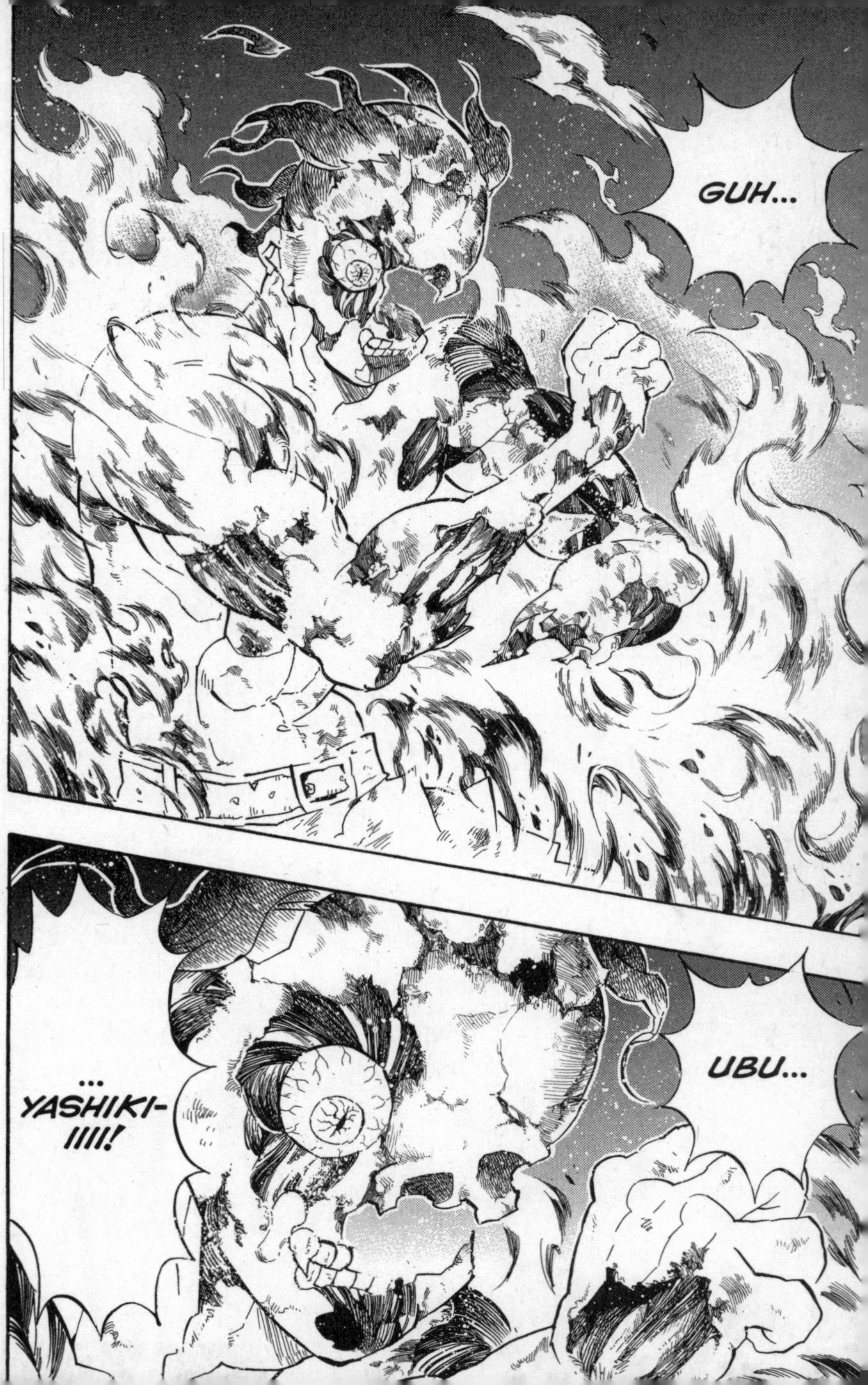
GUH...
UBU...
...YASHIKI-IIII!

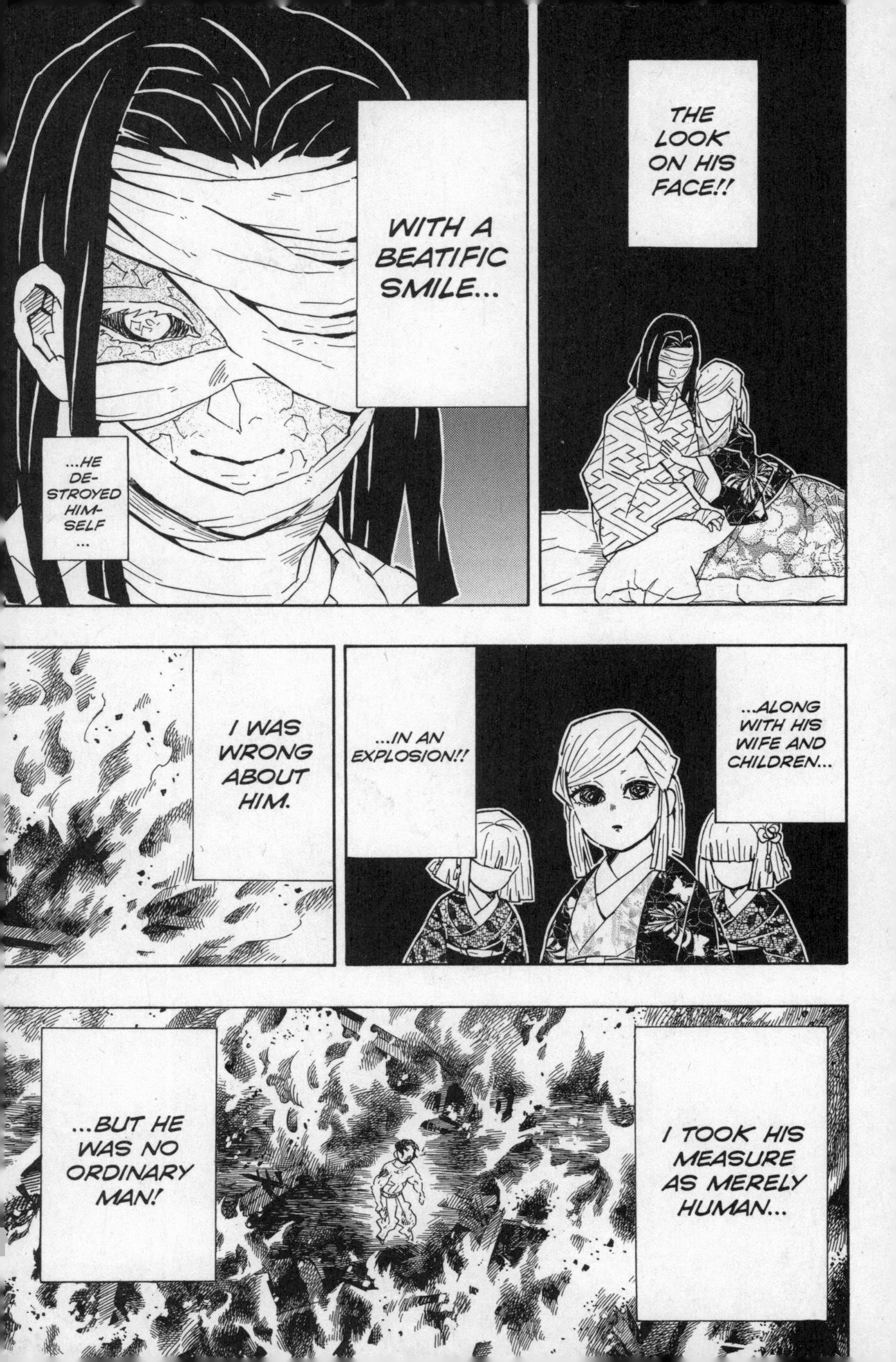
THE LOOK ON HIS FACE!!
WITH A BEATIFIC SMILE...
...HE DESTROYED HIMSELF ...
...ALONG WITH HIS WIFE AND CHILDREN...
...IN AN EXPLOSION!!
I WAS WRONG ABOUT HIM.
I TOOK HIS MEASURE AS MERELY HUMAN...
...BUT HE WAS NO ORDINARY MAN!

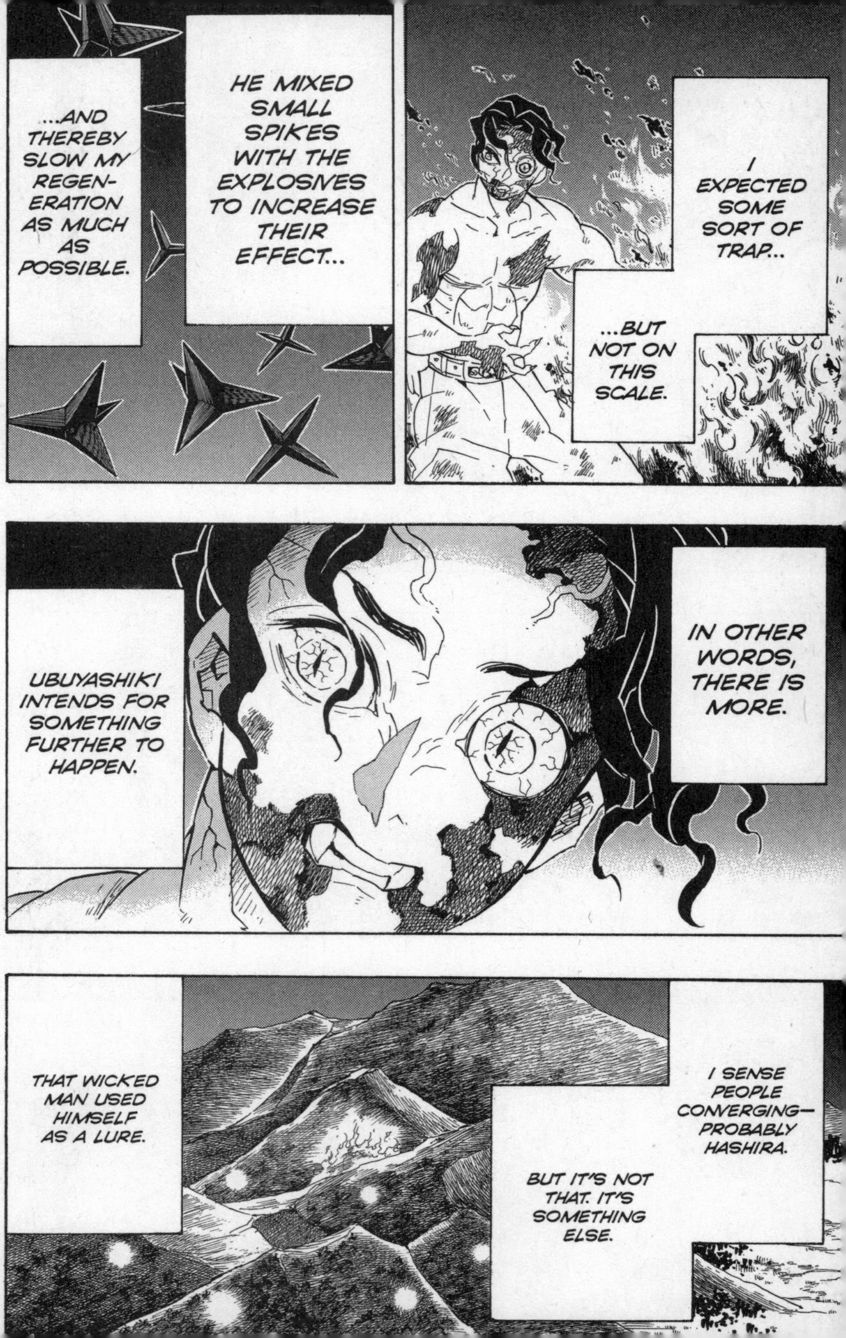
I EXPECTED SOME SORT OF TRAP...
...BUT NOT ON THIS SCALE.
HE MIXED SMALL SPIKES WITH THE EXPLOSIVES TO INCREASE THEIR EFFECT...
...AND THEREBY SLOW MY REGEN-ERATION AS MUCH AS POSSIBLE.
IN OTHER WORDS, THERE IS MORE.
UBUYASHIKI INTENDS FOR SOMETHING FURTHER TO HAPPEN.
I SENSE PEOPLE CONVERGING—PROBABLY HASHIRA.
BUT IT'S NOT THAT. IT'S SOMETHING ELSE.
THAT WICKED MAN USED HIMSELF AS A LURE.

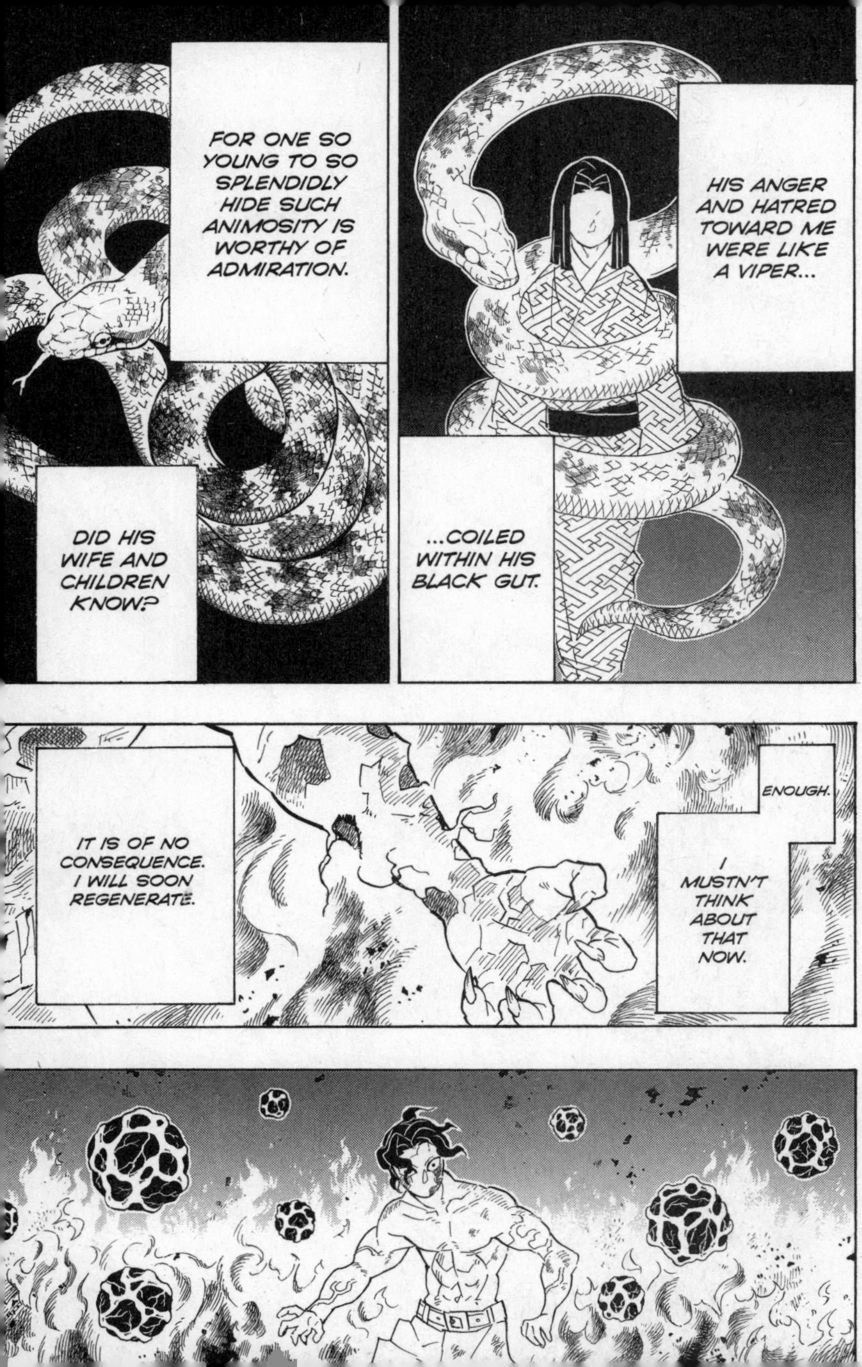
HIS ANGER AND HATRED TOWARD ME WERE LIKE A VIPER...
...COILED WITHIN HIS BLACK GUT.
FOR ONE SO YOUNG TO SO SPLENDIDLY HIDE SUCH ANIMOSITY IS WORTHY OF ADMIRATION.
DID HIS WIFE AND CHILDREN KNOW?
ENOUGH.
I MUSTN'T THINK ABOUT THAT NOW.
IT IS OF NO CONSEQUENCE. I WILL SOON REGENERATE.

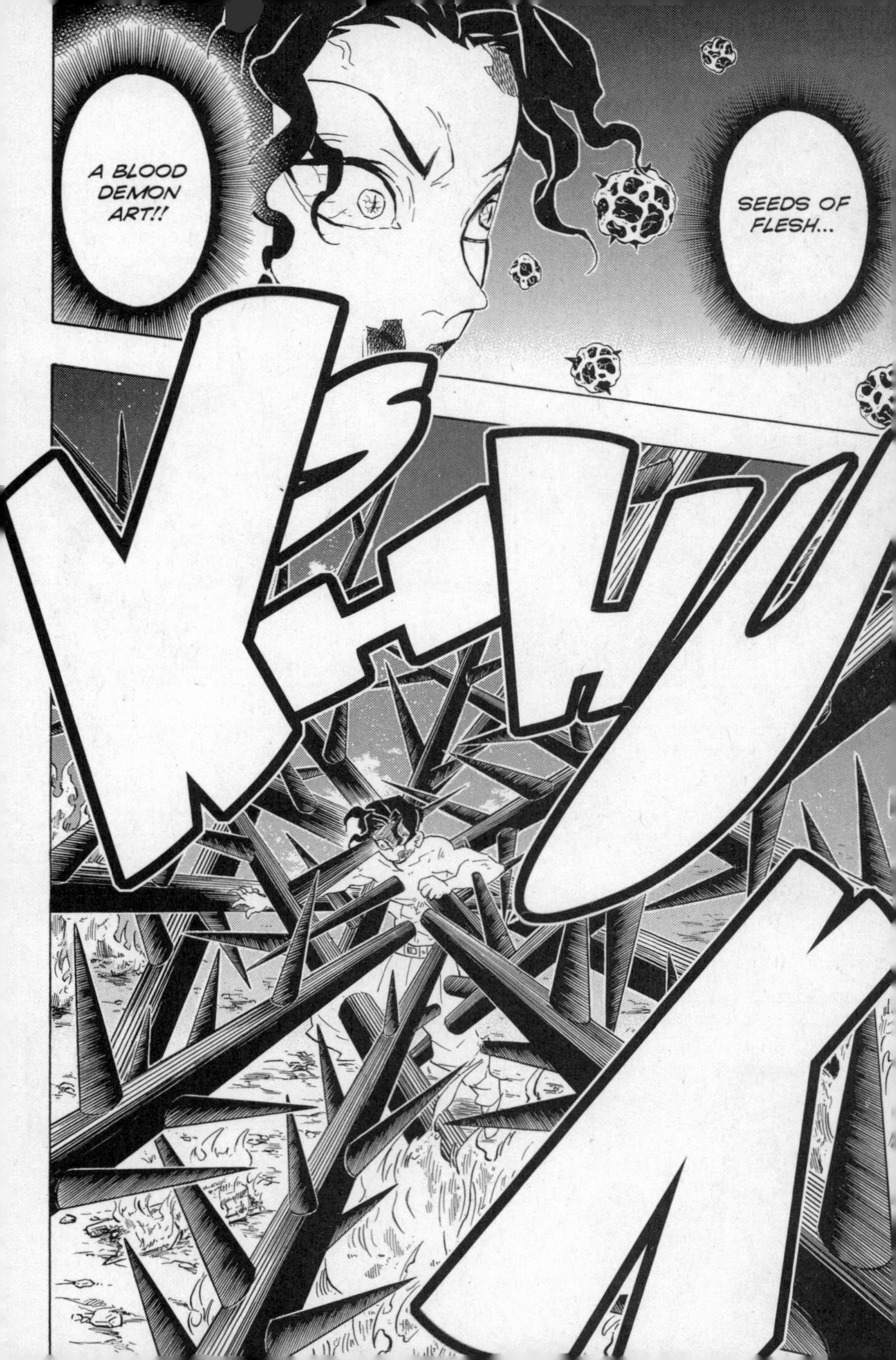
SEEDS OF FLESH...
A BLOOD DEMON ART!!

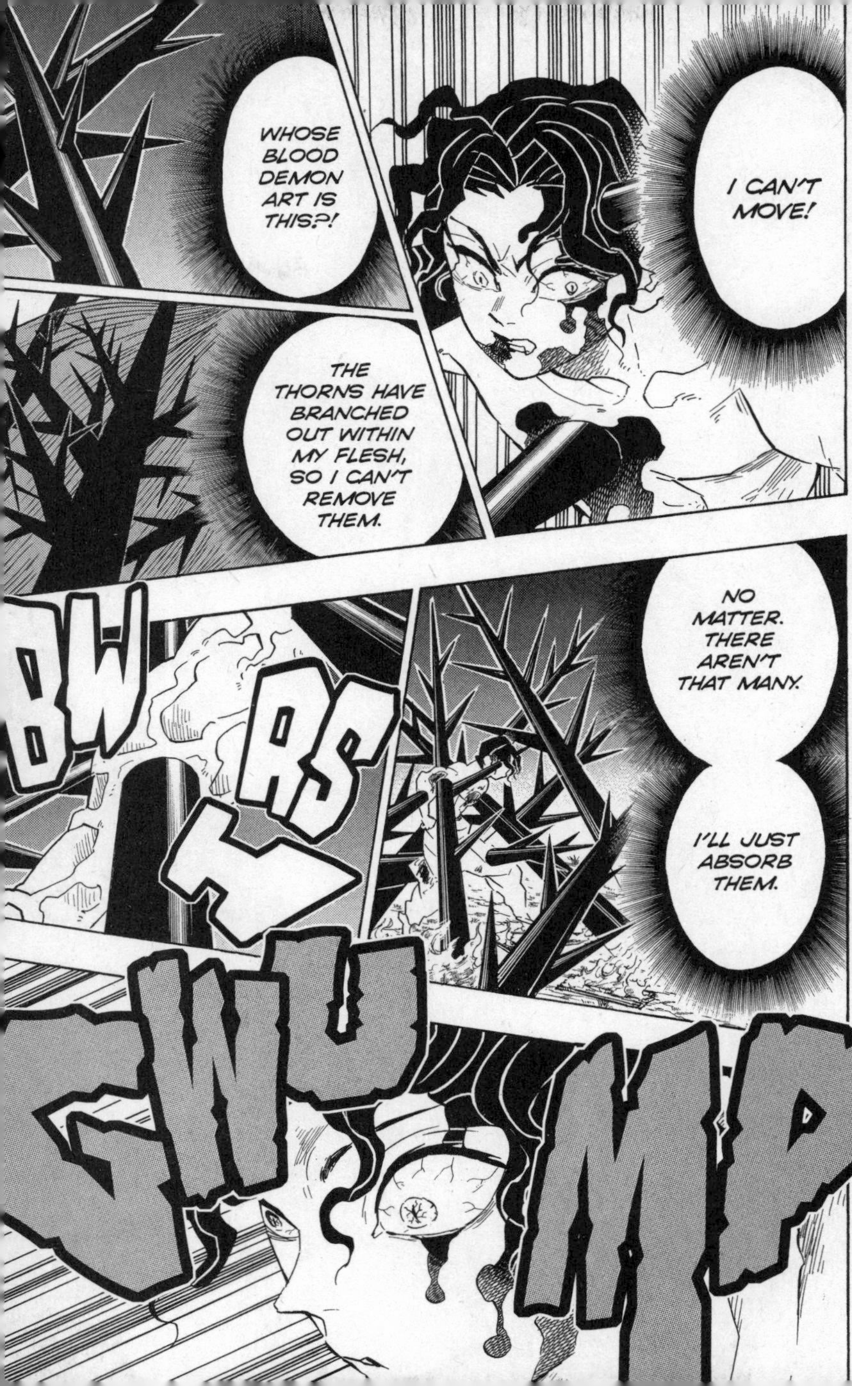
I CAN'T MOVE!
WHOSE BLOOD DEMON ART IS THIS?!
THE THORNS HAVE BRANCHED OUT WITHIN MY FLESH, SO I CAN'T REMOVE THEM.
NO MATTER. THERE AREN'T THAT MANY.
I'LL JUST ABSORB THEM.

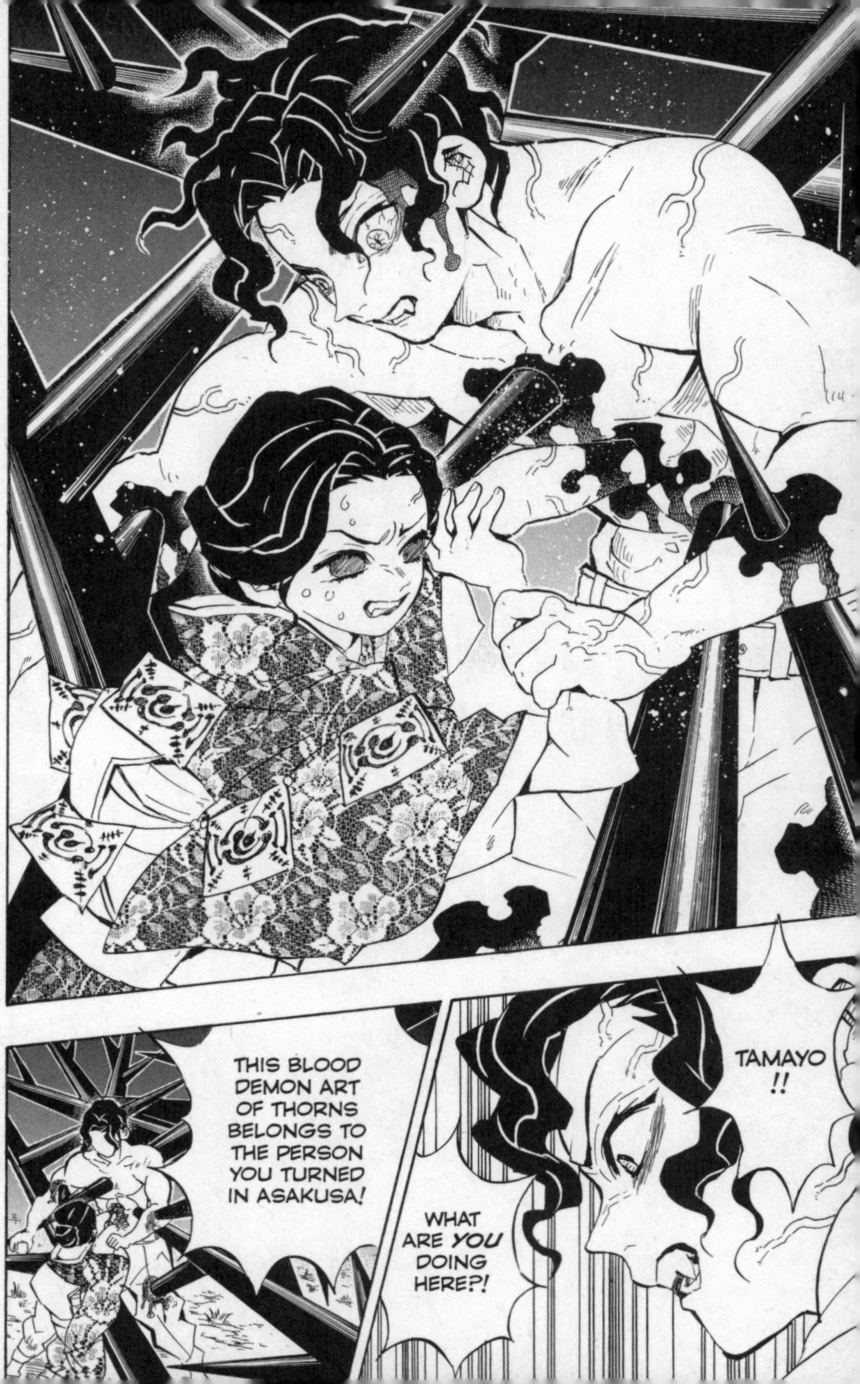
TAMAYO!!
WHAT ARE YOU DOING HERE?!
THIS BLOOD DEMON ART OF THORNS BELONGS TO THE PERSON YOU TURNED IN ASAKUSA!

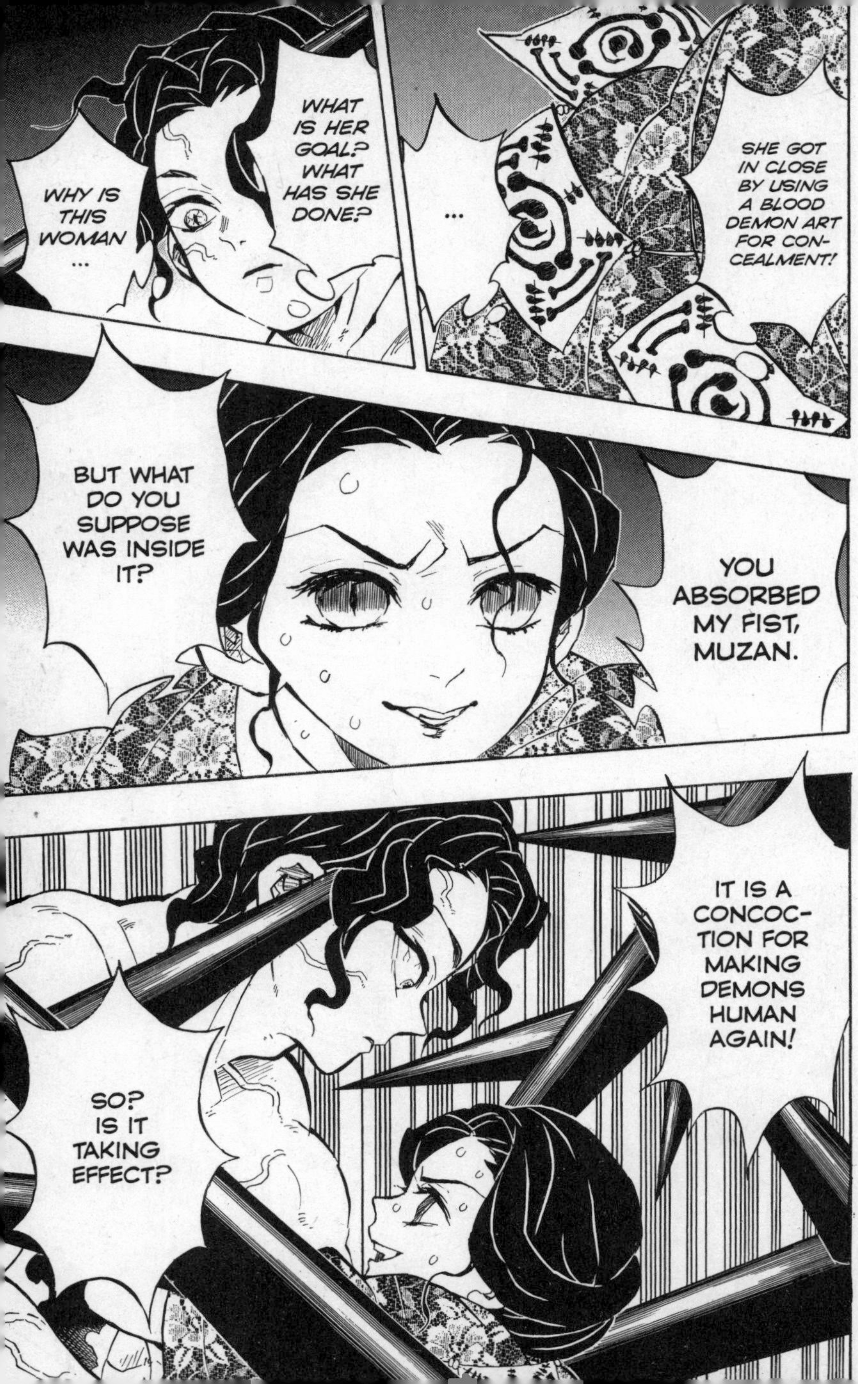
SHE GOT IN CLOSE BY USING A BLOOD DEMON ART FOR CONCEALMENT!
...
WHAT IS HER GOAL? WHAT HAS SHE DONE?
WHY IS THIS WOMAN ...
YOU ABSORBED MY FIST, MUZAN.
BUT WHAT DO YOU SUPPOSE WAS INSIDE IT?
IT IS A CONCOCTION FOR MAKING DEMONS HUMAN AGAIN!
SO? IS IT TAKING EFFECT?

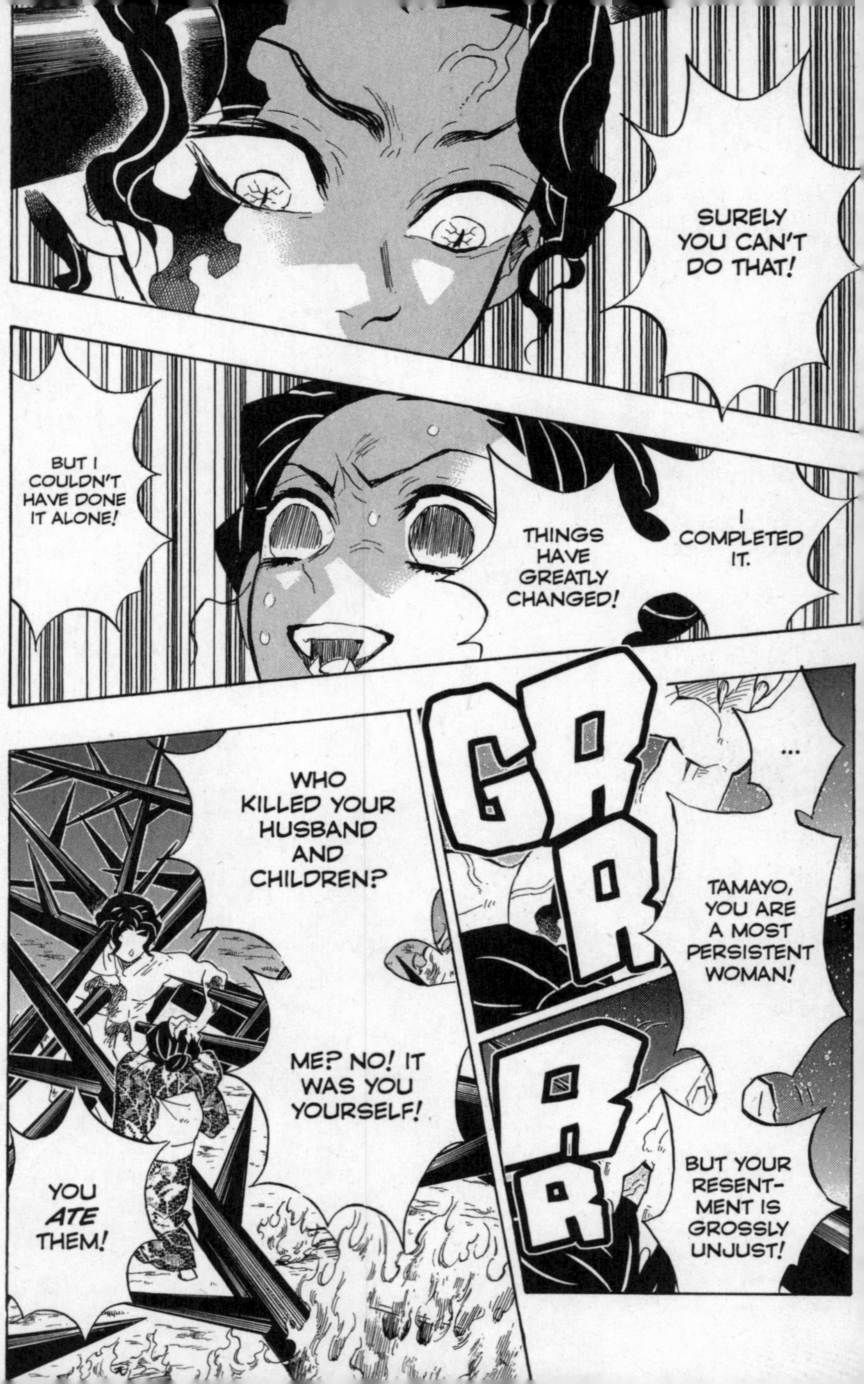
SURELY YOU CAN'T DO THAT!
I COMPLETED IT.
THINGS HAVE GREATLY CHANGED!
BUT I COULDN'T HAVE DONE IT ALONE!
...
GRRR
TAMAYO, YOU ARE A MOST PERSISTENT WOMAN!
BUT YOUR RESENT-MENT IS GROSSLY UNJUST!
WHO KILLED YOUR HUSBAND AND CHILDREN?
ME? NO! IT WAS YOU YOURSELF!
YOU *ATE* THEM!

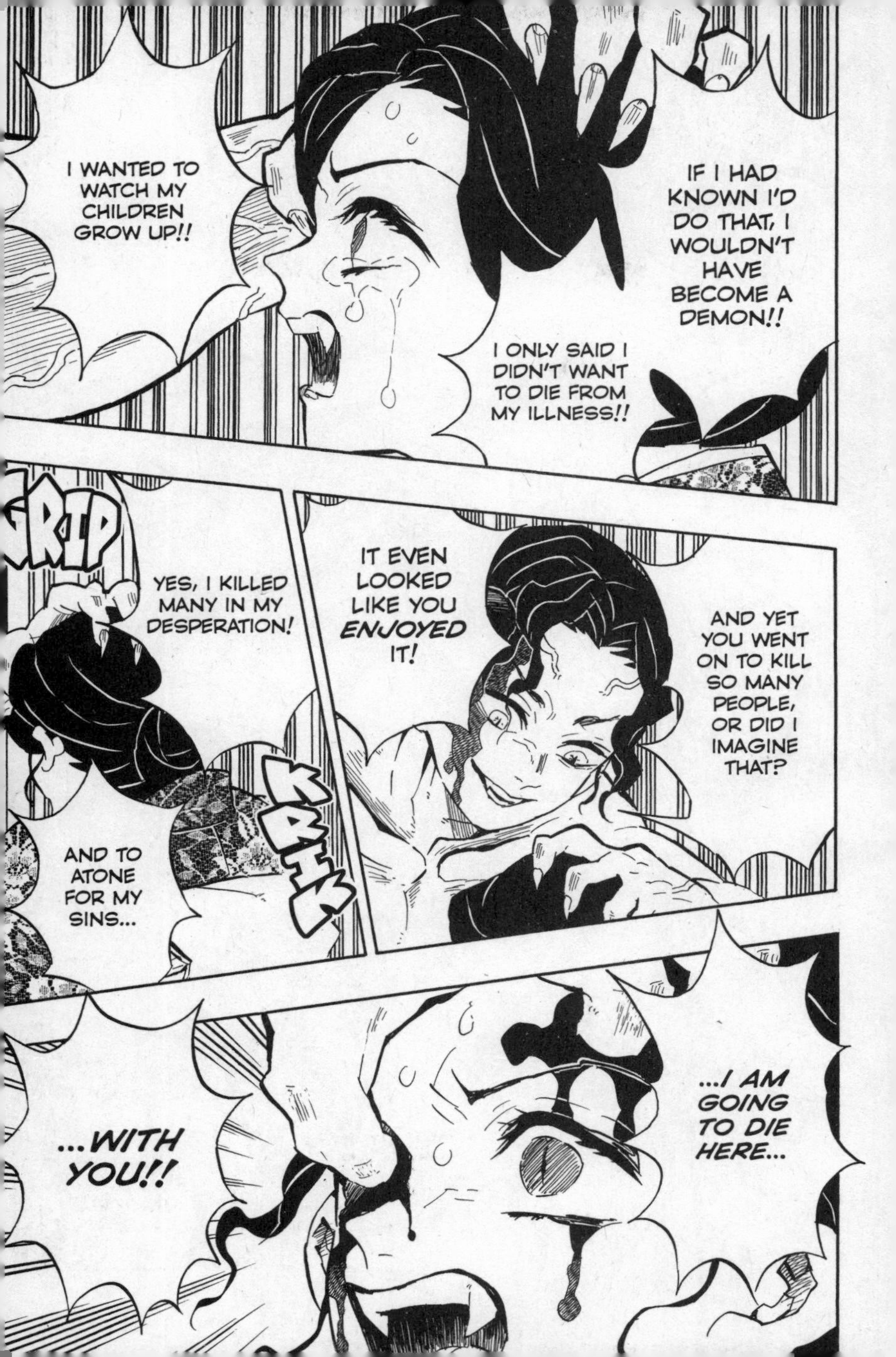
IF I HAD KNOWN I'D DO THAT, I WOULDN'T HAVE BECOME A DEMON!!
I ONLY SAID I DIDN'T WANT TO DIE FROM MY ILLNESS!!
I WANTED TO WATCH MY CHILDREN GROW UP!!
AND YET YOU WENT ON TO KILL SO MANY PEOPLE, OR DID I IMAGINE THAT?
IT EVEN LOOKED LIKE YOU *ENJOYED* IT!
GRIP
YES, I KILLED MANY IN MY DESPERATION!
KRIK
AND TO ATONE FOR MY SINS...
...*I AM GOING TO DIE HERE...*
...WITH YOU!!

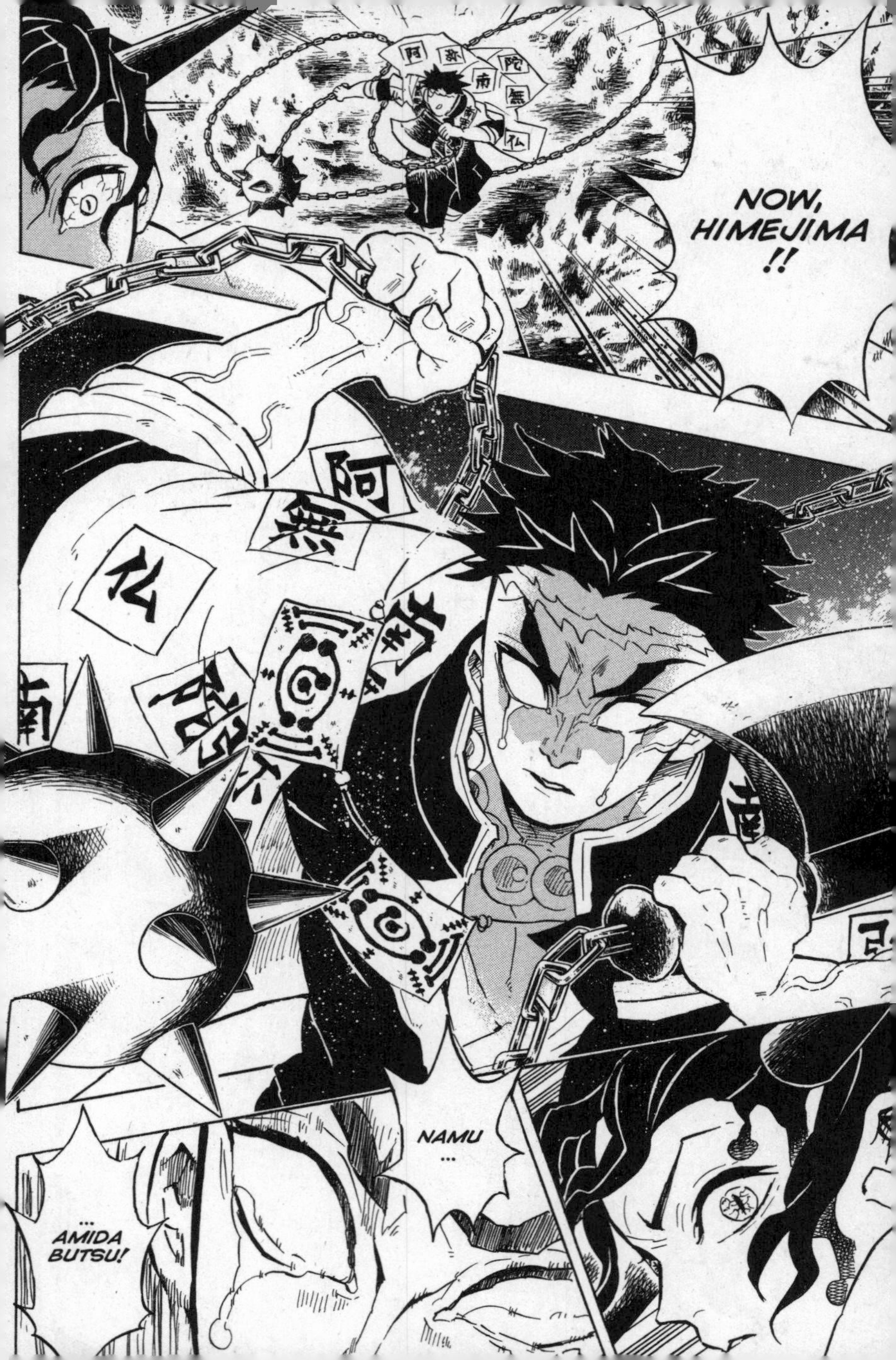
NOW, HIMEJIMA!!
NAMU ...
... AMIDA BUTSU!

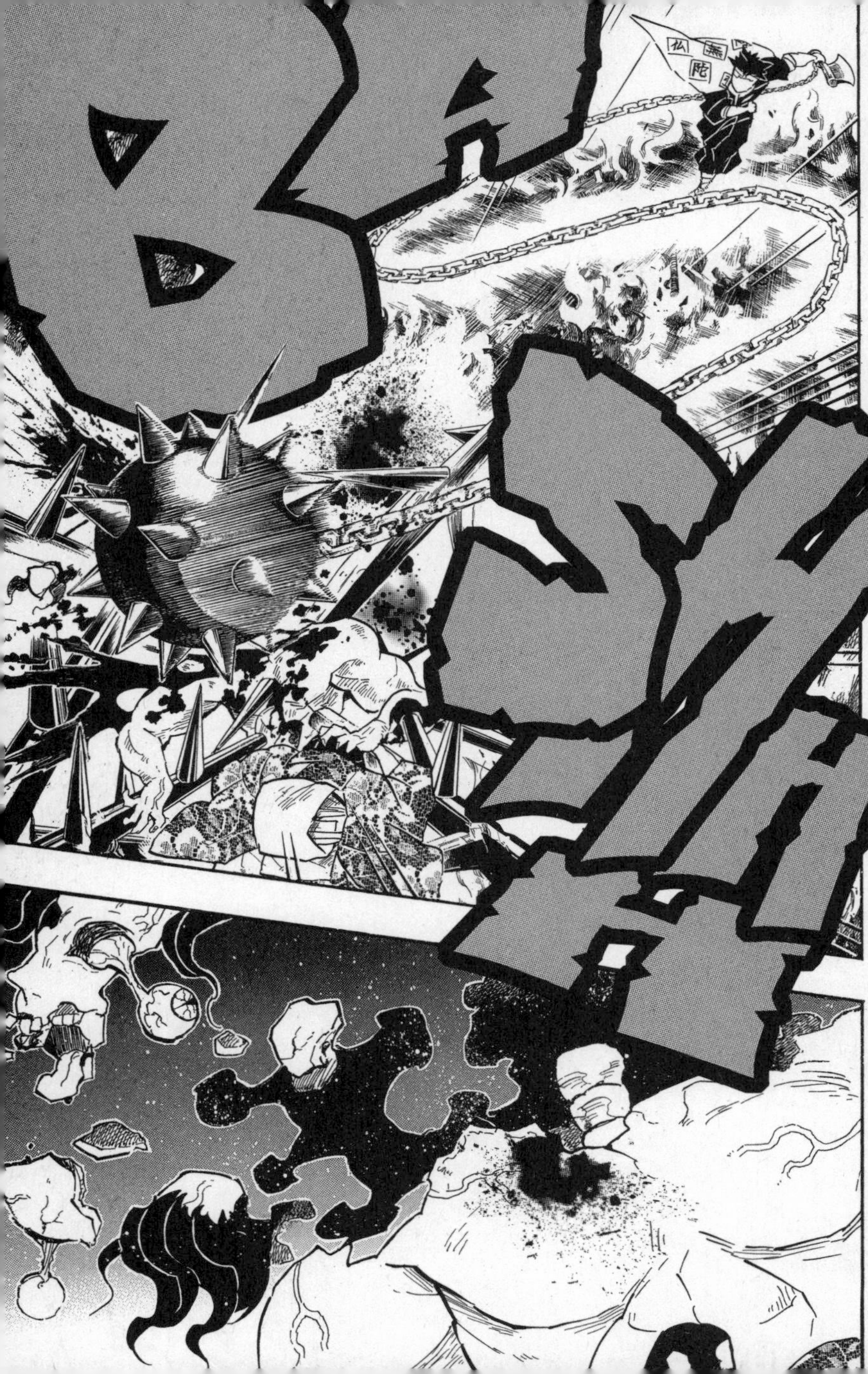

Yushiro isn't with Tamayo this time. He cannot refuse a request from the person he loves.

CHAPTER 139: FALLING

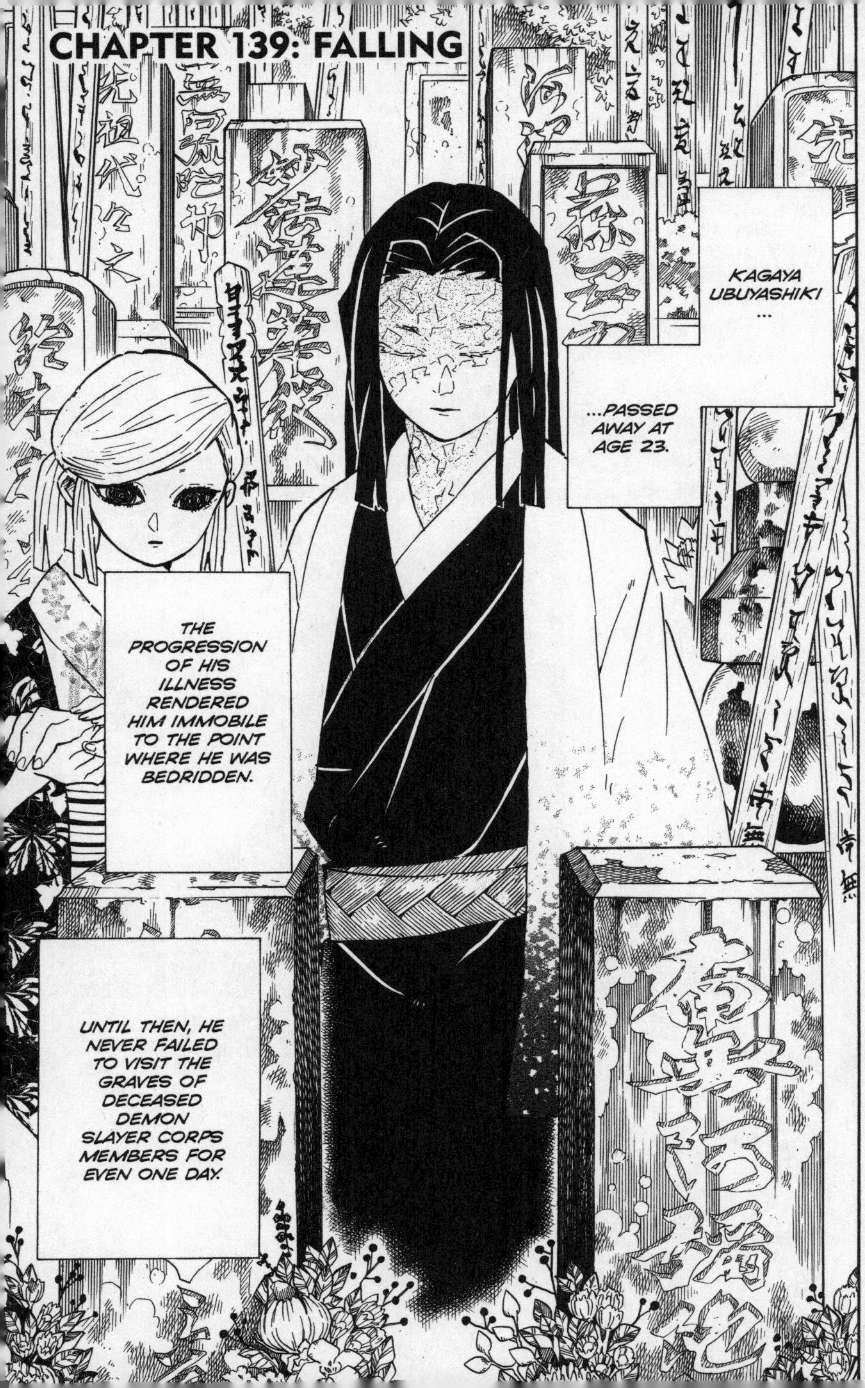
KAGAYA UBUYASHIKI …
…PASSED AWAY AT AGE 23.
THE PROGRESSION OF HIS ILLNESS RENDERED HIM IMMOBILE TO THE POINT WHERE HE WAS BEDRIDDEN.
UNTIL THEN, HE NEVER FAILED TO VISIT THE GRAVES OF DECEASED DEMON SLAYER CORPS MEMBERS FOR EVEN ONE DAY.

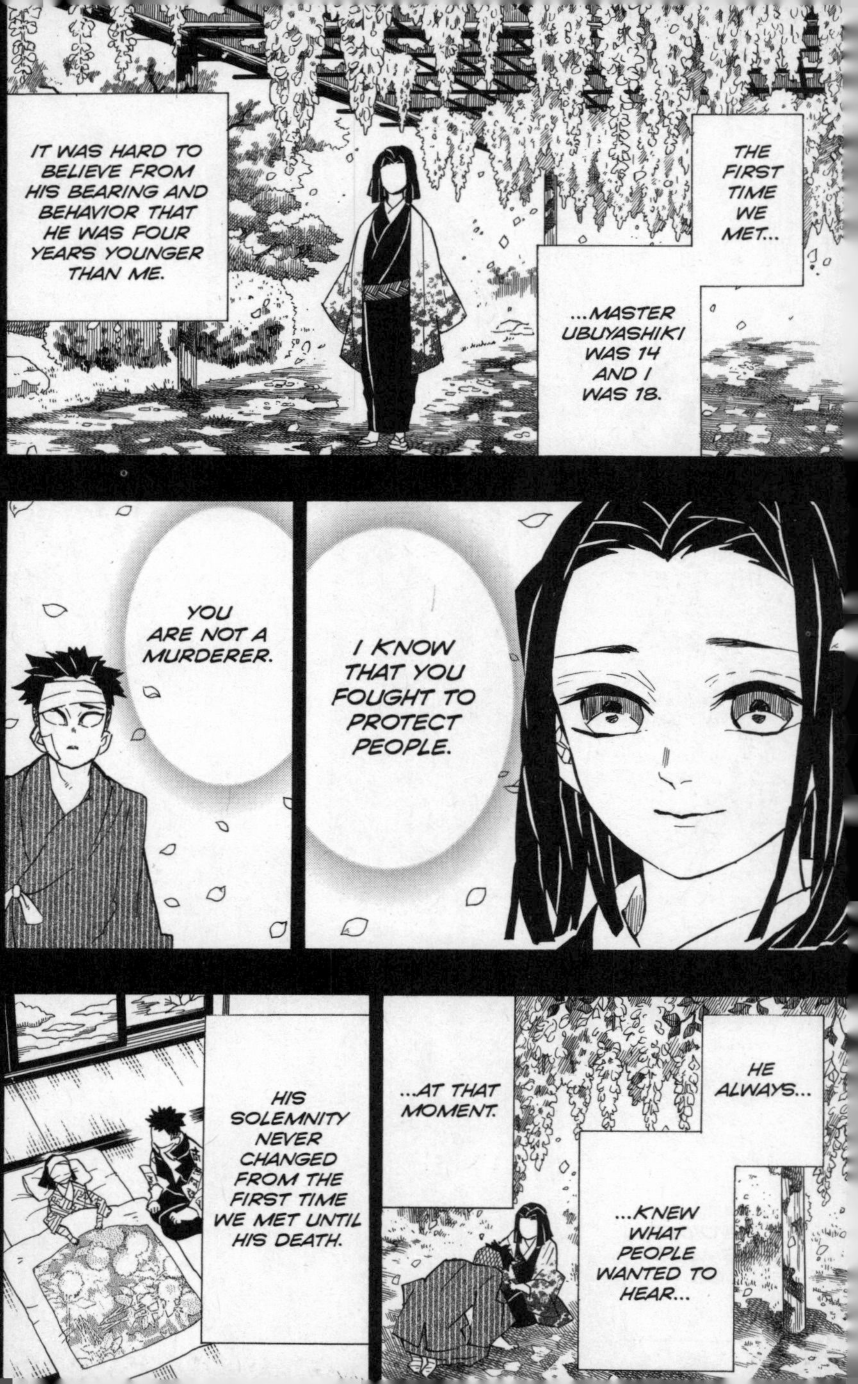
THE FIRST TIME WE MET...
...MASTER UBUYASHIKI WAS 14 AND I WAS 18.
IT WAS HARD TO BELIEVE FROM HIS BEARING AND BEHAVIOR THAT HE WAS FOUR YEARS YOUNGER THAN ME.
I KNOW THAT YOU FOUGHT TO PROTECT PEOPLE.
YOU ARE NOT A MURDERER.
HE ALWAYS...
...KNEW WHAT PEOPLE WANTED TO HEAR...
...AT THAT MOMENT.
HIS SOLEMNITY NEVER CHANGED FROM THE FIRST TIME WE MET UNTIL HIS DEATH.

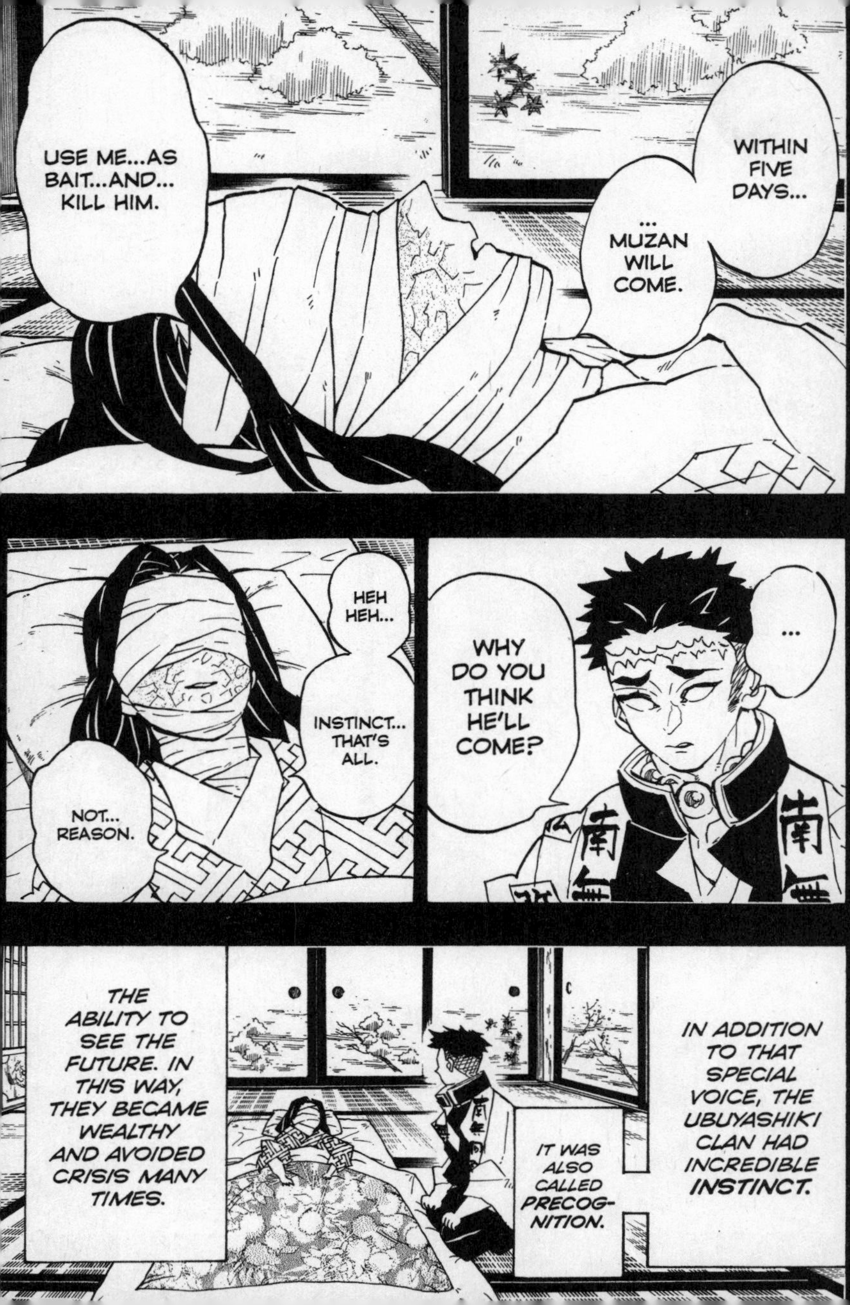
WITHIN FIVE DAYS...
... MUZAN WILL COME.
USE ME...AS BAIT...AND... KILL HIM.
...
WHY DO YOU THINK HE'LL COME?
HEH HEH...
INSTINCT... THAT'S ALL.
NOT... REASON.
IN ADDITION TO THAT SPECIAL VOICE, THE UBUYASHIKI CLAN HAD INCREDIBLE INSTINCT.
IT WAS ALSO CALLED PRECOG-NITION.
THE ABILITY TO SEE THE FUTURE. IN THIS WAY, THEY BECAME WEALTHY AND AVOIDED CRISIS MANY TIMES.

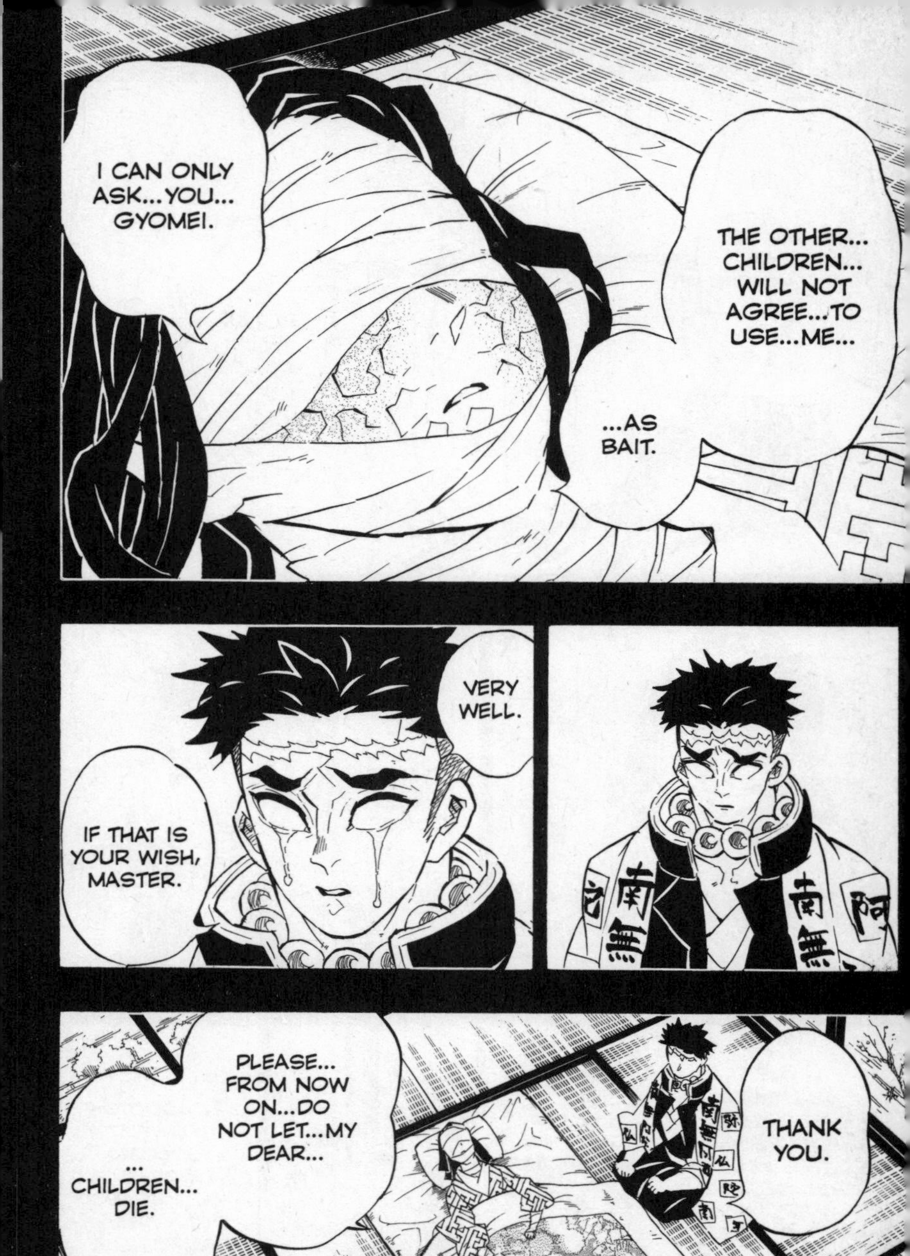
THE OTHER... CHILDREN... WILL NOT AGREE...TO USE...ME...
...AS BAIT.
I CAN ONLY ASK...YOU... GYOMEI.
VERY WELL.
IF THAT IS YOUR WISH, MASTER.
THANK YOU.
PLEASE... FROM NOW ON...DO NOT LET...MY DEAR...
... CHILDREN... DIE.

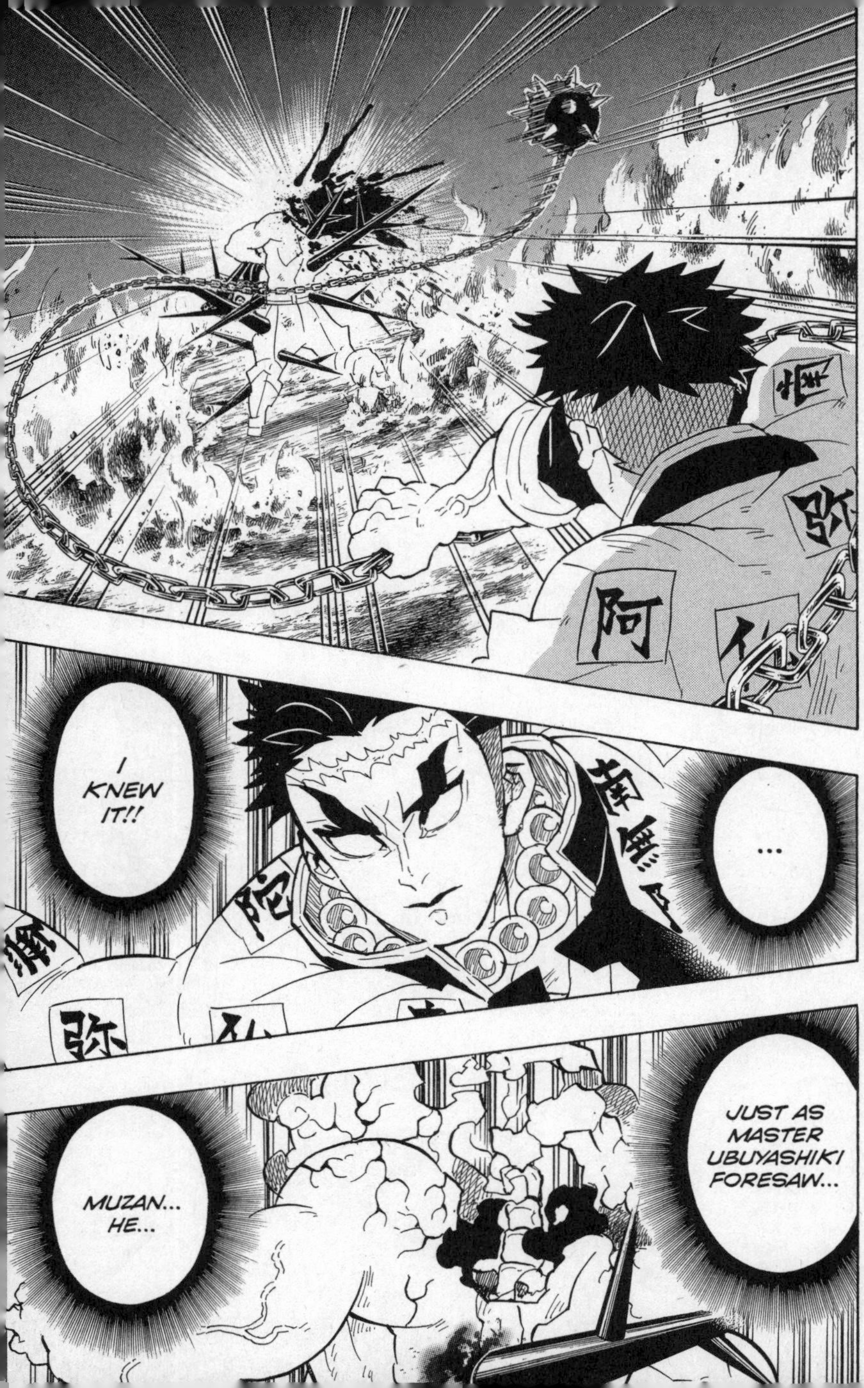
...
I KNEW IT!!
JUST AS MASTER UBUYASHIKI FORESAW...
MUZAN... HE...

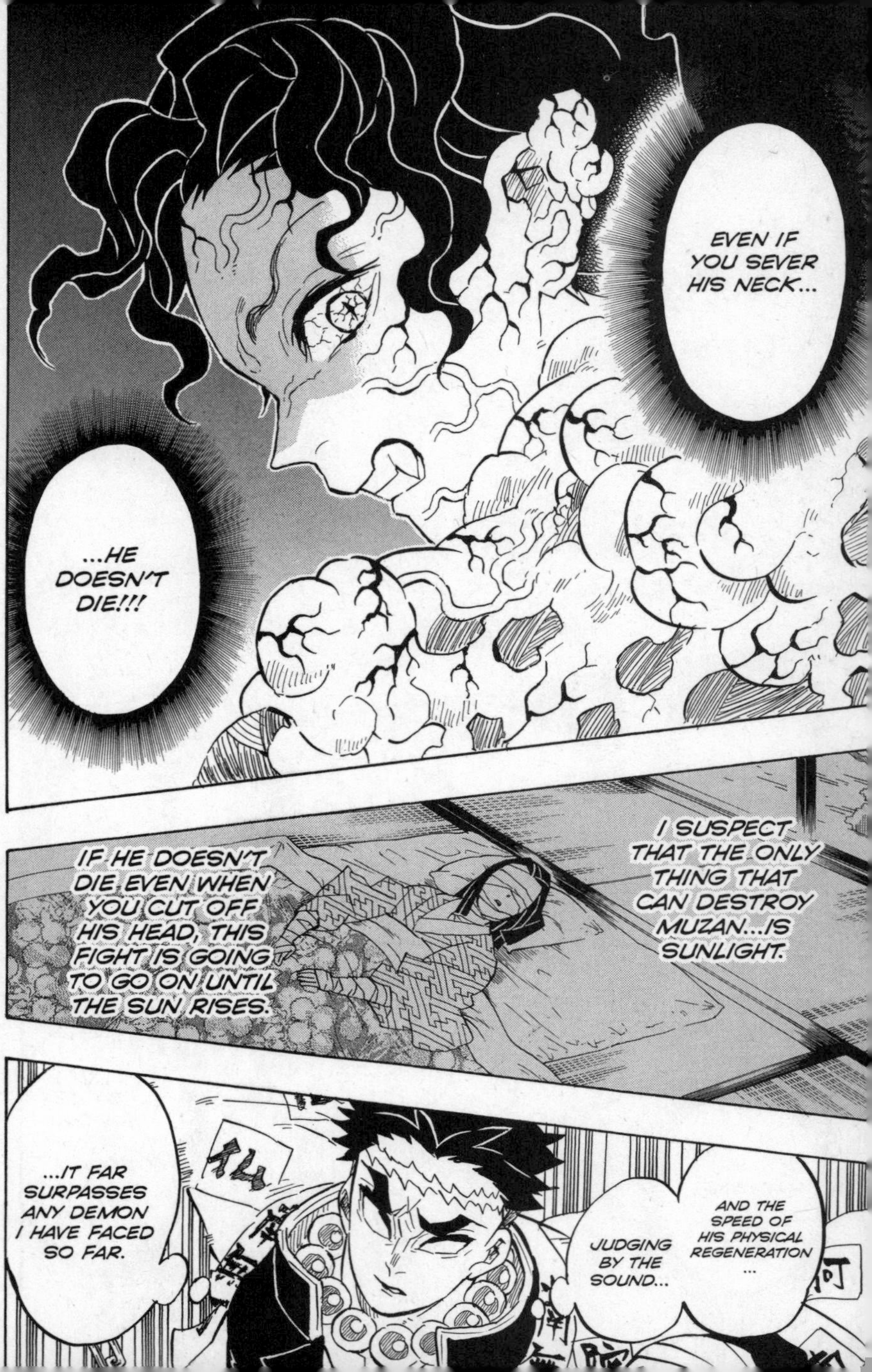
EVEN IF YOU SEVER HIS NECK...
...HE DOESN'T DIE!!!
I SUSPECT THAT THE ONLY THING THAT CAN DESTROY MUZAN...IS SUNLIGHT.
IF HE DOESN'T DIE EVEN WHEN YOU CUT OFF HIS HEAD, THIS FIGHT IS GOING TO GO ON UNTIL THE SUN RISES.
AND THE SPEED OF HIS PHYSICAL REGENERATION ...
JUDGING BY THE SOUND...
...IT FAR SURPASSES ANY DEMON I HAVE FACED SO FAR.

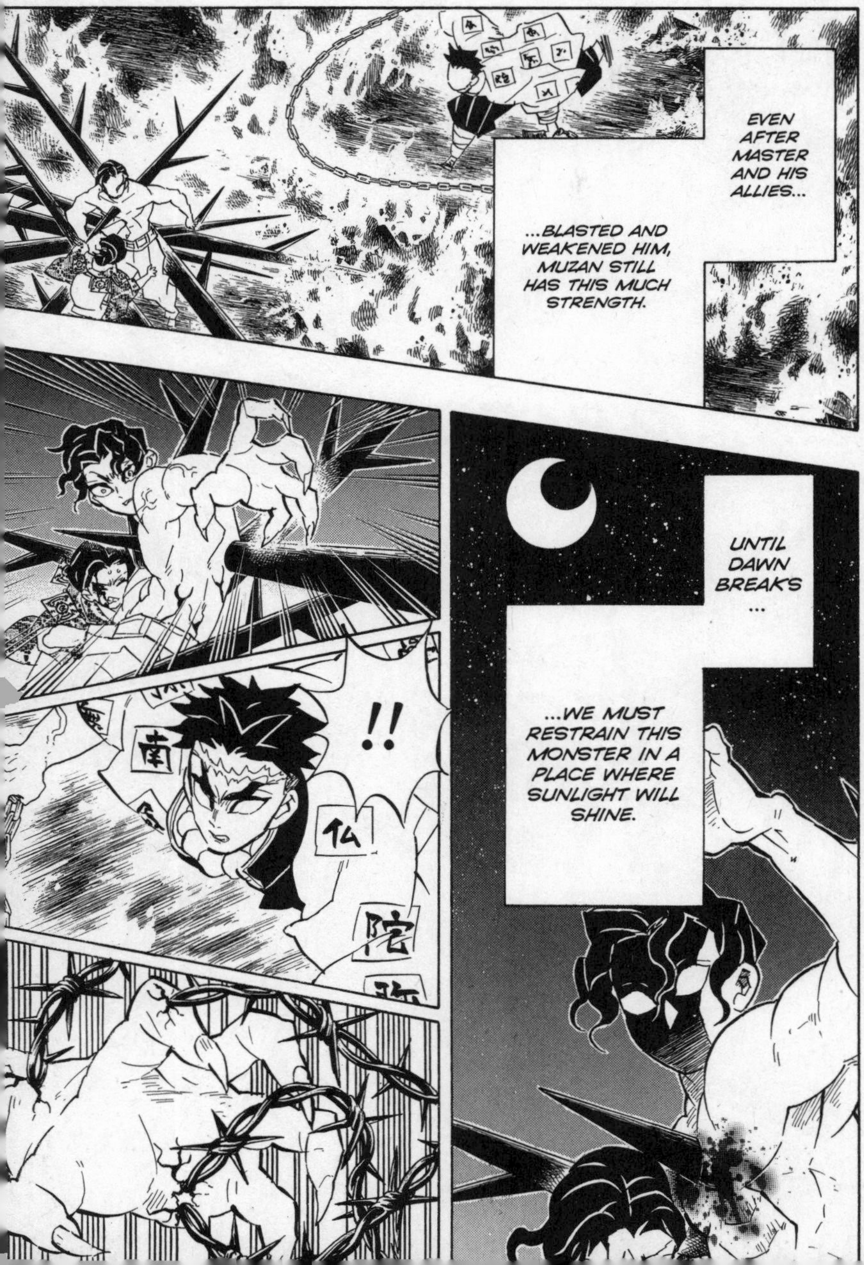
EVEN AFTER MASTER AND HIS ALLIES...
...BLASTED AND WEAKENED HIM, MUZAN STILL HAS THIS MUCH STRENGTH.
UNTIL DAWN BREAKS ...
...WE MUST RESTRAIN THIS MONSTER IN A PLACE WHERE SUNLIGHT WILL SHINE.
南
!!
仏
陀

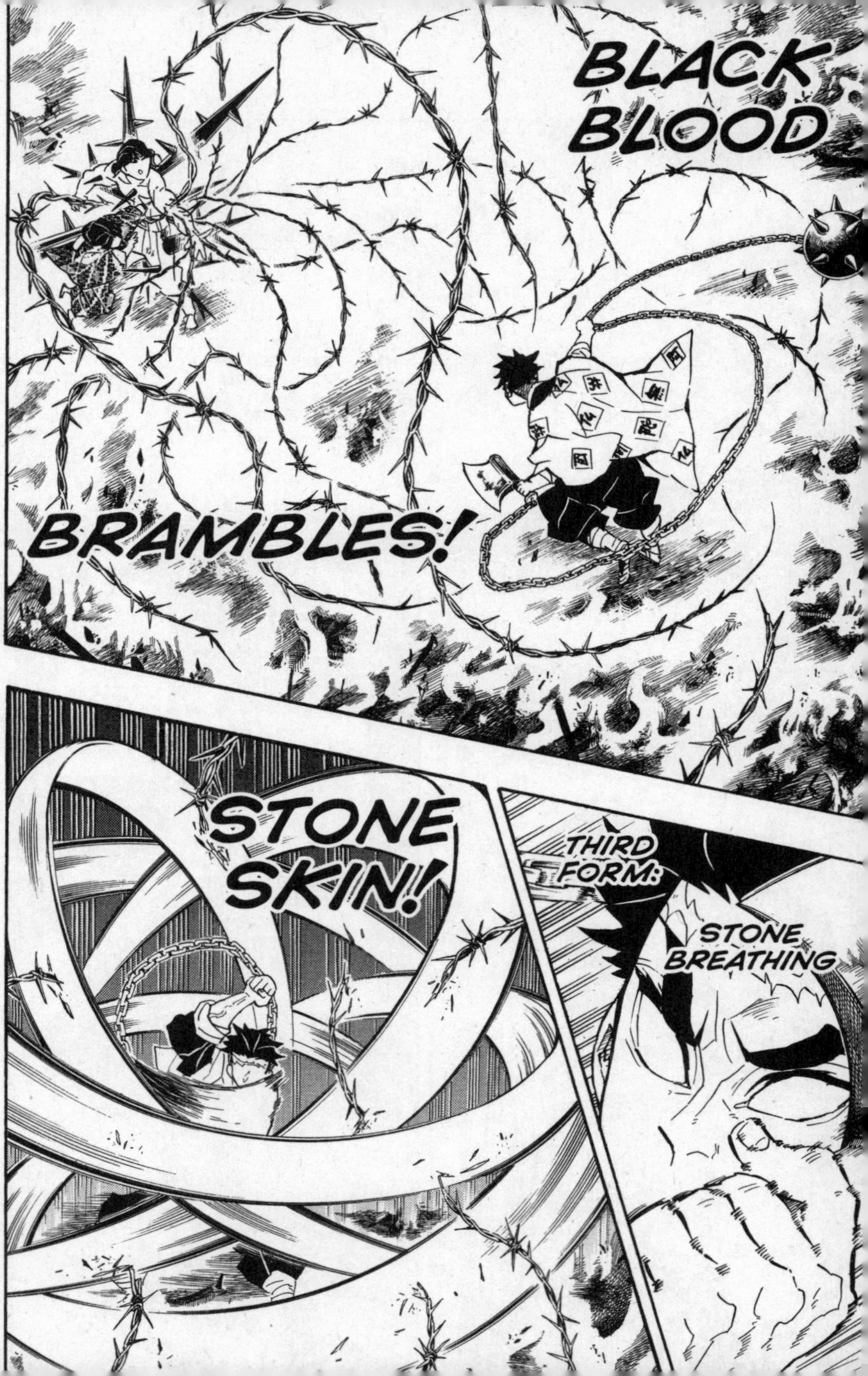
BLACK BLOOD
BRAMBLES!
STONE BREATHING
THIRD FORM:
STONE SKIN!

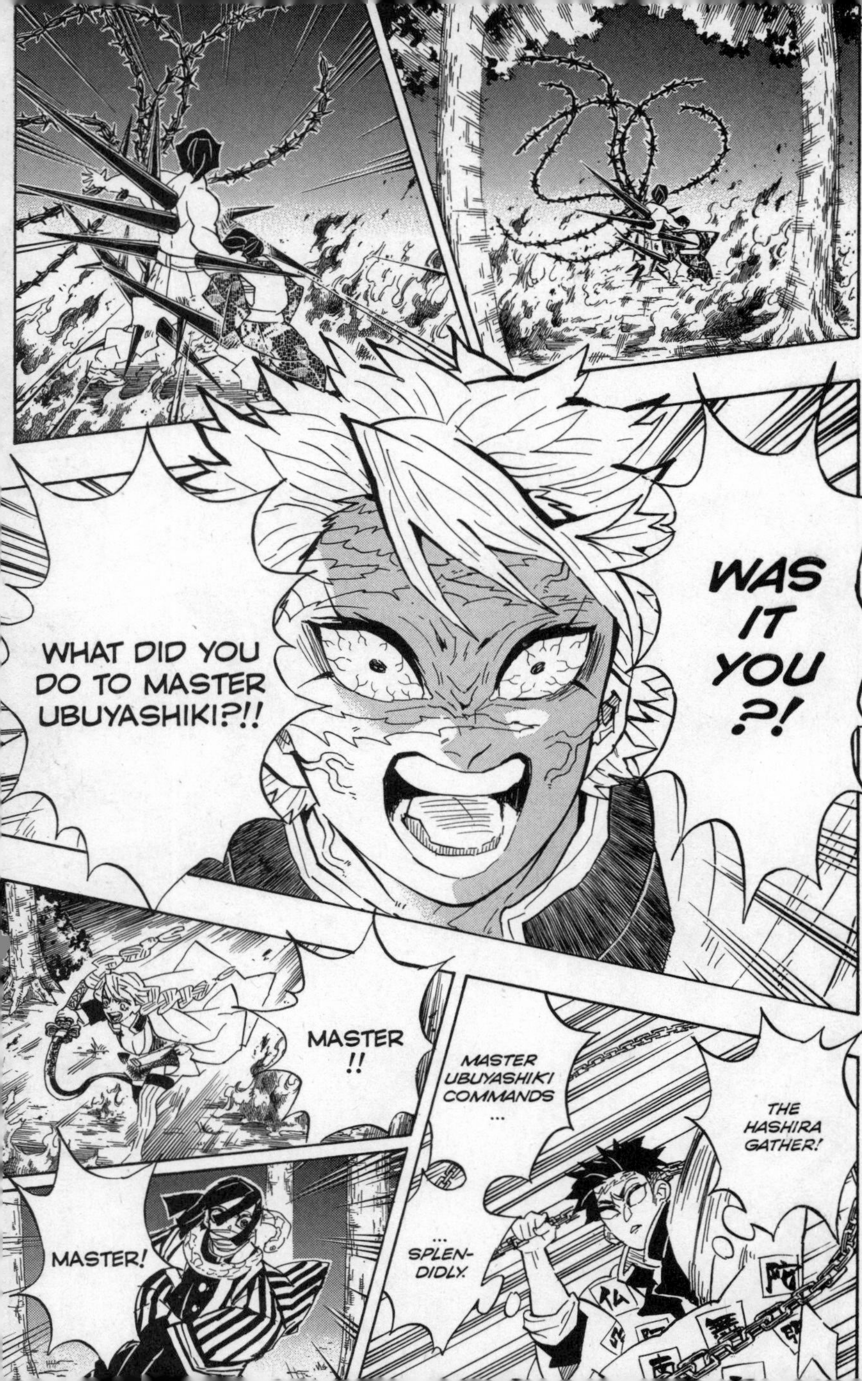
WAS IT YOU?!
WHAT DID YOU DO TO MASTER UBUYASHIKI?!!
THE HASHIRA GATHER!
MASTER UBUYASHIKI COMMANDS...
...SPLENDIDLY.
MASTER!!
MASTER!

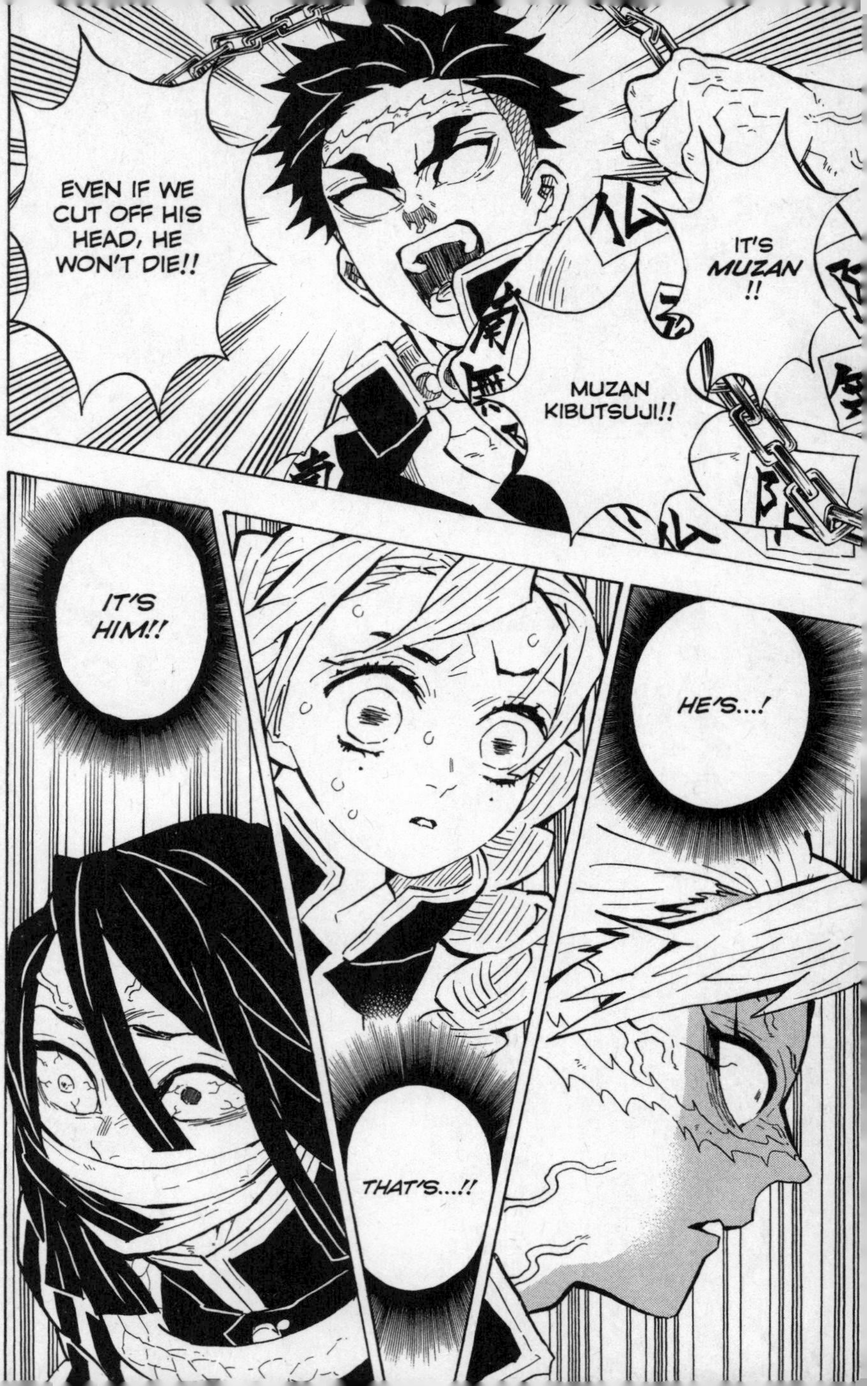
IT'S MUZAN!!
MUZAN KIBUTSUJI!!
EVEN IF WE CUT OFF HIS HEAD, HE WON'T DIE!!
HE'S...!
THAT'S...!!
IT'S HIM!!

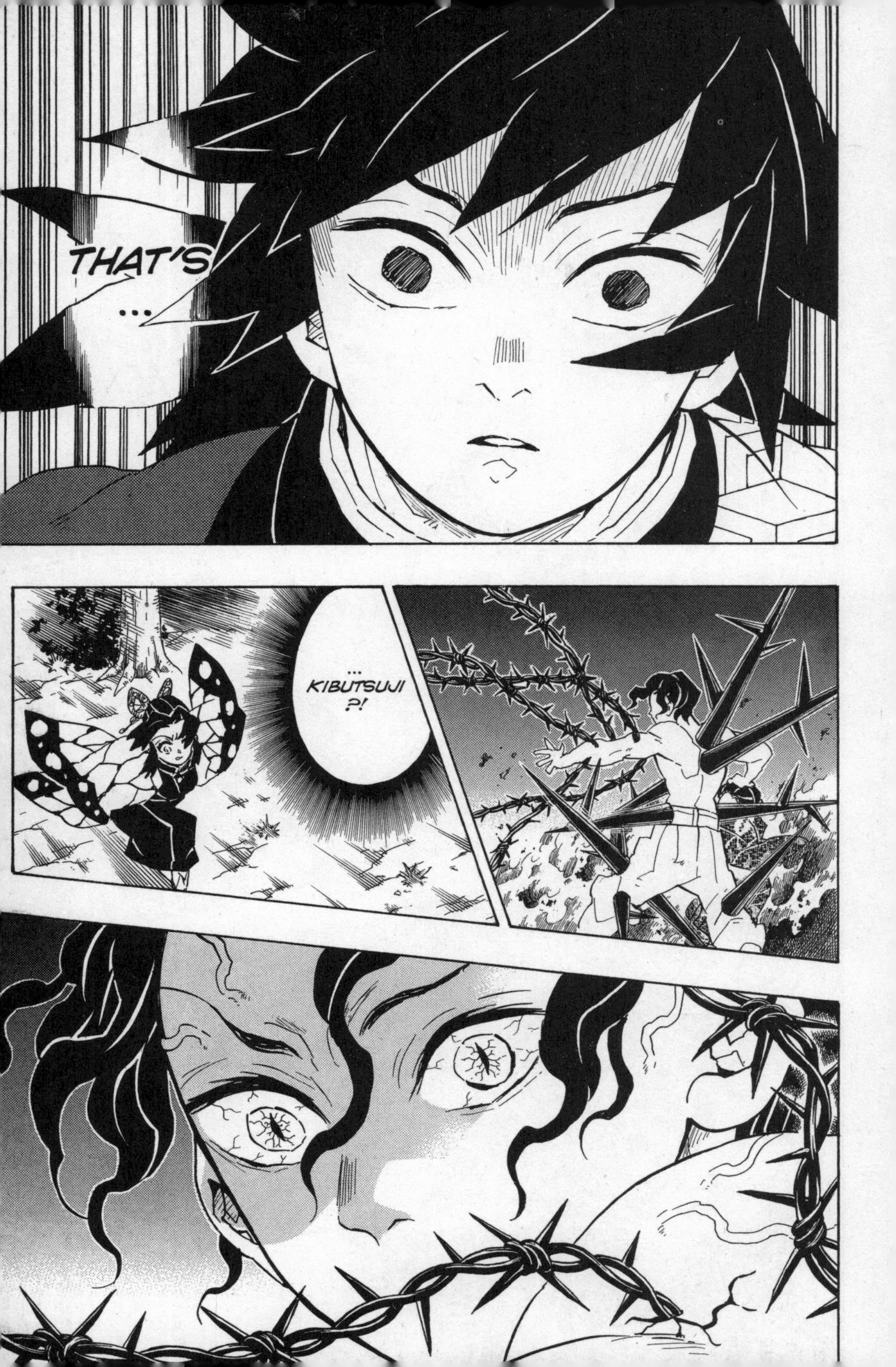
THAT'S
...
... KIBUTSUJI ?!

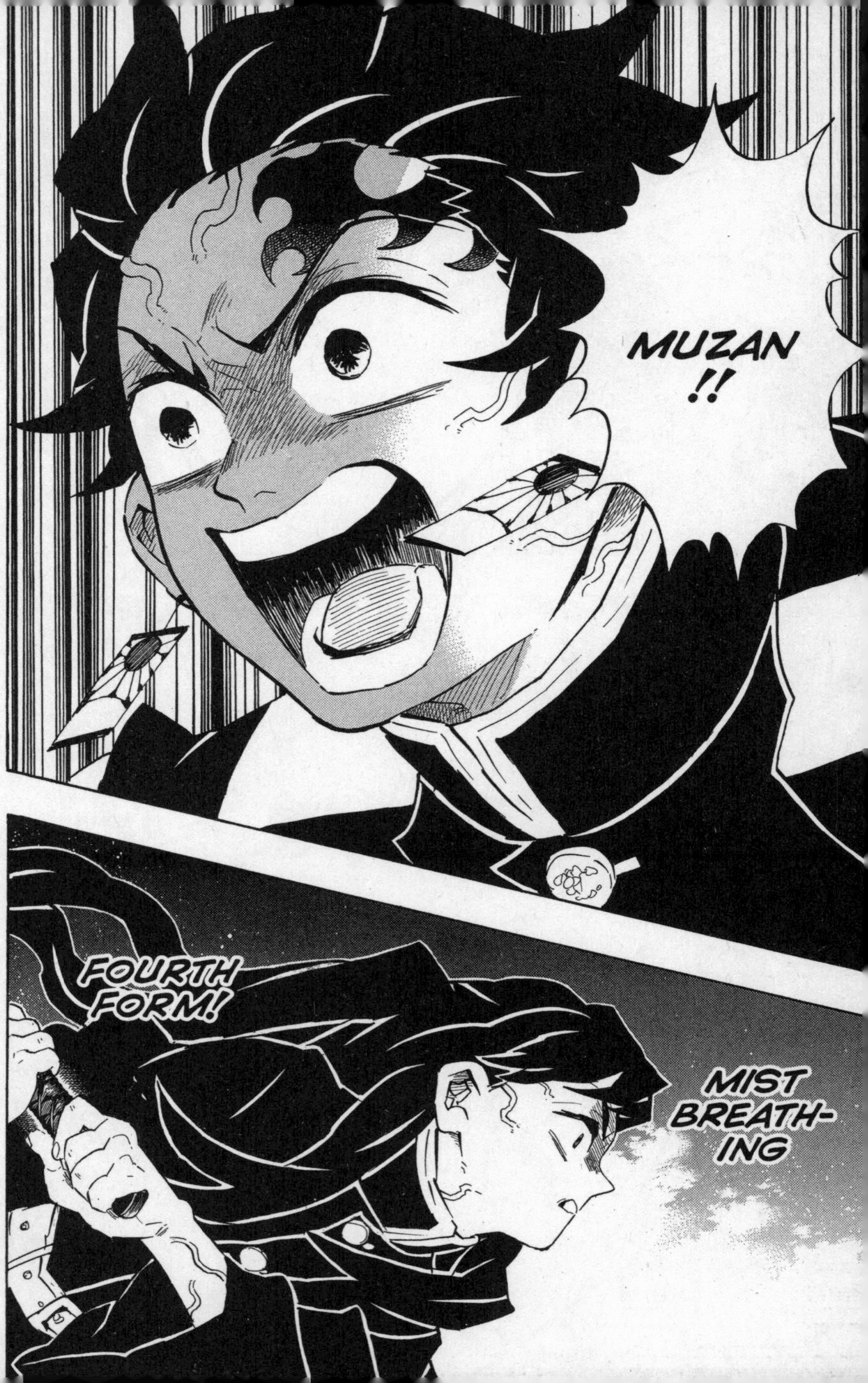
MUZAN !!
MIST BREATHING
FOURTH FORM!

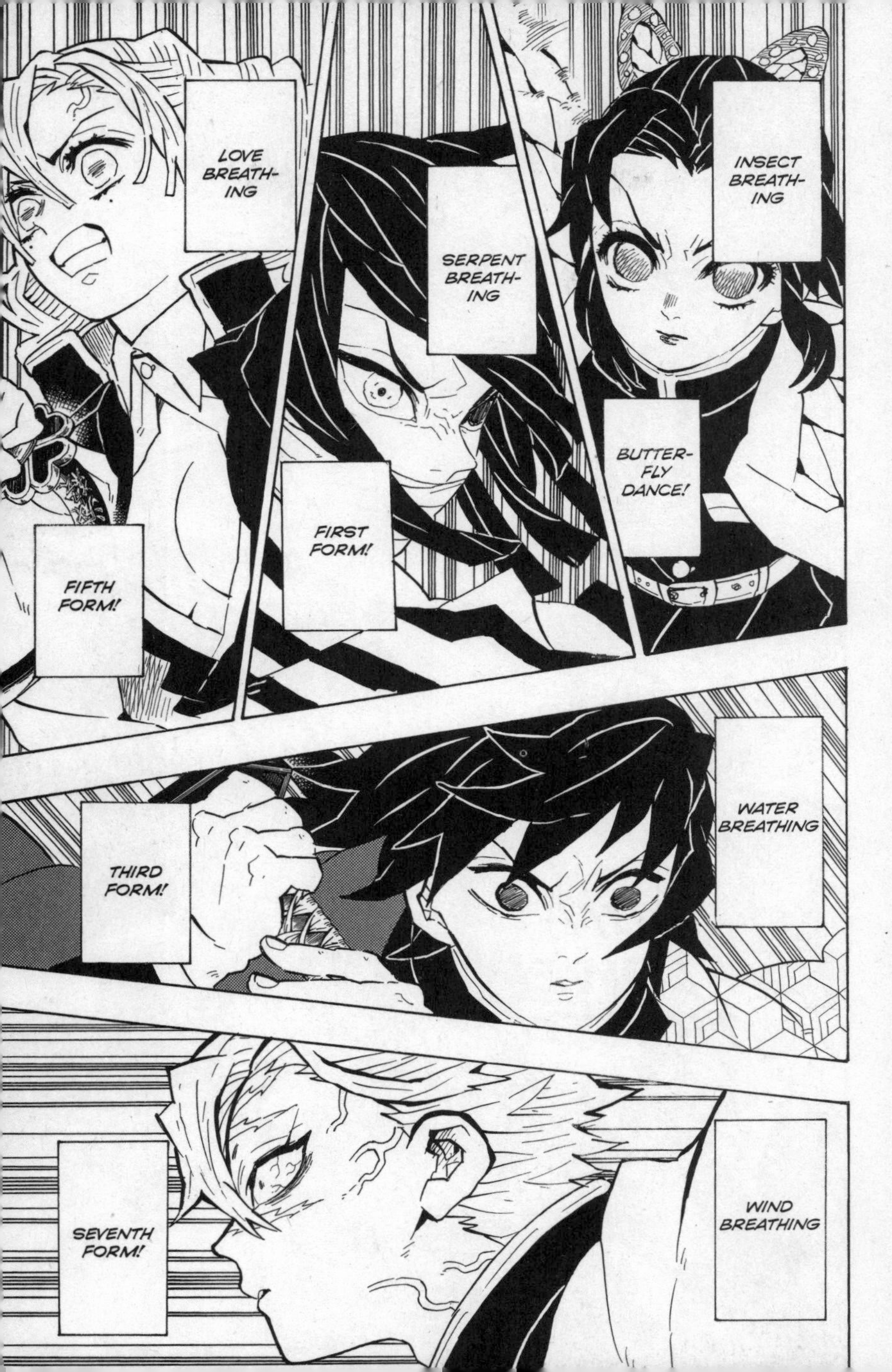
INSECT BREATH-ING
BUTTER-FLY DANCE!
SERPENT BREATH-ING
FIRST FORM!
LOVE BREATH-ING
FIFTH FORM!
WATER BREATHING
THIRD FORM!
WIND BREATHING
SEVENTH FORM!

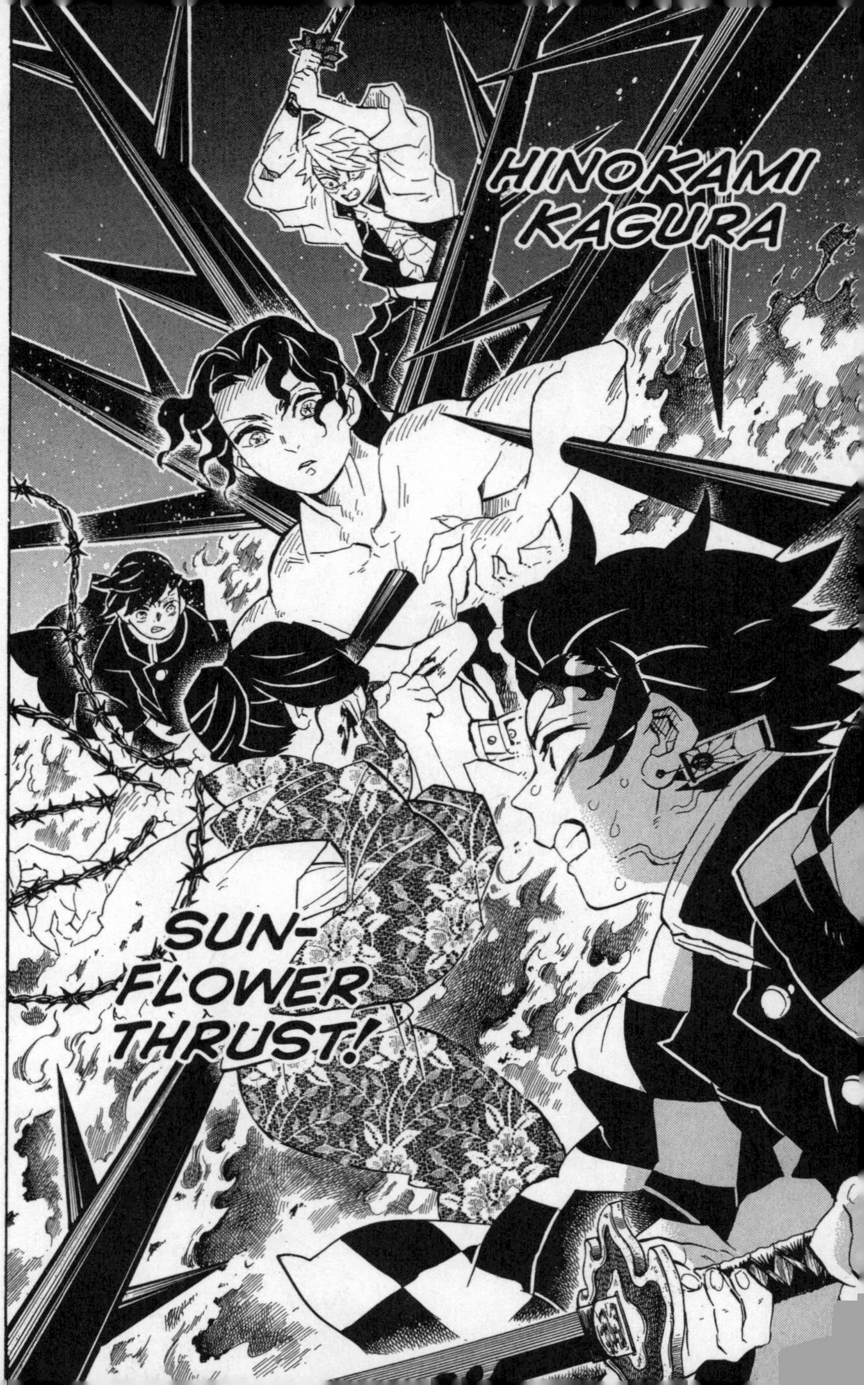
HINOKAMI KAGURA
SUN-FLOWER THRUST!

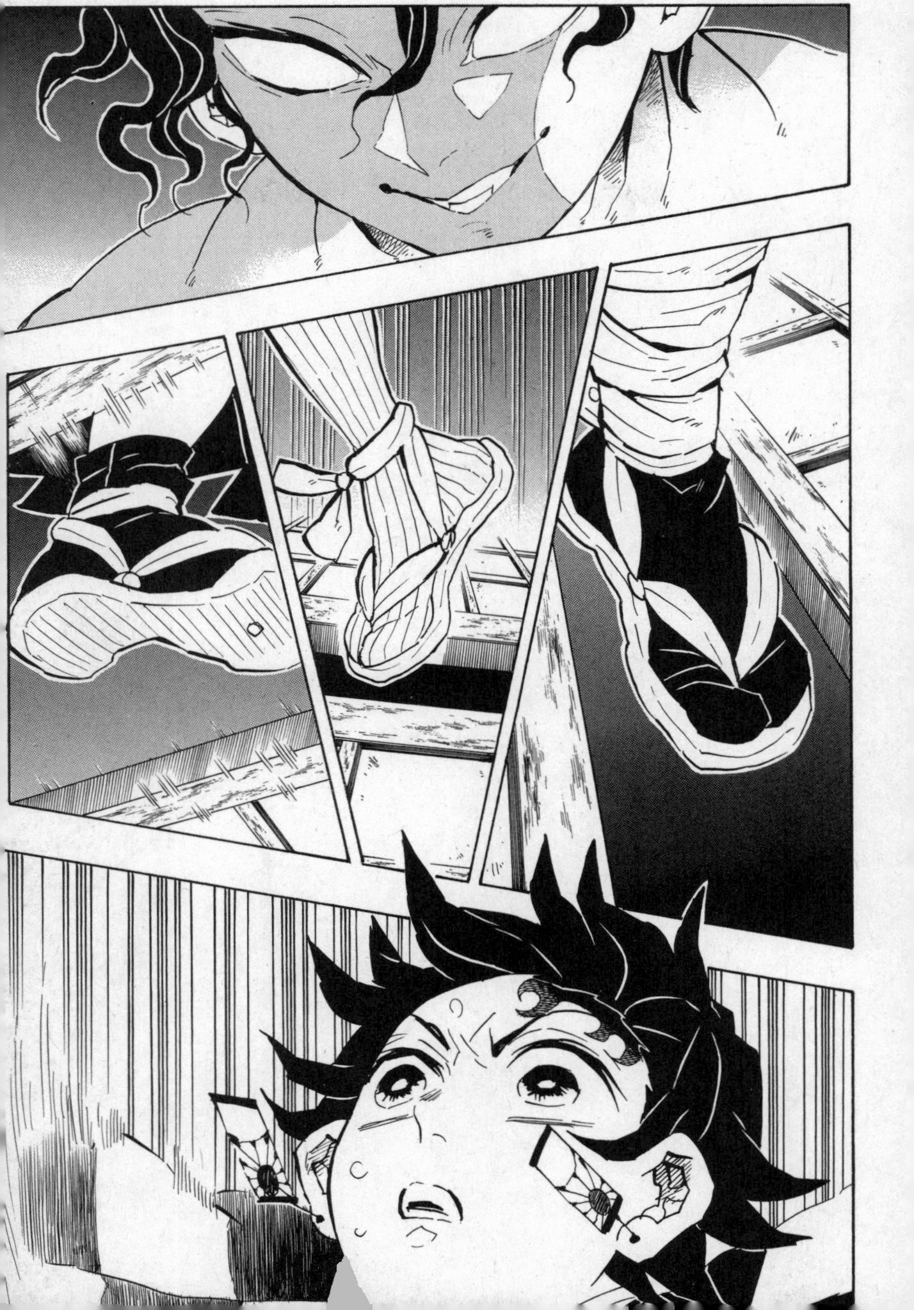

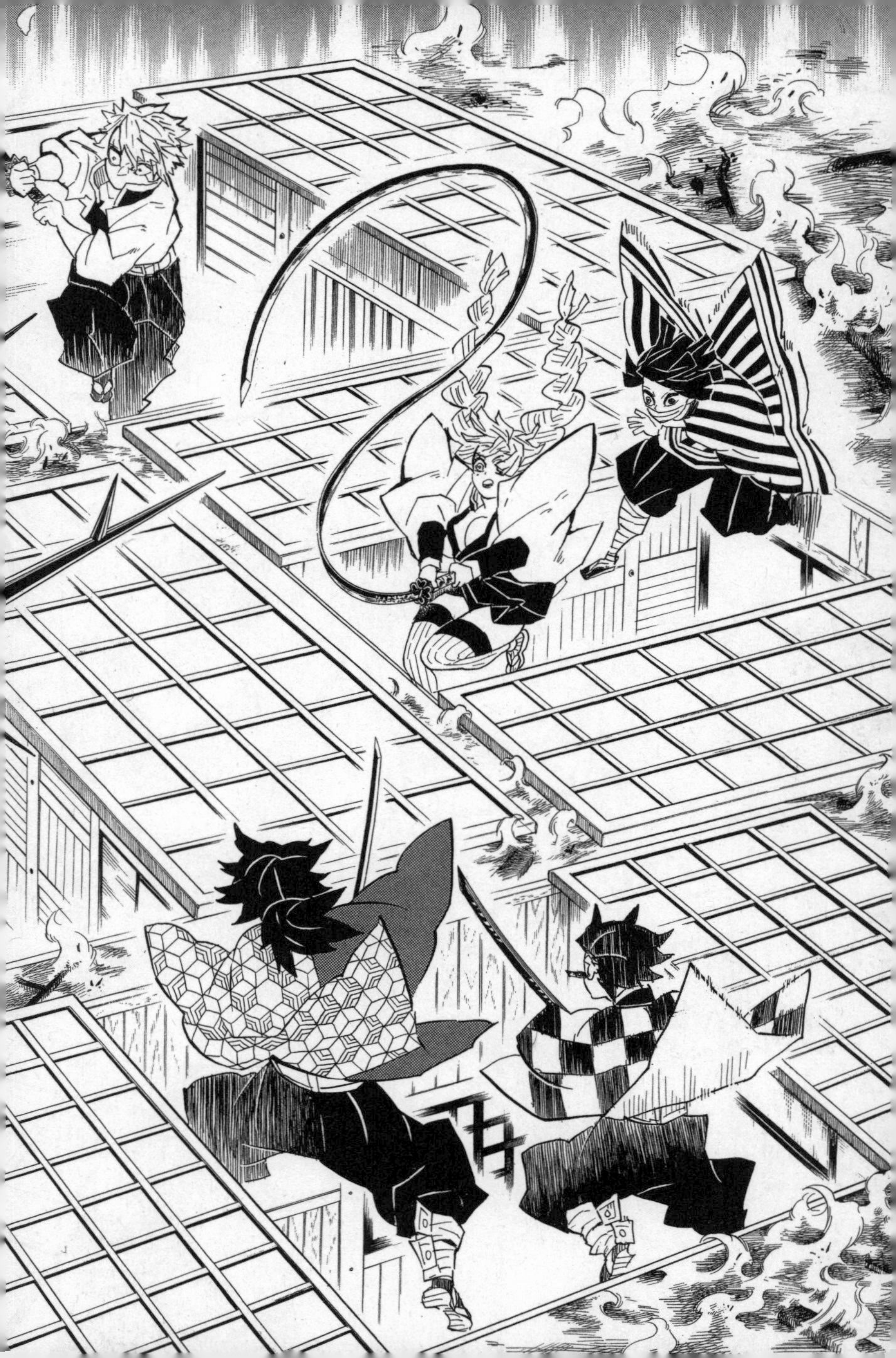

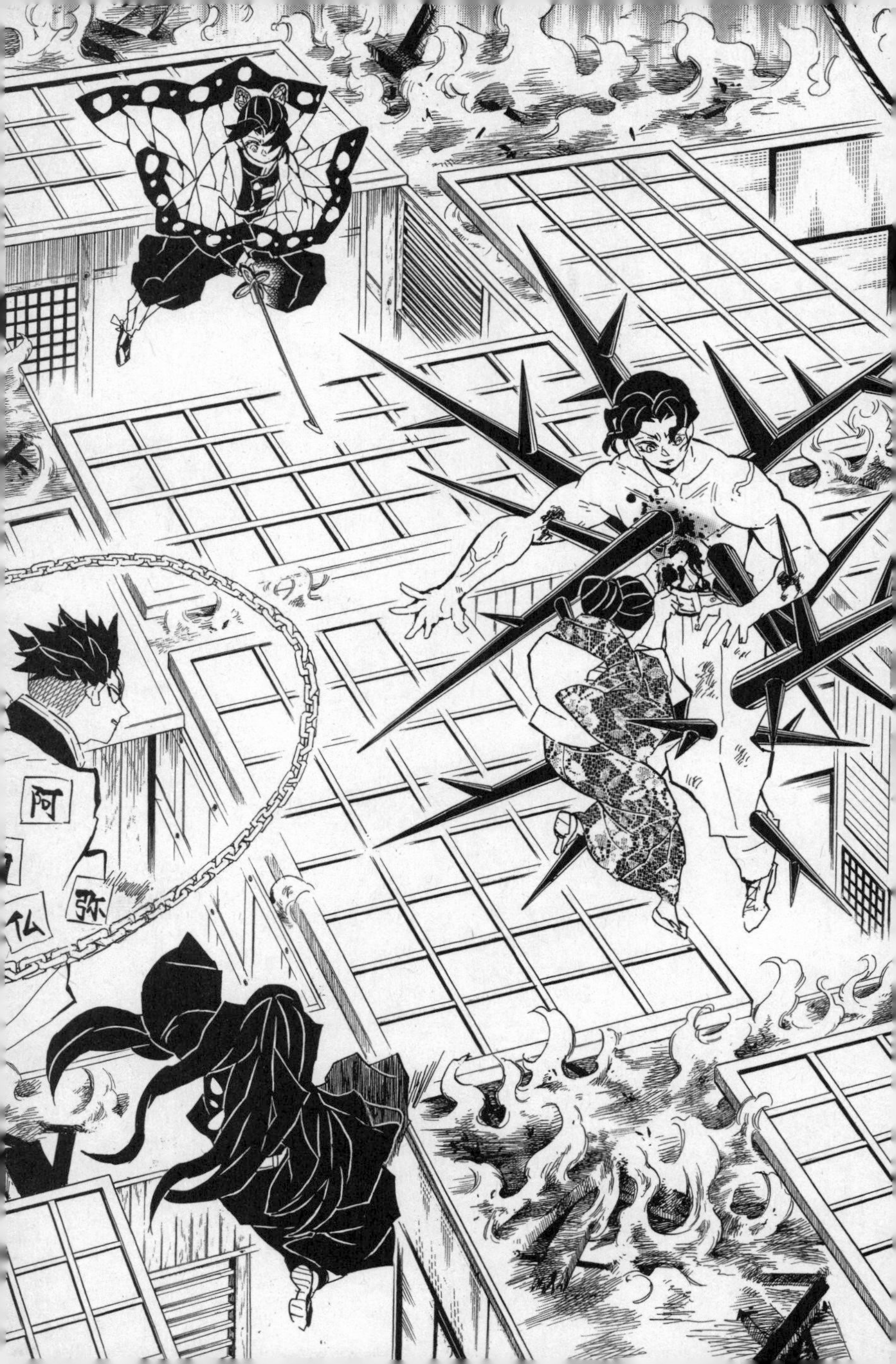

阿
弥
仏

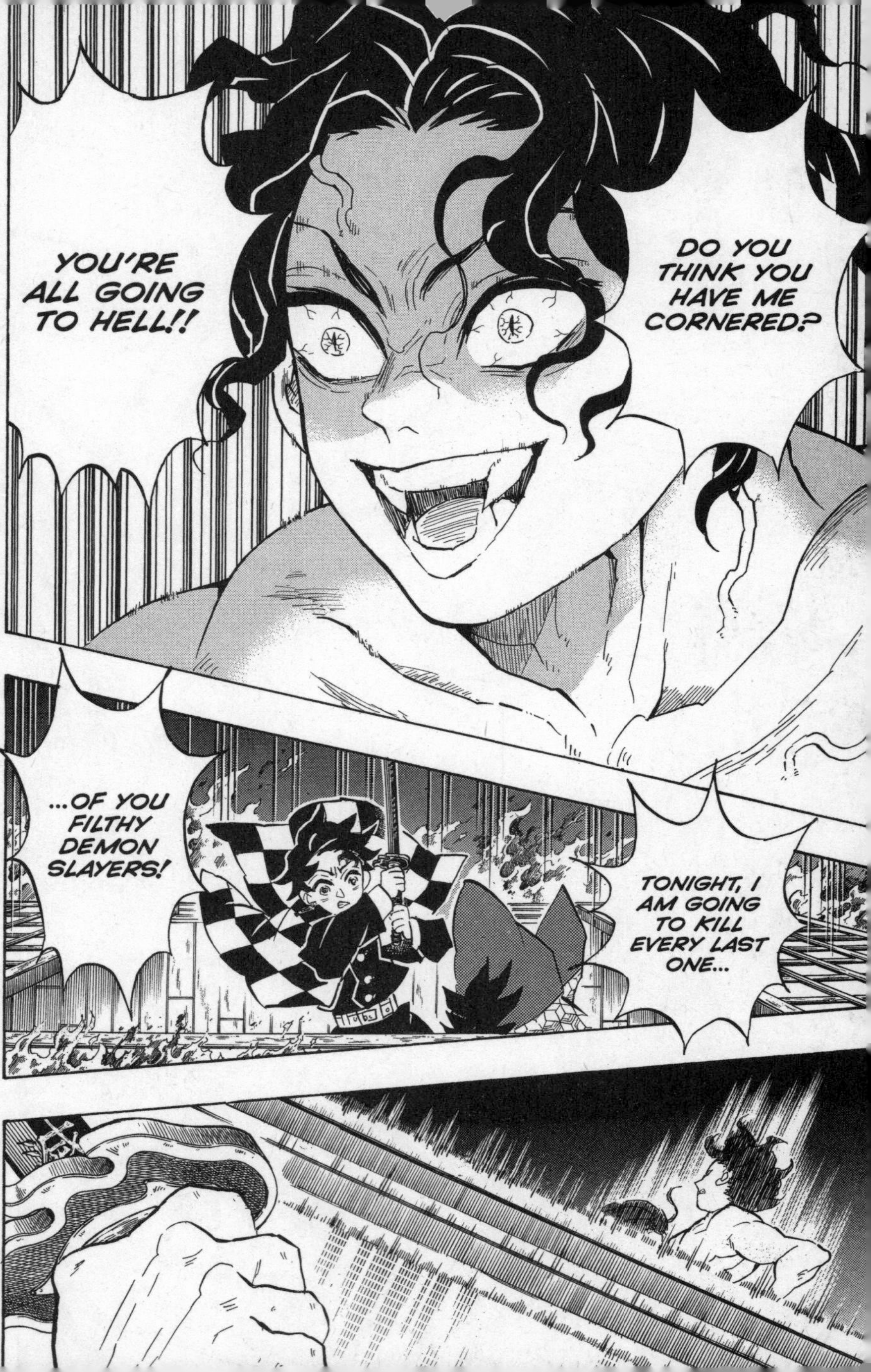
DO YOU THINK YOU HAVE ME CORNERED?
YOU'RE ALL GOING TO HELL!!
TONIGHT, I AM GOING TO KILL EVERY LAST ONE...
...OF YOU FILTHY DEMON SLAYERS!

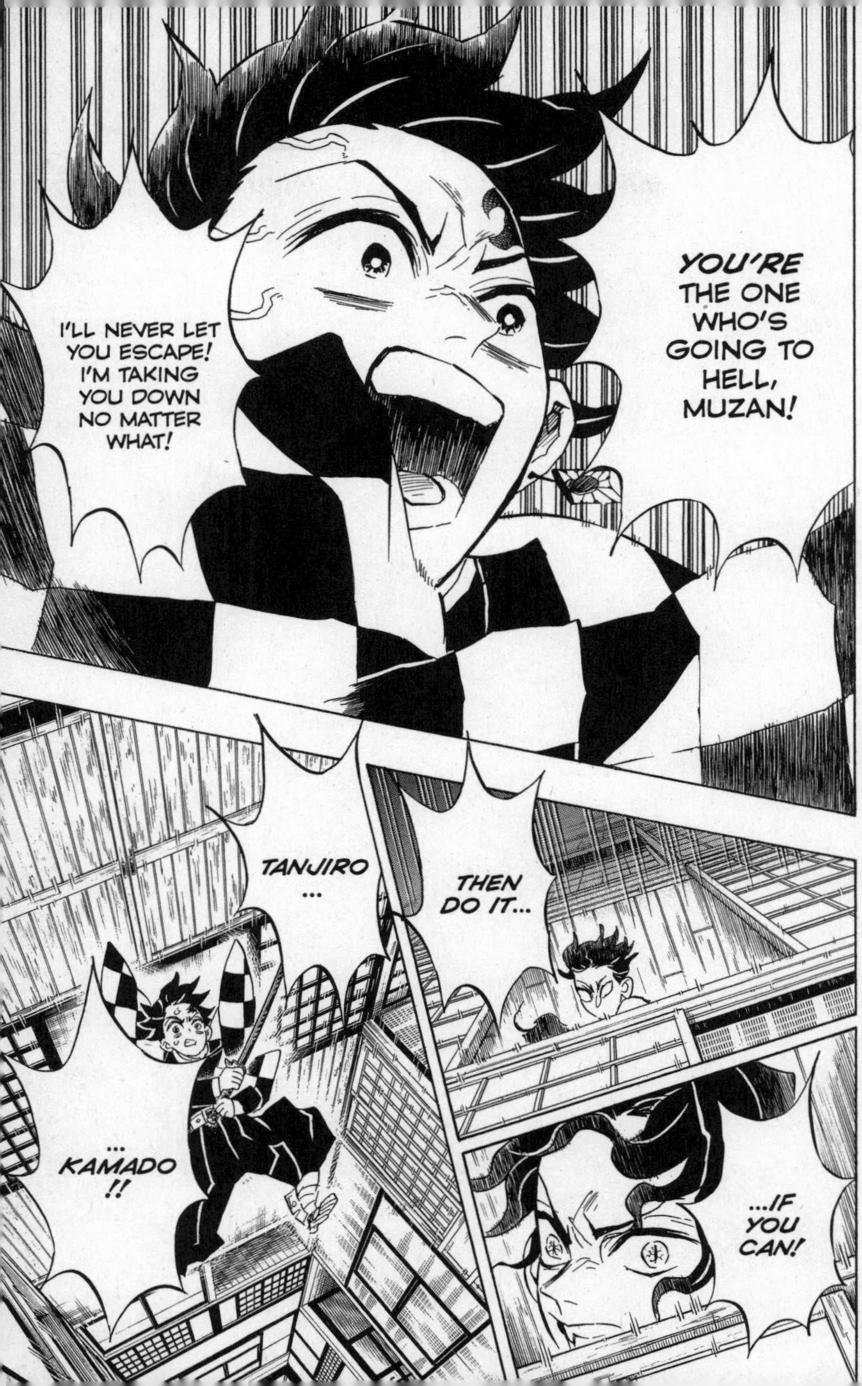
YOU'RE THE ONE WHO'S GOING TO HELL, MUZAN!
I'LL NEVER LET YOU ESCAPE! I'M TAKING YOU DOWN NO MATTER WHAT!
THEN DO IT...
...IF YOU CAN!
TANJIRO ...
... KAMADO !!

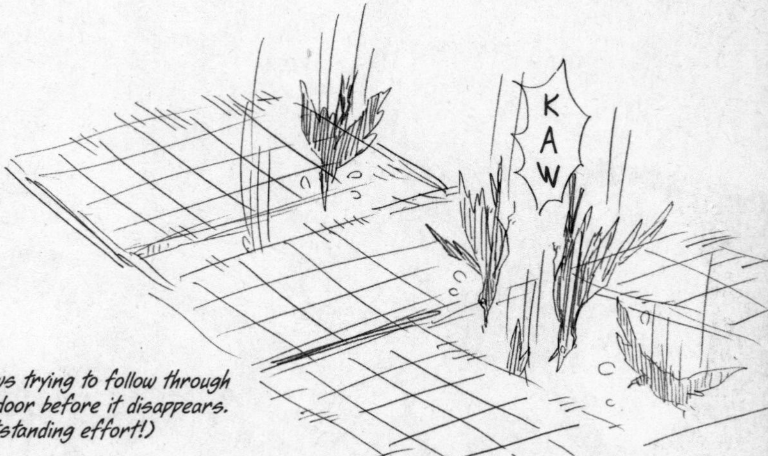
KAW

Crows trying to follow through
the door before it disappears.
(Outstanding effort!)

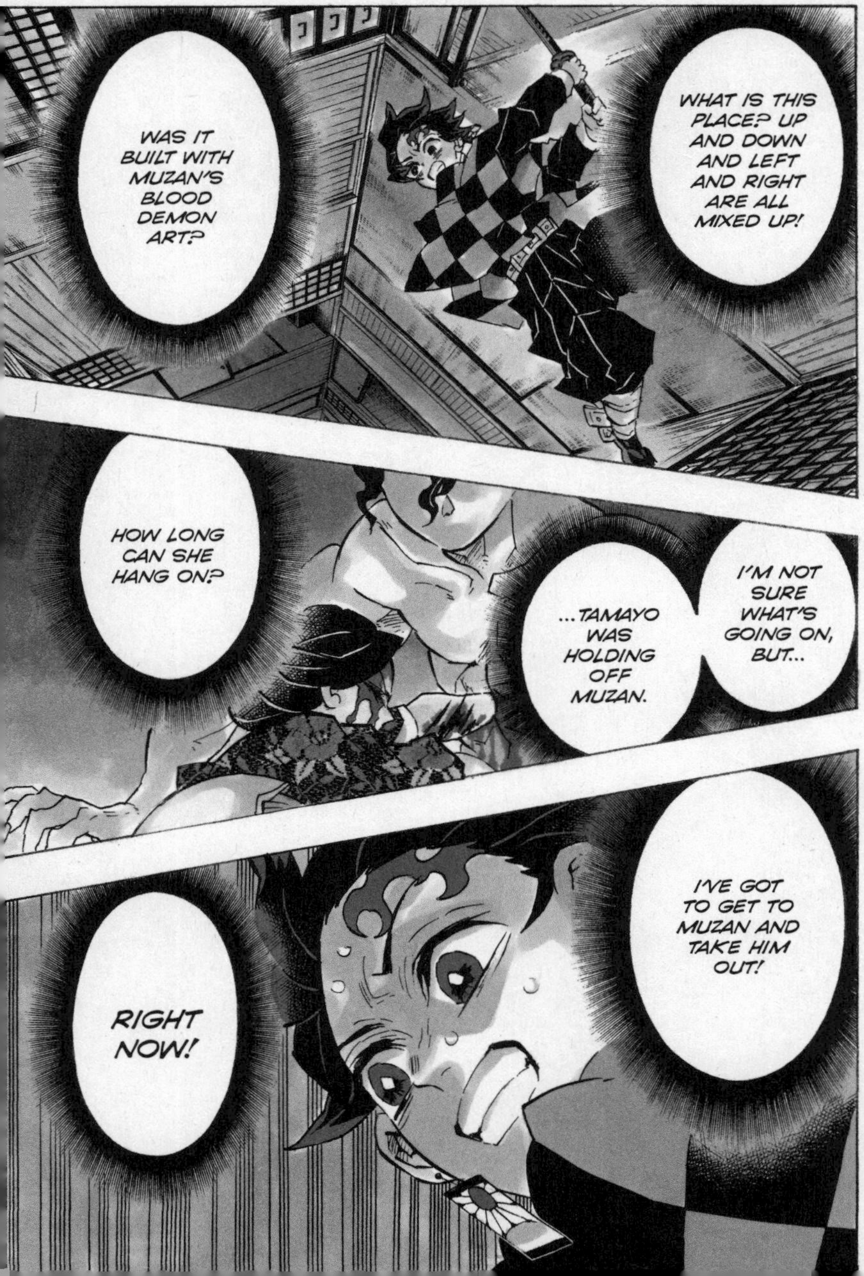
WHAT IS THIS PLACE? UP AND DOWN AND LEFT AND RIGHT ARE ALL MIXED UP!
WAS IT BUILT WITH MUZAN'S BLOOD DEMON ART?
I'M NOT SURE WHAT'S GOING ON, BUT...
...TAMAYO WAS HOLDING OFF MUZAN.
HOW LONG CAN SHE HANG ON?
I'VE GOT TO GET TO MUZAN AND TAKE HIM OUT!
RIGHT NOW!

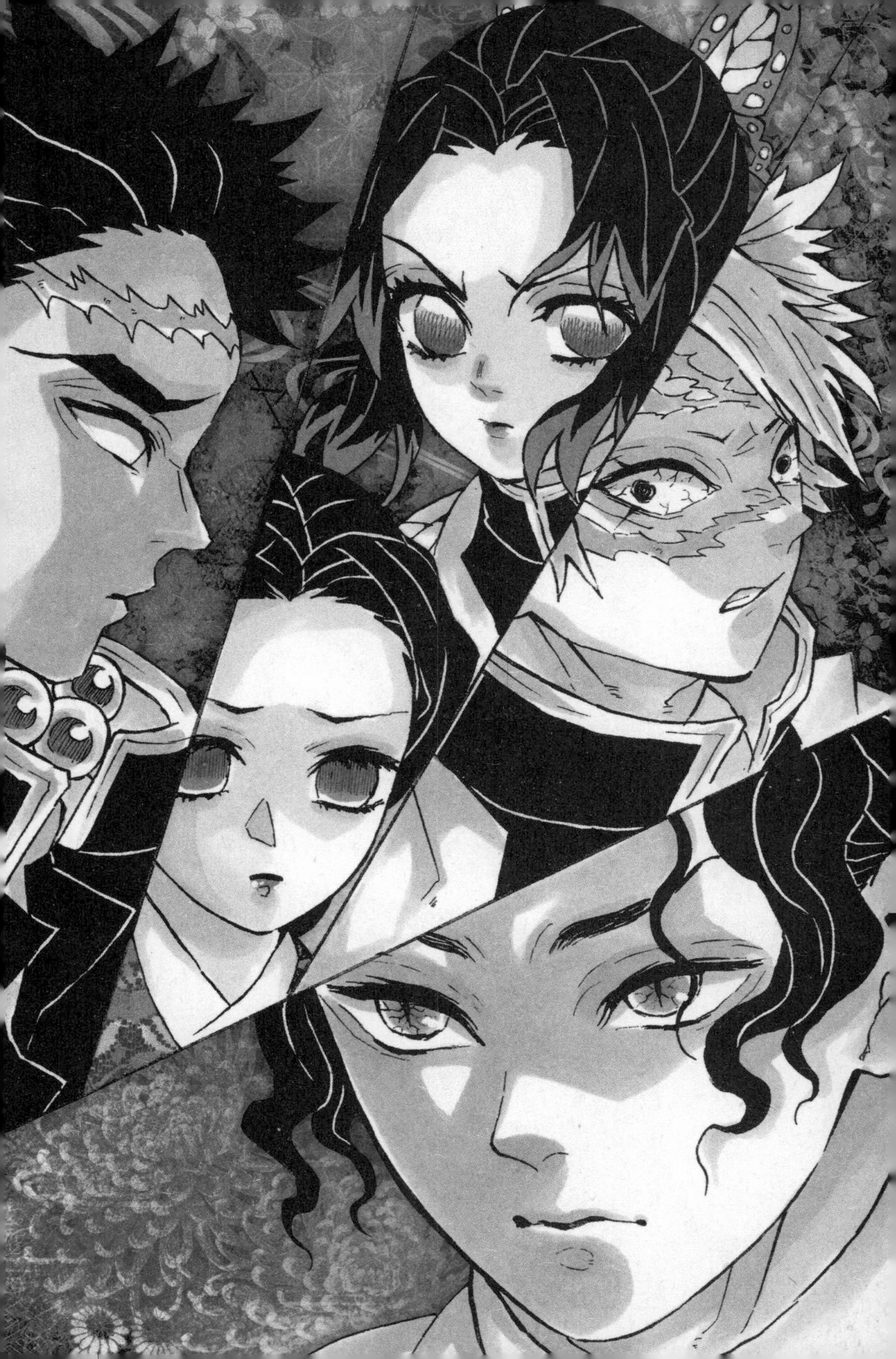

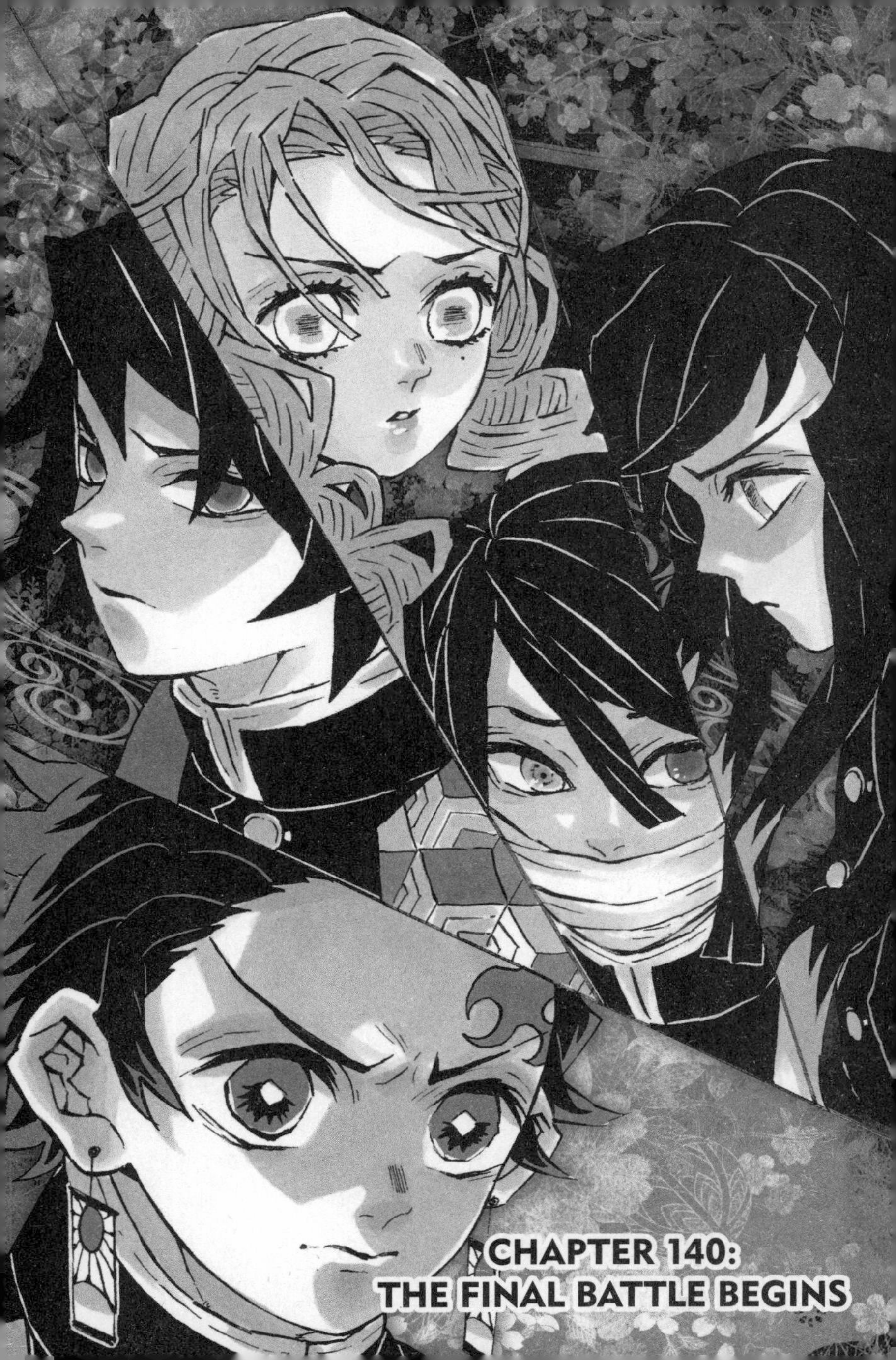

CHAPTER 140: THE FINAL BATTLE BEGINS

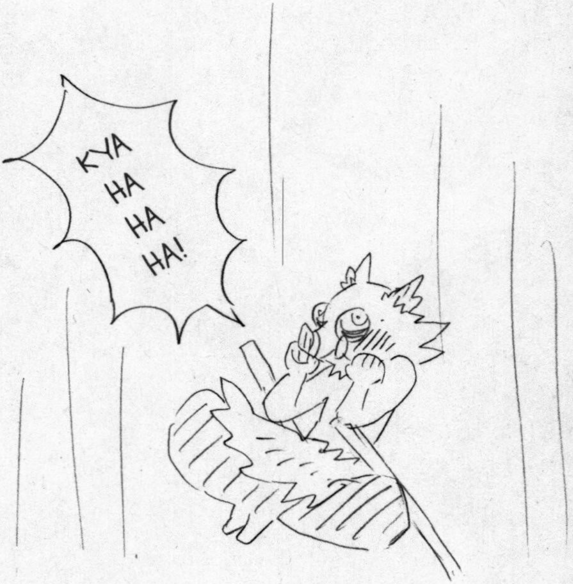
KYA HA HA HA!

All of the corps members whom Nakime caught this time fell into Infinity Castle. The moment when the floor suddenly dropped was fun, so Inosuke laughed.

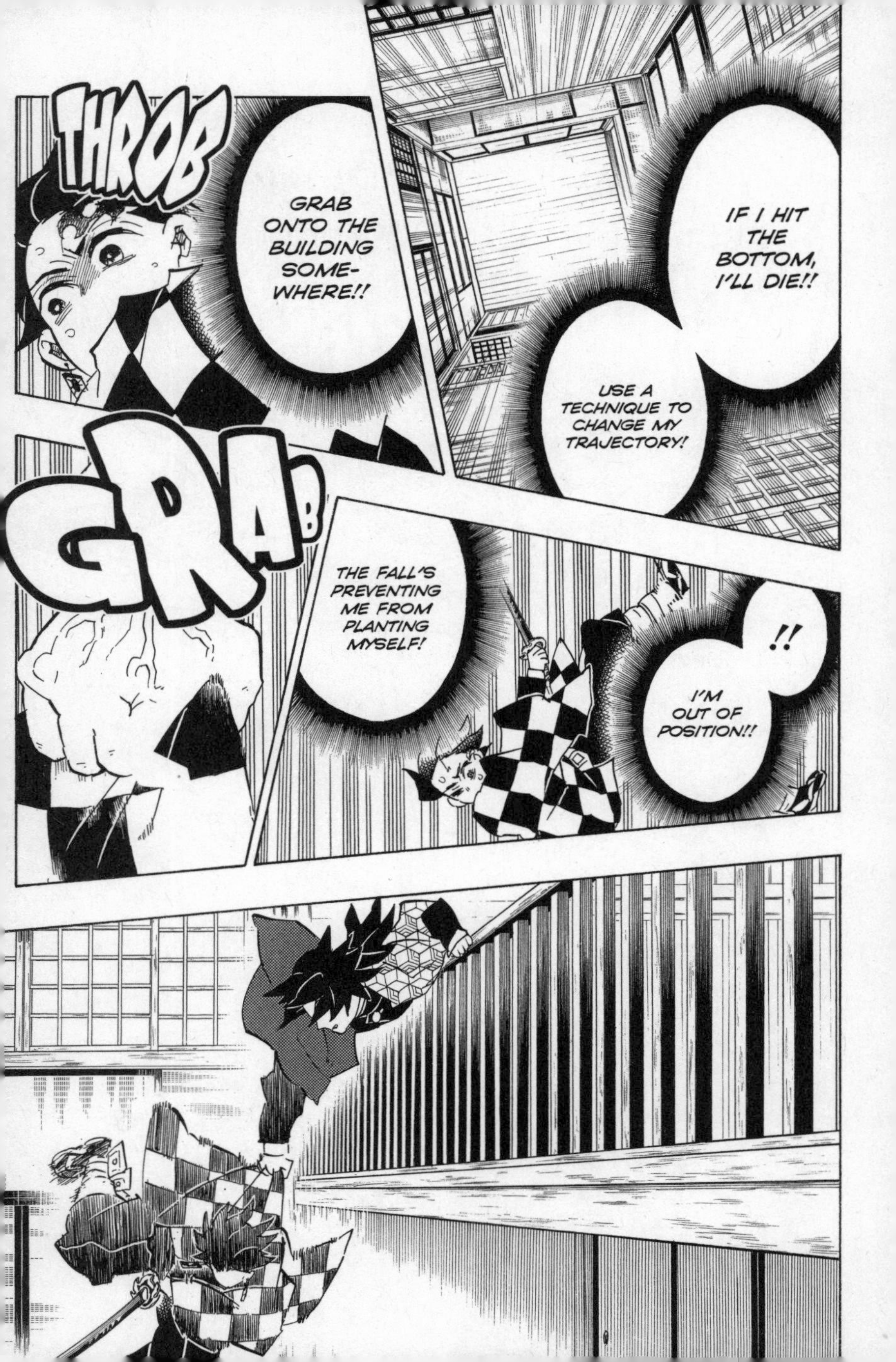
IF I HIT THE BOTTOM, I'LL DIE!!
USE A TECHNIQUE TO CHANGE MY TRAJECTORY!
THROB
GRAB ONTO THE BUILDING SOME-WHERE!!
!!
I'M OUT OF POSITION!!
THE FALL'S PREVENTING ME FROM PLANTING MYSELF!
GRAB

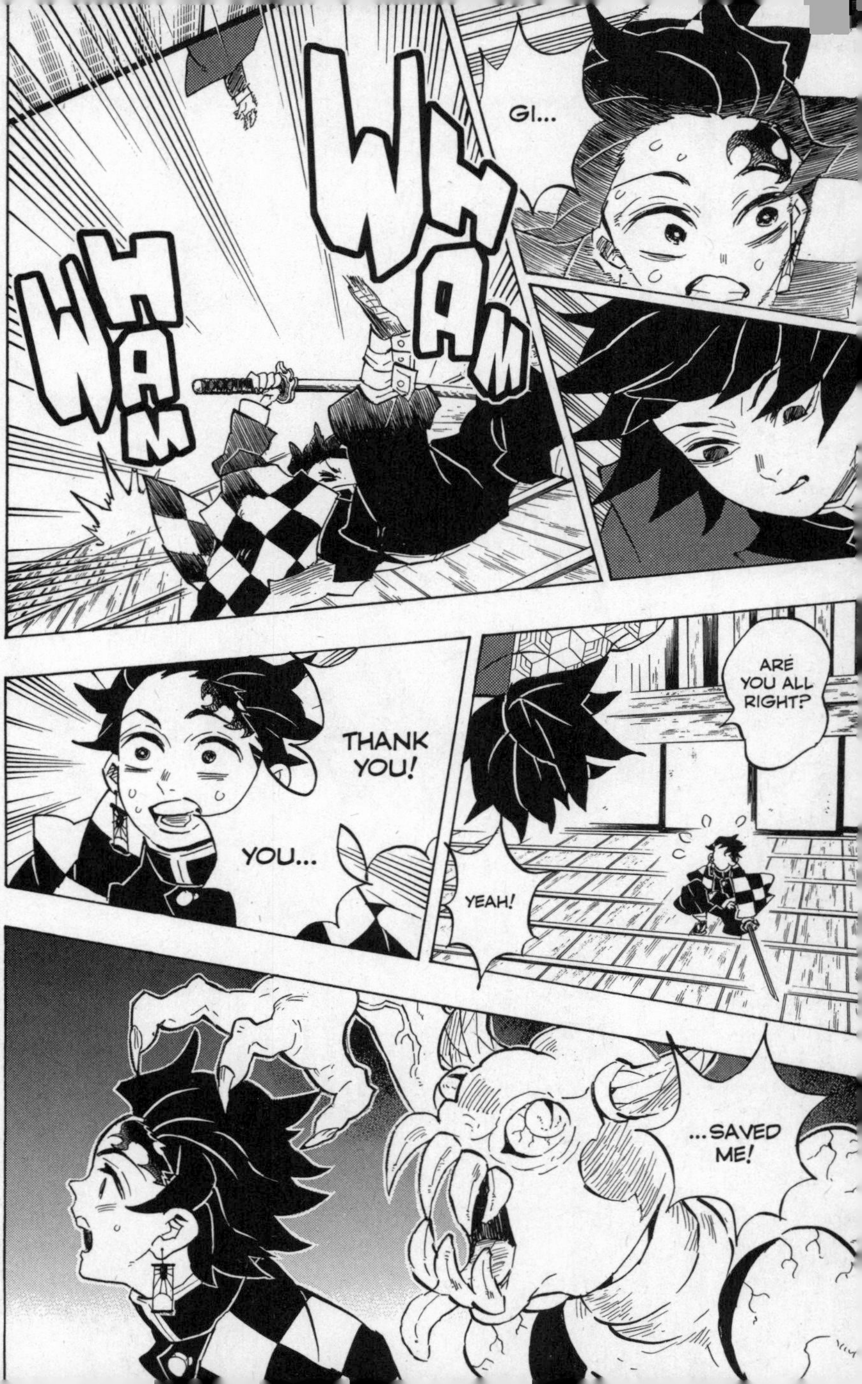
GI...
WHAM
WHAM
ARE YOU ALL RIGHT?
YEAH!
THANK YOU!
YOU...
...SAVED ME!

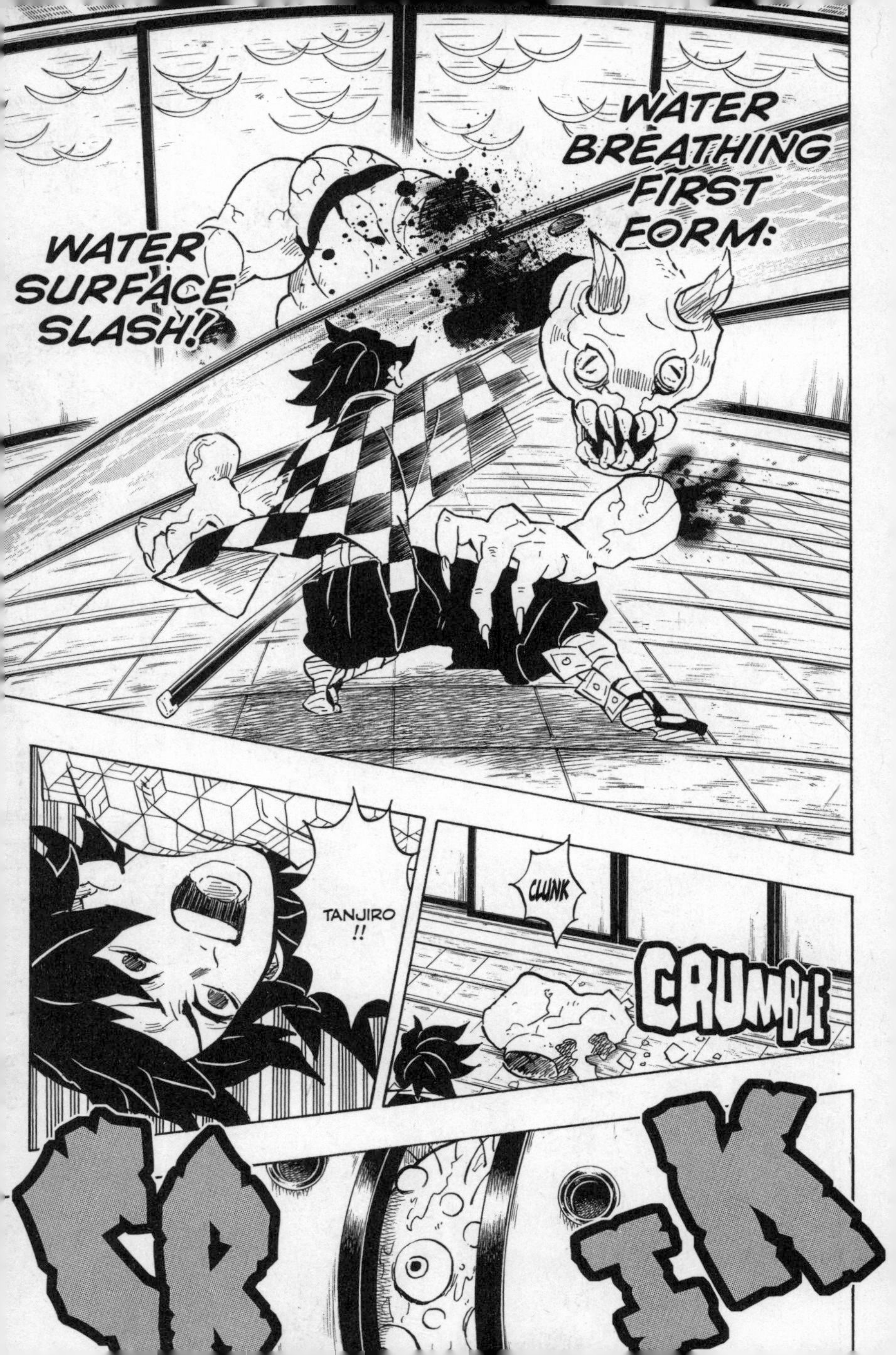
WATER BREATHING FIRST FORM:
WATER SURFACE SLASH!!
CLUNK
CRUMBLE
TANJIRO !!
CRIK

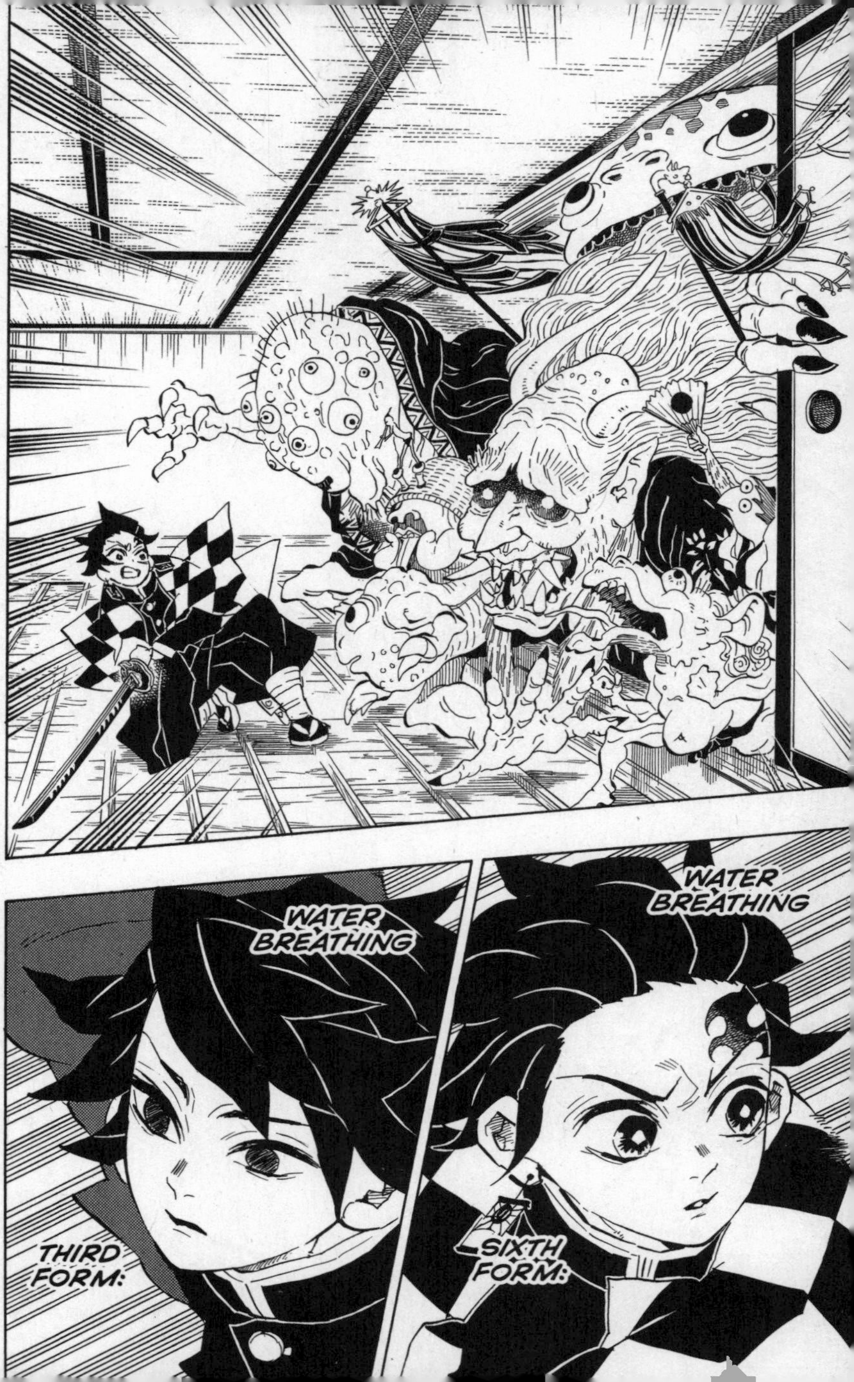
WATER BREATHING
SIXTH FORM:
WATER BREATHING
THIRD FORM:

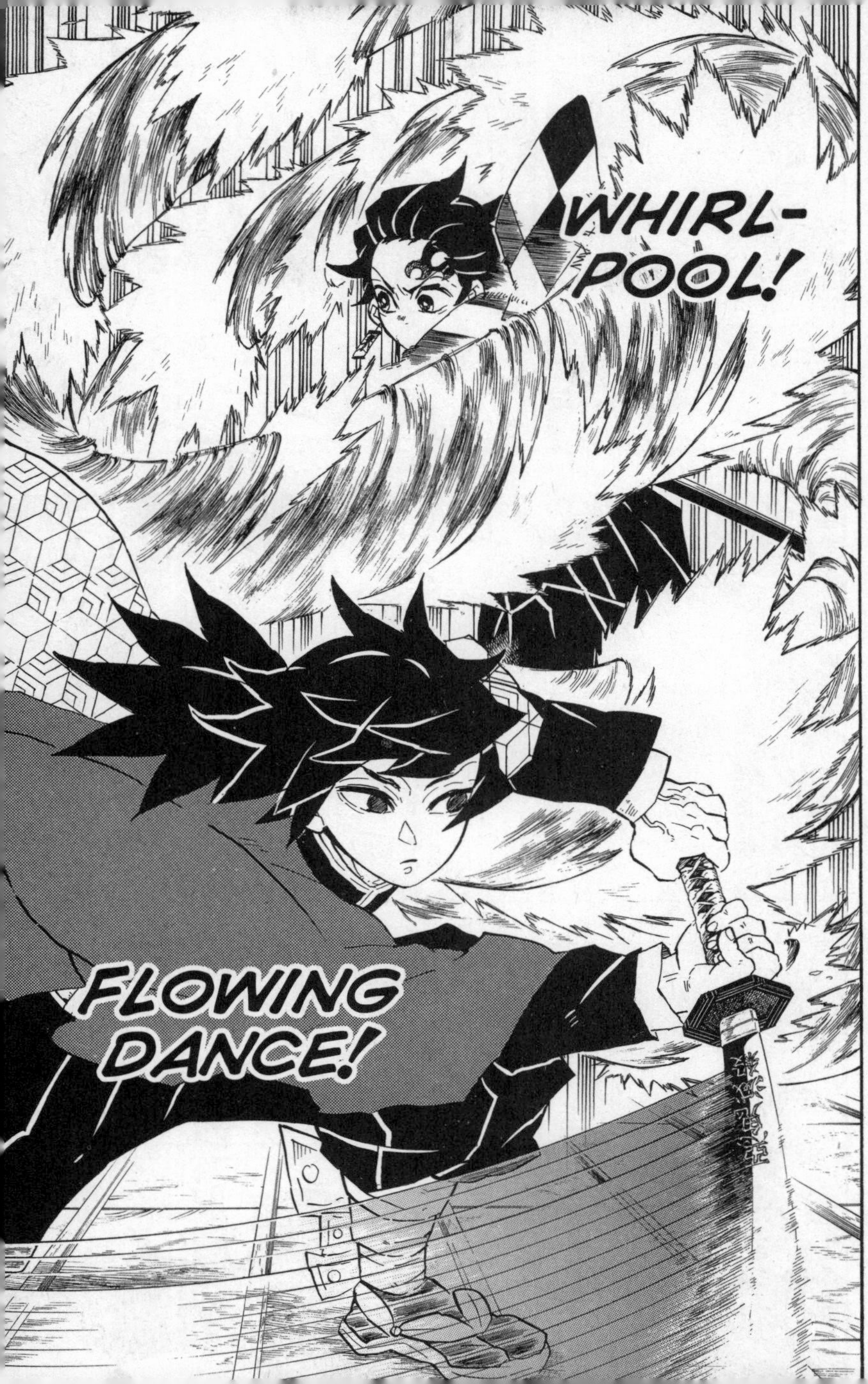
WHIRL-
POOL!
FLOWING
DANCE!

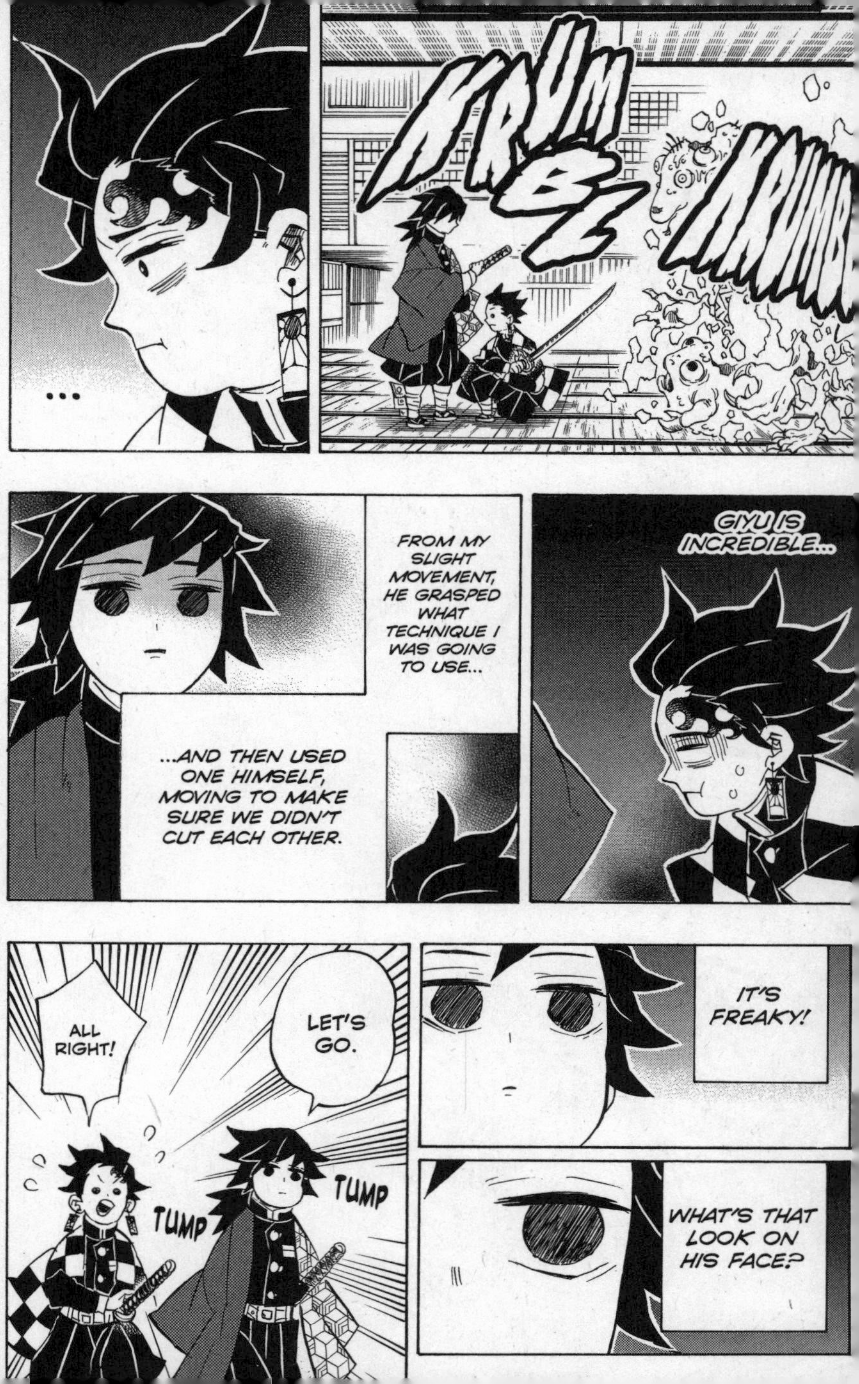
KRUMB
KRUMBLE
...
GIYU IS INCREDIBLE...
FROM MY SLIGHT MOVEMENT, HE GRASPED WHAT TECHNIQUE I WAS GOING TO USE...
...AND THEN USED ONE HIMSELF, MOVING TO MAKE SURE WE DIDN'T CUT EACH OTHER.
IT'S FREAKY!
WHAT'S THAT LOOK ON HIS FACE?
LET'S GO.
ALL RIGHT!
TUMP
TUMP

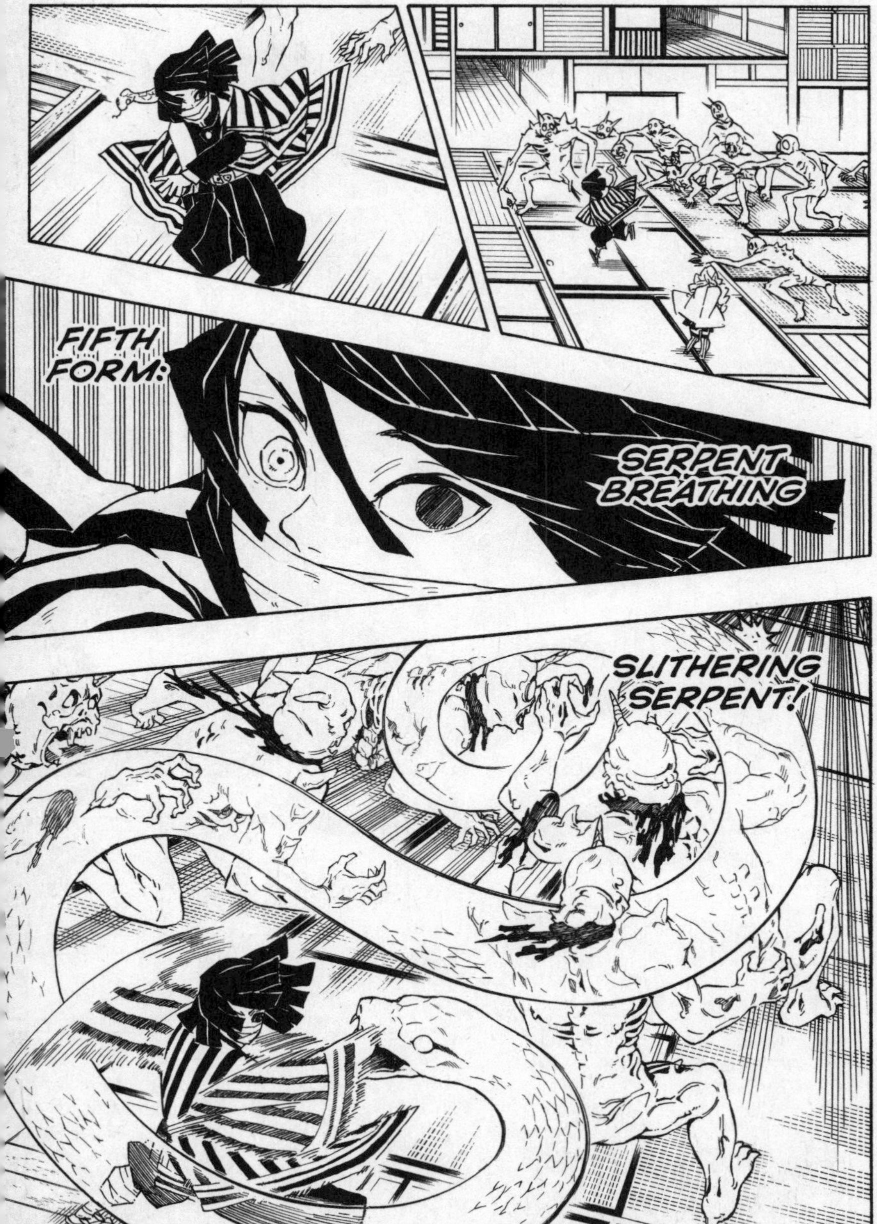
SERPENT BREATHING
FIFTH FORM:
SLITHERING SERPENT!

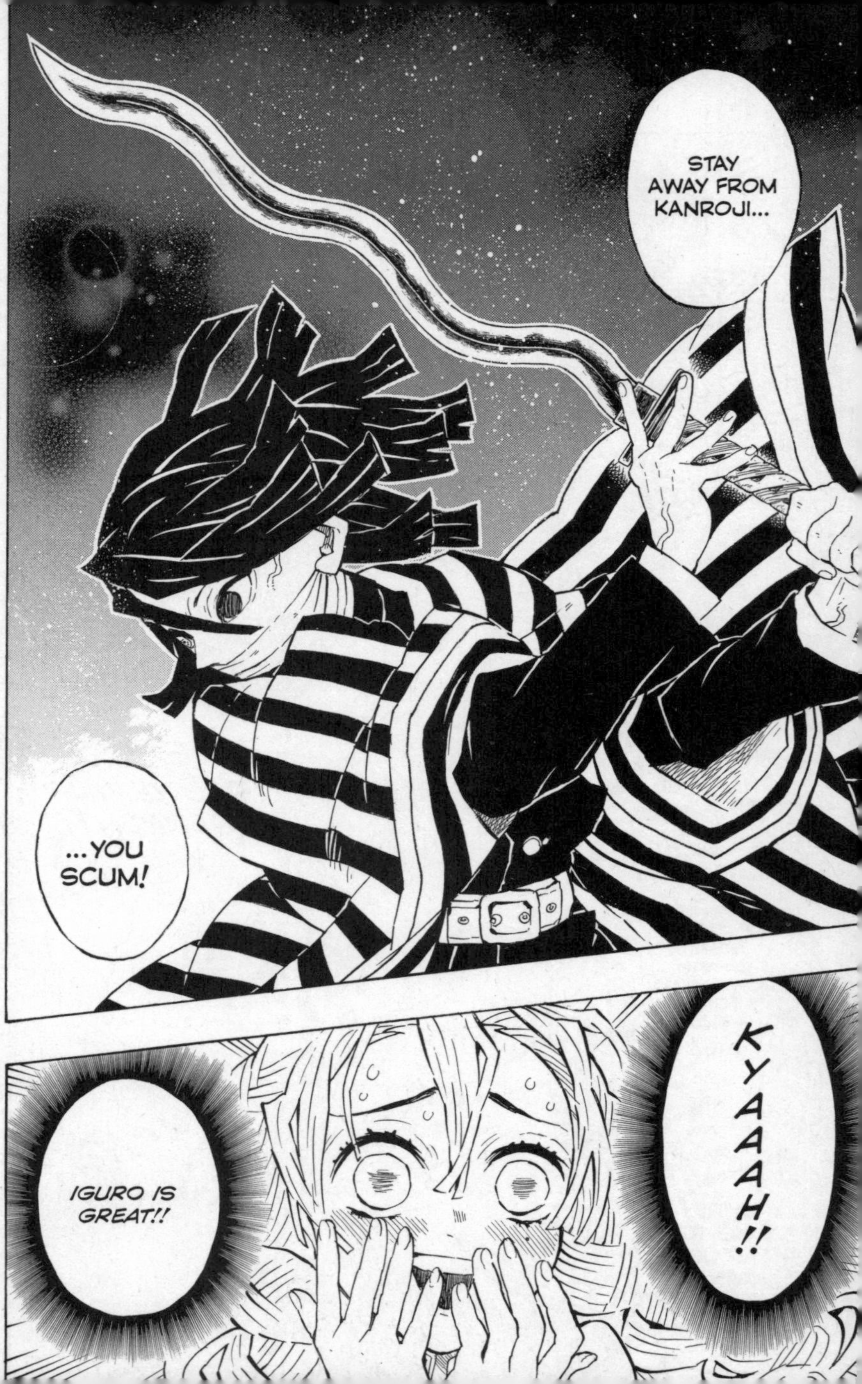
STAY AWAY FROM KANROJI...
...YOU SCUM!
KYAAAH!!
IGURO IS GREAT!!

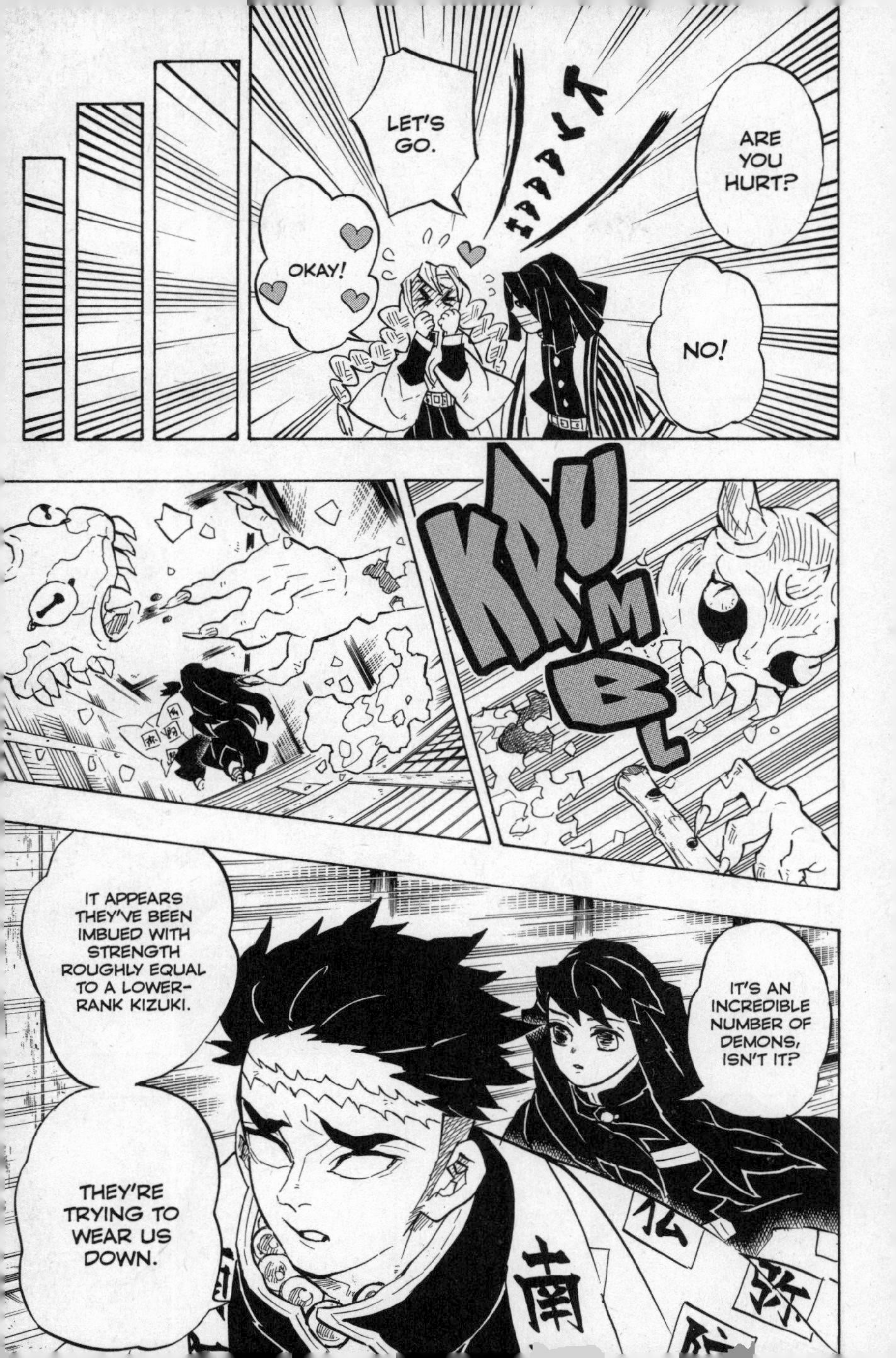
ARE YOU HURT?
KYAAAH
NO!
LET'S GO.
OKAY!
KRUMBL
IT'S AN INCREDIBLE NUMBER OF DEMONS, ISN'T IT?
IT APPEARS THEY'VE BEEN IMBUED WITH STRENGTH ROUGHLY EQUAL TO A LOWER-RANK KIZUKI.
THEY'RE TRYING TO WEAR US DOWN.

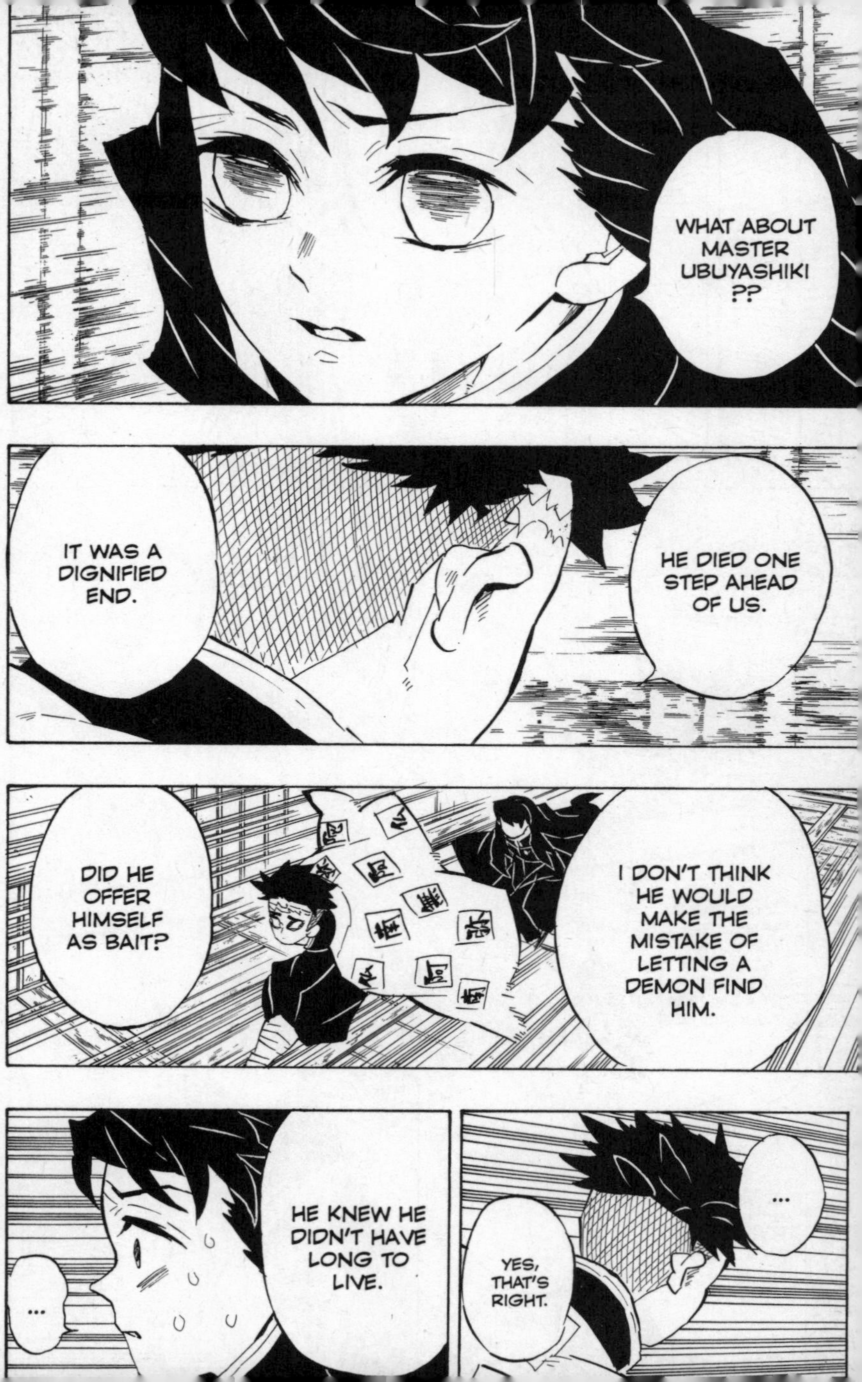
WHAT ABOUT MASTER UBUYASHIKI ??
HE DIED ONE STEP AHEAD OF US.
IT WAS A DIGNIFIED END.
I DON'T THINK HE WOULD MAKE THE MISTAKE OF LETTING A DEMON FIND HIM.
DID HE OFFER HIMSELF AS BAIT?
...
YES, THAT'S RIGHT.
HE KNEW HE DIDN'T HAVE LONG TO LIVE.
...

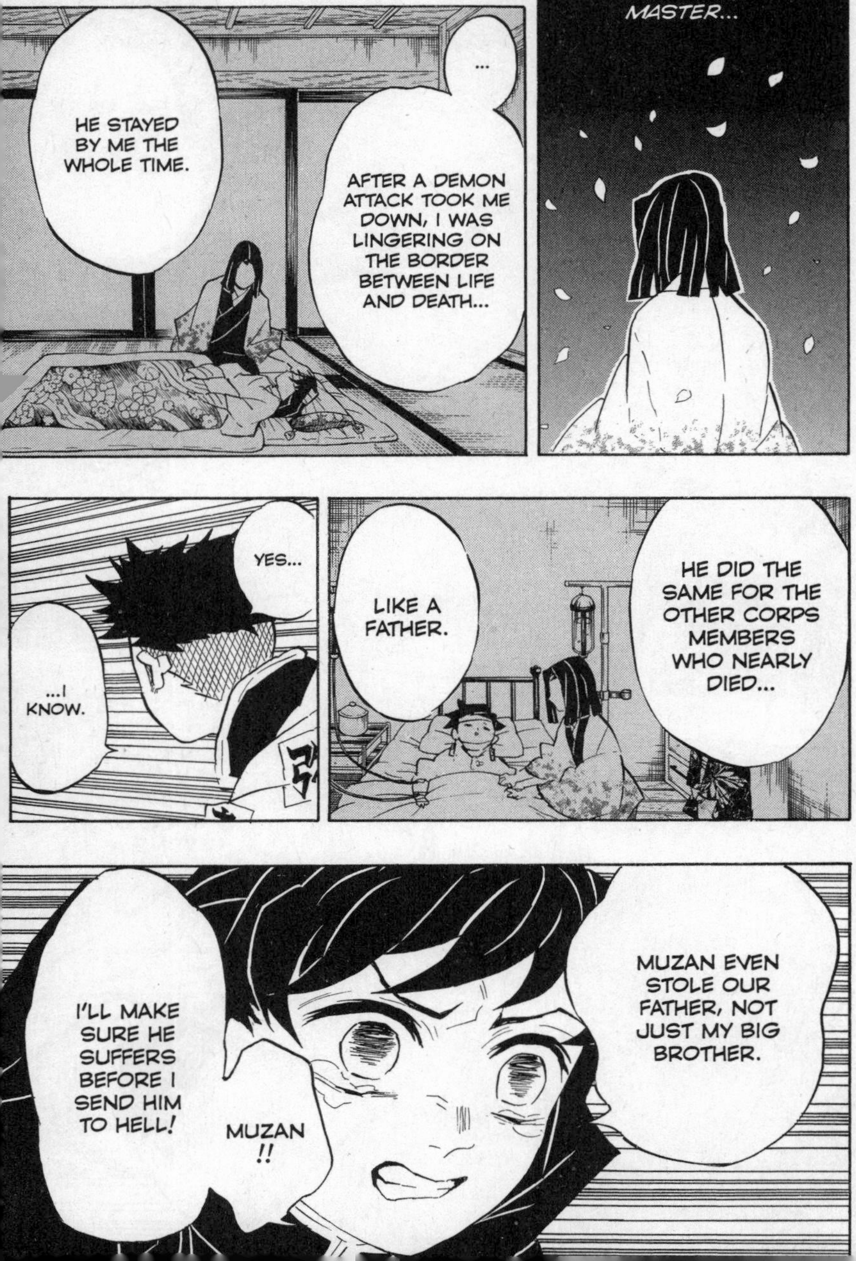
MASTER...
...
AFTER A DEMON ATTACK TOOK ME DOWN, I WAS LINGERING ON THE BORDER BETWEEN LIFE AND DEATH...
HE STAYED BY ME THE WHOLE TIME.
HE DID THE SAME FOR THE OTHER CORPS MEMBERS WHO NEARLY DIED...
LIKE A FATHER.
YES...
...I KNOW.
MUZAN EVEN STOLE OUR FATHER, NOT JUST MY BIG BROTHER.
MUZAN!!
I'LL MAKE SURE HE SUFFERS BEFORE I SEND HIM TO HELL!

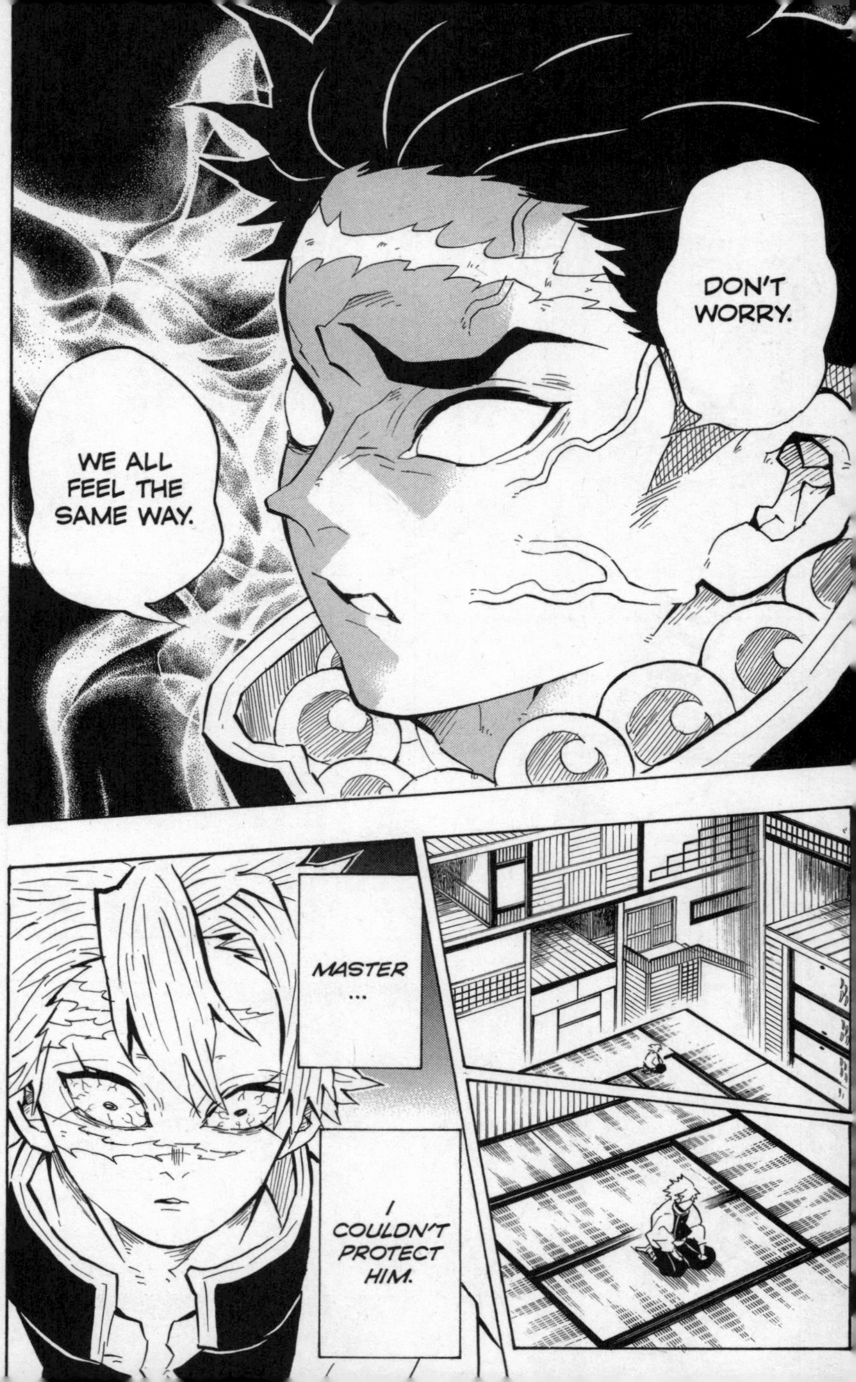
DON'T WORRY.
WE ALL FEEL THE SAME WAY.
MASTER ...
I COULDN'T PROTECT HIM.

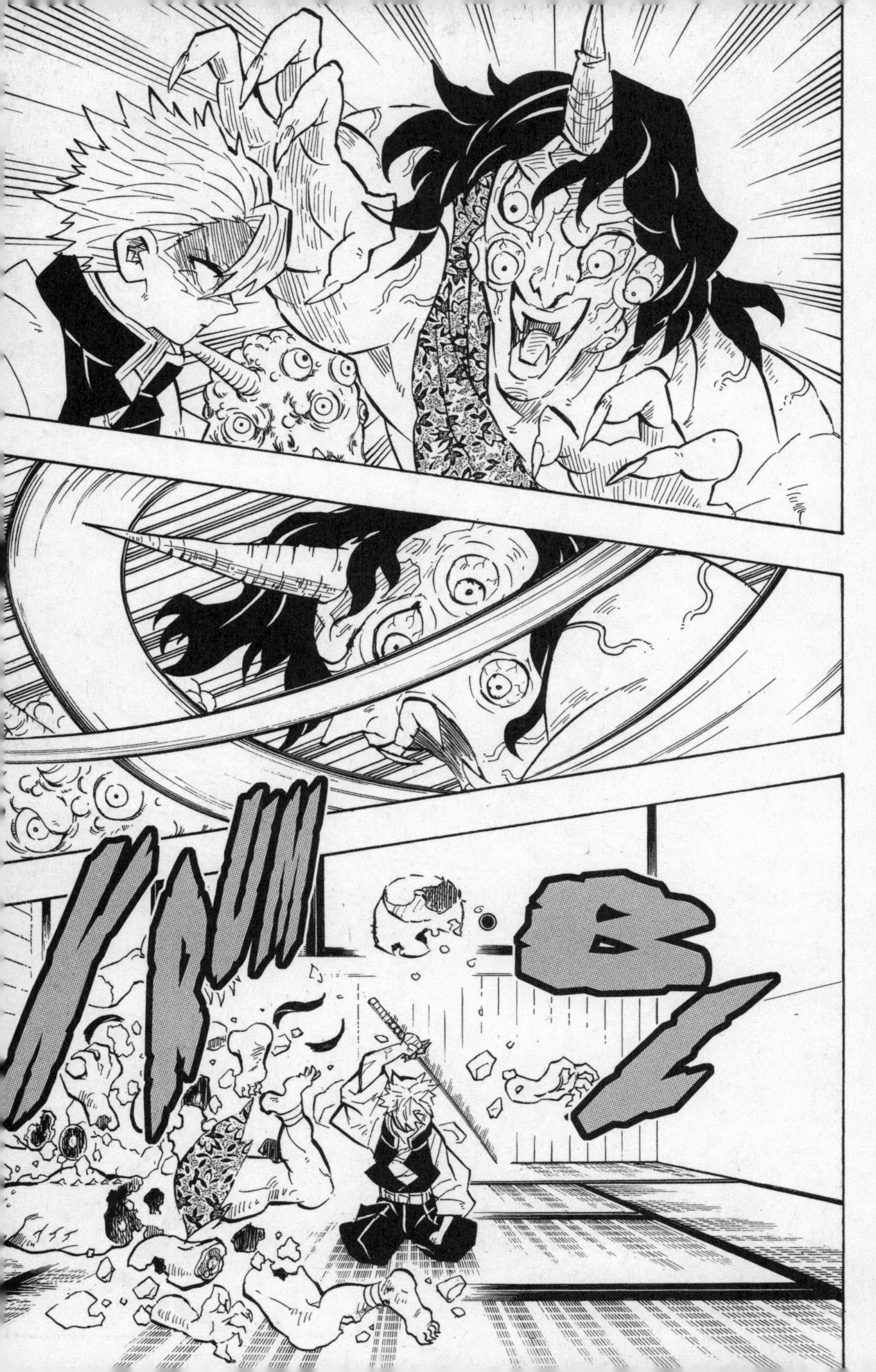

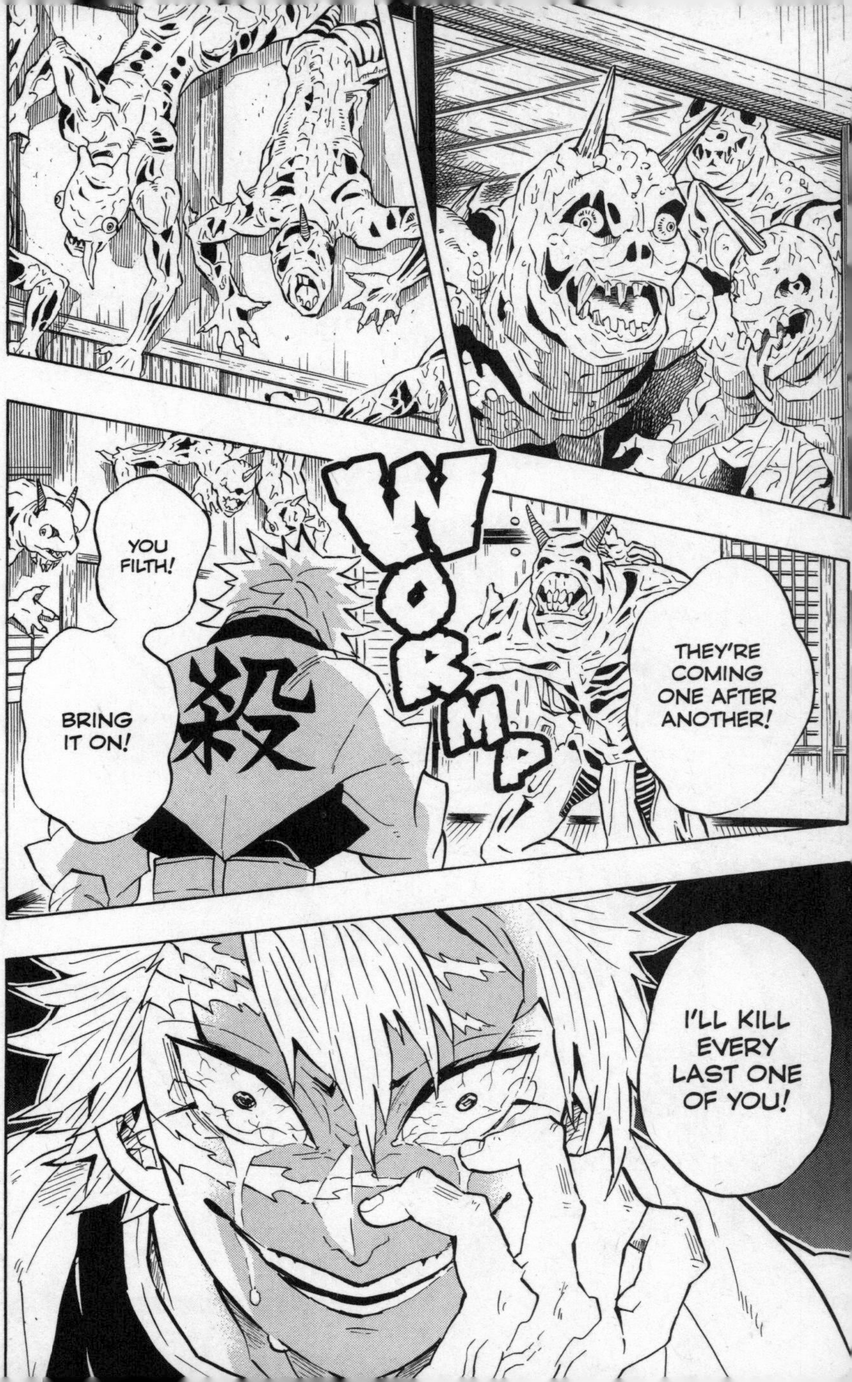
THEY'RE COMING ONE AFTER ANOTHER!
WORMP
YOU FILTH!
BRING IT ON!
殺
I'LL KILL EVERY LAST ONE OF YOU!

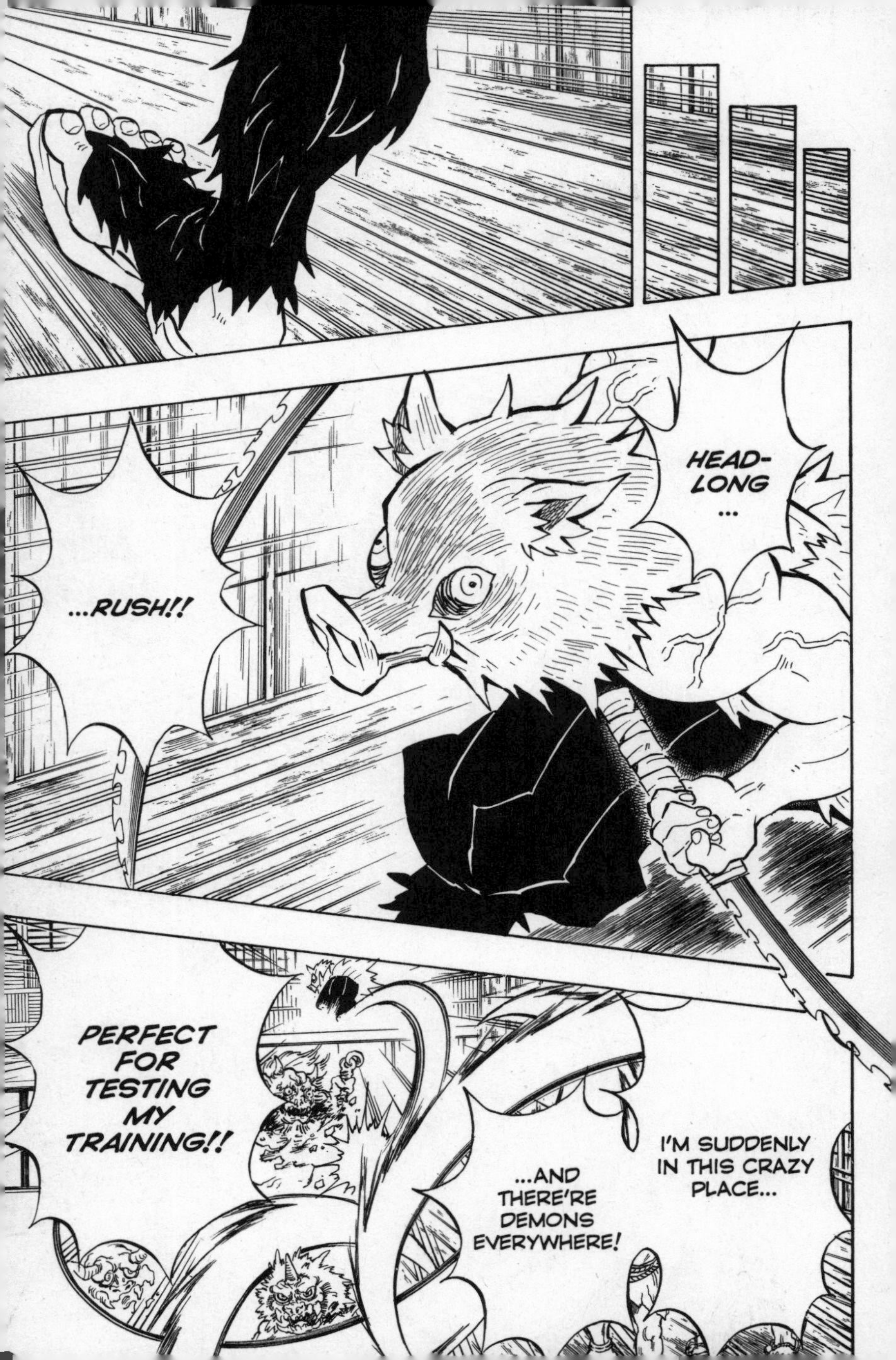
HEAD-LONG ...
...RUSH!!
I'M SUDDENLY IN THIS CRAZY PLACE...
...AND THERE'RE DEMONS EVERYWHERE!
PERFECT FOR TESTING MY TRAINING!!

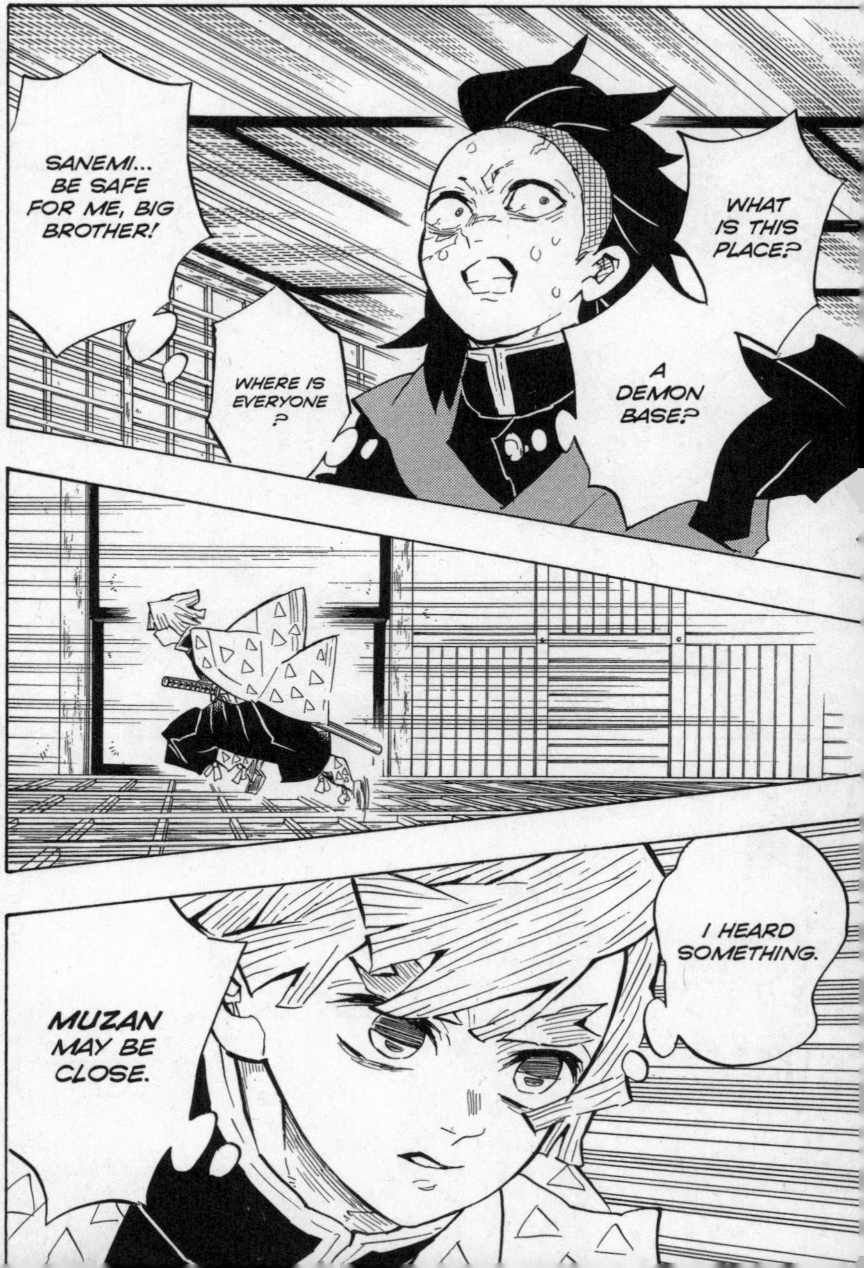
WHAT IS THIS PLACE?
A DEMON BASE?
WHERE IS EVERYONE?
SANEMI... BE SAFE FOR ME, BIG BROTHER!
I HEARD SOMETHING.
MUZAN MAY BE CLOSE.

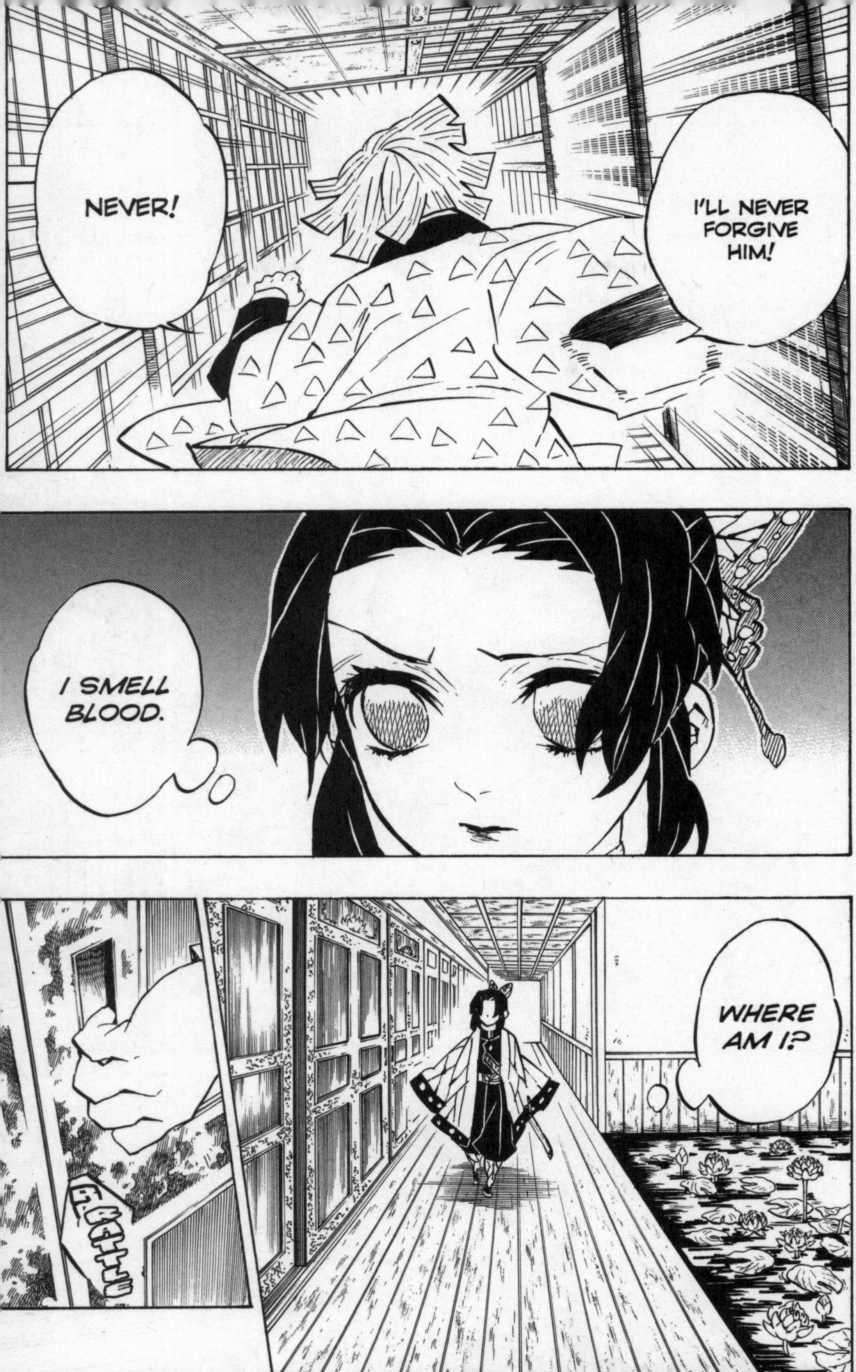
I'LL NEVER FORGIVE HIM!
NEVER!
I SMELL BLOOD.
WHERE AM I?

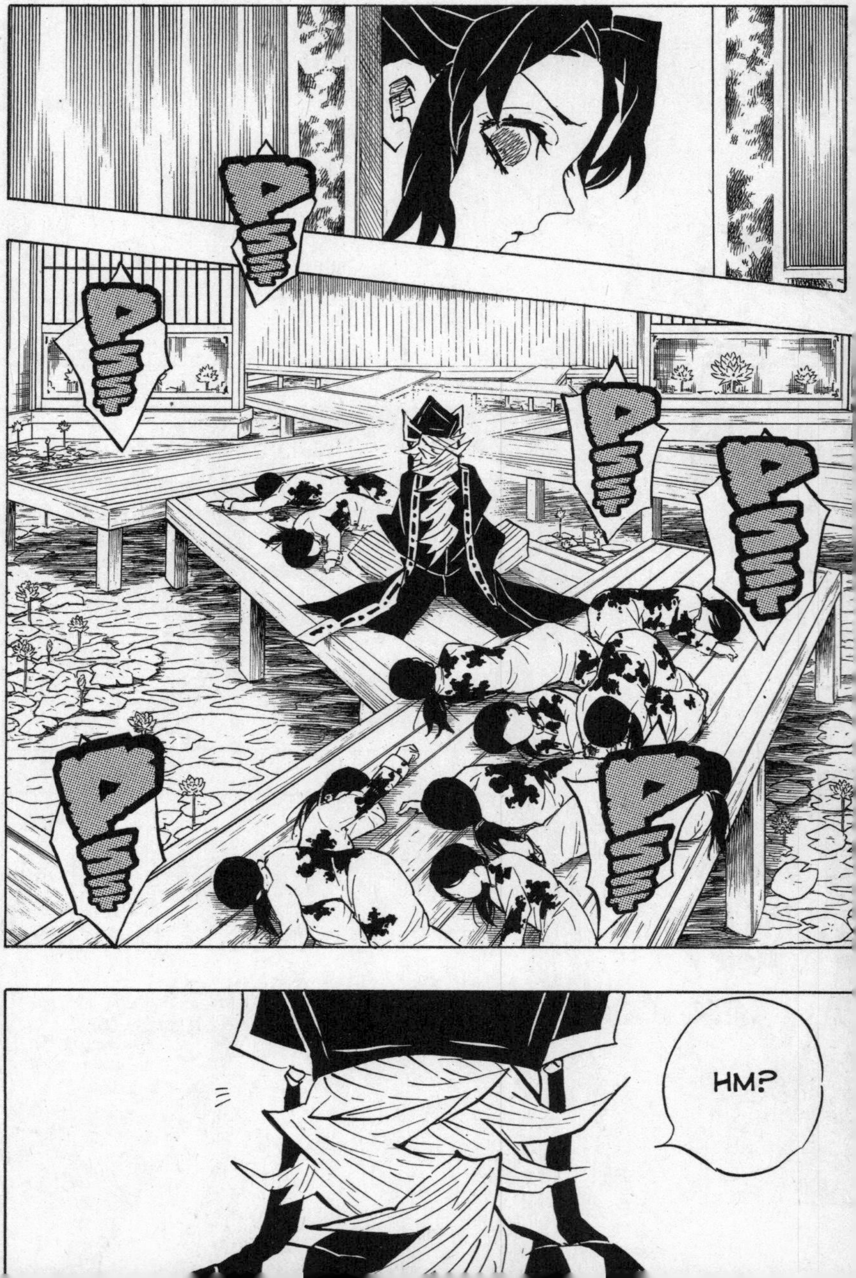
PSST
PSST
PSST
PSST
PSST
PSST
HM?

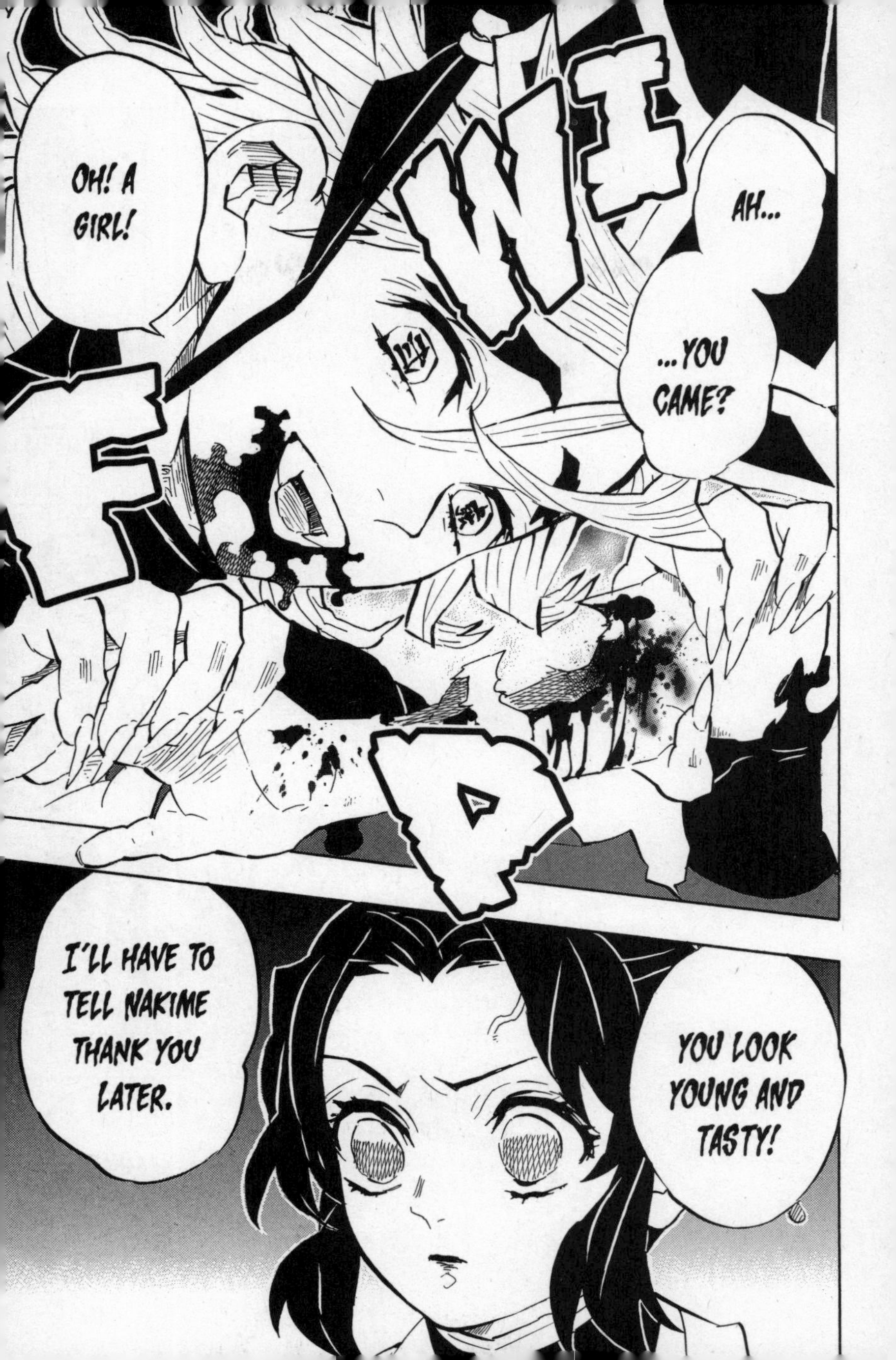
AH...
...YOU CAME?
OH! A GIRL!
YOU LOOK YOUNG AND TASTY!
I'LL HAVE TO TELL NAKIME THANK YOU LATER.

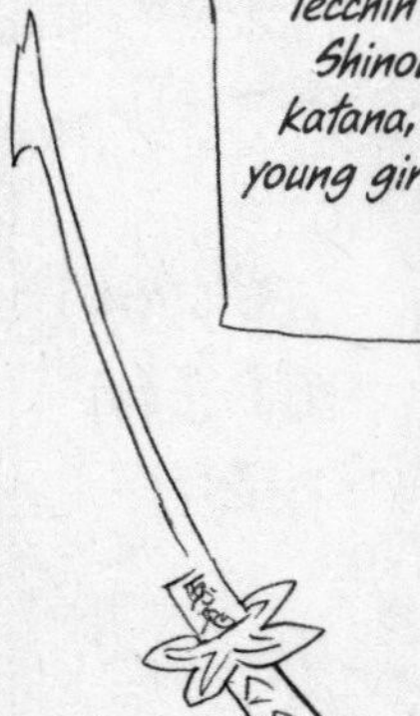

Tecchin made Shinobu's katana, which young girls love.

Shinobu doesn't have strong muscles when it comes to swinging her sword, so she can't cut off a demon's head. However, she is amazingly strong at pushing and thrusting, with the power to pierce rock. It's faster than the Water Breathing technique called Drop Ripple Thrust.

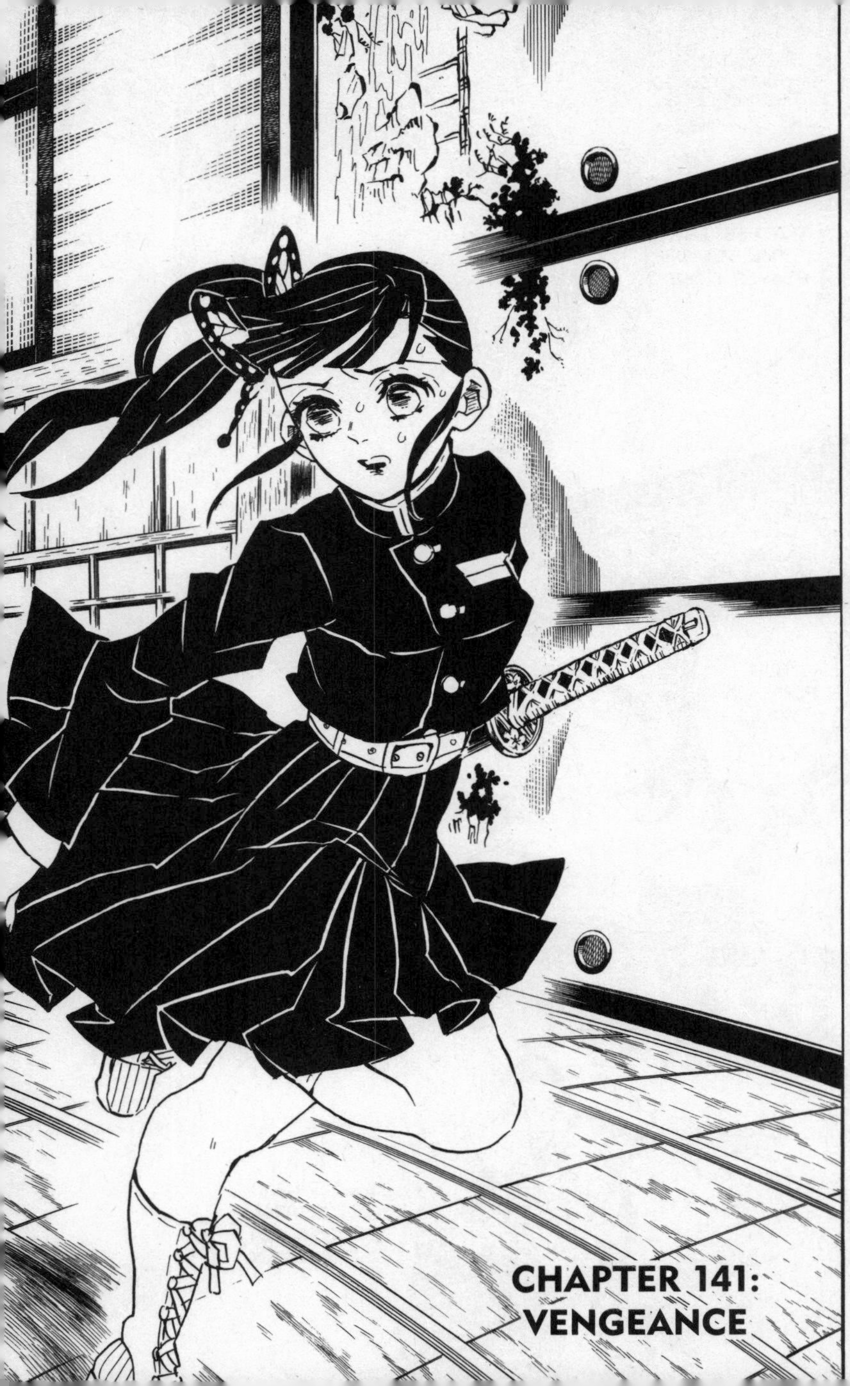
CHAPTER 141:
VENGEANCE

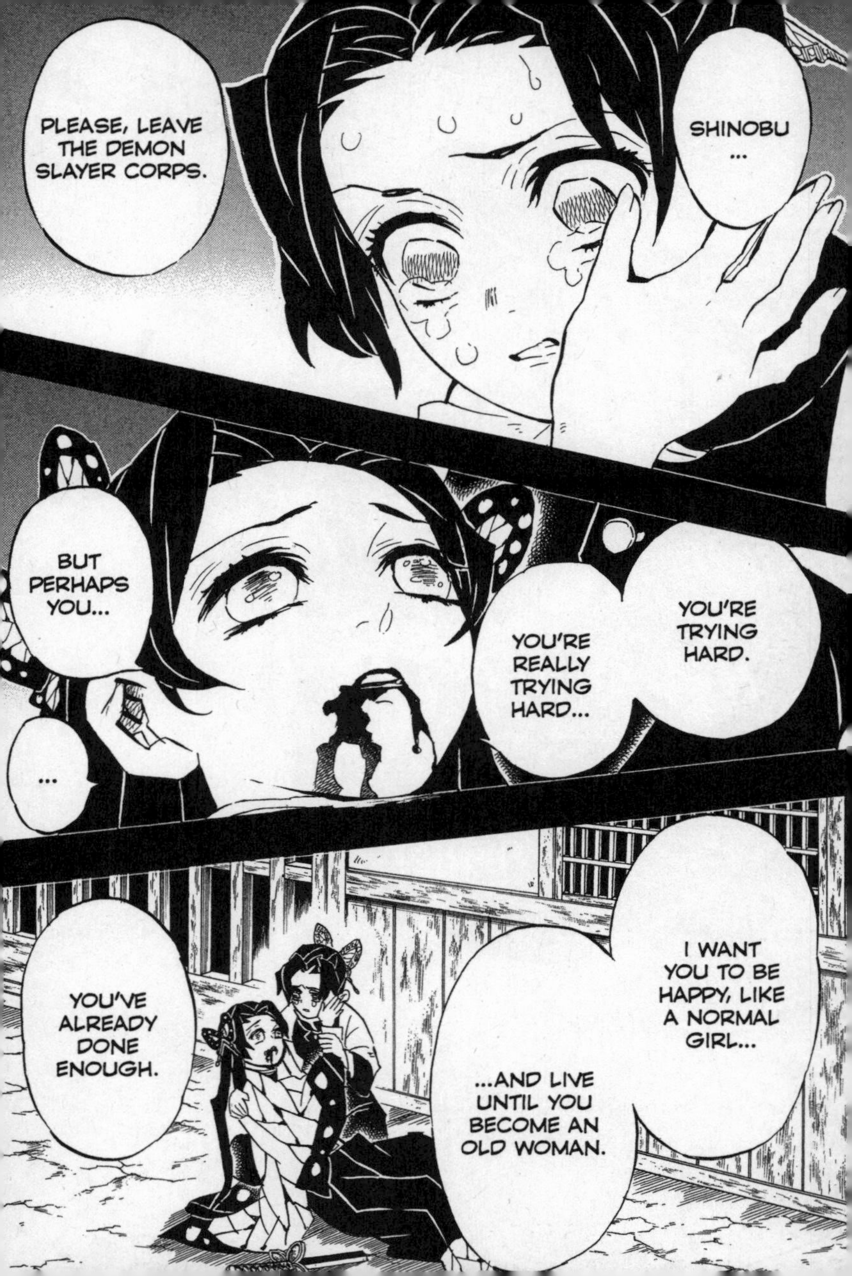
SHINOBU ...
PLEASE, LEAVE THE DEMON SLAYER CORPS.
YOU'RE TRYING HARD.
YOU'RE REALLY TRYING HARD...
BUT PERHAPS YOU...
...
I WANT YOU TO BE HAPPY, LIKE A NORMAL GIRL...
...AND LIVE UNTIL YOU BECOME AN OLD WOMAN.
YOU'VE ALREADY DONE ENOUGH.

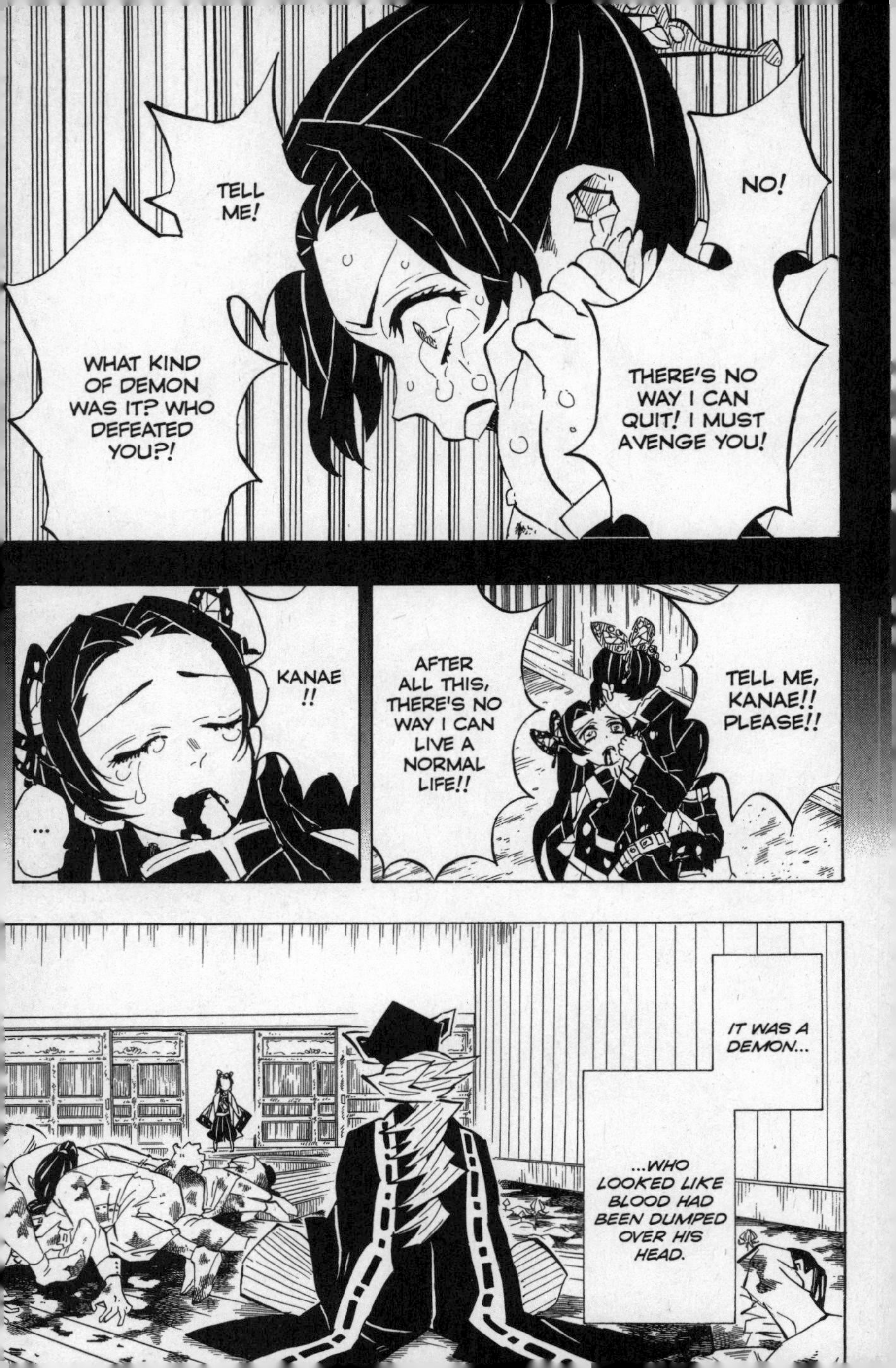
NO!
THERE'S NO WAY I CAN QUIT! I MUST AVENGE YOU!
TELL ME!
WHAT KIND OF DEMON WAS IT? WHO DEFEATED YOU?!
TELL ME, KANAE!! PLEASE!!
AFTER ALL THIS, THERE'S NO WAY I CAN LIVE A NORMAL LIFE!!
KANAE!!
...
IT WAS A DEMON...
...WHO LOOKED LIKE BLOOD HAD BEEN DUMPED OVER HIS HEAD.

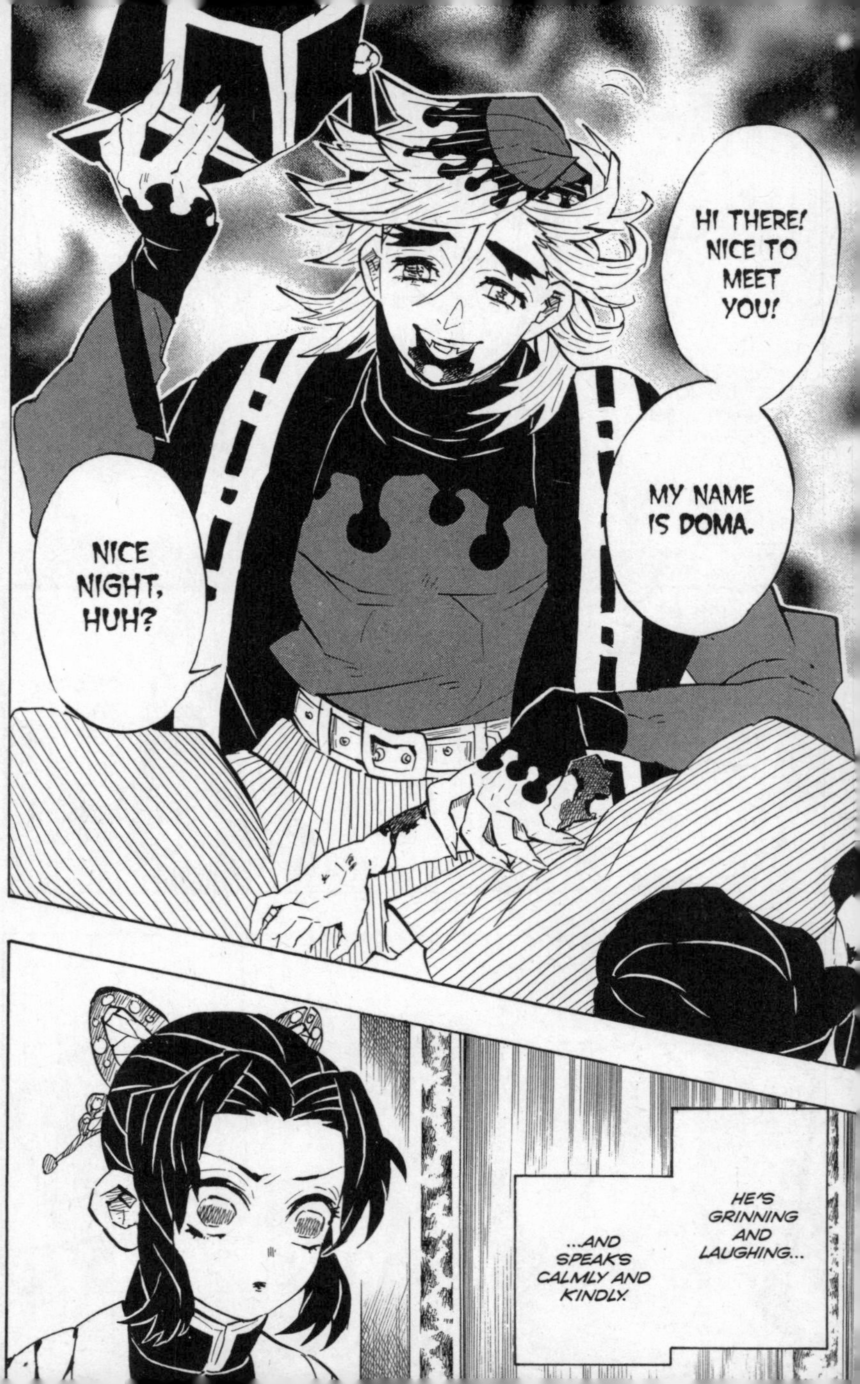
HI THERE! NICE TO MEET YOU!
MY NAME IS DOMA.
NICE NIGHT, HUH?
HE'S GRINNING AND LAUGHING...
...AND SPEAKS CALMLY AND KINDLY.

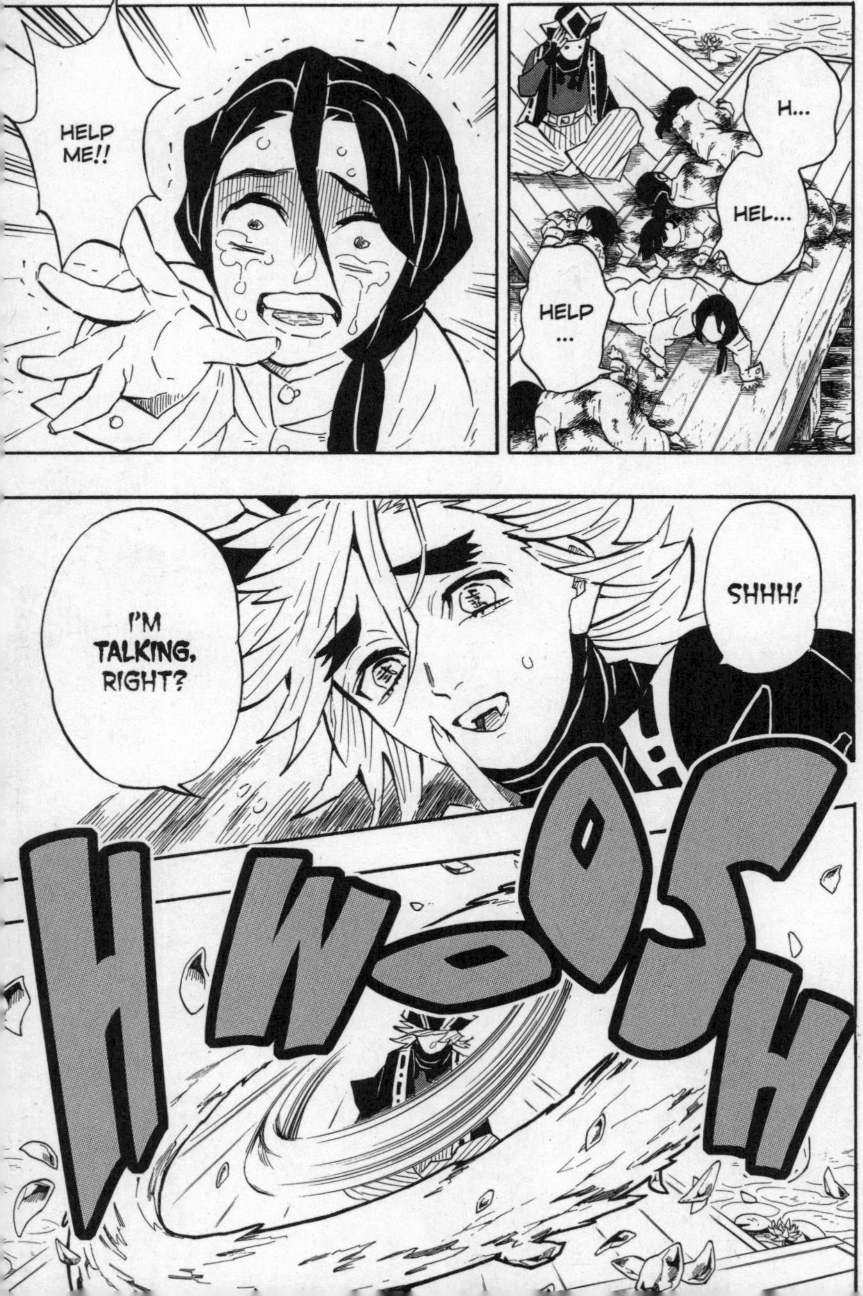
H...
HEL...
HELP ...
HELP ME!!
SHHH!
I'M TALKING, RIGHT?
WHOOSH

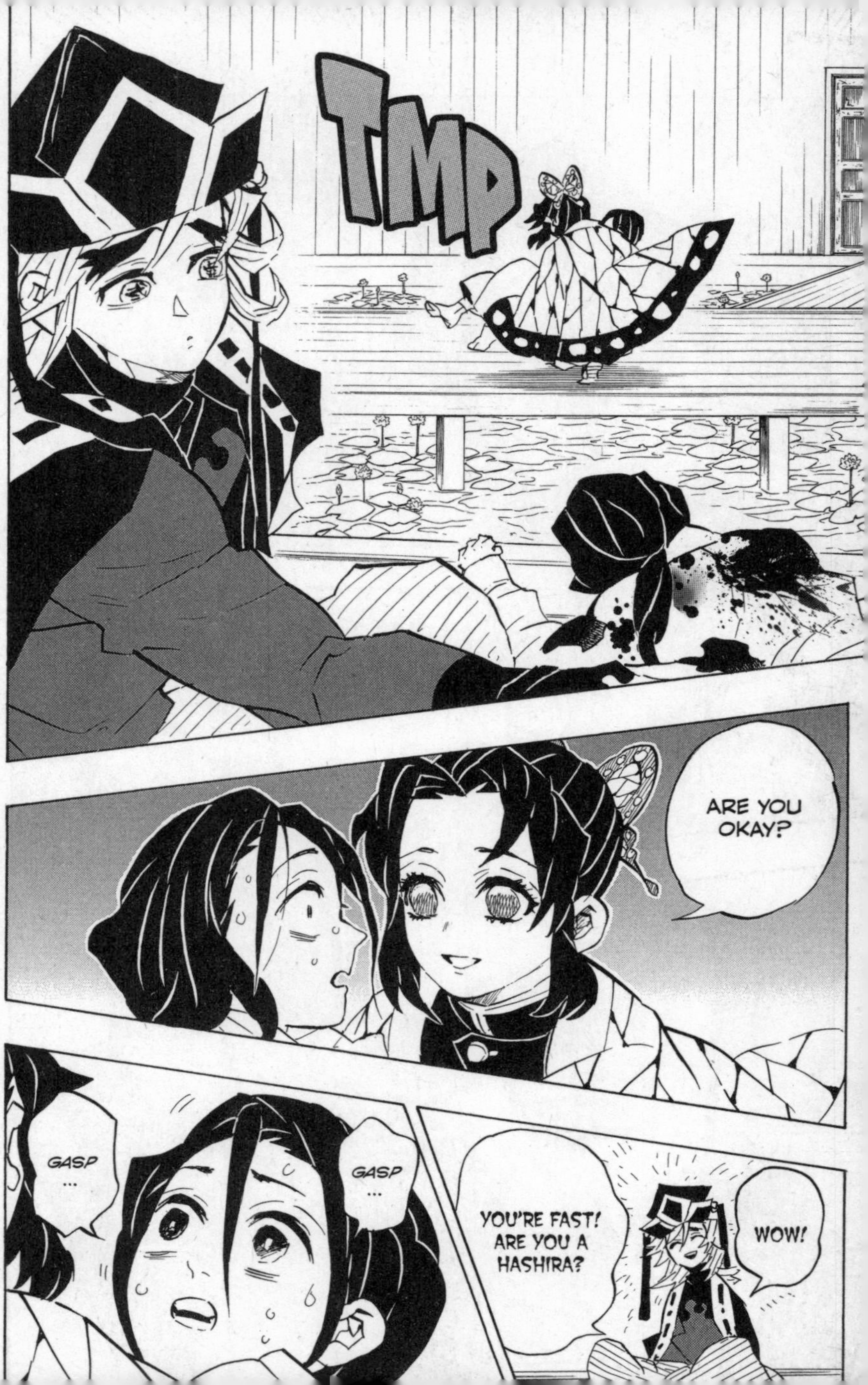
TMP
ARE YOU OKAY?
WOW!
YOU'RE FAST! ARE YOU A HASHIRA?
GASP ...
GASP ...

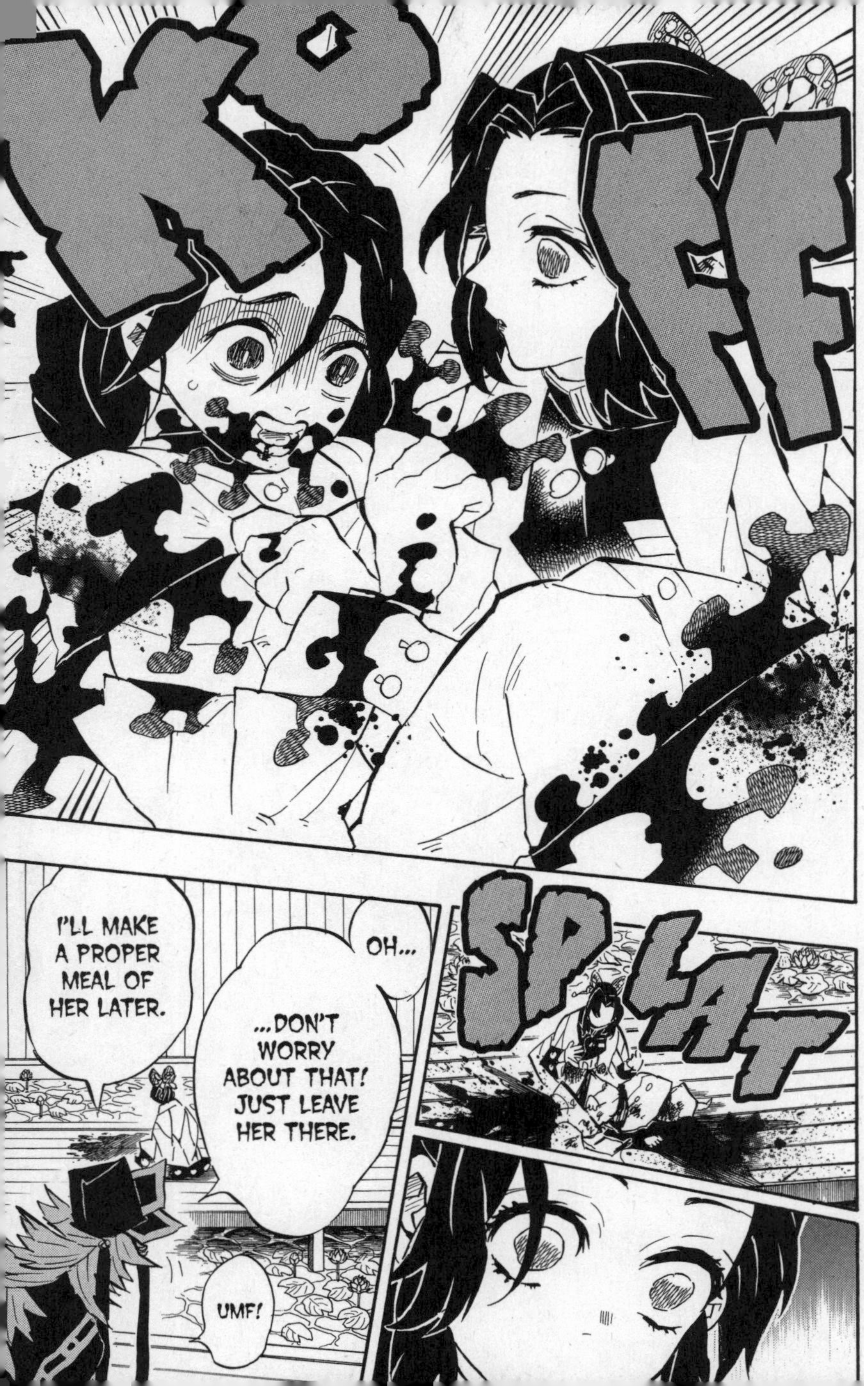
SPLAT
OH...
...DON'T WORRY ABOUT THAT! JUST LEAVE HER THERE.
I'LL MAKE A PROPER MEAL OF HER LATER.
UMF!

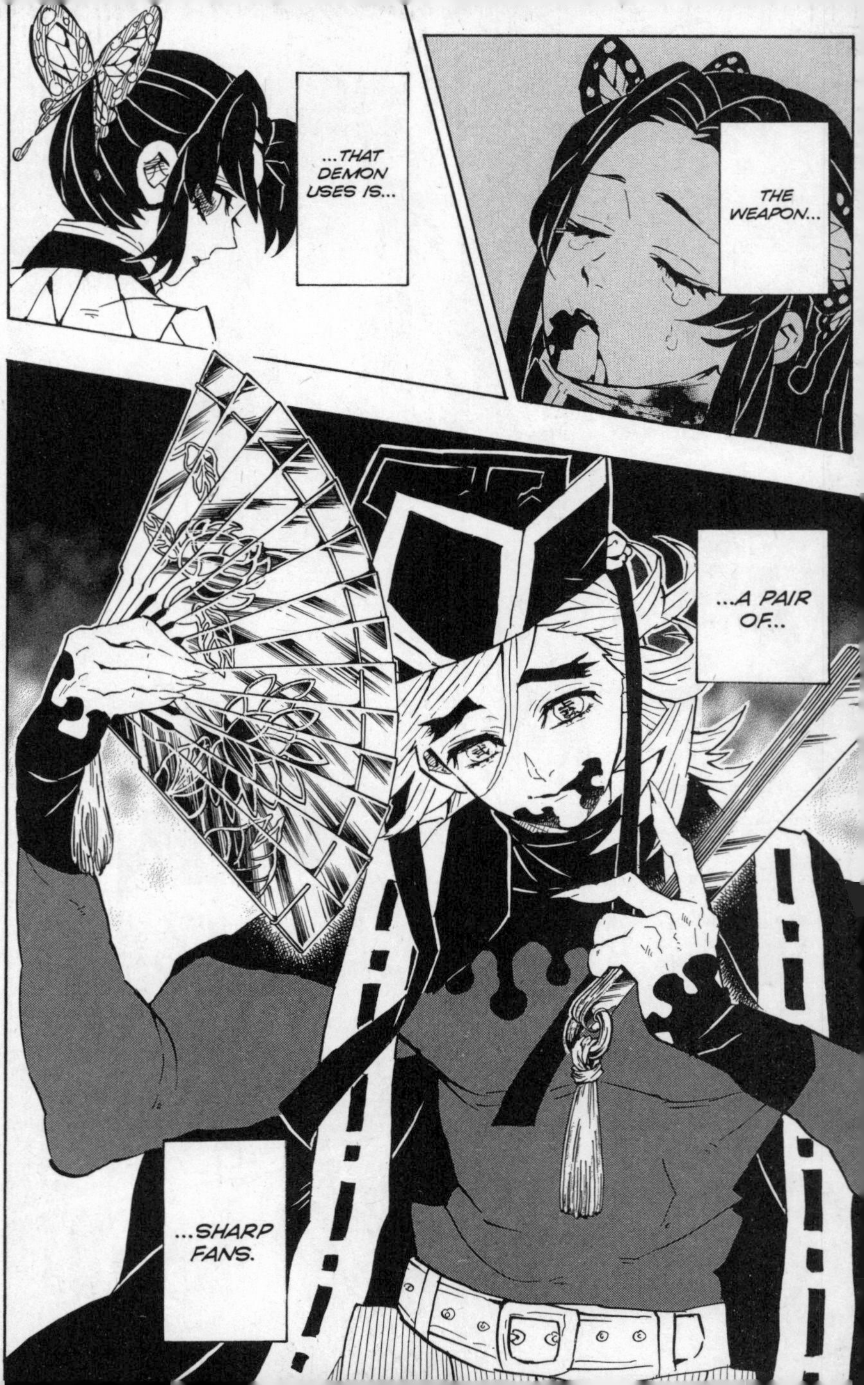
THE WEAPON...
...THAT DEMON USES IS...
...A PAIR OF...
...SHARP FANS.

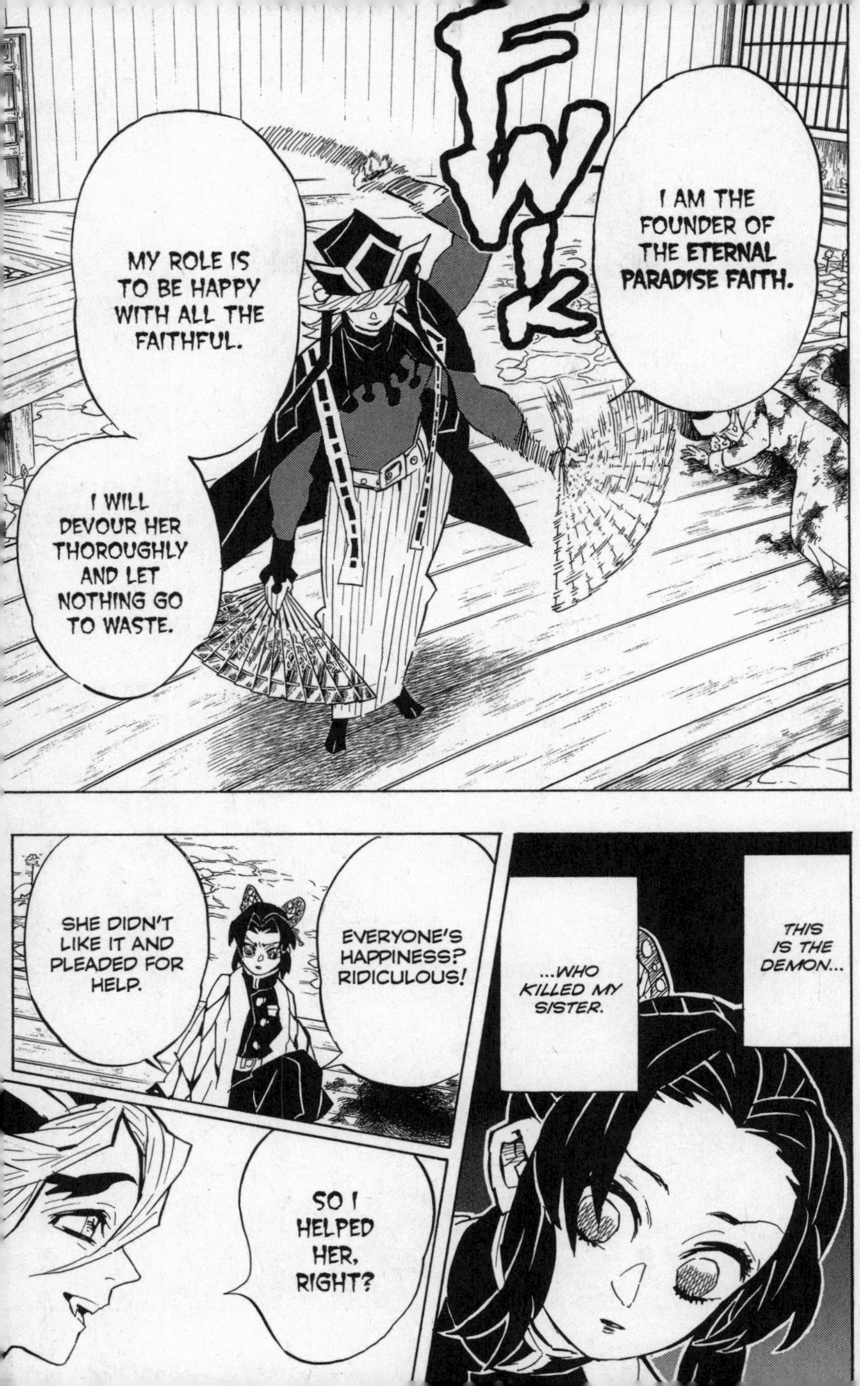
I AM THE FOUNDER OF THE ETERNAL PARADISE FAITH.
FWK
MY ROLE IS TO BE HAPPY WITH ALL THE FAITHFUL.
I WILL DEVOUR HER THOROUGHLY AND LET NOTHING GO TO WASTE.
THIS IS THE DEMON...
...WHO KILLED MY SISTER.
EVERYONE'S HAPPINESS? RIDICULOUS!
SHE DIDN'T LIKE IT AND PLEADED FOR HELP.
SO I HELPED HER, RIGHT?

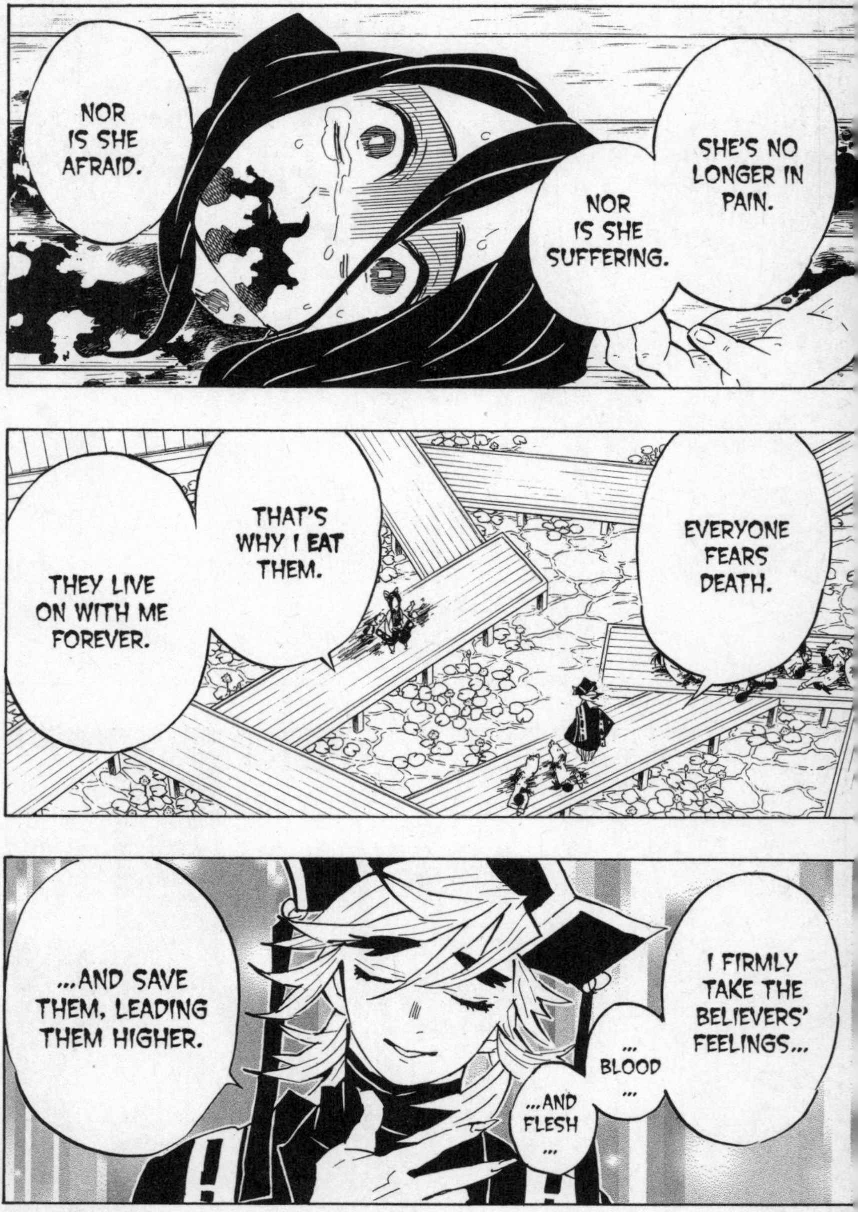
SHE'S NO LONGER IN PAIN.
NOR IS SHE SUFFERING.
NOR IS SHE AFRAID.
EVERYONE FEARS DEATH.
THAT'S WHY I EAT THEM.
THEY LIVE ON WITH ME FOREVER.
I FIRMLY TAKE THE BELIEVERS' FEELINGS...
...BLOOD...
...AND FLESH...
...AND SAVE THEM, LEADING THEM HIGHER.

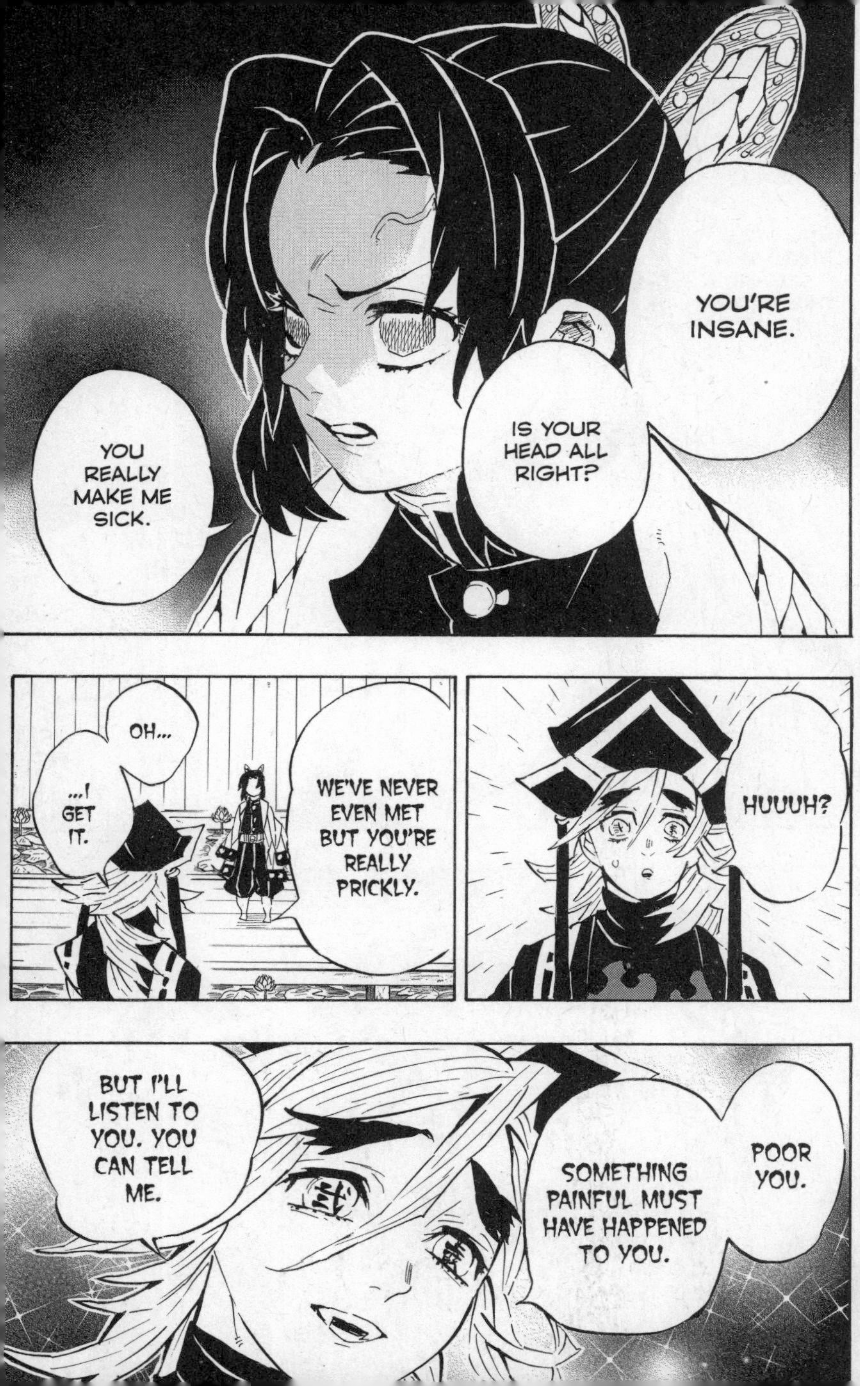
YOU'RE INSANE.
IS YOUR HEAD ALL RIGHT?
YOU REALLY MAKE ME SICK.
HUUUH?
WE'VE NEVER EVEN MET BUT YOU'RE REALLY PRICKLY.
OH...
...I GET IT.
POOR YOU.
SOMETHING PAINFUL MUST HAVE HAPPENED TO YOU.
BUT I'LL LISTEN TO YOU. YOU CAN TELL ME.

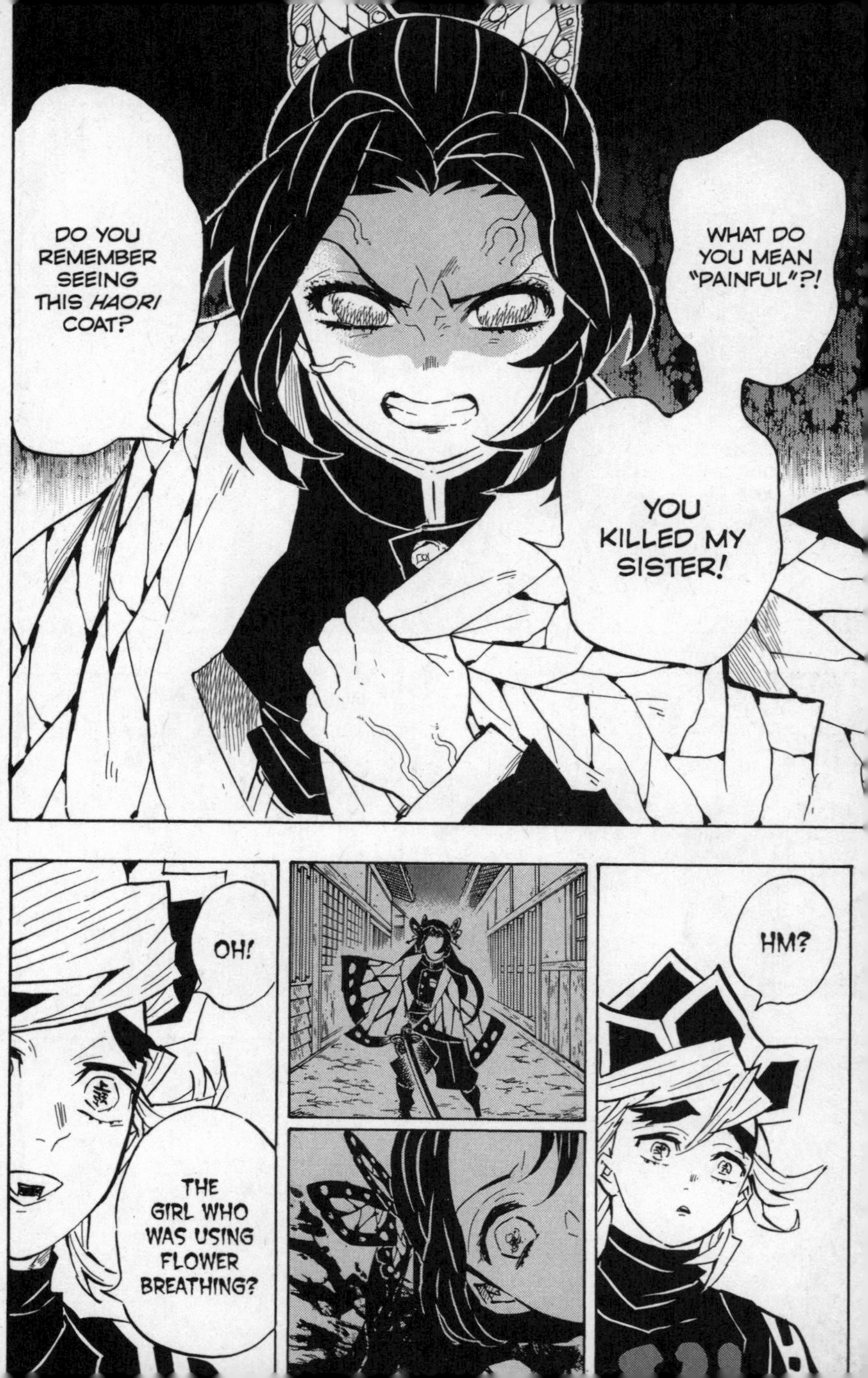
WHAT DO YOU MEAN "PAINFUL"?!
YOU KILLED MY SISTER!
DO YOU REMEMBER SEEING THIS *HAORI* COAT?
HM?
OH!
THE GIRL WHO WAS USING FLOWER BREATHING?

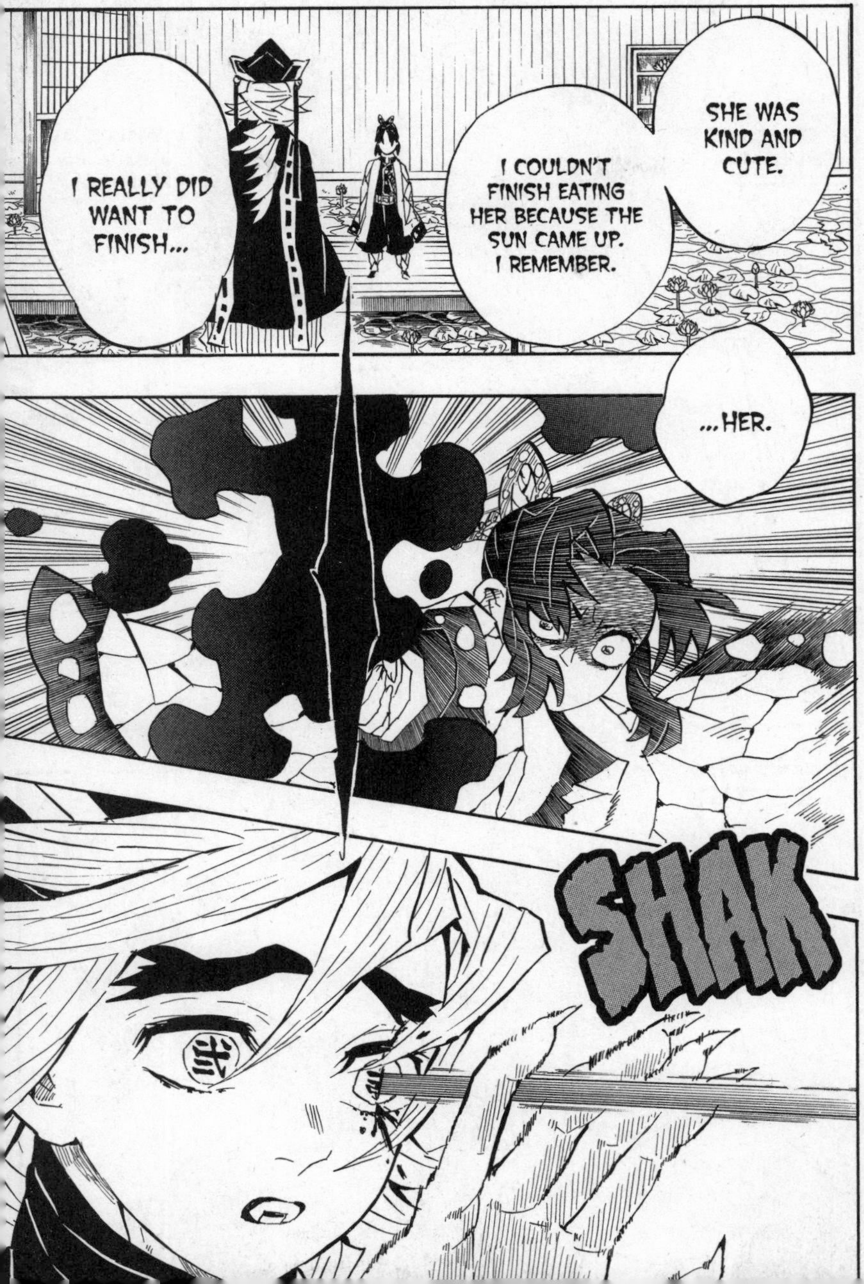
SHE WAS KIND AND CUTE.
I COULDN'T FINISH EATING HER BECAUSE THE SUN CAME UP. I REMEMBER.
I REALLY DID WANT TO FINISH...
...HER.
SHAK

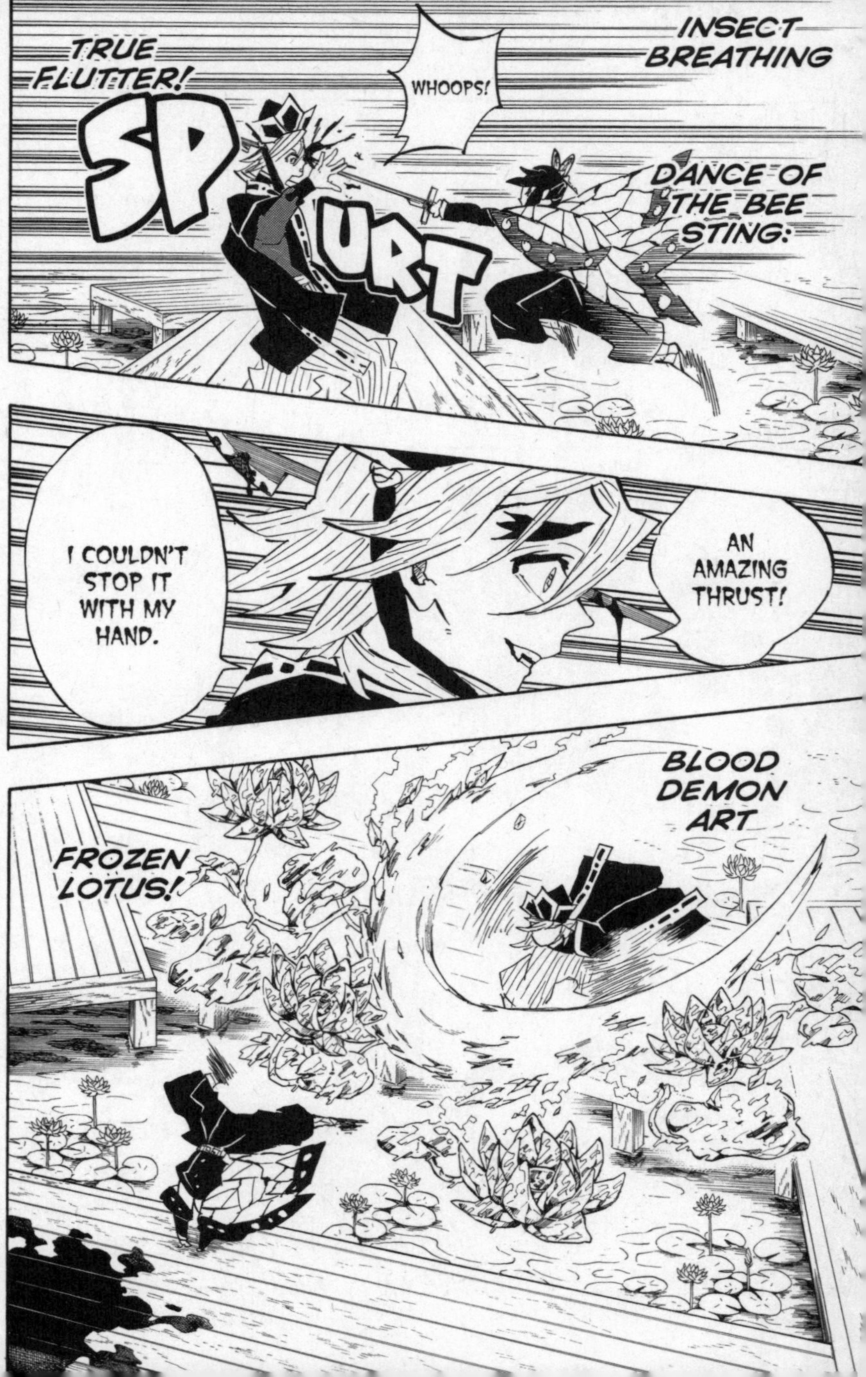
INSECT BREATHING
DANCE OF THE BEE STING:
WHOOPS!
TRUE FLUTTER!
SPURT
AN AMAZING THRUST!
I COULDN'T STOP IT WITH MY HAND.
BLOOD DEMON ART
FROZEN LOTUS!

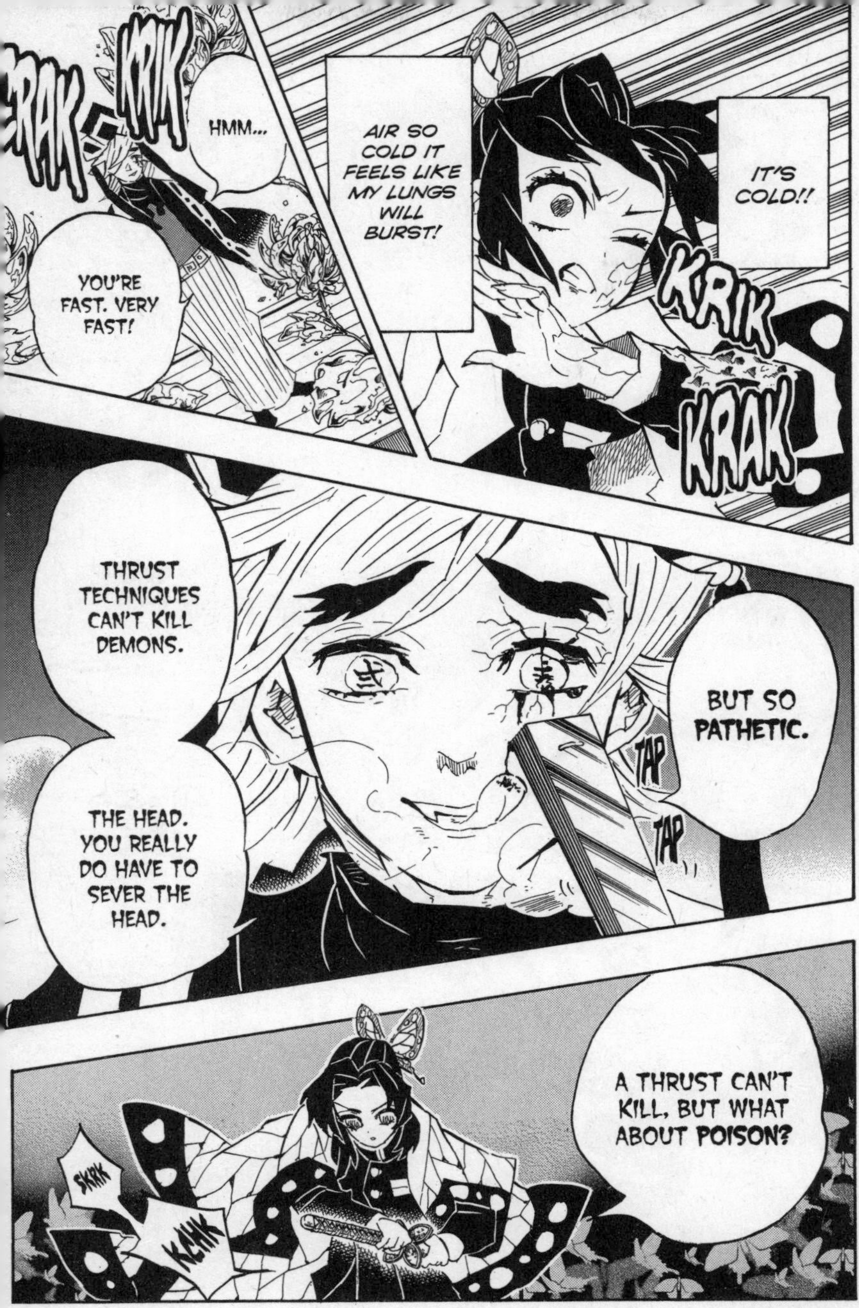
IT'S COLD!!
AIR SO COLD IT FEELS LIKE MY LUNGS WILL BURST!
KRIK
KRAK
KRIK
RAK
HMM...
YOU'RE FAST. VERY FAST!
BUT SO PATHETIC.
TAP
TAP
THRUST TECHNIQUES CAN'T KILL DEMONS.
THE HEAD. YOU REALLY DO HAVE TO SEVER THE HEAD.
A THRUST CAN'T KILL, BUT WHAT ABOUT POISON?
SKRK
KCHK

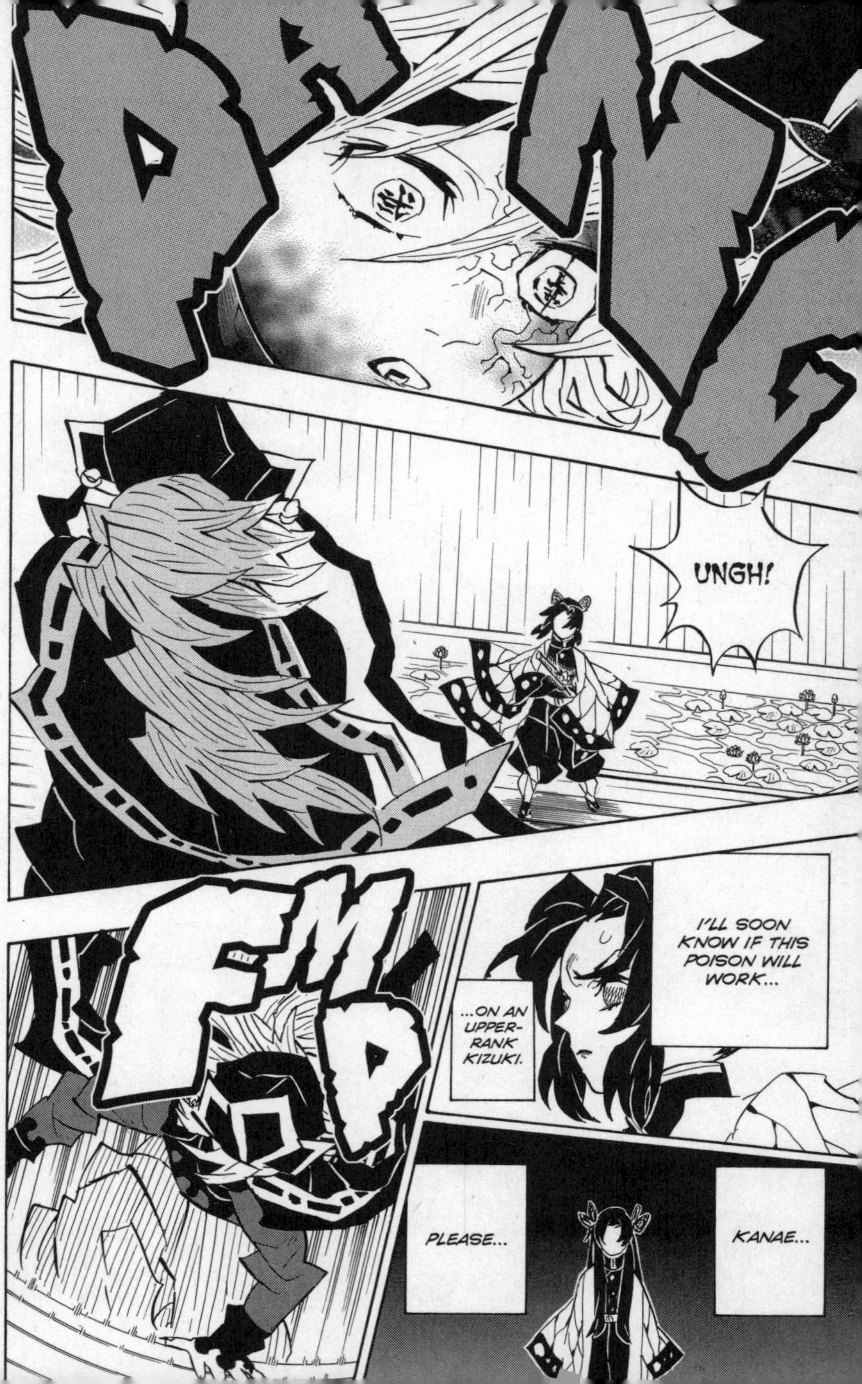
UNGH!
I'LL SOON KNOW IF THIS POISON WILL WORK...
...ON AN UPPER-RANK KIZUKI.
KANAE...
PLEASE...

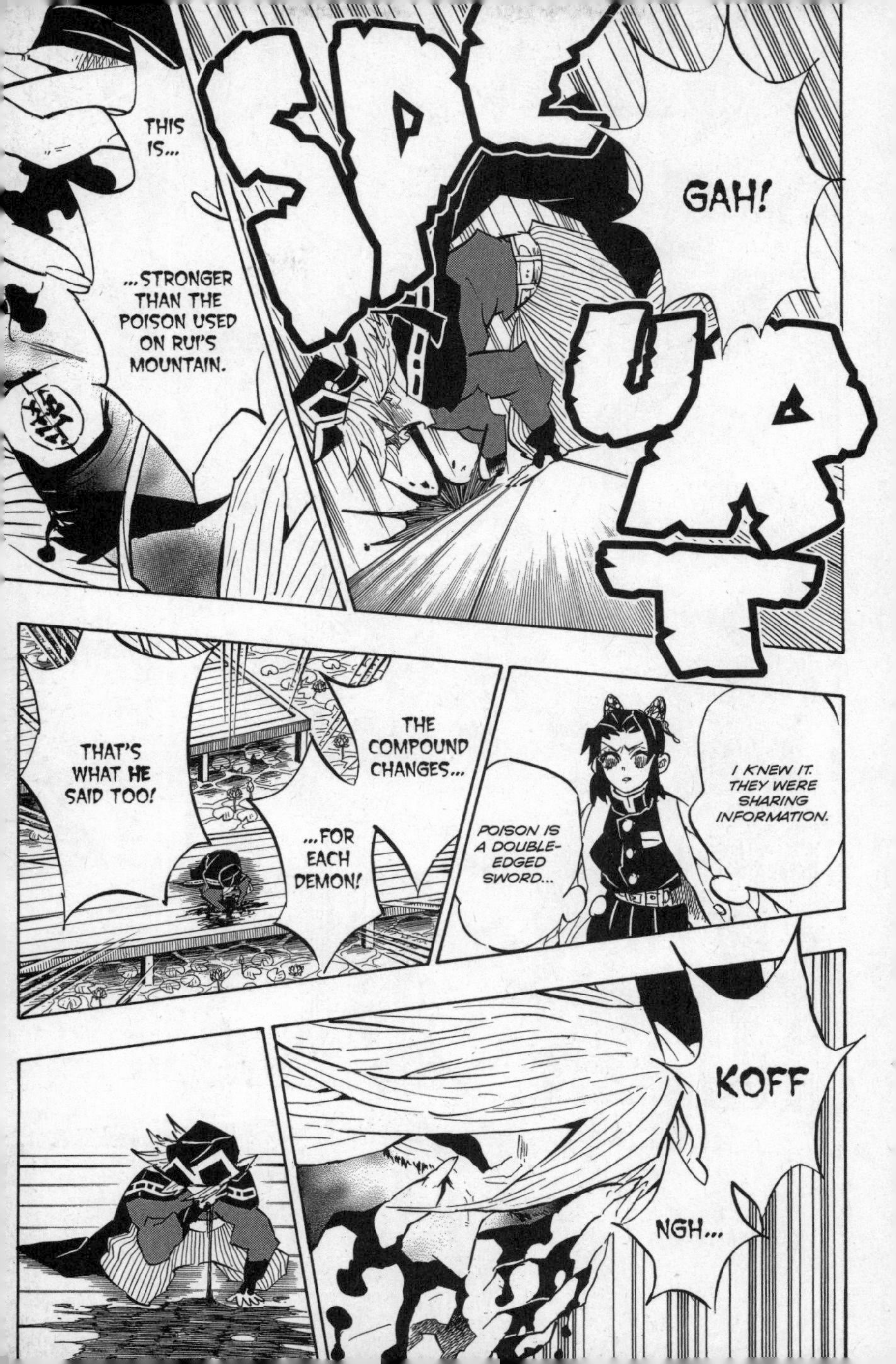
GAH!
THIS IS...
...STRONGER THAN THE POISON USED ON RUI'S MOUNTAIN.
I KNEW IT. THEY WERE SHARING INFORMATION.
POISON IS A DOUBLE-EDGED SWORD...
THE COMPOUND CHANGES...
...FOR EACH DEMON!
THAT'S WHAT HE SAID TOO!
KOFF
NGH...

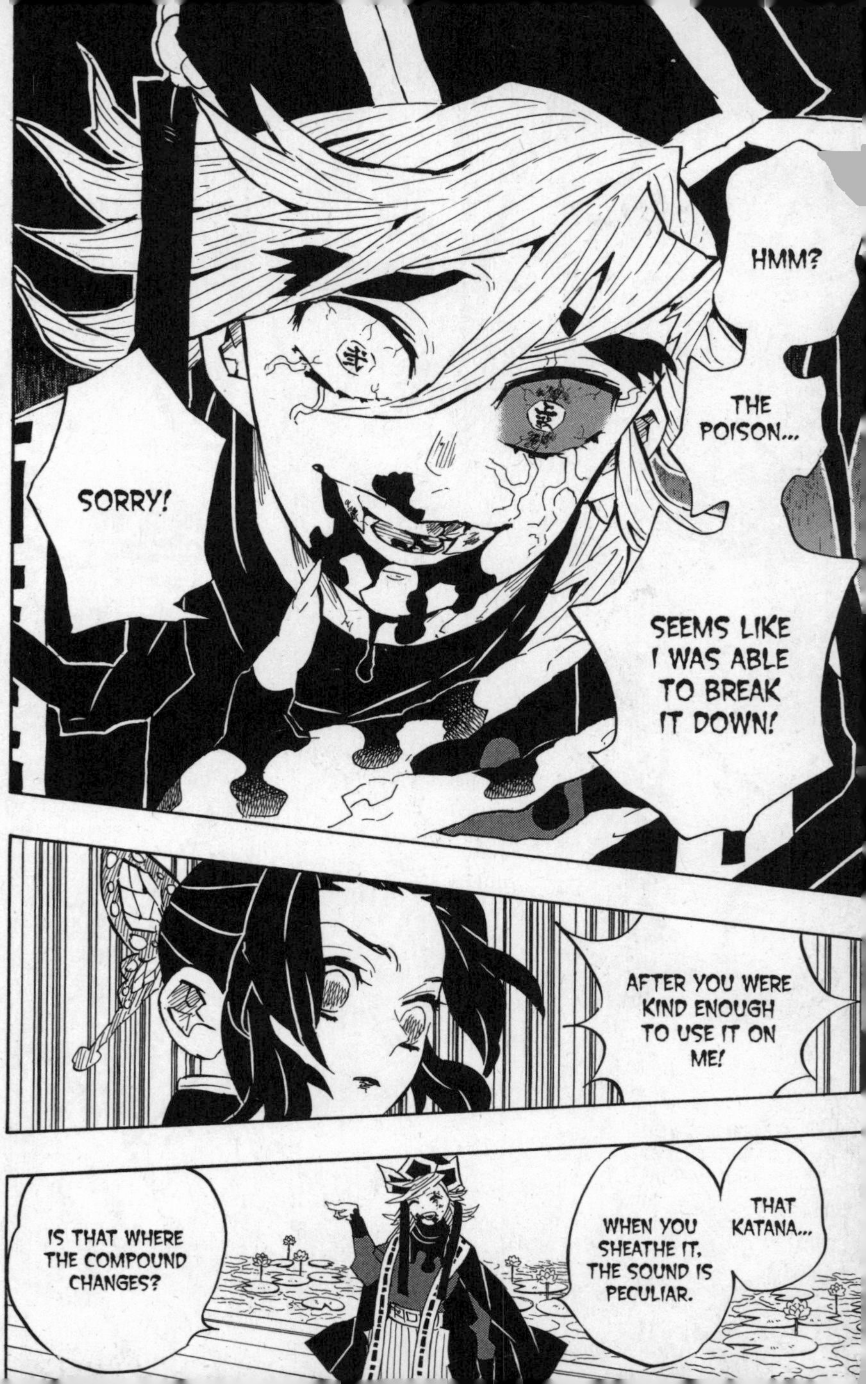
HMM?
THE POISON...
SEEMS LIKE I WAS ABLE TO BREAK IT DOWN!
SORRY!
AFTER YOU WERE KIND ENOUGH TO USE IT ON ME!
THAT KATANA...
WHEN YOU SHEATHE IT, THE SOUND IS PECULIAR.
IS THAT WHERE THE COMPOUND CHANGES?

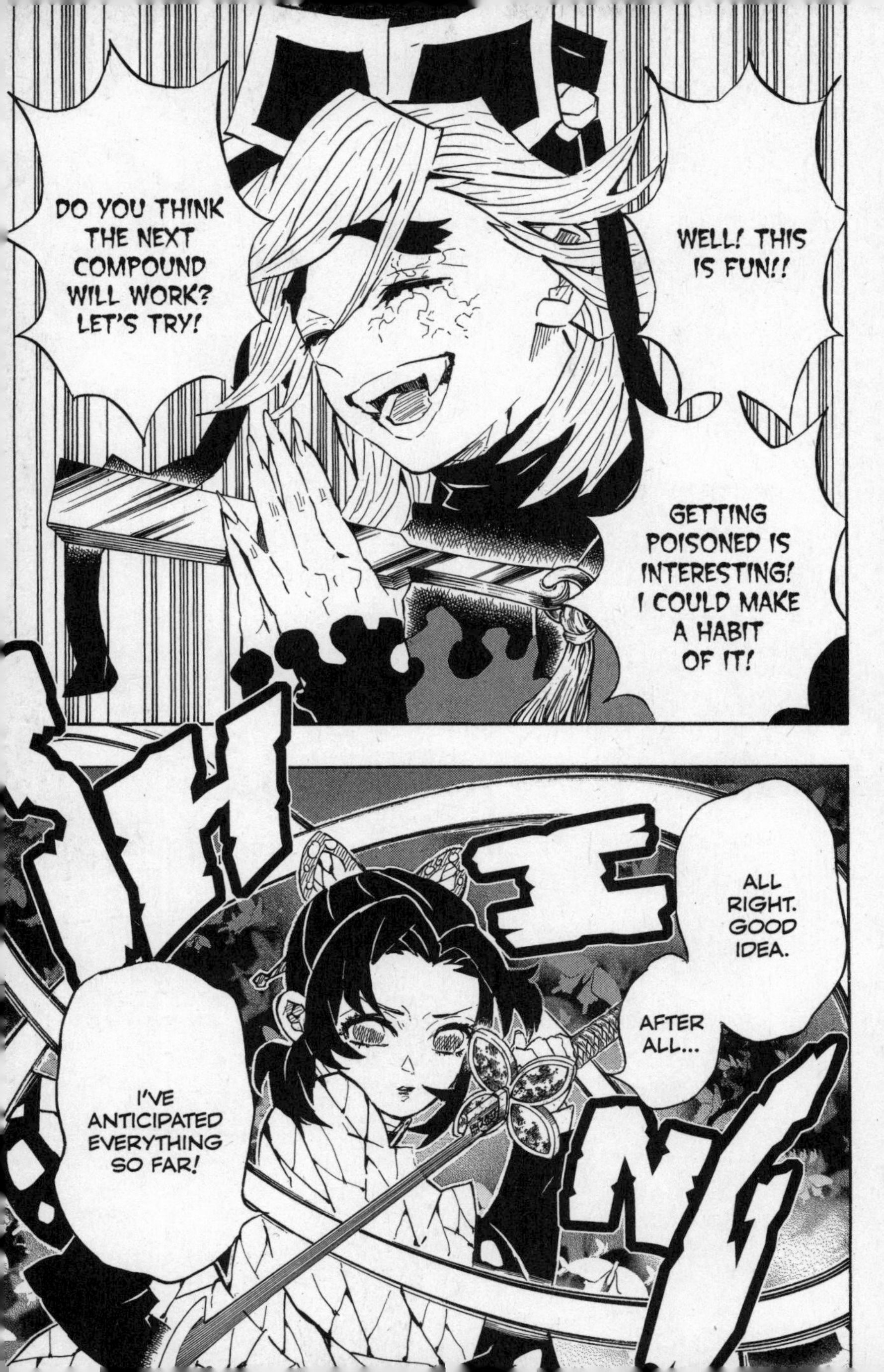
WELL! THIS IS FUN!!
GETTING POISONED IS INTERESTING! I COULD MAKE A HABIT OF IT!
DO YOU THINK THE NEXT COMPOUND WILL WORK? LET'S TRY!
ALL RIGHT. GOOD IDEA.
AFTER ALL...
I'VE ANTICIPATED EVERYTHING SO FAR!

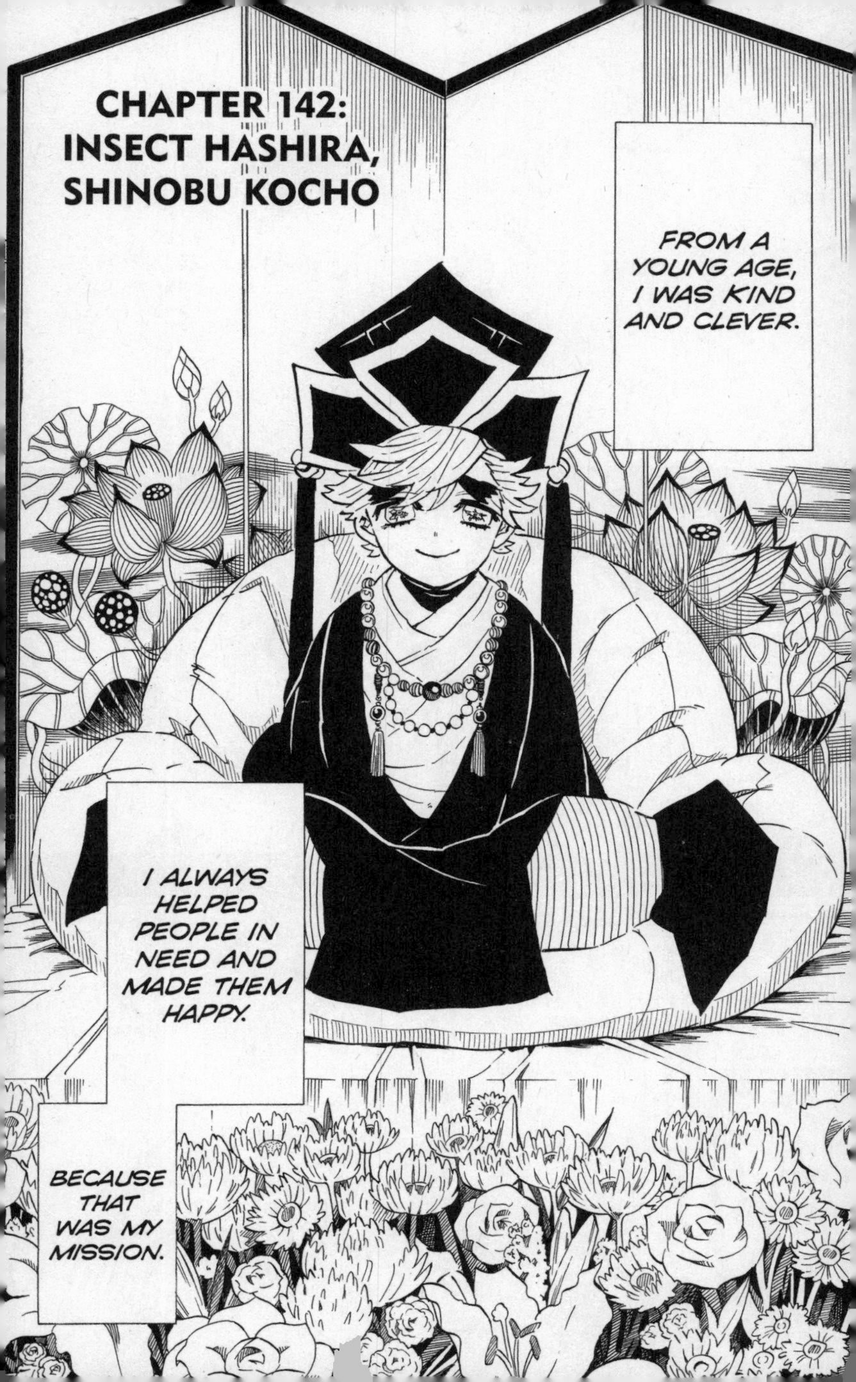
CHAPTER 142: INSECT HASHIRA, SHINOBU KOCHO
FROM A YOUNG AGE, I WAS KIND AND CLEVER.
I ALWAYS HELPED PEOPLE IN NEED AND MADE THEM HAPPY.
BECAUSE THAT WAS MY MISSION.

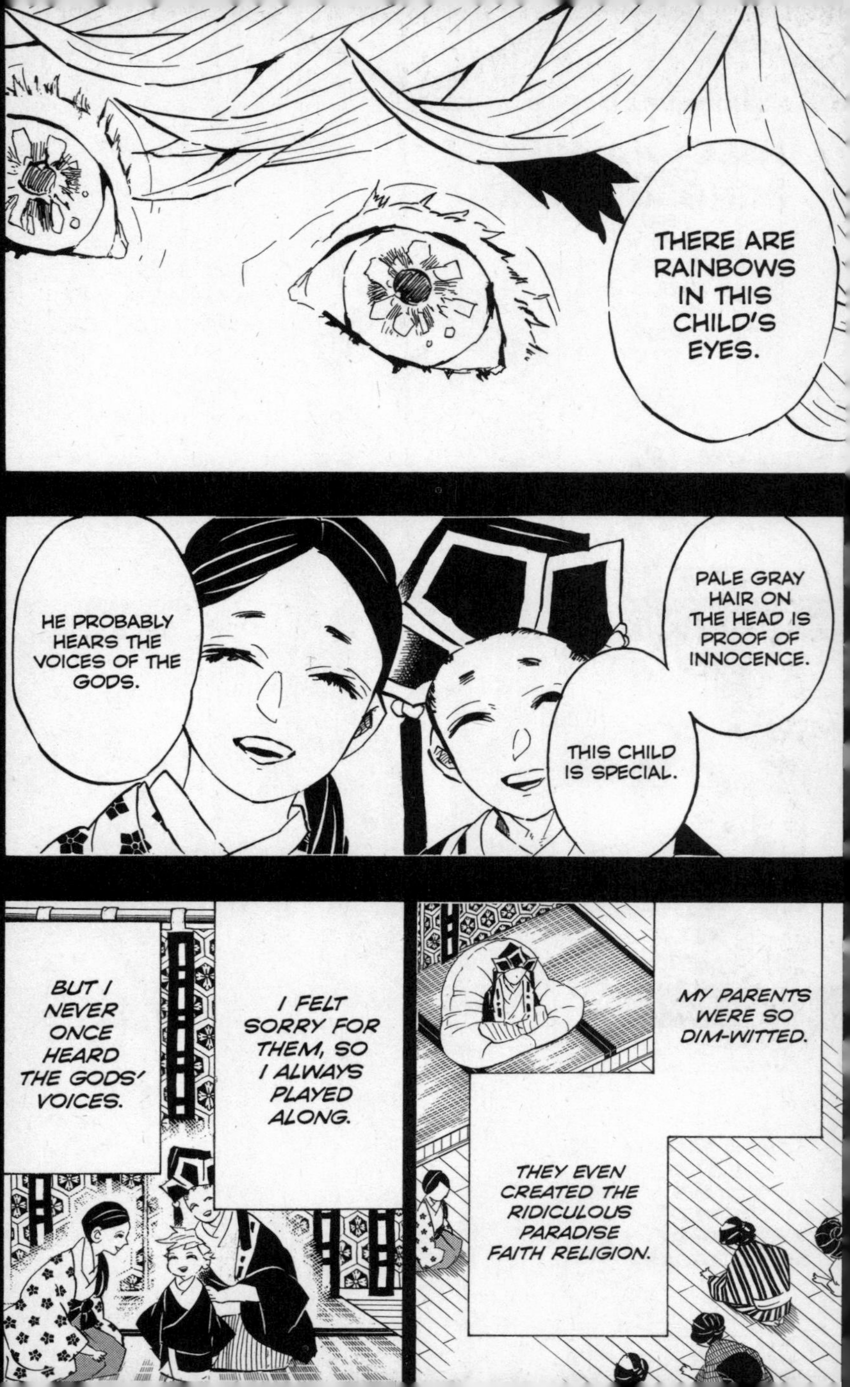
THERE ARE RAINBOWS IN THIS CHILD'S EYES.
PALE GRAY HAIR ON THE HEAD IS PROOF OF INNOCENCE.
THIS CHILD IS SPECIAL.
HE PROBABLY HEARS THE VOICES OF THE GODS.
MY PARENTS WERE SO DIM-WITTED.
THEY EVEN CREATED THE RIDICULOUS PARADISE FAITH RELIGION.
I FELT SORRY FOR THEM, SO I ALWAYS PLAYED ALONG.
BUT I NEVER ONCE HEARD THE GODS' VOICES.

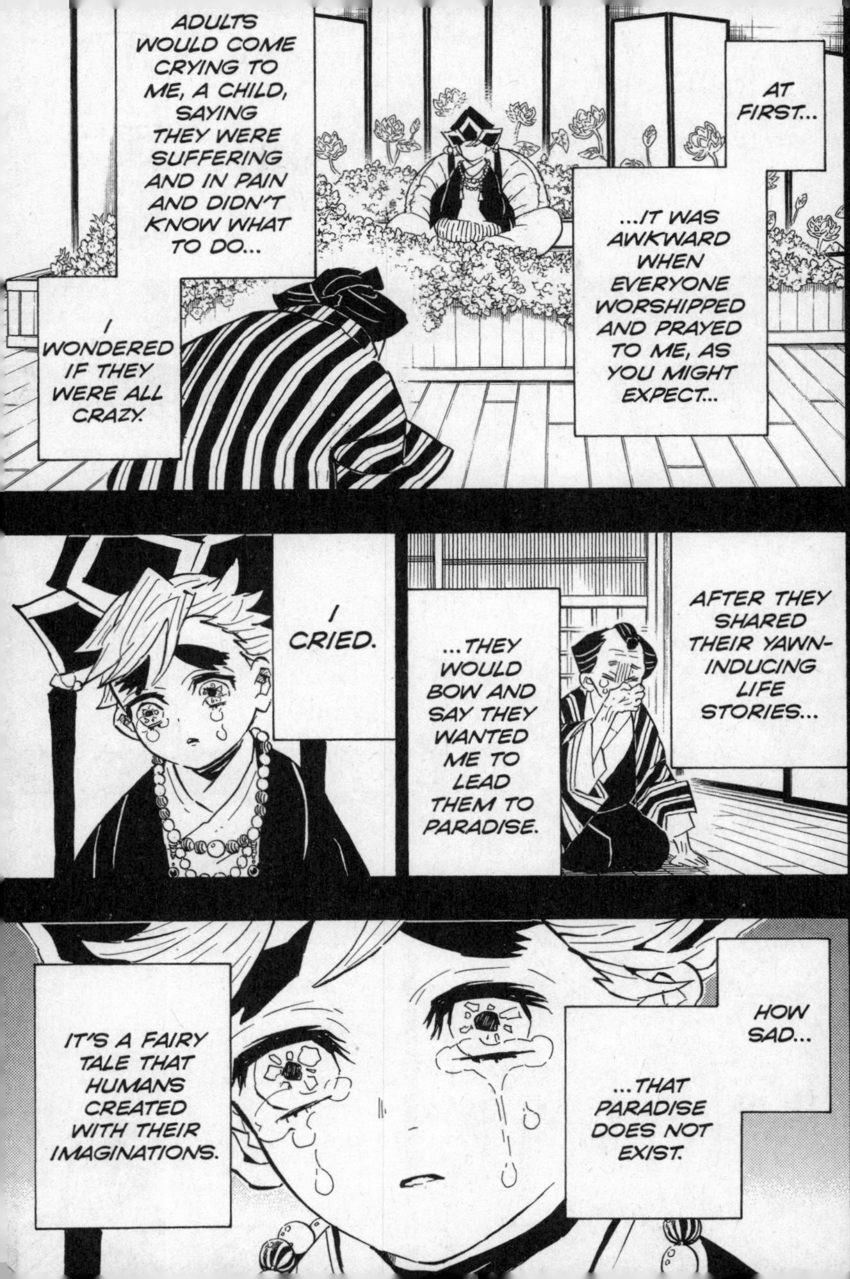
AT FIRST...
...IT WAS AWKWARD WHEN EVERYONE WORSHIPPED AND PRAYED TO ME, AS YOU MIGHT EXPECT...
ADULTS WOULD COME CRYING TO ME, A CHILD, SAYING THEY WERE SUFFERING AND IN PAIN AND DIDN'T KNOW WHAT TO DO...
I WONDERED IF THEY WERE ALL CRAZY.
AFTER THEY SHARED THEIR YAWN-INDUCING LIFE STORIES...
...THEY WOULD BOW AND SAY THEY WANTED ME TO LEAD THEM TO PARADISE.
I CRIED.
HOW SAD...
...THAT PARADISE DOES NOT EXIST.
IT'S A FAIRY TALE THAT HUMANS CREATED WITH THEIR IMAGINATIONS.

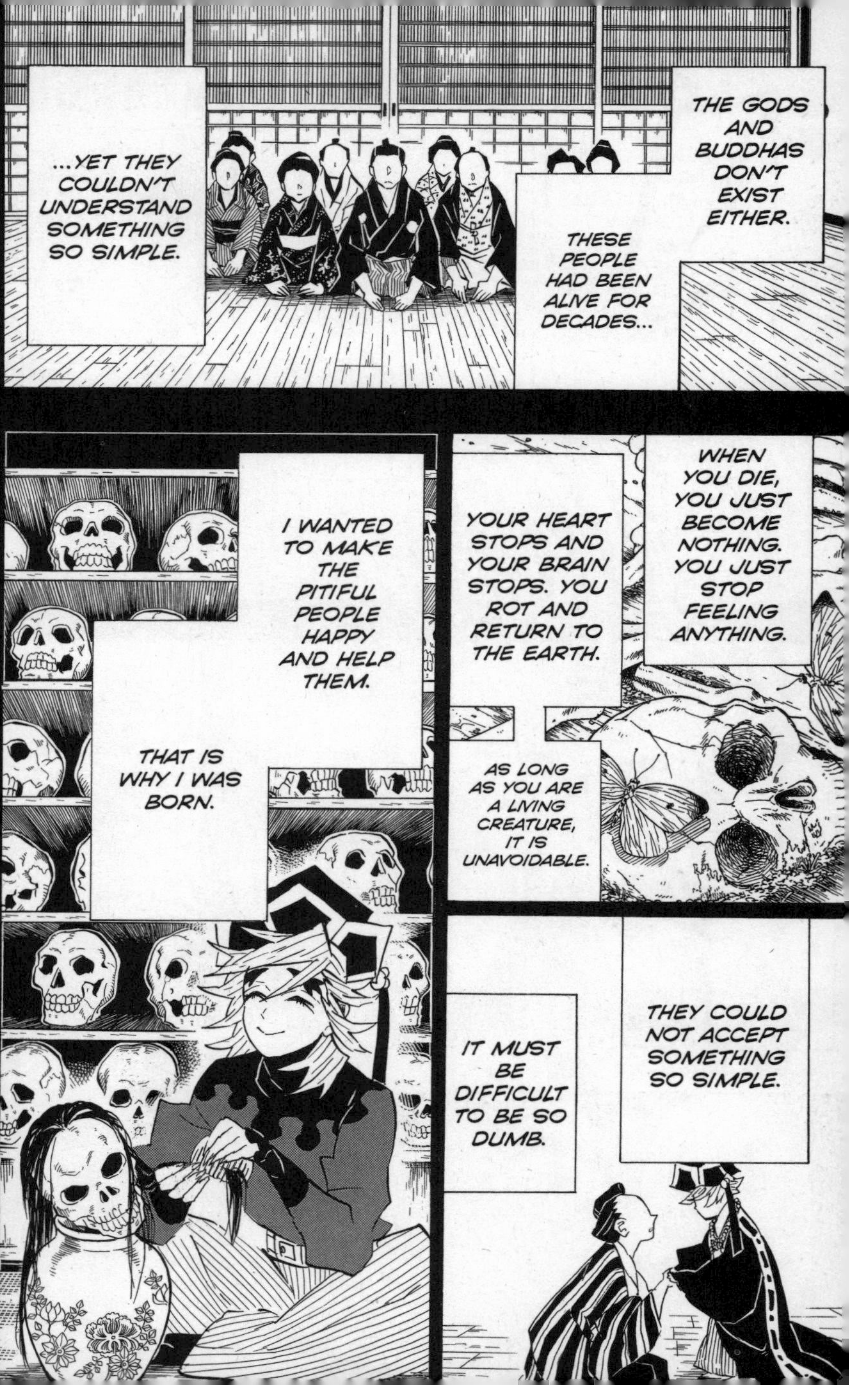
THE GODS AND BUDDHAS DON'T EXIST EITHER.
THESE PEOPLE HAD BEEN ALIVE FOR DECADES...
...YET THEY COULDN'T UNDERSTAND SOMETHING SO SIMPLE.
WHEN YOU DIE, YOU JUST BECOME NOTHING. YOU JUST STOP FEELING ANYTHING.
YOUR HEART STOPS AND YOUR BRAIN STOPS. YOU ROT AND RETURN TO THE EARTH.
AS LONG AS YOU ARE A LIVING CREATURE, IT IS UNAVOIDABLE.
THEY COULD NOT ACCEPT SOMETHING SO SIMPLE.
IT MUST BE DIFFICULT TO BE SO DUMB.
I WANTED TO MAKE THE PITIFUL PEOPLE HAPPY AND HELP THEM.
THAT IS WHY I WAS BORN.

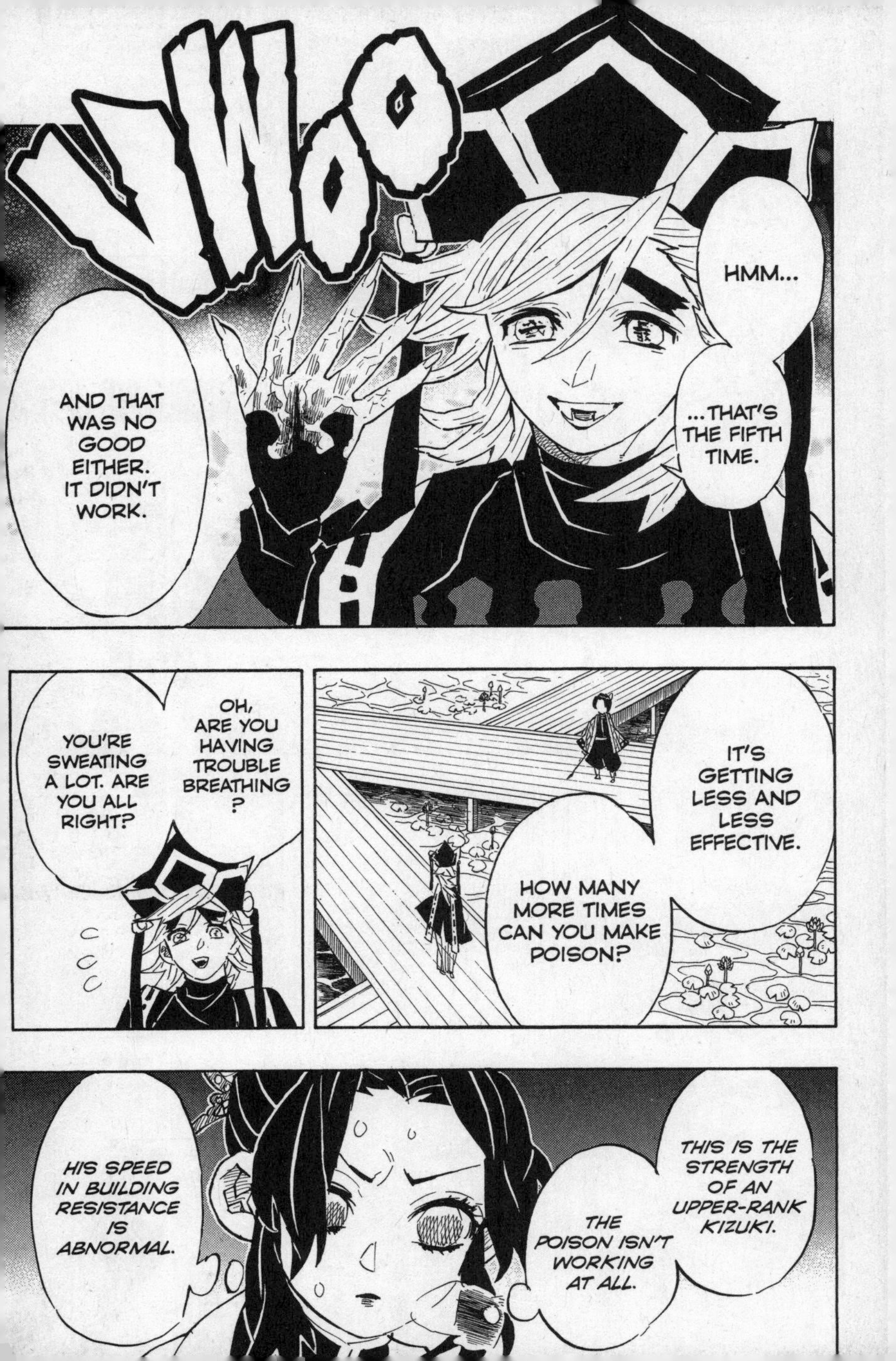
VWOO
HMM...
...THAT'S THE FIFTH TIME.
AND THAT WAS NO GOOD EITHER. IT DIDN'T WORK.
IT'S GETTING LESS AND LESS EFFECTIVE.
HOW MANY MORE TIMES CAN YOU MAKE POISON?
OH, ARE YOU HAVING TROUBLE BREATHING?
YOU'RE SWEATING A LOT. ARE YOU ALL RIGHT?
THIS IS THE STRENGTH OF AN UPPER-RANK KIZUKI.
THE POISON ISN'T WORKING AT ALL.
HIS SPEED IN BUILDING RESISTANCE IS ABNORMAL.

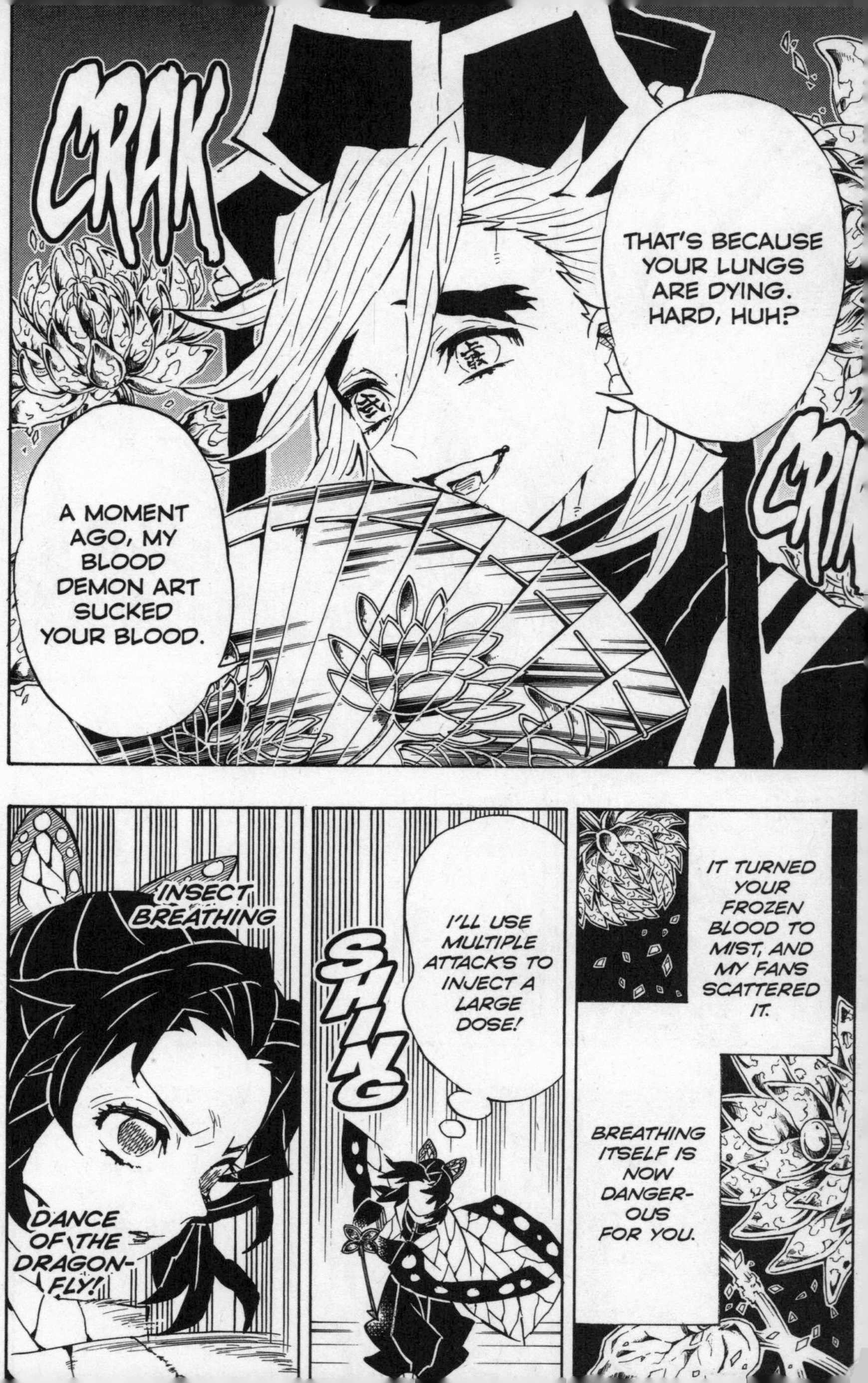
THAT'S BECAUSE YOUR LUNGS ARE DYING. HARD, HUH?
CRAK
A MOMENT AGO, MY BLOOD DEMON ART SUCKED YOUR BLOOD.
IT TURNED YOUR FROZEN BLOOD TO MIST, AND MY FANS SCATTERED IT.
BREATHING ITSELF IS NOW DANGER-OUS FOR YOU.
I'LL USE MULTIPLE ATTACKS TO INJECT A LARGE DOSE!
SHING
INSECT BREATHING
DANCE OF THE DRAGON-FLY!

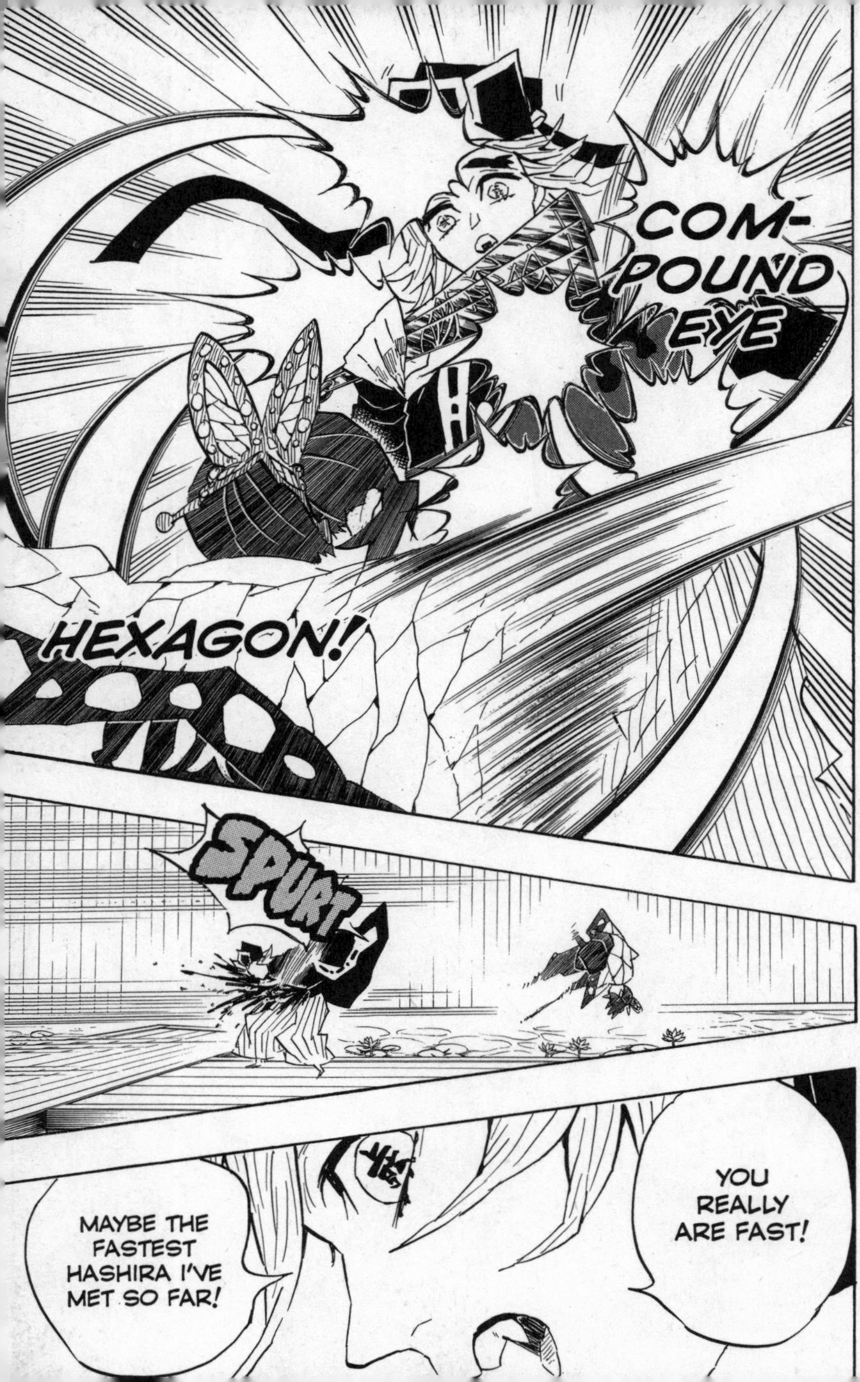
COM-POUND EYE
HEXAGON!
SPURT
YOU REALLY ARE FAST!
MAYBE THE FASTEST HASHIRA I'VE MET SO FAR!

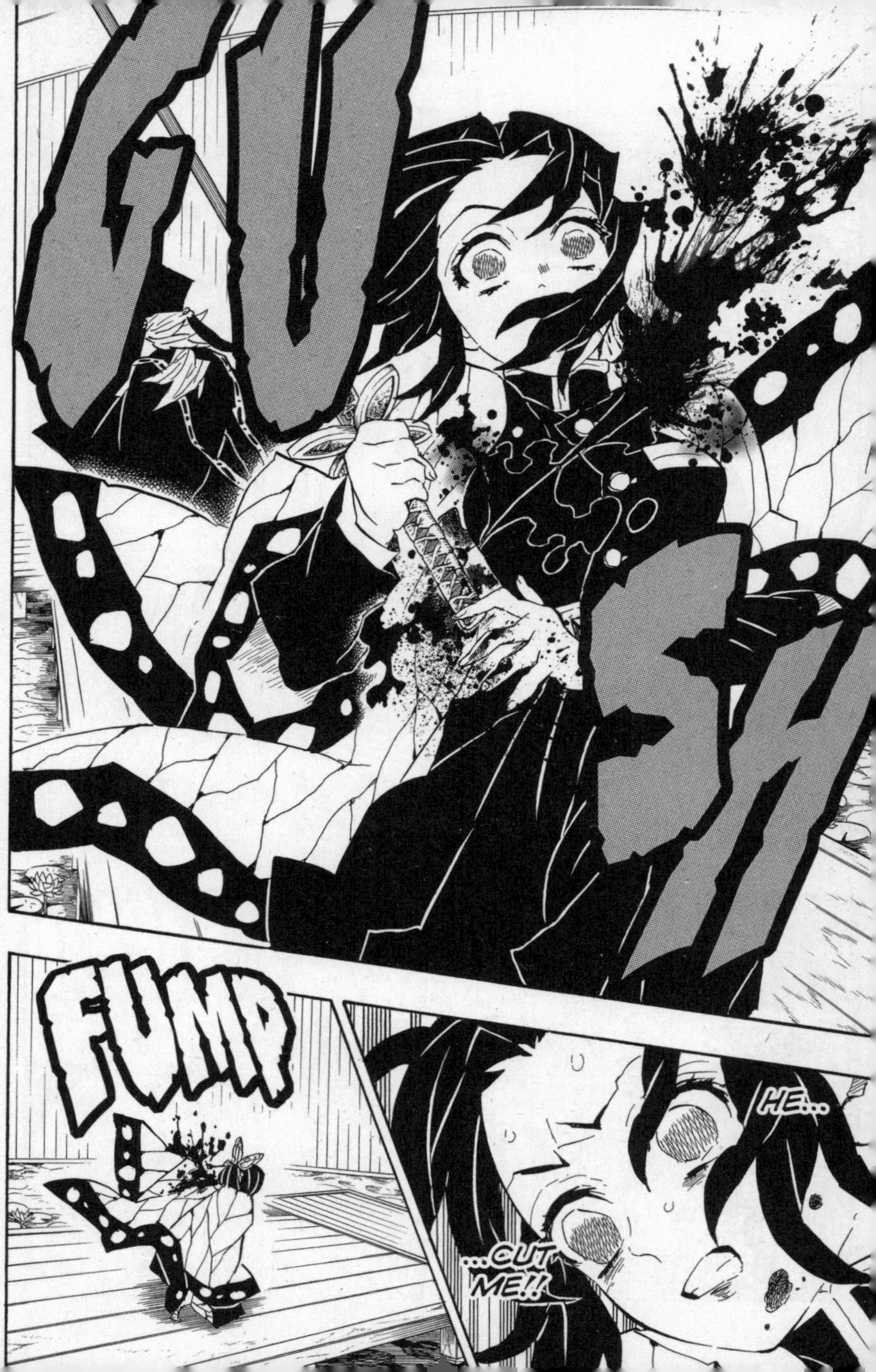
GUSH
HE...
...CUT ME!!
FUMP

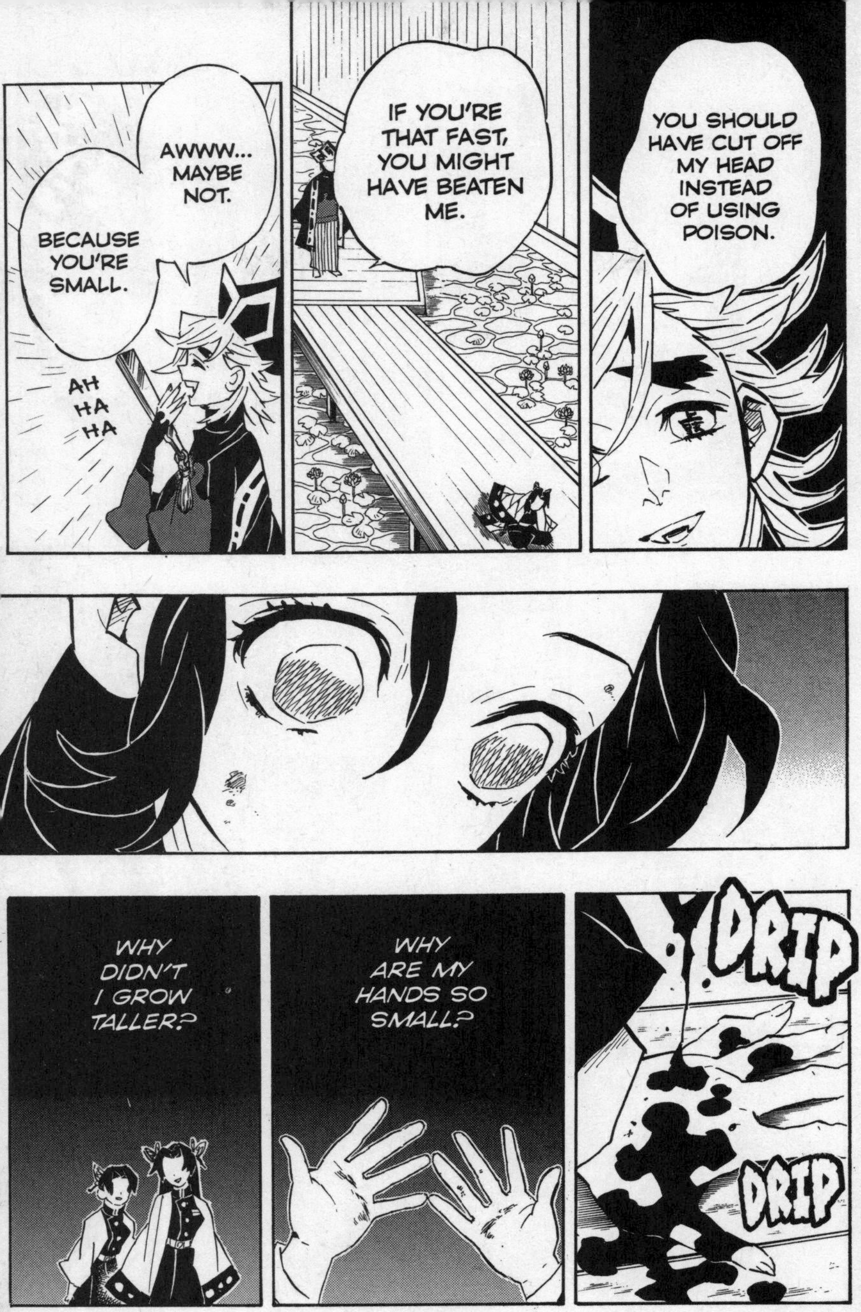
YOU SHOULD HAVE CUT OFF MY HEAD INSTEAD OF USING POISON.
IF YOU'RE THAT FAST, YOU MIGHT HAVE BEATEN ME.
AWWW... MAYBE NOT.
BECAUSE YOU'RE SMALL.
AH HA HA
DRIP
DRIP
WHY ARE MY HANDS SO SMALL?
WHY DIDN'T I GROW TALLER?

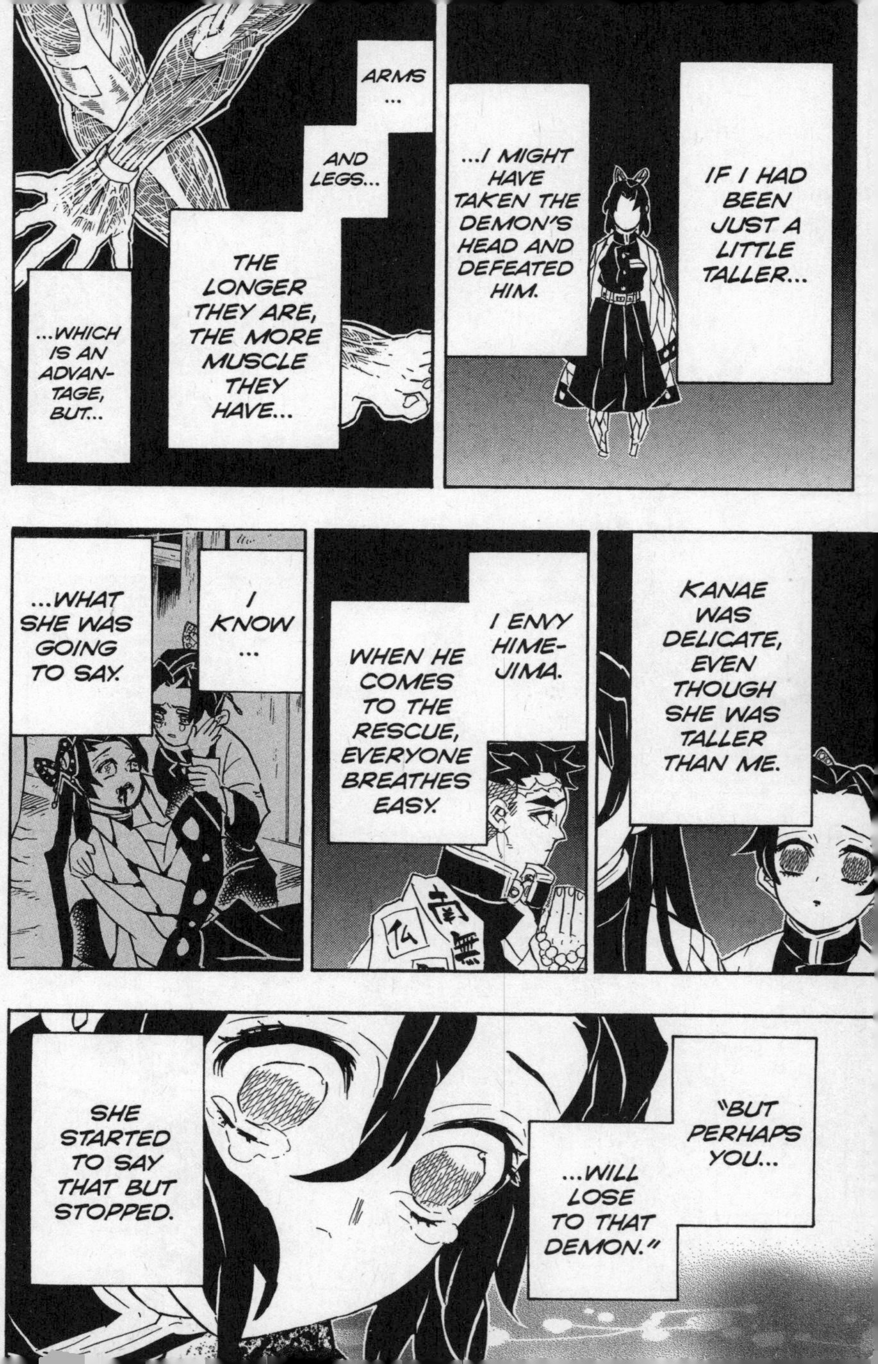
IF I HAD BEEN JUST A LITTLE TALLER...
...I MIGHT HAVE TAKEN THE DEMON'S HEAD AND DEFEATED HIM.
ARMS...
AND LEGS...
THE LONGER THEY ARE, THE MORE MUSCLE THEY HAVE...
...WHICH IS AN ADVAN-TAGE, BUT...
KANAE WAS DELICATE, EVEN THOUGH SHE WAS TALLER THAN ME.
I ENVY HIME-JIMA.
WHEN HE COMES TO THE RESCUE, EVERYONE BREATHES EASY.
I KNOW...
...WHAT SHE WAS GOING TO SAY.
"BUT PERHAPS YOU...
...WILL LOSE TO THAT DEMON."
SHE STARTED TO SAY THAT BUT STOPPED.

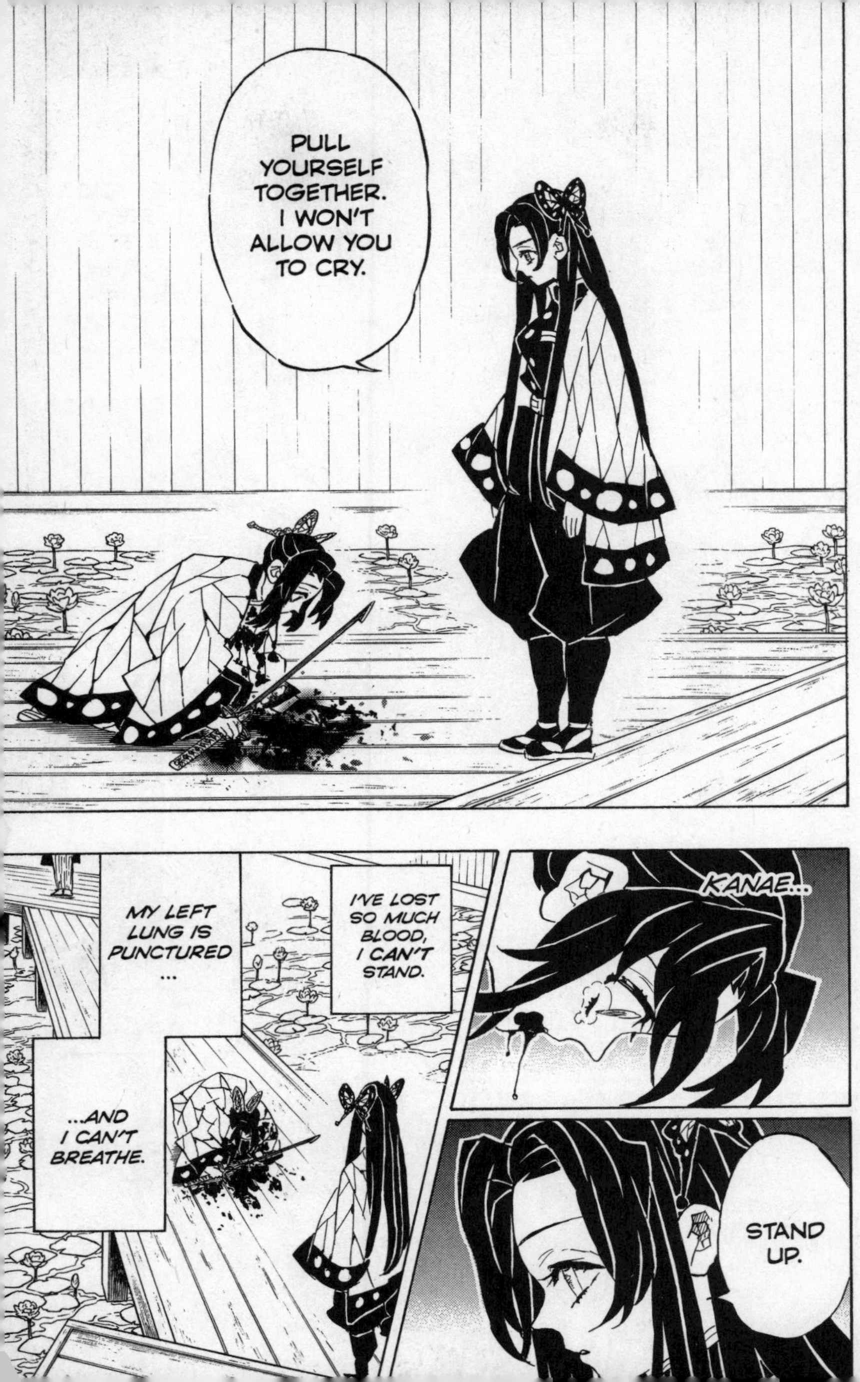
PULL YOURSELF TOGETHER. I WON'T ALLOW YOU TO CRY.
KANAE...
STAND UP.
I'VE LOST SO MUCH BLOOD, I CAN'T STAND.
MY LEFT LUNG IS PUNCTURED ...
...AND I CAN'T BREATHE.

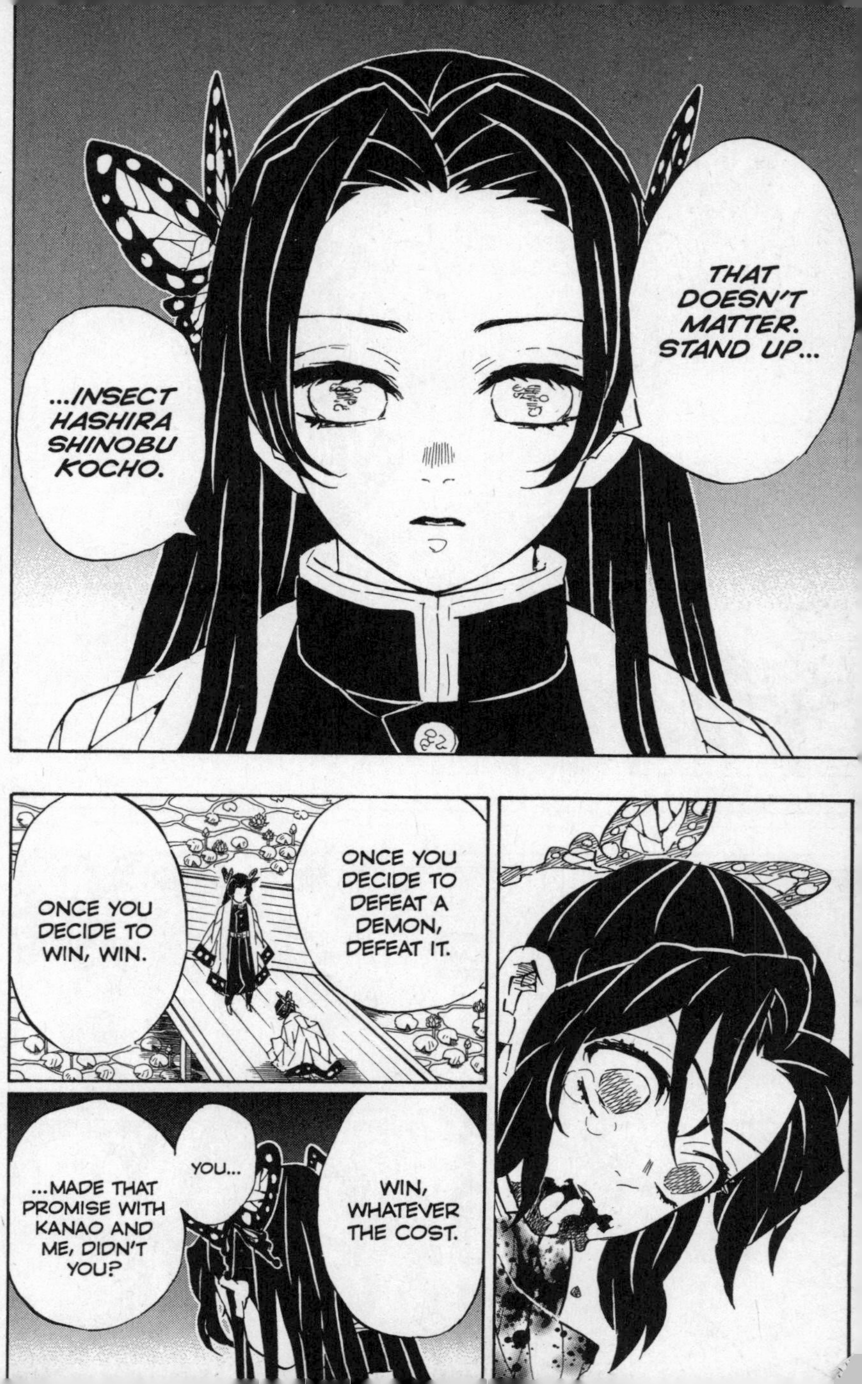
THAT DOESN'T MATTER. STAND UP...
...INSECT HASHIRA SHINOBU KOCHO.
ONCE YOU DECIDE TO DEFEAT A DEMON, DEFEAT IT.
ONCE YOU DECIDE TO WIN, WIN.
WIN, WHATEVER THE COST.
YOU...
...MADE THAT PROMISE WITH KANAO AND ME, DIDN'T YOU?

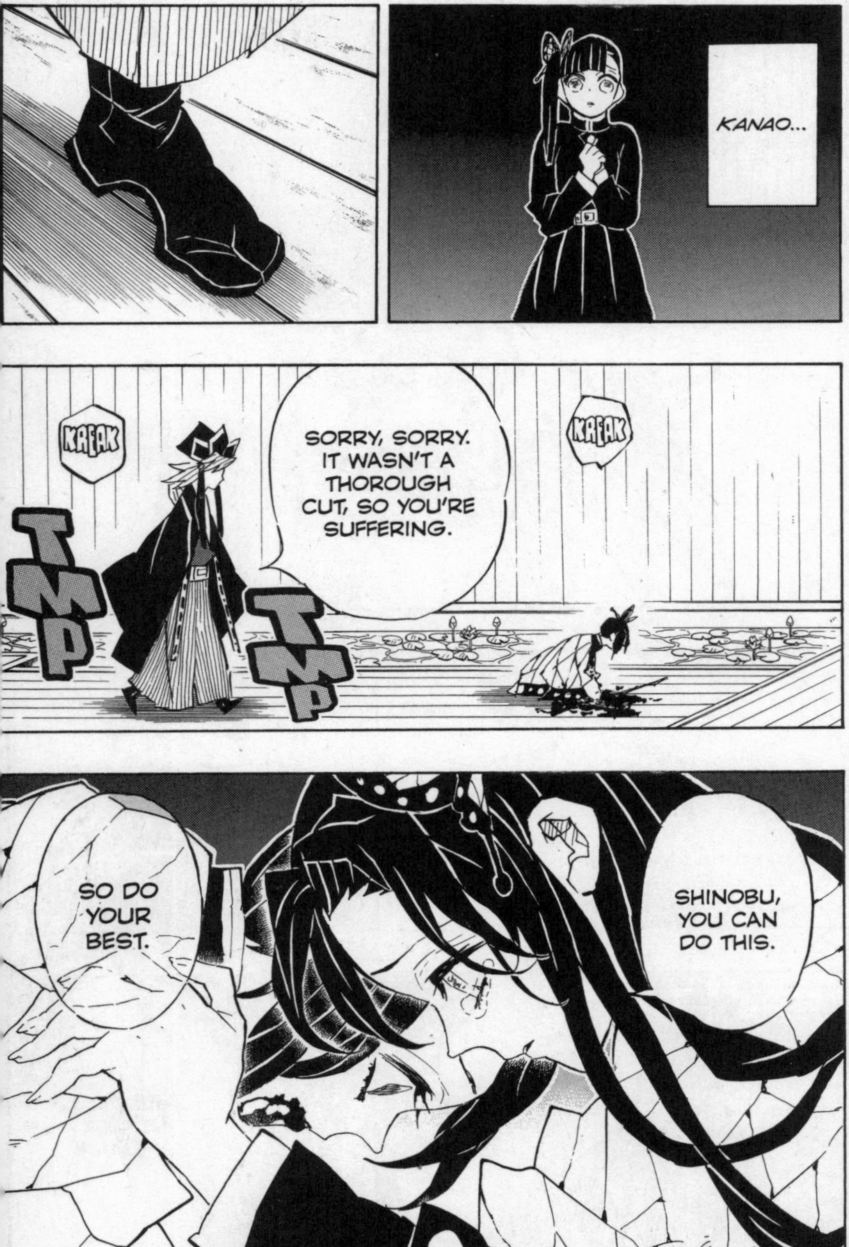
KANAO...
KREAK
SORRY, SORRY. IT WASN'T A THOROUGH CUT, SO YOU'RE SUFFERING.
TMP
KREAK
TMP
SHINOBU, YOU CAN DO THIS.
SO DO YOUR BEST.

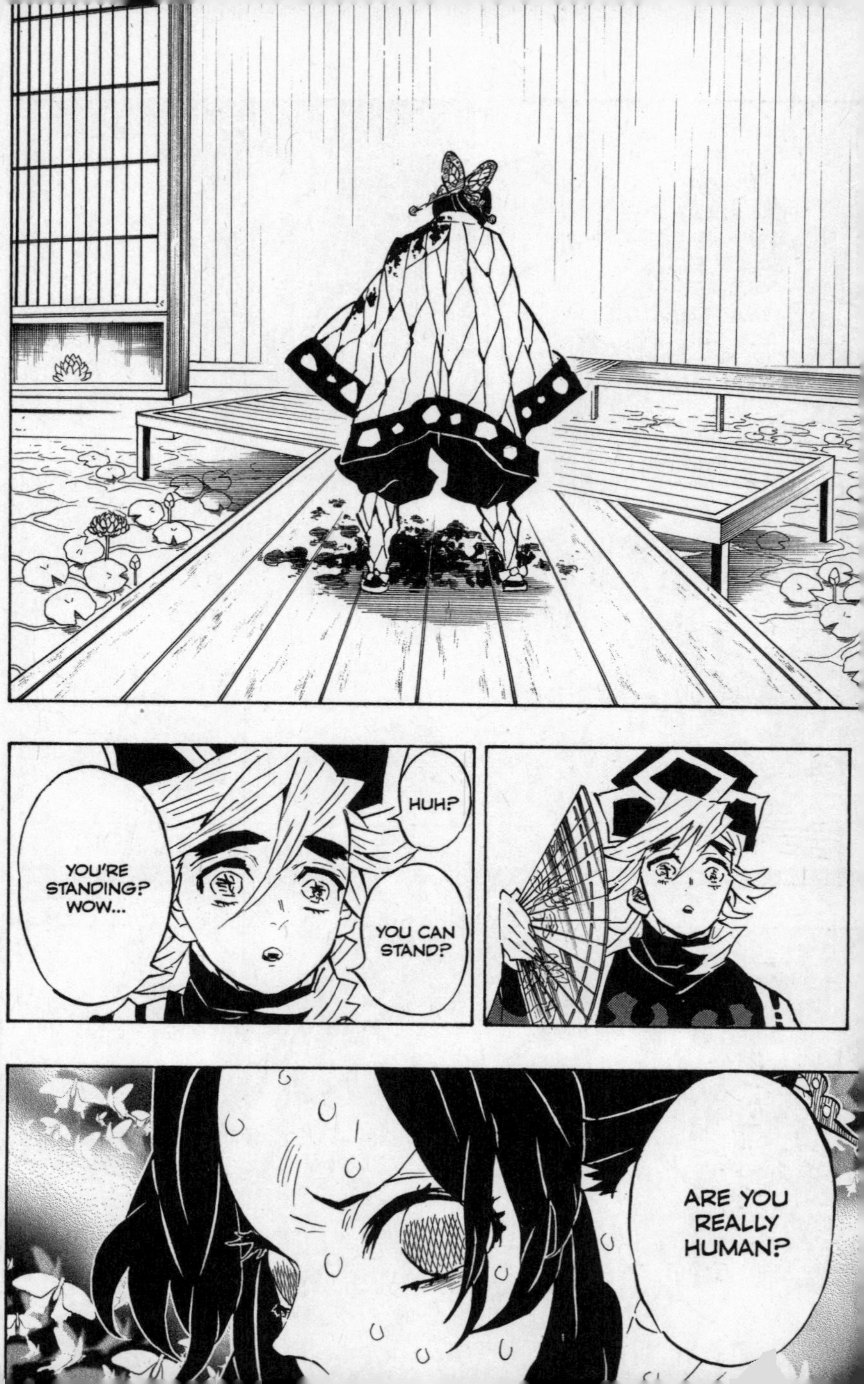
HUH?
YOU CAN STAND?
YOU'RE STANDING? WOW...
ARE YOU REALLY HUMAN?

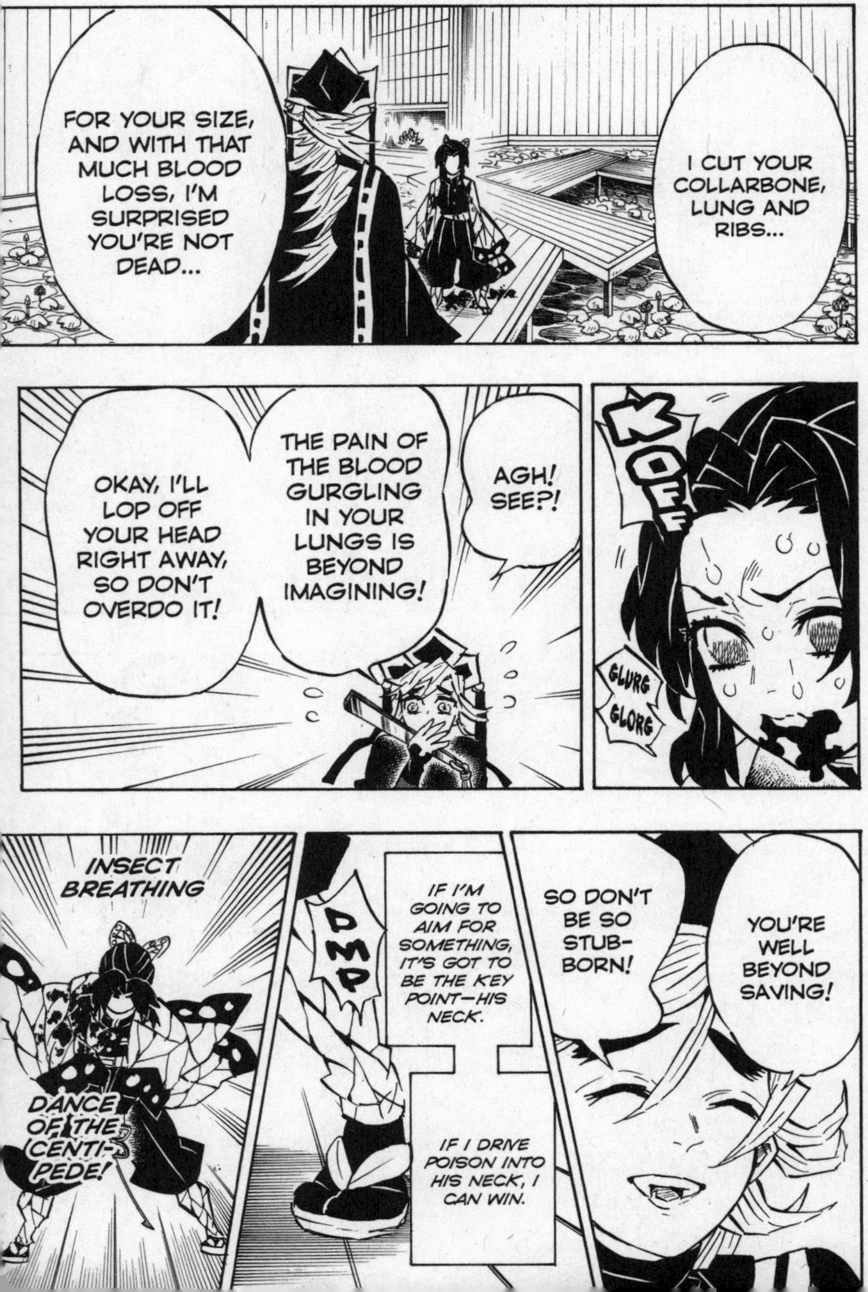
I CUT YOUR COLLARBONE, LUNG AND RIBS...
FOR YOUR SIZE, AND WITH THAT MUCH BLOOD LOSS, I'M SURPRISED YOU'RE NOT DEAD...
KOFF
GLURG GLORG
AGH! SEE?!
THE PAIN OF THE BLOOD GURGLING IN YOUR LUNGS IS BEYOND IMAGINING!
OKAY, I'LL LOP OFF YOUR HEAD RIGHT AWAY, SO DON'T OVERDO IT!
YOU'RE WELL BEYOND SAVING!
SO DON'T BE SO STUB-BORN!
IF I'M GOING TO AIM FOR SOMETHING, IT'S GOT TO BE THE KEY POINT—HIS NECK.
DMP
IF I DRIVE POISON INTO HIS NECK, I CAN WIN.
INSECT BREATHING
DANCE OF THE CENTI-PEDE!

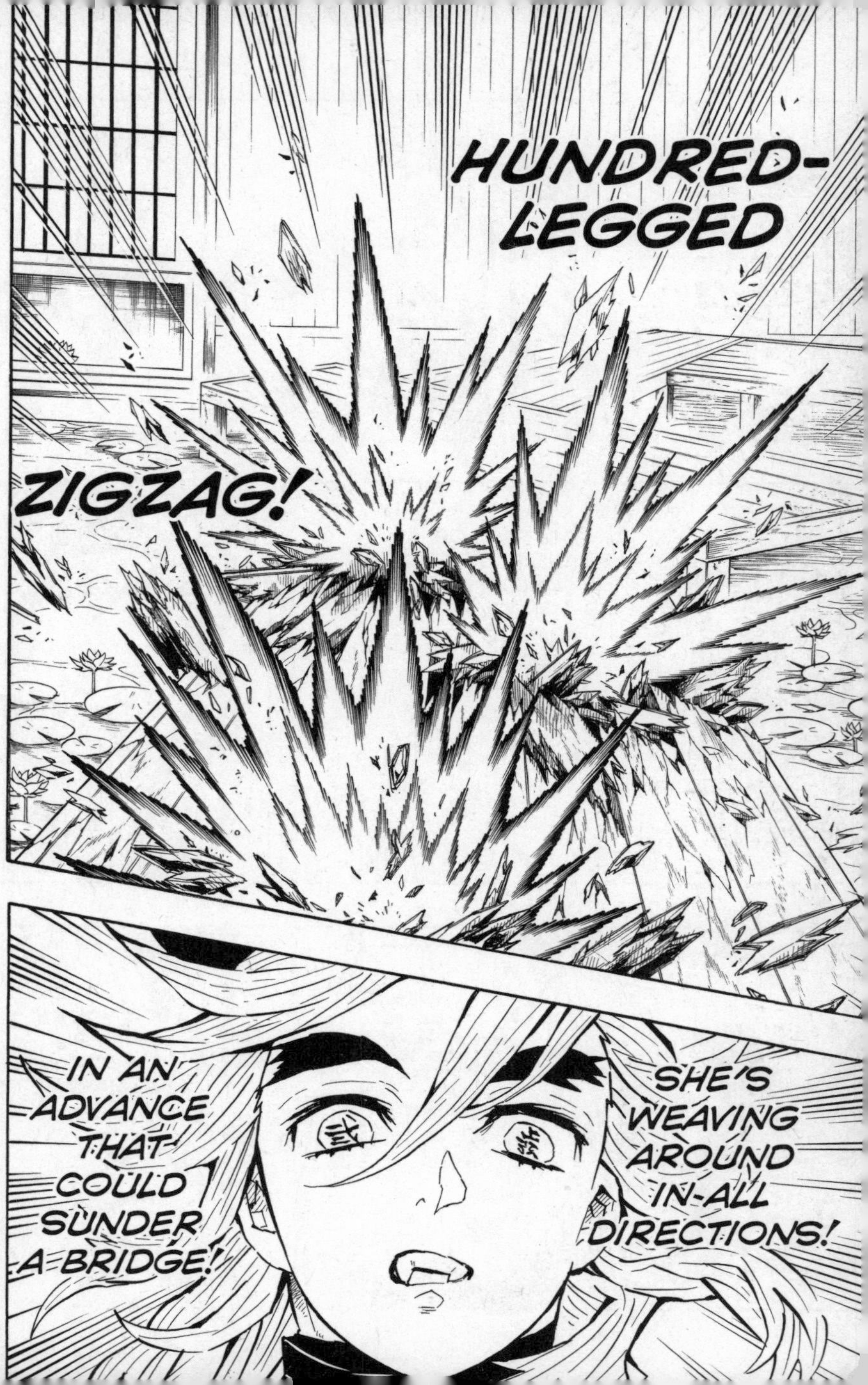
HUNDRED-LEGGED
ZIGZAG!
SHE'S WEAVING AROUND IN ALL DIRECTIONS!
IN AN ADVANCE THAT COULD SUNDER A BRIDGE!

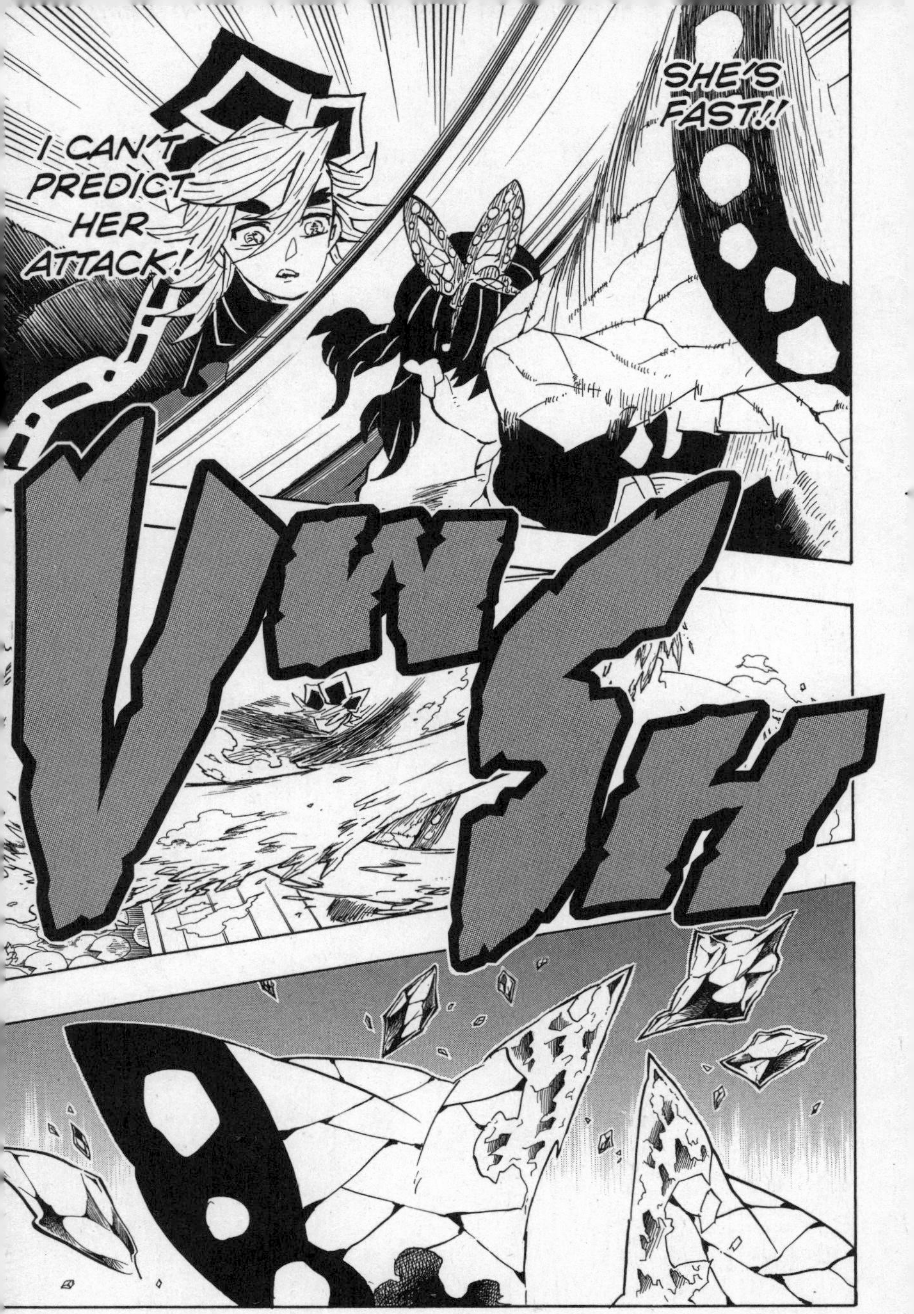
SHE'S FAST!!
I CAN'T PREDICT HER ATTACK!
VWSH

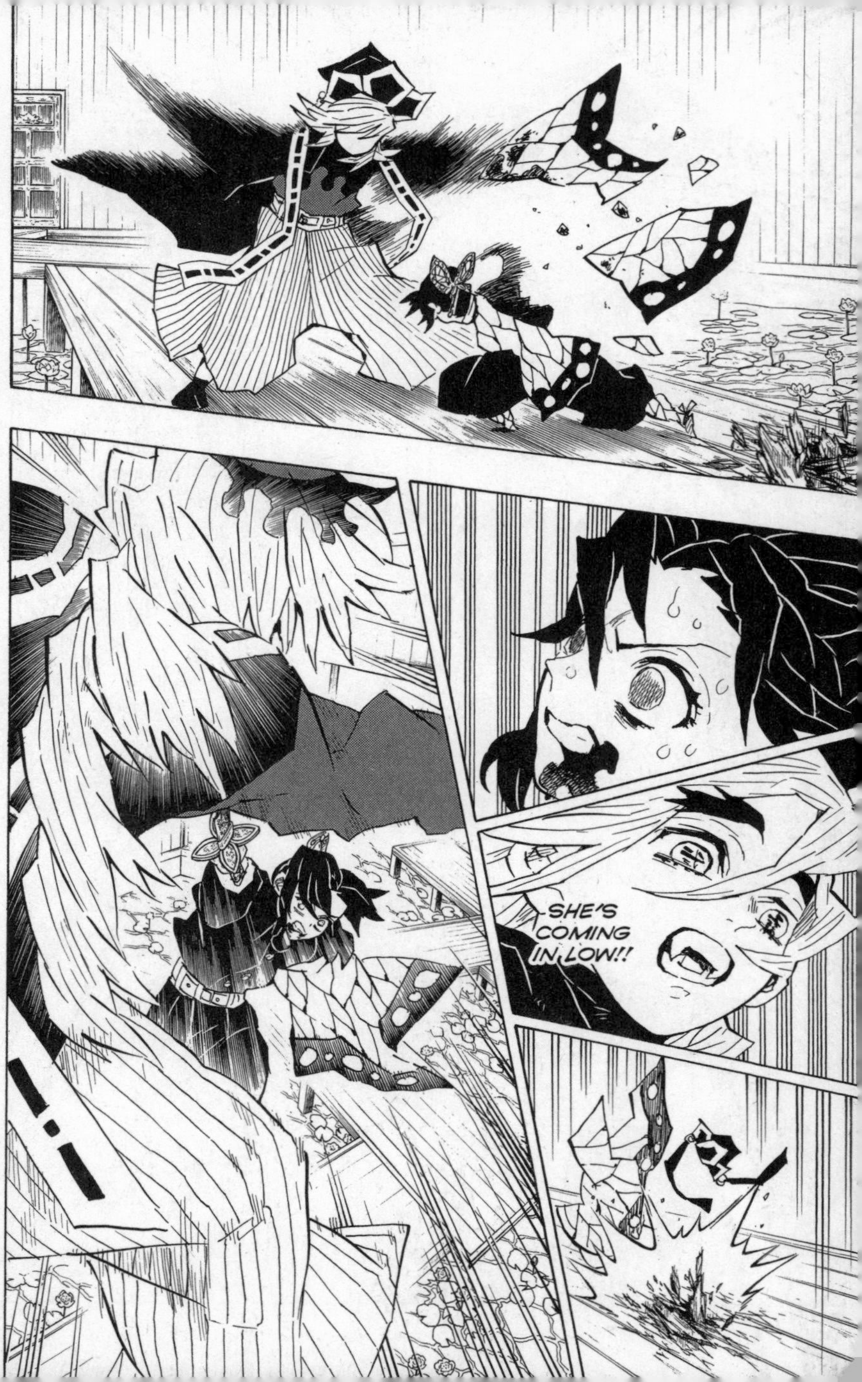
SHE'S COMING IN LOW!!

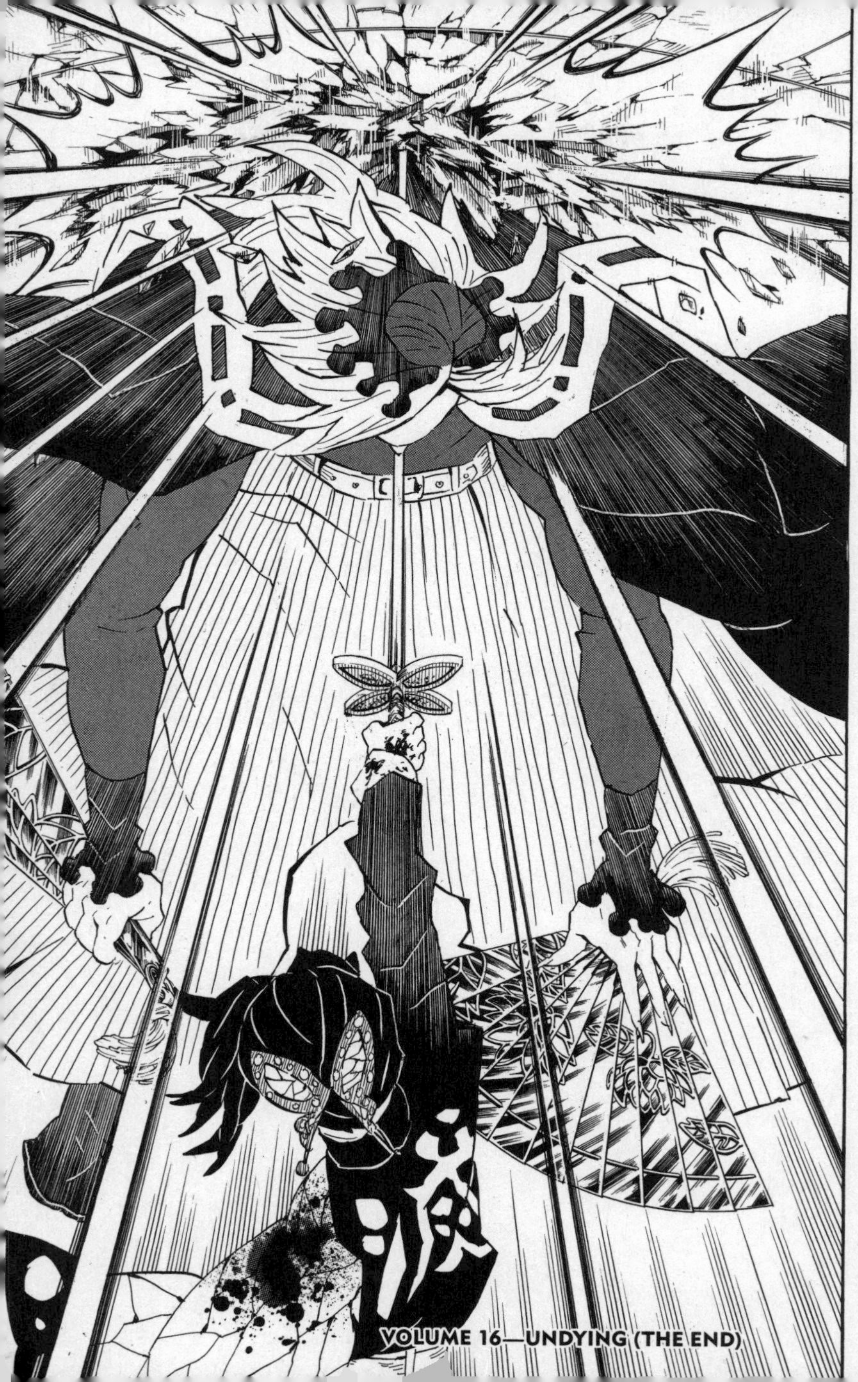

VOLUME 16—UNDYING (THE END)

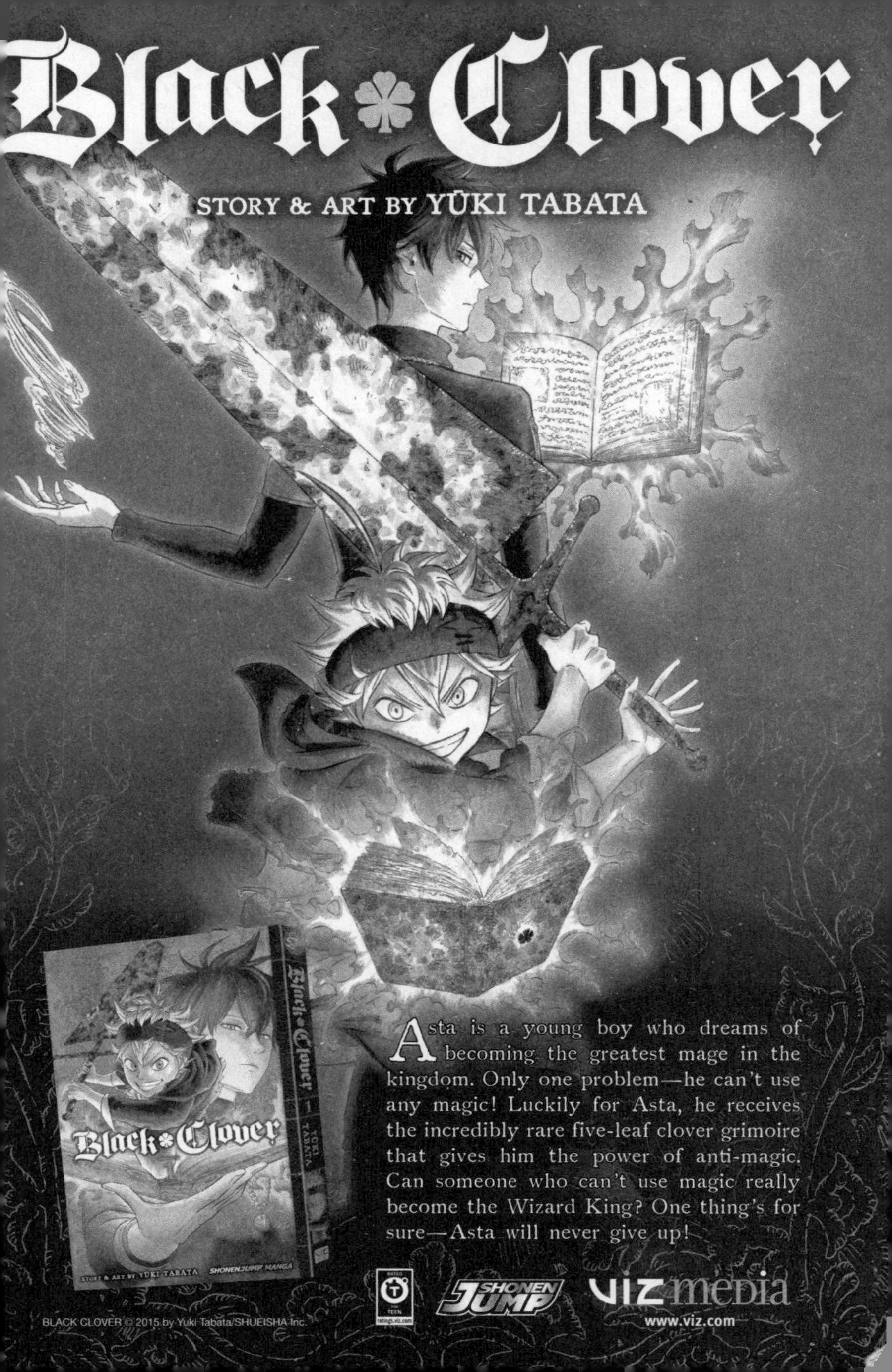
Black Clover
STORY & ART BY YŪKI TABATA
Asta is a young boy who dreams of becoming the greatest mage in the kingdom. Only one problem—he can't use any magic! Luckily for Asta, he receives the incredibly rare five-leaf clover grimoire that gives him the power of anti-magic. Can someone who can't use magic really become the Wizard King? One thing's for sure—Asta will never give up!
Black Clover
STORY & ART BY YŪKI TABATA
SHONENJUMP MANGA
RATED T FOR TEEN
ratings.viz.com
SHONEN JUMP
VIZ media
www.viz.com
BLACK CLOVER © 2015 by Yuki Tabata/SHUEISHA Inc.

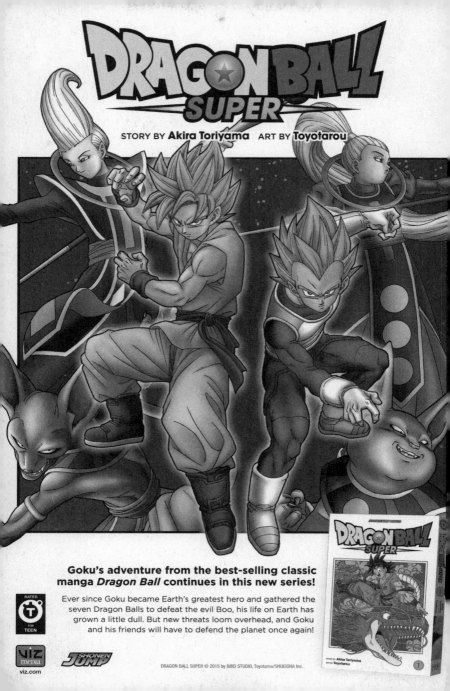

Goku's adventure from the best-selling classic manga *Dragon Ball* continues in this new series!

Ever since Goku became Earth's greatest hero and gathered the seven Dragon Balls to defeat the evil Boo, his life on Earth has grown a little dull. But new threats loom overhead, and Goku and his friends will have to defend the planet once again!

YOU'RE READING THE
WRONG WAY!

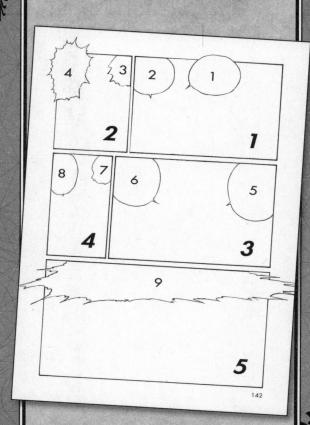

DEMON SLAYER: KIMETSU NO YAIBA
reads from right to left, starting in the
upper-right corner. Japanese is read from
right to left, meaning that action, sound
effects and word-balloon order are com-
pletely reversed from English order.